Programmer's Guide
to NCurses

Programmer's Guide to NCurses

Dan Gookin

1807
WILEY
2007
BICENTENNIAL

Wiley Publishing, Inc.

Programmer's Guide to NCurses

Published by

Wiley Publishing, Inc.

10475 Crosspoint Boulevard

Indianapolis, IN 46256

www.wiley.com

ISBN: 978-0-470-10759-1

Manufactured in the United States of America

10 9 8 7 6 5 4 3 2 1

About the Author

Dan Gookin has been writing about technology for over 20 years. He's contributed articles to numerous high-tech magazines and written more than 100 books on personal computers, many of them accurate.

Dan combines his love of writing with his gizmo fascination to create books that are informative, entertaining, and not boring. Having sold more than 14 million titles translated into more than 30 languages, Dan can attest that his method of crafting computer tomes does seem to work.

Perhaps his most famous title is the original *DOS For Dummies*, published in 1991. It became the world's fastest-selling computer book, at one time moving more copies per week than the *New York Times* #1 bestseller (though as a reference, it could not be listed on the *NYT* Bestseller list). From that book spawned the entire line of *For Dummies* books, which remains a publishing phenomenon to this day.

Dan's most recent titles include *Word 2007 For Dummies*, *Laptops For Dummies*, 2nd Edition, and *PCs For Dummies*, 10th Edition. He also maintains the vast and helpful Web page www.wambooli.com.

Dan holds a degree in Communications/Visual Arts from the University of California, San Diego. Presently he lives in the Pacific Northwest, where he enjoys spending time with his boys in the gentle woods of Idaho.

Credits

Acquisitions Editor
Kit Kemper

Development Editor
Lisa Thibault

Technical Editor
Thomas Dickey

Production Editor
Felicia Robinson

Copy Editor
C.M. Jones

Editorial Manager
Mary Beth Wakefield

Production Manager
Tim Tate

Vice President and Executive Group Publisher
Richard Swadley

Vice President and Executive Publisher
Joseph B. Wikert

Project Coordinator
Erin Smith

Graphics and Production Specialists
Sean Decker
Carrie A. Foster
Brooke Graczyk
Denny Hager
Stephanie D. Jumper
Alicia B. South

Quality Control Technicians
Cynthia Fields
John Greenough

Proofreading and Indexing
Broccoli Information Management
Sossity R. Smith

Anniversary Logo Design
Richard Pacifico

Contents

Acknowledgments

I'd like to thank Thomas Dickey for his marvelous work augmenting my dive into the NCurses library. I truly appreciate his participation in this project and admire him not only for maintaining NCurses but working to assist others with their questions and problems. Thank you, Thomas!

Introduction

The NCurses library is a programming tool you can use in UNIX distributions as well as in Windows under `CYGWIN` to program, control, and manipulate text on the terminal screen. With NCurses you can control interactive I/O, organize information into windows on the screen, use color to highlight text and organize information, and even use a mouse to further refine input. It's all possible with NCurses.

This book presents NCurses in two parts. The first part is a 14-chapter tutorial that covers enough of the basic NCurses library to get you started and more. The second part is an A to Z reference of more than 175 NCurses functions. It is *not* a rehash of the man pages but descriptions and examples based on my own research. The reference is cross-referenced, and the entire book is indexed.

I've created this book so that it will be the only Curses reference you'll need. Feel free to mark up the pages, dog-ear, and put sticky notes where necessary. This is *your* book!

Assumptions

This book assumes that you're using a UNIX-like operating system (Linux, FreeBSD, Mac OS X, or some other OS based on UNIX).

Most UNIX operating systems today use a graphical user interface (GUI), though for programming Curses you'll need to have access to a terminal screen. This can be a terminal window inside the GUI. Make sure you know how to open such a beast.

Curses or NCurses?

The Curses library of terminal control functions has been with UNIX since the early 1980s. As such, it was part of the older versions of UNIX, which required complex licenses and such to be used.

NCurses is the *New* Curses software emulation of the original Curses and is available from the GNU folks at the Free Software Foundation. Odds are pretty good that the computer system you're using employs NCurses, not the original Curses. Because of that, this book uses NCurses to refer to the library and its functions.

The book is current with NCurses version 5.5.

Conventions

In this book, you'll find the following conventions used:

- C language keywords, function names, or prompt commands are listed in monospace type, such as: if or newwin() or ls -l.

- Filenames are listed in monospaced caps, such as A.OUT or GOODBYE.C. Directory and pathnames are also in small caps: ~/PROG/C/CURSES

- Program code appears with the source code filename first, followed by the code:

Listing I-1: box.c

```
1                    #include <ncurses.h>
2
3                    int main(void)
4                    {
5                                          initscr();
6
7                                          box(stdscr,'*','*');
8                                          refresh();
9                                          getch();
10
11                                         endwin();
12                                         return 0;
13                   }
```

The line numbers, to the left of the bar, are for reference only; do not type them. The code is to the right of the bar.

The programs in this book are short and to the point. As such, they rarely include comments. Even so, be sure to comment your own code and name your variables in a friendly way.

Some programs later in the book dispense with error-checking for some NCurses procedures. This is noted as a bad practice in real life but is done here to keep the code short and easy to read and type. In your code, always be sure to check for errors with those NCurses functions that can return errors, as noted in the text.

Compatibility Issues

I wrote this book on a G5 Mac running OS X. Programs were also tested on a FreeBSD computer as well as a system running Mandrake Linux. All the programs in this book work, but not all of them work well or identically on all systems. Even though NCurses is very universal, do not expect all the code here to fly perfectly on your computer.

If you encounter problems with NCurses on your OS, please refer to the OS Technical Support — or an online forum or Wikipedia — for assistance. Odds are pretty good that I don't have your same setup, so e-mailing me isn't going to get you anywhere.

As this book goes to press, I've already reported several dozen issues with NCurses on Mac OS X to the OS X developer support team, as well as to the NCurses maintenance team.

Contacting the Author

Here is my real e-mail address:

```
dgookin@wambooli.com
```

I cannot promise to answer all my e-mail, as I get a ton of it and most of it is for technical support, which is not my business. I do enjoy hearing feedback about my books, and I will answer questions about the books. I cannot, obviously, write your source code for you.

This book has a companion web page, which is shared with the site I use to support my C programming books. The page can be found at:

```
http://www.c-for-dummies.com/ncurses/
```

There you'll find supplemental material and bonus programs, plus perhaps an FAQ when one is warranted. The C Language forum has plenty of regulars who know C very well and are eager to help out beginners as well as old hands. Try visiting there first with your problems or questions regarding C.

Enjoy NCurses!

DAN

The Setup

This chapter covers a basic setup and organization for you to get started with NCurses programming. Here you'll find:

- An introduction to the terminal window in UNIX
- A smattering of basic shell commands
- Creating a special `curses` directory for this document's programs
- A review of available text editors
- The creation of a basic NCurses program
- A review of the gcc compiler and linking commands
- Re-editing source code and debugging exercises

The idea here is to show you how everything works and to get you comfortable programming with NCurses, even if you've never written a UNIX program before.

NCurses Is a UNIX Thing

You must have a UNIX-like operating system to work the samples and examples in this book.

Beyond this, note that you must also have the programming libraries installed for your operating system. Without those libraries, programming in NCurses just isn't gonna happen. Refer to your operating system's installation or setup program, such as /stand/sysinstall in FreeBSD, to install the C programming libraries for your operating system. If special extensions are required to get the NCurses library installed, use them!

NOTE It's possible to program NCurses in Windows when using the Cygwin environment. I've not toyed with Cygwin, so I'm unable to comment on it here. For more information, refer to www.cygwin.com.

Run (Don't Walk) to a Terminal Screen Near You

NCurses is about programming the terminal screen, so you'll need access to a terminal screen or window to run the programs.

You can either use one of the virtual terminals (which you can access on most PCs by pressing Alt+F1, Alt+F2, Alt+F3, and so on) or open a terminal window in the X Window System environment or in Mac OS X using the Terminal program. (See Figure 1-1.)

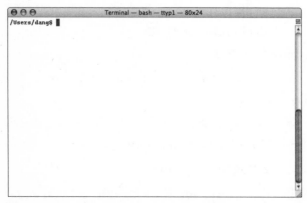

Figure 1-1: A terminal window for Mac OS X

Note that the terminal you choose can affect what NCurses does. Not all terminal types can, for example, do color or draw lines on the screen.

Know Something About the Shell

The program you use in the terminal screen is a *shell*. It displays a shell prompt and lets you type one of the gazillions of UNIX commands and what not — which is all basic UNIX stuff.

The following sections review basic shell operations and a smattering of commands. If you feel you already know this, skim up to the section titled "Make a Place for Your Stuff."

Some Shelly Stuff

For example, the standard Bourne shell may look like this:

```
$
```

The dollar sign is the prompt, and you type your commands after the prompt.

The Bash shell, popular with Linux, may look like this:

```
Bash-2.05a$
```

Or the shell may be customized to display your login name:

```
dang$
```

Or even the working directory:

```
/home/dang/$
```

Whatever!

No one really cares about which shell you use, but you should know enough shell commands to be able to do these things:

- Make directories
- Display a file's contents
- Copy files
- Rename files
- Remove files

It's beyond the scope of this book to teach you such stuff, though a handy list of popular shell commands is provided at the end of this chapter.

Note that this book does not display the shell prompt when you're directed to enter a command. Simply type the command; then press Enter to send the command to the shell program for processing.

It is always assumed that you press the Enter key to input the command.

> **NOTE** Please do check your typing! The shell is very fussy about getting things correct. In the Bash shell, you'll see a `command not found` error when you mistype something:
>
> ```
> -bash: tcc: command not found
> ```

Know Your History, Because You're Going to Repeat It

One handy shell feature you should take advantage of is the history. Various history commands allow you to recall previously typed text at the command prompt. This is commonly done as you edit, compile, re-edit, and recompile your code.

For example, most of the time you're using this book you'll be cycling through three sets of commands. First comes the editing:

```
vim goodbye.c
```

Then comes the compiling:

```
gcc -lncurses goodbye.c
```

Then comes the running:

```
./a.out
```

I'll cover these steps in detail later, but for now recognize that these commands are to be repeated over and over: Edit, compile, run (or test); then re-edit, recompile, and test again. To assist you in that task, employ your shell's history function.

In the Bash shell, for example, use the up arrow key on your keyboard to recall a previous command. To recall the second previous command, press the up arrow key twice. I'm not intimate with the other shells, so if you use the C shell or Bourne shell, review your documentation for any history commands available with those shells.

Make a Place for Your Stuff

Please do be organized and build yourself a handy little directory into which you can save, compile, and test the various programs presented in this document.

For example, in my home directory, I have the following set up:

```
$HOME/prog/c/ncurses
```

`$HOME` is the home directory, the shell variable that represents your account's home directory for most UNIX shells that I've played with. It can also be abbreviated as ~/ in some shells.

Then I have a subdirectory called `PROG`, which contains all my programming junk and test files. `PROG` contains subdirectories for C language programs, Perl programs, shell scripts, and whatever else I'm dabbling in.

The `C` subdirectory contains C programs and directories.

Finally, the `NCURSES` directory is where I built all the sample files for this book.

You should consider a similar setup for your system, even if it's just something like `$HOME/ncurses`. As long as you can keep all the sample files around and be able to access them later, you'll be a happy camper.

If you want to create a ~/`PROG/C/NCURSES` directory for your stuff, you can use the following command in your home directory:

```
mkdir -p prog/c/ncurses
```

The `-p` switch directs `mkdir` to build all parent directories to the final `NCurses` directory.

Using an Editor to Create an NCurses Program

There's no point in bothering with a fancy developer environment or IDE when you're programming NCurses. I think you'll be happier using the terminal window and a shell prompt, unless you've been totally corrupted by some IDE. Then you're on your own!

Picking an Editor

Since day one of UNIX, a text editor has been used to create code. That's what I recommend for this book. Any text editor will do, and most UNIX-like operating systems give you a smattering of editors to choose from:

- **ee.** The "easy editor" is a popular choice for many UNIX newcomers. No one will think any less of you for using ee, especially if you're using it with your C programming.

- **emacs.** This is the most popular choice, mostly because its commands are more word processor-like and you don't have to keep whacking the Escape key as you do in vi/vim.

- **vim.** This is my personal choice, simply because it's so damn raw and complex. As you get used to vim, though, it becomes a very powerful and handy tool. Plus it's common to all Unixes.

Whenever this book tells you to edit or create some source code, you'll use your favorite text editor to make it happen. (And please do create these programs in your NCurses directory, as covered in the previous section.)

If you don't know any editors, I recommend ee as the easiest. Otherwise, this book does not teach you how to use any text editor; I assume you'll figure that out on your own.

Creating Your First NCurses Program

Rather than just discuss all this stuff, why not get moving?

Use the cd command to change directories to the NCURSES directory you just created. You can confirm which directory you're using with the pwd command.

This is what I see on my screen:

```
/HOME/DANG/PROG/C/NCURSES
```

Your screen will probably show something different. The point is the same: You're in the NCURSES directory and ready to create some source code with your editor.

Source code is presented in this book as follows: First comes the filename, then the source code. To the left are line numbers for reference purposes only. Do not type the line numbers!

Use your editor to name (or create) the file; then input all the text *exactly* as shown in Listing 1-1.

Listing 1-1: GOODBYE.C

```
 1    #include <ncurses.h>
 2
 3    int main(void)
 4    {
 5        initscr();
 6        addstr(Goodbye, cruel C programming!);
 7
 8        endwin();
 9        return 0;
10    }
```

So if you're using vim, you would type:

```
vim goodbye.c
```

Then you would enter the text into the editor using your favorite, cryptic vim commands.

> **NOTE** Note that some compilers require there to be an extra blank line following the last line of code. This is not shown above or in any sample code in this document.

When you're done entering text, double-check to ensure that you didn't miss anything.

Note that from now on it's assumed that whenever you see source code as shown here, you are to type it and name it according to the source code heading. And, naturally, you don't have to type *every* program, only those you want to experiment with.

Some Deviations

The next step in the programming process is compiling and linking, handled deftly by the common GCC command. But before compiling and linking, consider a few sidetracks, just to get you oriented if you're not used to programming in UNIX.

Use the ls command to view the contents of your NCURSES directory.

The ls command displays or lists the files in the directory, one of which should be goodbye.c. Confirm that.

```
~/prog/c/ncurses$  ls
goodbye.c
~/prog/c/ncurses$
```

You can also use the *long* variation on the ls command to see more details.

```
~/prog/c/ncurses$  ls -l
total 8
-rw-r--r--   1 dang   dang   113 dec  7 13:02 goodbye.c
~/prog/c/ncurses$
```

Now you can see permissions, owner, group, file size, and date information for the GOODBYE.C file — all of which help to confirm the file's existence.

Finally, you can view the file's contents with the cat command:

```
~/prog/c/ncurses$   cat goodbye.c
#include <ncurses.h>

int main(void)
{
        initscr();
```

```
        addstr(Goodbye, cruel C programming!);

        endwin();
        return 0;
}
```

```
~/prog/c/ncurses$
```

And there is the file yet again on the screen.

Typing ls and cat are not required steps in the program-creation process. I just like to remind you of their use here, which I liken to peering into the mail drop box twice just to confirm that your mail actually made it into the box and is not somehow stuck on the hinged lid.

Time to compile!

Know Thy Compiler

The standard C compiler in the UNIX environment is gcc, the GNU C compiler. Here is how it works in this book: You will see source code listed, such as the goodbye.c program. You will immediately know to type it and compile it.

To compile, you will type something at the shell prompt, perhaps like this:

```
gcc goodbye.c -lncurses
```

That's the gcc command, your compiler.

The first option is the name of the source code file, the text file you created. In this case, it's named goodbye.c. The single, lowercase c denotes a standard C source code file, not C++.

Finally comes -lncurses, which tells the compiler to -l "link in" the NCurses library. *This is very important!* NCurses is not just a header file; it's also a *library*. And you must link in the library to have those NCurses functions work.

Use this command:

```
gcc goodbye.c -lncurses
```

And you're compiled. Or not.

Linking NCurses or Curses?

On most systems I've visited, both the CURSES and NCURSES libraries are the same thing, meaning that if you link in -lcurses instead of -lncurses, the results are the same. The only advantage here is that typing -lcurses saves you a keystroke. Otherwise, I recommend using -lncurses.

What Does the gcc Command Do?

The gcc command either outputs a slew of error messages or shows you nothing.

When you get a slew of error messages, you must re-edit the source file and try to work out whatever bugs you can. The compiler is brutally honest, but it's also nice in that it does give you a line number to show you where (approximately) you screwed up.

When gcc does nothing, the source code is properly compiled and linked. This is what you want.

In this case, I've tricked you into typing sloppy code so that you'll see an error message. Something like:

```
goodbye.c:6: macro 'addstr' used with too many (2) args
```

One variation of the gcc compiler yielded even more information:

```
goodbye.c:6:45: macro "addstr" passed 2 arguments, but takes just 1
```

These error messages are just oozing with information:

- goodbye.c tells you which source code file is offensive.
- The 6 tells you that the error is either in line 6 or the previous line. In the second example, the 45 tells you which column in the line is offensive — very specific.
- Then the error message itself; something is apparently wrong with the call to the addstr macro. Must fix.

NOTE If you didn't see the error message, you probably have been coding C for some time and just put the addstr() function's text in double quotes out of habit. Good for you!

Re-editing Your Source Code

In programming you do more re-editing than editing. In this case, the error was on purpose so I could show you how the compiler displays an error message. The fix is easy: Just edit the GOODBYE.C source code file again.

Don't forget to use your shell's history (if available) to recall that editing command!

> **NOTE** Here's a tip: Familiarize yourself with the editor's command that
> instantly jumps to a specific line number. Most of your editing will actually be
> re-editing, where the compiler directs you to a specific line number. If you
> know the line-number-jumping command, you can get there quickly to fix your
> source code and try (again) to compile it:
>
> In vim, the line number skipping command is nG, where n is the line number
> and G is Shift+G. Thus, typing 6G will get you right to line 6.

The line should read:

```
addstr("Goodbye, cruel C programming!");
```

Then you should save the file to disk and re-compile it. But nothing happens. That's good! However....

Where Is the Program?

The program gcc creates is named a.out. It's a binary file, and its permissions are all properly set so that the operating system knows it's a program file and not a slice of Velveeta.

Use the ls command to confirm that a.out exists, if you like.

To run the program, you need to focus on the current directory: ./A.OUT.

You can't just type a.out, because the operating system looks only to the search path for programs to run. So you must specifically direct tired old UNIX to look in the current directory — abbreviated by the . single dot — to run the program.

So ./ means "look in the current directory" and A.OUT means "run the file named a.out."

Of course, if you have the manual dexterity, you can always type a full pathname, something like:

```
~/prog/c/ncurses/a.out
```

This also runs the a.out program, but I believe you'll find typing ./A.OUT a lot easier.

Nothing happens, not even an error. Again, there is a problem and you need to re-edit and recompile.

Fixing Stuff (Again)

Fixing stuff (again) in this case means that you forgot a key NCurses command. (Or more properly, fixing it again here means that I didn't specify a command on purpose simply to drive this point home.)

The problem? You didn't use the `refresh()` function, which is a common blunder in NCurses programming. Only by using `refresh()` is the NCurses "window" updated and any text written to the screen displayed. So, back to the editor!

Insert the `refresh()` function after the `addstr()` function on line 6. Your code should look like Listing 1-2, complete.

Listing 1-2: goodbye.c

```
1    #include <ncurses.h>
2
3    int main(void)
4    {
5        initscr();
6        addstr("Goodbye, cruel C programming!");
7        refresh();
8
9        endwin();
10       return 0;
11   }
```

Double-check your work.

Remember that you can use your shell's history to quickly recall those common commands: your editor, your compiler, and the `./a.out` command.

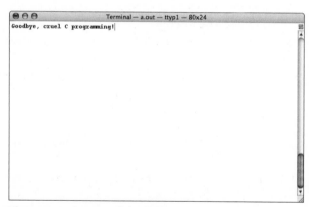

Figure 1-2: Output of the GOODBYE.C code.

Now it should work, and you'll see the string thrown up onto the screen via NCurses, as shown in Figure 1-2. Congratulations!

Don't Panic When You Still Don't See Anything!

Even with the refresh() function in the code, it's still possible that you won't see any program output. The problem isn't the program or even NCurses; it's your terminal.

Many terminals, such as xterm, support a feature known as *rmcup*. It restores the screen to what it looked like before a program was run. The situation also occurs with any full-screen terminal program, such as *man* or *less*; the program's text disappears after you quit the program, and the prompt "window" is restored.

Sadly, there is no handy way to switch off *rmcup* support from a terminal window. The terminfo file for the terminal needs to be recompiled to remove *rmcup* support, or a new terminfo file needs to be created in your home directory, one that lacks *rmcup* as an option.

The quick solution is to use the getch() function in your code. By inserting a line with getch() before the endwin() function, you can pause output and see what NCurses does before the program quits, as shown in Listing 1-3.

Listing 1-3: goodbye.c

```
1    #include <ncurses.h>
2
3    int main(void)
4    {
5        initscr();
6        addstr("Goodbye, cruel C programming!");
7        refresh();
8        getch();
9
10       endwin();
11       return 0;
12   }
```

The new line 8 was added, allowing the program to pause, and for you to read the output.

Many of the program examples in this book use getch() to pause output. But some programs do not; be sure to use getch() in your code to see output, or modify your terminfo file to disable the *rmcup* feature.

NOTE It might also help to be vocal about the *rmcup* feature for future releases of your operating system. While many folks may see *rmcup* as a handy thing, other users dislike it. The solution is to make the feature easy to disable. Let's hope that will be possible sooner than later.

Do You Think a.out Is a Goofy Name?

Yes, a.out is a goofy name, but that's because the compiler doesn't know any better.

For running the myriad test programs in this book, using a.out will be a blessing. It won't take up as much disk space as individually compiling each program and creating separate silly little programs, plus it means you can instantly recall the ./a.out command using your shell's history command.

But anyway, if you'd rather compile to a different output file, you need to specify the −o switch when you use gcc. It goes like this:

```
gcc goodbye.c -lncurses -o goodbye
```

gcc is still the compiler.

goodbye.c is the source code.

−lncurses directs the compiler to link in the *NCurses* library.

And finally, −o goodbye tells gcc to create the output file named goodbye as opposed to creating a.out.

Use the preceding command to accomplish this.

Do not forget the ./ prefix! Silly old UNIX needs to know where to find the file. So you must type ./GOODBYE to run the program.

By the way, the output file doesn't have to be the same name as the source code file. You could use the following command if you like:

```
gcc goodbye.c -lncurses -o cloppyfeen
```

This creates the program file named cloppyfeen from the source code found in goodbye.c., so what you name the final program file can be anything you like.

All Done!

That pretty much does it for your whirlwind introduction to NCurses programming using the C language in the UNIX environment. This chapter has imparted the following knowledge, stuff that you'll need to carry with you throughout the remainder of this document:

General Info

Keep in mind that it's a good idea to keep your learning NCurses files in your special NCURSES directory. This is assumed.

Do remember those handy shell history commands. You'll be doing a lot of repetitious commands here, and pressing the up arrow key is a lot easier than retyping boring old UNIX commands.

And from now on, I will not be reminding you to specifically input, compile, and run the sample programs. There may be other, specific instructions given in the text, but whenever you see source code, it's assumed that you can type it in and run it if you want to learn more.

Handy Shell Commands to Know

cat	Displays a text file (source code) to the screen
clear	Clears the screen
cp	Copies a file
ls -l	Lists files in the long format
ls	Lists files
mv	Moves or renames a file
rm	Removes (deletes) a file

Source Code Tidbits

End the source code file with .C to show that it's a C language source code file. (Some editors, such as vim, may even recognize this and bless you with color-coded, in context contents as you edit.)

The main() function is an int and must return a value to the shell via either return or the exit() function.

If you use the exit() function, remember to include the STDLIB.H header file at the top of your source code.

If the program seems not to display anything, remember to add a getch() function before the endwin() function.

Compiling Tips

The compiler used in this book is gcc.

You must link in the NCurses library by using the -lncurses option to properly compile these programs.

The program file produced is always named a.out.

You must type ./a.out to test run the program file.

You can use the -o compiler option to specify the name of the output file as something different from a.out.

The compiler command format is:

```
gcc filename.c -lncurses
```

You supply the filename according to the source code name given in this document.

CHAPTER 2

Basic I/O, the NCurses Way

NCurses allows you full control over terminal screen (or window) but only if you heed its rules! There is a definite way to set up an NCurses program and some specific tricks and traps to know. Also, you must use NCurses' own I/O functions to display text as well as read input from the keyboard.

The Skeleton

The majority of NCurses programs have the same basic skeleton, which looks something like this:

```
#include <ncurses.h>

int main(void)
{
    initscr();          /* Initialize ncurses */

                /* i/o and other programming done here */

    endwin();           /* Properly close ncurses */
    return 0;           /* cough up return value for the shell */
}
```

The bookends are the two functions `initscr()` and `endwin()`. Between them you can stuff all the NCurses commands and functions that your little heart desires, plus the usual hoard of C programming commands — with the exception of the standard I/O commands. No, you must use NCurses' own I/O commands for NCurses to work. But more on that later.

```
#include <ncurses.h>
```

You must include the NCURSES.H header file so that the compiler doesn't choke on your NCurses functions.

> **NOTE** Please note that including the NCURSES.H header file does not automatically link in the NCurses library. No, you must do that with the −lncurses switch when you compile (as covered in Chapter 1). There is a difference between the header and library files!

The NCurses header file does a few nifty tricks. First, it automatically includes the following other header files:

```
stdio.h
unctrl.h
stdarg.h
stddef.h
```

Therefore, there is no need to re-include these header files in your source code. In fact, if you do, you may end up slowing things down and creating files much larger than they need to be. So if you're tempted to do this:

```
#include <stdio.h>
#include <ncurses.h>
```

Do only this instead:

```
#include <ncurses.h>
```

Also, the NCURSES.H file defines such things as TRUE, FALSE, OK, ERR, and other useful constants. It contains definitions for structures you'll be using later. Plus, it includes many other wonderful and useful goodies. If you have the time, peruse the header file, which can be found at /USR/INCLUDE/ NCURSES.H.

The initscr() Function

The initscr() function initializes NCurses. It does not clear the terminal screen. Instead, it sets up internal memory structures and interfaces between the NCurses functions and your computer's terminal I/O thingy.

Two important items initscr() creates are called the *standard screen* and the *current screen*. Both of these are internal structures used by NCurses to efficiently display information on the terminal screen.

The standard screen, or stdscr, is the default output window for NCurses, as shown in Figure 2-1. As you'll discover later in Chapter 8, all NCurses output commands, and a select few input commands, are window oriented. The standard screen is the main window you'll use, and it's exactly the same size as the terminal screen. The initscr() function creates the standard screen and uses the variable stdscr to reference it.

The standard screen, however, is not the same as the terminal window, and stuff you write to the standard screen doesn't appear on the terminal window. Well, not right away.

The refresh() command is required to update text on the terminal window, letting you see what NCurses has done. What refresh() does is to check for new text has been output by NCurses and update that text on the current screen, or curscr, as shown in Figure 2-2.

The current screen is NCurses's internal representation of what is believed to be on the terminal screen, or what the user sees, as shown in Figure 2-2. The refresh() function is responsible for updating the current screen, which then updates what is shown to the user.

Like the standard screen, the current screen is an NCurses window. But unlike stdscr, it's uncommon (and not recommended) to output directly to curscr. There are many reasons for this, as you'll learn later in this book.

In addition to the standard screen and current screen, there is something called the *virtual screen*. The virtual screen exists for efficiency's sake. It contains updated information, only those items changed or *touched* in a certain window and which are waiting to be updated on the current screen, as shown in Figure 2-3.

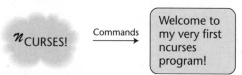

Figure 2-1: The standard screen is the default window for NCurses text output commands.

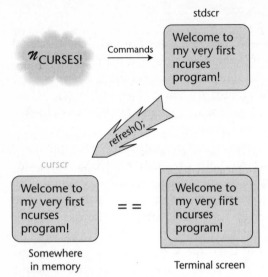

Figure 2-2: The current screen holds an approximation of what NCurses believes to be on the terminal window.

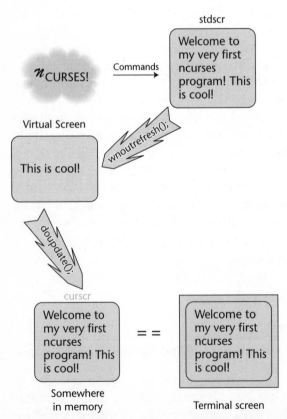

Figure 2-3: How the virtual screen helps keep text output efficient

Internally, the refresh() function consists of two commands. The first is wnoutrefresh(), which updates only the changed portions of a window or the standard screen to the virtual screen. The second half of the refresh() function is doupdate(), which makes the current screen match the virtual screen's updates. Again, this is done to keep text output efficient. The other way would be to update the complete terminal screen each time new text is output, which can be maddeningly slow on some terminals.

All this terminology (standard screen, current screen, virtual screen, wnoutrefresh() and doupdate()) can be overwhelming. Don't let it get to you now. It's merely the internal mechanisms by which NCurses works. As another example, consider the source code for GOODBYE.C as shown in Chapter 1:

```
1    #include  <ncurses.h>
2
3    int main(void)
4    {
5        initscr();
6        addstr("Goodbye, cruel C programming!");
7        refresh();
8        getch();
9
10       endwin();
11       return 0;
12   }
```

In line 5, the initscr() function configures NCurses and creates both the stdscr and curscr.

Text is written to the stdscr using the addstr() function in line 6.

The refresh() command in line 7 updates both the virtual screen, which immediately updates the current screen and, in the end, the terminal window so that you can see the text.

In line 8, everything pauses with getch(), waiting for the user to press Enter.

The endwin() function shuts NCurses down in line 10, but endwin() deserves its own section and explanation.

The initscr() Function's Exceptions

For starting out, it's easy to remember that initscr() is the function that initializes NCurses for your code. But initscr() isn't alone; it has a twin function called newterm().

The newterm() function sets up NCurses just as initscr() does, but it allows you more control over the input and output sources. Therefore, it's kind of an advanced function, and, if you're curious, you can look it up in Appendix A. Otherwise, it does not appear in the tutorial portion of this book.

Also, `initscr()` isn't necessarily the very first NCurses function you'll use in your code. There are several functions in NCurses that must be used *before* `initscr()`. These functions are mentioned under the definition of `initscr()` in Appendix A, and more information on each function can be found in that appendix as well.

The endwin() Function

The cleanup hitter in the NCurses line up is the `endwin()` function. It undoes any modifications that NCurses has made to your terminal, and does other tidying up.

It's very important that you finish your NCurses program with this command!

If you neglect to use `endwin()`, your terminal's behavior becomes unpredictable. (This is the voice of experience here.) So be very, very sure that you use `endwin()` when your program is done — especially if you're programming some large, monster program with several exit holes.

Note that the standard C output functions — `putc()`, `puts()`, `printf()`, and so on — do output text when NCurses is active, though by doing so NCurses would be confused about what's on the display. Therefore, it's better not to use such output functions while NCurses is actively outputting text.

Incidentally, `endwin()` need not be the end of your NCurses program. It's possible to use `endwin()` to merely suspend NCurses and return to the terminal. When the `refresh()` function is used after `endwin()`, it reactivates NCurses visual mode, though you must still use another `endwin()` function to properly end your program. The entry for `endwin()` in Appendix A explains more about this feature.

The refresh() Function

Rare is the NCurses program without a `refresh()` function. It's almost required. `refresh()` updates the screen, noting any changes between what you want on the screen and what's there and writing the difference.

Use the following code in Listing 2-1 to create the `cls` program.

Listing 2-1: cls.c

```
1    #include  <ncurses.h>
2
3    int main(void)
4    {
5         initscr();
6         refresh();
7
8         endwin();
9         return 0;
10   }
```

Yes, indeed, the program clears the screen. Here's how. When `initscr()` runs, it initializes `stdscr`, the default window, to all blanks and it sets the cursor to the *home* position, top row, left-most column. The `refresh()` function updates `stdscr` to the current screen and the terminal display, which has the effect of clearing the screen and homing the cursor.

Writing Text

Here are three popular NCurses text output functions:

```
addch(ch);
addstr(*str);
printw(format,var[,var...]);
```

The `addch()` function places (or adds) a single character to the display.

`addstr()` adds an entire string, essentially calling `addch()` over and over until the entire string is coughed up. You've already seen `addstr()` in use with the `goodbye.c` program in Chapter 1. It's similar to the `puts()` function in C, though a newline (`\n`) isn't automatically appended to the string.

`printw()` is the NCurses version of the `printf()` function. It outputs a formatted string to the display.

NCurses sports more text output functions, but for getting started these three basic functions are fine.

Tossing Up Text One Stupid Character at a Time

I love marquee programs. But rather than write a really fancy one, I'll just show you how `addch()` can blurt out one character at a time as the following program in Listing 2-2 demonstrates.

Listing 2-2: ADD1.C

```
1    #include  <ncurses.h>
2
3    int main(void)
4    {
5        char text[] = "Greetings from NCurses!";
6        char *t;
7
8        initscr();            /* initialize NCurses */
9        t = text;             /* initialize the pointer */
10
11       while(*t)             /* loop through the whole string */
12       {
```

(continued)

Listing 2-2 *(continued)*

```
13              addch(*t);        /* put one char to curscr */
14              t++;              /* increment the pointer */
15              refresh();        /* update the screen */
16              napms(100);       /* delay a bit to see the display */
17      }                     /* end while */
18      getch();              /* wait here */
19
20      endwin();             /* clean up NCurses */
21      return 0;             /* keep the shell happy */
22  }
```

This program inches through a string of text using a pointer t. The pointer allows each character in the string to be displayed one at a time via the addch() function.

The napms() function pauses output one-tenth of a second between each character displayed, which helps to drive home the nature of addch(). I'll cover napms() in more detail in the next section.

> **NOTE** Note the importance of refresh()! You cannot see what's on the screen until you refresh!

Pausing for a Side-trip

In addition to all the fun screen (and soon-to-come keyboard) frivolity, NCurses also features a variable pausing function, napms(). Such a cute name!

```
napms(ms)
```

The napms() function pauses program execution for ms milliseconds. So the statement:

```
napms(1000);
```

causes program execution to pause for one whole second. The statement:

```
napms(100);
```

used in the code for ADD1.C pauses execution for only a paltry $1/10^{th}$ second.

Change the value of napms() in line 16 of the ADD1.C code in Listing 2-3 to see how it affects the program's output.

Blurping Text

There's no point in using addch() to display an entire line of text. That's because there's also the addstr() function, which takes care of the tedious task for you.

Listing 2-3: ADD2.C

```
1    #include  <ncurses.h>
2
3    int main(void)
4    {
5        char text1[] = "Oh give me a clone!\n";
6        char text2[] = "Yes a clone of my own!";
7
8        initscr();
9        addstr(text1);     /* add the first string */
10       addstr(text2);     /* add the second string */
11       refresh();         /* display the result */
12       getch();        /* wait */
13
14       endwin();
15       return 0;
16   }
```

Note the comments in Listing 2-3: The string is *added* with the addstr() function, not displayed. The string gets displayed only when refresh() updates the current screen.

Another thing to note: The \n at the end of the first string did, indeed, move the cursor down to the next line.

This next program example in Listing 2-4 contains a subtle variation on the ADD2.C code.

Listing 2-4: ADD3.C

```
1    #include  <ncurses.h>
2
3    int main(void)
4    {
5        char text1[] = "Oh give me a clone!\n";
6        char text2[] = "Yes a clone of my own!";
7
8        initscr();
9        addstr(text1);     /* add the first string */
10       addstr(text2);     /* add the second string */
11       move(2,0);         /* cursor to row 3, column 1 */
12       addstr("With the Y chromosome changed to the X.");
```

(continued)

Listing 2-4 *(continued)*

```
13          refresh();        /* display the result */
14          getch();
15
16          endwin();
17          return 0;
18      }
```

I added the move() function in line 11, which changes the cursor's location on the standard screen window. I also added another addstr() function at line 12 to write the next line of text.

The move() Function

There are many cursors in NCurses. For example, each window has its own cursor and that cursor location stays the same in each window regardless of what happens to the cursor in other windows.

In the code for ADD3.C shown in Listing 2-4, the newline displayed by addstr() in line 9 moves the cursor on the standard screen window from the end of the current line of text, down to the start of the next line — as you would expect.

In line 11 of ADD3.C, the move() function moves the cursor's location. Here is the format of the move() function:

```
move(y,x)
```

y is a row value, going up and down the screen.

x is a column value, going left to right across the screen.

The upper-left corner of the screen is coordinate 0,0. And, of course, the total number of rows and columns depends on your terminal configuration, though there is a way to discover it, as I'll show you in Chapter 4. Figure 2-4 also helps illustrate how the coordinates work out.

> **NOTE** It's important to remember that the move() **function puts the row first, or Y, X (if you're used to Cartesian coordinates). Think *row, column* as opposed to *X, Y*.**

The Old Formatted Text Trick

In NCurses, the printw() function can be used just like printf() to display strings of text, variables, formatted text, and all that sort of junk. If you know printf(), you also know printw() — but remember that in NCurses the printw() function is the one you want to use. Check out Listing 2-5 to see how this works.

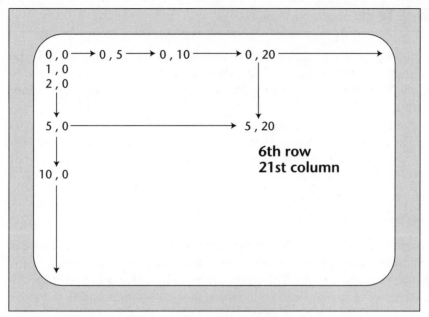

Figure 2-4: Plotting window coordinates in NCurses

Listing 2-5: YODA.C

```
1     #include  <ncurses.h>
2
3     int main(void)
4     {
5         int yoda = 874;
6         int ss = 65;
7
8         initscr();
9         printw("Yoda is %d years old\n",yoda);
10        printw("He has collected %d years\n",yoda-ss);
11        printw("of Social Security.");
12        refresh();
13        getch();
14
15        endwin();
16        return 0;
17    }
```

Nothing truly new here. The `printw()` function works just as you would expect `printf()` to work.

Reading Text

There is nothing really magical about writing text to the screen. Well, the
move() function is pretty cool. But the really cool stuff — especially if you're
weary of a lack of single-character input functions in C — comes with reading
text in from the keyboard.

Here are some NCurses console input functions:

getch()

getstr(*str)

getnstr(*str,length)

scanw(format,var[,var...])

The getch() function returns a single character from the console. There is
no need to press the Enter key, because the character is read right away.

The getstr() and getnstr() functions read in a string of text from the
console. Of the two, use getnstr(), which measures input and is therefore
more secure than the straight getstr() function.

Finally, scanw() works just like the standard I/O function scanf(). It
allows formatted input.

There are other NCurses functions for console input. Some help you shape
input, which I'll get into later in this book. For now I'm just going to demonstrate the basic commands listed here.

The Silly Typewriter Program

Nothing best demonstrates "one character in/one character out" than a simple, stupid typewriter program, such as the one in Listing 2-6.

Listing 2-6: TYPEWRITER.C

```
1     #include  <ncurses.h>
2
3     int main(void)
4     {
5          char ch;
6
7          initscr();
8          addstr("Type a few lines of text\n");
9          addstr("Press ~ to quit\n");
10         refresh();
11
12         while( (ch = getch()) != '~')
13              ;
14
15         endwin();
```

Listing 2-6 *(continued)*

```
16        return 0;
17    }
```

Note the while loop here. Basically, it's saying to read all character input until the ~ character is received; then bail. Try the program out:

```
Type a few lines of text
Press ~ to quit
```

Pressing Enter may result in a return instead of a return/line feed combination. That's fine; the program is more about I/O than actually editing text.

Note, however, that getch() in its natural state does display the text you've input; there is no need to use refresh() when getch() is reading text.

The getch() function doesn't always display text as it's typed. It's possible in NCurses to turn off echo on input. I'll cover that in Chapter 7.

Consuming a String Whole

The getstr() function works similarly to the standard gets() function, which simply takes keyboard input and stuffs it into a buffer — and without bounds checking, I might add. I demonstrate the function in Listing 2-7, but for security reasons, in your real programs, please use the getnstr() function instead, which is shown in the next section.

Listing 2-7: STRING1.C

```
1     #include  <ncurses.h>
2
3     int main(void)
4     {
5         char first[24];
6         char last[32];
7
8         initscr();
9         addstr("What is your first name? ");
10        refresh();
11        getstr(first);
12
13        addstr("What is your last name? ");
14        refresh();
15        getstr(last);
16
17        printw("Pleased to meet you, %s %s!",first,last);
18        refresh();
19        getch();
20
21        endwin();
22        return 0;
23    }
```

In this program, only 24 characters are allocated for first name storage, then 32 for last name. Please be sane about this and try not to type any super-long names!

Also note the positioning of the refresh() functions. Like getch(), get-str() normally displays its input as you type, so there's no need to refresh() after or during the function.

```
What is your first name? Clark

What is your last name? Kent

Pleased to meet you, Clark Kent!
```

And it pretty much works as you would expect it to.

Swallowing Only So Much of a String

Rather than risk some idiot typing 3,000 characters of text for his first name (the latter part of which is a worm program designed to hijack your computer), use the getnstr() function instead of getstr(). That n in there means "accept only *n* characters of input," a wise and logical addition to the input command.

Listing 2-8 shows a subtle modification of the previous string1.c program.

Listing 2-8: STRING2.C

```
1     #include  <ncurses.h>
2
3     int main(void)
4     {
5         char first[4];
6         char last[4];
7
8         initscr();
9         addstr("Enter the first 3 letters of your first name? ");
10        refresh();
11        getnstr(first,3);
12
13        addstr("Enter the first 3 letters of your last name? ");
14        refresh();
15        getnstr(last,3);
16
17        addstr("Your secret agent name is ");
18        printw("%s%s",first,last);
19        addch('!');
20        refresh();
21        getch();
22
```

Listing 2-8 *(continued)*

```
23        endwin();
24        return 0;
25    }
```

The size of the input buffers, `first` and `last`, is set to 4 characters. That's 3 letters plus the null \0 at the end of the string.

Note the format for `getnstr()`: First comes the character buffer, then the maximum character count. Users can still backspace and erase after reaching that number of characters, but if they try to type any more, the computer beeps at them (or the screen flashes).

The `printw()` function displays the two short strings.

Finally `addch()` is used to display the exclamation point.

The Obligatory scanw() Program

I'm not a big `scanf()` fan (as you already know if you've read my C programming books); therefore you're not going to be seeing much of `scanw()` outside of this section. Given that, Listing 2-9 shows the obligatory demonstration of `scanw()`.

Listing 2-9: SUSHI.C

```
1     #include <ncurses.h>
2
3     #define UNI 4.5
4
5     int main(void)
6     {
7         int pieces;
8
9         initscr();
10
11        addstr("SUSHI BAR");
12        move(3,0);
13        printw("We have Uni today for $%.2f.\n",UNI);
14        addstr("How many pieces would you like? ");
15        refresh();
16
17        scanw("%d",&pieces);
18        printw("You want %d pieces?\n",pieces);
19        printw("That will be $%.2f!",UNI*(float)pieces);
20        refresh();
21        getch();
22
23        endwin();
24        return 0;
25    }
```

Again, this could just be a simple `scanf()` program, though `scanw()` is used instead. I've not much more to say about it, mostly because, as I've already mentioned, I'm not a big `scanf()` fan.

TIP The big flub everyone makes with `scanf()`/`scanw()` is forgetting the ampersand before nonarray variable names. That one will cost you a core dump or three if you don't catch it.

CHAPTER 3

Formatting Text

NCurses not only puts text up on the screen; it also lets you put text on the screen with *style*. While the style may not be as elaborate as the styles offered in a GUI word processor, it is enough to add emphasis, fun, and perhaps a wee bit o' color to what would otherwise be boring terminal text.

Text Abuse with Text Attributes

There are three useful functions that control the tone of the text displayed on the screen:

```
attrset(attr)
attron(attr)
attroff(attr)
```

The `attrset()` function sets text attributes. It directs NCurses to apply the attribute(s) specified to all text displayed from that point onward.

The `attron()` and `attroff()` functions turn specific text attributes on or off, respectively.

There is some confusion regarding whether to use `attrset()` or `attron()` to apply text attributes. You can use either one. For example:

```
attrset(A_BOLD);
```

```
attron(A_BOLD);
```

Both these statements apply the bold text attribute to any text displayed afterward. The difference is that `attrset()` *turns off* all other attributes previously applied, leaving only bold applied to the text, while `attron()` *adds* the bold attribute to any attributes already applied to the text.

More than Boring Black and White (but Not Much)

When you start up NCurses, the text output is displayed using the normal (A_NORMAL) text attribute. That equates to the standard white text on a black background or however you have your terminal configured (for example, green text on a white background or whatever).

But that's so boring!

Table 3-1 lists the basic (noncolor) text attributes you can apply to text using the `attrset()` or `attron()` functions.

Table 3-1: NCurses Text Attributes

ATTRIBUTE NAME	WHAT IT DOES
A_ALTCHARSET	Displays text using an alternative character set (defined by your terminal)
A_BLINK	Annoying blinking text
A_BOLD	Bright text, bold text, thick text (depending on terminal type)
A_DIM	Dimmed text (not as bright as regular text)
A_INVIS	"Hidden text" (available only on certain terminals)
A_NORMAL	Normal text
A_REVERSE	Inverse text
A_STANDOUT	Same as `standout()`
A_UNDERLINE	Underline text
A_PROTECT	"Protected text," available only on certain terminals, prevents text from being overwritten.
A_HORIZONTAL	
A_LEFT	
A_LOW	
A_RIGHT	
A_TOP	
A_VERTICAL	Not implemented

The attributes listed in Table 3-1 are used with the attrset(), attron(), and attroff() functions to control the appearance of text on the screen. attron() and attroff() are used to set and reset individual attributes. attrset() is used to override any previous text attributes and set a new attribute for all text.

Some attributes are defined by the XSI (X/Open System Interface) but not yet implemented, at least not in any version of NCurses I've found. These are: A_HORIZONTAL, A_LEFT, A_LOW, A_RIGHT, A_TOP, and A_VERTICAL. (These are "highlighted modes," and I'm not really certain what that means.)

Testing Some Attributes

You can use the following program in Listing 3-1 as a base or test bed for testing the various attributes listed in Table 3-1.

Listing 3-1: twinkle.c

```
1    #include <ncurses.h>
2
3    int main(void)
4    {
5        initscr();
6
7        attron(A_BOLD);
8        addstr("Twinkle, twinkle little star\n");
9        attron(A_BLINK);
10       addstr("How I wonder what you are.\n");
11       attroff(A_BOLD);
12       addstr("Up above the world so high,\n");
13       addstr("Like a diamond in the sky.\n");
14       attrset(A_NORMAL);
15       addstr("Twinkle, twinkle little star\n");
16       addstr("How I wonder what you are.\n");
17       refresh();
18       getch();
19       endwin();
20       return 0;
21   }
```

The important thing to remember about this code is that an attribute stays on until you turn it off, either via attroff() or attrset(). Otherwise, the attributes are slapped on to all text output after the attribute function is used, which can be seen in Figure 3-1.

A_BOLD displays the text foreground in bold.

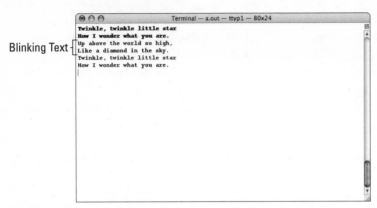

Figure 3-1: Output of the `twinkle.c` code

A_BLINK blinks the text on and off. Note that your terminal definition, or GUI terminal preferences panel, may disable this feature. It's generally accepted that blinking text is perhaps the most irritating attribute you can ever assign to anything on the screen.

> **NOTE** Note that text attributes affect only text, not the spaces or "blanks" between words.

Multiple-Attribute Mania

You don't have to issue multiple `attrset()`, `attron()`, or `attroff()` functions to apply or remove multiple attributes. Thanks to the unique bit patterns of the attribute constants in NCurses, text attributes can be applied all at once by using a logical OR between each attribute you want in a single `attron()` or `attrset()` function.

For example, if you want your text bold and blinking, you can use:

```
attrset(A_BOLD | A_BLINK);
```

Here, both the bold and blink attributes are specified, meaning any text displayed after that statement will boldly blink (highly irritating). See Listing 3-2 as an example.

Listing 3-2: `annoy.c`

```
1    #include <ncurses.h>
2
3    #define COUNT 5
4
5    int main(void)
```

Listing 3-2 *(continued)*

```
 6    {
 7        char text[COUNT][10] = { "Do", "you", "find", "this", "silly?" };
 8        int a,b;
 9
10        initscr();
11
12        for(a=0;a<COUNT;a++)
13        {
14            for(b=0;b<COUNT;b++)
15            {
16                if(b==a) attrset(A_BOLD | A_UNDERLINE);
17                printw("%s",text[b]);
18                if(b==a) attroff(A_BOLD | A_UNDERLINE);
19                addch(' ');
20            }
21            addstr("\b\n");
22        }
23        refresh();
24        getch();
25
26        endwin();
27        return 0;
28    }
```

Here's some sample output:

```
Do you find this silly?
Do you find this silly?
Do you find this silly?
Do you find this silly?
Do you find this silly?
```

Any number of attributes (including color) can be applied in a single `attron()` or `attrset()` command and likewise turned off via `attroff()` or `standend()`. Simply specify the | (logical OR) between the attribute constants.

Can It Do Color?

Of course, NCurses can do color! The question is whether or not the terminal can. Fortunately, the NCurses library comes with the tools to assist you in determining whether or not the terminal is color blind or rainbow ready.

```
has_colors()
```

The `has_colors()` function returns a logical TRUE if the terminal is able to display colored text, FALSE otherwise. (Both TRUE and FALSE are defined in NCURSES.H, so don't fret over them or redefine them in your code.)

After determining whether the terminal has colors, you need to start up NCurses color abilities. Here's the function that does that, aptly named:

```
start_color()
```

The start_color() function returns OK if the color functions are properly initialized. (And OK is defined in NCURSES.H.) So after successful completion of the start_color() command, you can use color attributes on text and to shade the background.

The following program in Listing 3-3 determines whether your terminal can do colors in NCurses and can start the color routines. If so, the program tells you how many colors and color combinations you can use. (More on that in the next section.)

Listing 3-3: colortest.c

```
1    #include <ncurses.h>
2    #include <stdlib.h>
3
4    void bomb(char *msg);
5
6    int main(void)
7    {
8        initscr();
9
10   /* first test for color ability of the terminal */
11       if(!has_colors())
12           bomb("Terminal cannot do colors\n");
13
14   /* next attempt to initialize curses colors */
15       if(start_color() != OK)
16           bomb("Unable to start colors.\n");
17
18   /* colors are okay; continue */
19       printw("Colors have been properly initialized.\n");
20       printw("Congratulations!\n");
21       printw("NCurses reports that you can use %d colors,\n",COLORS);
22       printw("and %d color pairs.",COLOR_PAIRS);
23       refresh();
24       getch();
25
26       endwin();
27       return 0;
28   }
29
30   void bomb(char *msg)
31   {
32       endwin();
33       puts(msg);
34       exit(1);
35   }
```

Here's the output I see on my computer:

```
Colors have been properly initialized.
Congratulations!

NCurses reports that you can use 8 colors,

and 64 color pairs.
```

Note the use of the COLORS and COLOR_PAIRS. These constants are set when start_color() checks to see how many colors are available to the terminal, as well as how much space is left for storing color information in the NCurses attr_t variable type. The next section explains the difference between COLORS and COLOR_PAIRS.

Colors and Color Pairs

In NCurses, the COLORS and COLOR_PAIRS constants report how many colors the terminal can display and how many color combinations (foreground + background — a *color pair*) can be defined. This may not be the way you've dealt with text colors in the past, so pay attention!

The COLORS value reflects the basic set of colors available to the terminal. The typical PC reports only eight colors available. These are the standard eight text colors used on PCs since the first IBM PC color graphics adapter set the standard back in 1981. The colors are listed in Table 3-2, along with their NCurses constant names and values.

Table 3-2: NCurses Colors

NCURSES NUMBER	PC BIOS NUMBER	PC NAME	NCURSES NAME
0	0	Black	COLOR_BLACK
1	4	Red	COLOR_RED
2	2	Green	COLOR_GREEN
3	6	Brown	COLOR_YELLOW
4	1	Blue	COLOR_BLUE
5	5	Magenta	COLOR_MAGENTA
6	3	Cyan	COLOR_CYAN
7	7	White	COLOR_WHITE

It's important to remember that the COLORS value tells you how many colors are available, yet the colors are numbered starting with zero. So the range of colors available is 0 through COLORS minus one.

A *color pair* is simply a combination of foreground and background color attributes. Each combination is a color pair and assigned a number from 1 through the value of COLOR_PAIRS minus 1.

For example, the color pair COLOR_YELLOW, COLOR_RED indicates yellow text on a red background. To assign those colors as a text attribute, you must first associate them with a color pair number. This is done with the init_pair function:

```
init_pair(pair,f,b)
```

The init_pair() function assigns two colors to color pair number pair. f is the foreground, or text, color; b is the background color.

```
init_pair(1,COLOR_YELLOW,COLOR_RED);
```

The preceding statement defines color pair number 1 as yellow text on a red background.

The next step is to apply the color attribute to the text. This is done by using the attrset() or attron() function just as you would apply any other text attribute. The key, however, is to use the COLOR_PAIR(n) constant:

```
attrset(COLOR_PAIR(1));
```

The preceding statement applies the color attributes assigned to color pair 1 to the text that follows. If COLOR_PAIR(1) is defined as yellow text on a red background, that's the attribute taken by the text.

To apply a different color to the text, use init_pair() to set up foreground and background colors for a color pair. Then use the COLOR_PAIR(n) constant with attrset() or attron() to apply that color pair combination to your text.

Eight or Sixteen Colors?

While NCurses may report only eight colors available, on most terminals there are twice as many colors to choose from. The secret is to apply the bold text attribute (A_BOLD) with a color pair.

The bold text attribute affects only the foreground text color. It gives you access to the eight *brighter* versions of the standard eight (or however many) text colors available.

For example, if color pair 1 is defined as Magenta on Black, applying bold to the text attribute yields pink on black text:

```
attrset(COLOR_PAIR(1) | A_BOLD);
```

The other foreground text colors become brighter versions of their original colors when logically OR'd with the A_BOLD attribute. Brown actually becomes yellow, and black becomes a midtone gray.

Spruce Up Some Text!

The color-pair stuff is only confusing when you're reading about it. The best way to understand the way NCurses applies color is, naturally, with a test program such as Listing 3-4.

Listing 3-4: `colorme.c`

```
1    #include <ncurses.h>
2    #include <stdlib.h>
3
4    void bomb(int r);
5
6    int main(void)
7    {
8        initscr();
9        start_color();
10
11       init_pair(1,COLOR_BLACK,COLOR_RED);
12       init_pair(2,COLOR_BLUE,COLOR_BLACK);
13       attrset(COLOR_PAIR(1));
14       addstr("My name is Mr. Black!\n");
15       attrset(COLOR_PAIR(2));
16       addstr("My name is Mr. Blue!\n");
17       attrset(COLOR_PAIR(1));
18       addstr("How do you do?\n");
19       attrset(COLOR_PAIR(2));
20       addstr("How do I do ");
21       attron(A_BOLD);
22       addstr("what");
23       attroff(A_BOLD);
24       addch('?');
25       refresh();
26       getch();
27
28       endwin();
29       return 0;
30   }
```

Note that I'm not using any error-checking with `start_color()` in line 10. In this code, I'm assuming that you know whether or not your terminal can do color. In the code you plan on releasing, it's wise to check for color and have your programs behave accordingly.

This basic program contains a simple back-and-forth conversation between two color pairs, shown in Figure 3-2. Be mindful of the parenthesis in the `attrset(COLOR_PAIR(n))` statements.

Notice how the color attributes affect only the text put to the screen. The red background doesn't "splash" out the rest of the line, and the foreground color, like other text attributes, affects only characters, not the blanks or white space between text.

A Color Thing Your Terminal Probably Cannot Do

NCurses has a treat for you when you're lucky enough to have a terminal that can define its own text colors. For example, you can define pink text and use it if you like. This is done via the `init_color()` function. The problem is that this function doesn't appear to be supported on many terminals. That can be confirmed with another function, `can_change_color()`, which returns a logical `TRUE` or `FALSE` depending on whether the terminal has the color-changing ability:

```
if(!can_change_color())
    bomb("Unable to do color change.\n");
```

Now if you can get it to work, the `init_color()` function comes into play, wherein you can create your own unique text colors. That function looks something like this:

```
init_color(color,r,g,b);
```

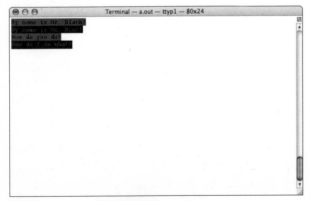

Figure 3-2: Sample output for `colorme.c` code

The values passed to init_color() are all short integers. The first color represents the new color number. It must be in the range of zero to COLOR minus 1. Then come values for the red (r), green (g), and blue (b) arguments, each of which ranges from 0 to 1000, representing the intensity of that particular color.

So, for example, the following call to init_color() defines (or redefines) color number 2 as a dark gray:

```
init_color(2,250,250,250);
```

The following source code in Listing 3-5 demonstrates how init_color is used to define the color pink for color code 1.

Listing 3-5: color_me.c

```
1    #include <ncurses.h>
2
3    #define NEW_COLOR 1
4    #define RED 1000
5    #define GREEN 750
6    #define BLUE 750
7
8    int main(void)
9    {
10       initscr();
11       start_color();
12       if(!can_change_color())
13           addstr("This probably won't work, but anyway:\n");
14
15       init_color(NEW_COLOR,RED,GREEN,BLUE);
16
17       init_pair(1,NEW_COLOR,COLOR_BLACK);
18       attrset(COLOR_PAIR(1));
19       printw("This is the new color %d.\n",NEW_COLOR);
20       refresh();
21       getch();
22
23       endwin();
24       return 0;
25   }
```

The init_color() function is used in line 15 to create the new color "pink" by mixing 1000 points of red with 750 points each of blue and green, which works out to be pink. Then that color is put to use by the init_pair() function, and the printw() function should display its text in the new color.

On my terminal, which cannot change text color values, the new color shows up as red, which is the default for color 1 anyway. I would call that a failure.

Coloring a Window

In addition to coloring text, NCurses' color attributes can be applied to windows as well, including the standard screen, the default window you see in NCurses. (The standard screen is the same size as the terminal screen.)

The function to fill the standard screen window with color (or any text attribute) is:

```
bkgd()
```

The bkdg() function, as its name suggests, sets the background attributes for the standard screen. Every screen location is filled with the attribute(s) specified, whether they're plain text attributes or color.

Screen Background Color

To set the background color, you must do three things, two of which you already know:

1. First, activate color. Use the has_color() command if necessary to determine whether the console can do colors. If so, use start_color() to put NCurses into rainbow mode.

2. Second, use init_pair() to create the color pair(s) you want to use, setting foreground and background colors.

3. Third, use bkgd() to color the entire window.

The code shown in Listing 3-6 demonstrates how background color is set.

Listing 3-6: bgcolor1.c

```
1     #include <ncurses.h>
2
3     int main(void)
4     {
5          initscr();
6
7          start_color();
8          init_pair(1,COLOR_WHITE,COLOR_BLUE);
9          bkgd(COLOR_PAIR(1));
10         refresh();
11         getch();
12
13         endwin();
14         return 0;
15    }
```

The result should be a solid blue screen, top to bottom. Any text added at this point appears with the color attribute applied automatically, in this case with white text on a blue background.

Press the Enter key to end the program; then modify the code to add some text. For example, insert the following before line 10:

```
addstr("So this is what a color screen looks like?\n");
```

The text appears on the screen with the same attribute: white text on a blue background.

More than Solid

Now if the solid screen bores you, it's possible to use the bkgd() function to fill each character space on the screen with a given character. That's because the argument to the bkgd() function is a chtype character.

The NCurses chtype is a special type of variable that includes both an attribute and a character. So, if you like, you can specify a single character as the background attribute for a window.

Modify the BGCOLOR1.C source code and change line 9 to read:

```
bkgd('.');
```

Upon running the program, you'll see the window's background filled with dots or periods. They appear between words as well because it's the dot that defines the window's background "attribute."

To combine the dot and the color pair, modify line 9 to read:

```
bkgd(COLOR_PAIR(1) | '.');
```

The | in the code is the *logical OR*. It takes the value of COLOR_PAIR(1) and logically ORs it with the character code for a period. You can also use the logical OR to apply other attributes or characters for the bkgd() function. (See Appendix C for more information on the chtype variable in NCurses.)

Changing Color on the Fly

The bkgd() function affects all attributes and unused character places on the screen. Any text you've written stays on the screen as text; only the attributes are changed, as Listing 3-7 demonstrates:

Listing 3-7: bgcolor2.c

```
1    #include <ncurses.h>
2
3    int main(void)
4    {
5        initscr();
6
7        start_color();
8        init_pair(1,COLOR_WHITE,COLOR_BLUE);
9        init_pair(2,COLOR_GREEN,COLOR_WHITE);
10       init_pair(3,COLOR_RED,COLOR_GREEN);
11       bkgd(COLOR_PAIR(1));
12       addstr("I think that I shall never see\n");
13       addstr("a color screen as pretty as thee.\n");
14       addstr("For seasons may change\n");
15       addstr("and storms may thunder;\n");
16       addstr("But color text shall always wonder.");
17       refresh();
18       getch();
19
20       bkgd(COLOR_PAIR(2));
21       refresh();
22       getch();
23
24       bkgd(COLOR_PAIR(3));
25       refresh();
26       getch();
27
28       endwin();
29       return 0;
30   }
```

The program initially displays some text on the screen, blue on a white background. Press the Enter key and the colors change to green on a white background — but the text is unchanged. Press Enter again and the text color changes to red, the background to green. Ugly, but it proves that you can change the screen color without bothering any printed text.

Noise, Too!

NCurses doesn't have sound routines (at least not yet), but there is an audible way to attract attention to your programs, a way beyond text attributes and colors. Two functions do the job.

The beep() function, as you can guess, simply beeps the terminal's speaker. Or, if you're from the ancient days, it would ring the bell on the teletype! Either way, it's getting the user's attention.

The flash() function is newer than beep, designed to get attention by flashing the screen, supposedly to assist the hearing impaired in recognizing alerts. Sadly, flash() isn't implemented on every terminal, so it may just beep the speaker on your computer. The one way to find out is to run a test program such as Listing 3-8.

Listing 3-8: notice.c

```
1    #include <ncurses.h>
2
3    int main(void)
4    {
5        initscr();
6
7        addstr("Attention!\n");
8        beep();
9        refresh();
10       getch();
11       addstr("I said, ATTENTION!\n");
12       flash();
13       refresh();
14       getch();
15       endwin();
16       return 0;
17   }
```

After you see Attention! on the screen, you should hear the beep. Press Enter to see I said, ATTENTION! and look for the flash. On my computer, I just heard another beep. Press Enter again to end the program.

Around the Window

One of the things that make NCurses appeal to programmers is the control it offers, not only over the text you display but over the location of that text as well. The key is moving the cursor. Secondary to that, of course, is knowing how big the terminal screen (or, in NCurses, the standard screen window) can be, so that you keep all your text visible.

Measuring the Standard Screen

If you're going to be moving the cursor hither, thither, and yon, it helps to know the dimensions of your terminal screen. Not every terminal is going to be exactly like yours, and it's an especially bad thing to assume that all terminals follow the dimensions of the standard PC text screen's 25 rows by 80 columns.

In NCurses the terminal screen isn't part of the equation. Instead, a window is used called the *standard screen*, which coincidentally is just the same size and dimensions as the terminal's screen. (Yes, this may seem trivial at this point, but soon you'll discover NCurses window functions, wherein all this makes much more sense.)

The Size of the Window Is Y by X

To discover the size of any window in NCurses, the following function can be used:

```
getmaxyx(win,y,x)
```

The `getmaxyx()` function returns the dimensions of the window `win` in rows and columns, where `y` is the row and `x` is the column. That the function is named `getmaxyx()` should help you remember that Y, or rows, comes first.

The `win` argument is the name of a specific window in NCurses. For the terminal screen, you use the standard screen window, which is named `stdscr`.

The `y` and `x` arguments are `int` variables (not pointers) that will hold the maximum number of rows and columns in the named window. (See Listing 4-1.)

Listing 4-1: `screensize.c`

```
 1    #include <ncurses.h>
 2
 3    int main(void)
 4    {
 5         int x,y;
 6
 7         initscr();
 8
 9         getmaxyx(stdscr,y,x);
10         printw("Window size is %d rows, %d columns.\n",y,x);
11         refresh();
12         getch();
13
14         endwin();
15         return 0;
16    }
```

Here's what I see for output:

```
Windows size is 24 rows, 80 columns.
```

That's my terminal window's size; yours may be different. Because my terminal window is in a graphical window in a GUI, I can resize it. When I do and make the window wider, rerunning the program reports the new results:

```
Windows size is 24 rows, 85 columns.
```

The point here is to remember that it's a *bad thing* to guess the terminal's size. Write your code so that your program uses `getmaxyx()` to determine the screen size and save those values in variables; do not use constants!

And Now: the Shortcut

The `getmaxyx()` function can read the dimensions of any NCurses window, but because the standard screen is special, there are two NCurses constants you can use as well (refer to Listing 4-2):

LINES

COLS

The value of the LINES constant is equal to the number of rows on the standard screen window and, therefore, the terminal screen.

The value of COLS is equal to the number of columns on the standard screen window, as well as the terminal.

Listing 4-2: `stdscrsize.c`

```
1     #include <ncurses.h>
2
3     int main(void)
4     {
5         initscr();
6
7         printw("Window size is %d rows, %d columns.\n",LINES,COLS);
8         refresh();
9         getch();
10
11        endwin();
12        return 0;
13    }
```

The output is the same as from the SCREENSIZE.C code, though LINES and COLS are always specific to the standard screen.

Do remember that the Y constant is LINES, not ROWS.

Moving the Cursor Around

In NCurses, the cursor — that thing that tells curses where to put the next character on the screen — is moved around via the move() function but also by most commands that put text to the screen. As you've seen in early chapters, putting a \n to the screen moves the text down to the next line. Nothing surprising there.

To provide basic cursor control, there is only one command:

```
move(y,x)
```

You've already seen this command at work in Chapter 2, and there's really nothing to it. But in this chapter I'll add three more interesting commands that combine moving the cursor with slapping down text:

```
mvaddch(y,x,ch)

mvaddstr(y,x,*str)

mvprintw(y,x,format,arg[...])
```

Oh, you could probably guess how they go, but I love sample programs, and the urge to create them is just *too great!* So follow along and learn a tad bit more about moving the cursor in NCurses.

Watch Out! I've Got You Cornered!

There are four corners on the standard screen: upper left, upper right, lower left, and lower right. And you know what would just look lovely in each corner? Why, an asterisk, that's what. Just like the program in Listing 4-3 demonstrates:

Listing 4-3: `corners1.c`

```
1      #include <ncurses.h>
2
3      int main(void)
4      {
5          int rows,cols;
6
7          initscr();
8          getmaxyx(stdscr,rows,cols);
9          rows--;
10         cols--;
11
12         move(0,0);              /* UL corner */
13         addch('*');
14         refresh();
15         napms(500);            /* pause half a sec. */
16
17         move(0,cols);          /* UR corner */
18         addch('*');
19         refresh();
20         napms(500);
21
22         move(rows,0);          /* LL corner */
23         addch('*');
24         refresh();
25         napms(00);
26
27         move(rows,cols);        /* LR corner */
```

Listing 4-3 *(continued)*

```
28        addch('*');
29        refresh();
30        getch();
31
32        endwin();
33        return 0;
34    }
```

The program slaps down an asterisk in every corner of the screen.

Line 12 isn't necessary; NCurses initializes the cursor at the *home* location of 0,0 when the standard screen window is created by `initscr()`. Even so, I recommend using a `move(0,0);` statement in your code just in case future editions of NCurses change and because it's never really a good idea to assume anything in your code.

Some Compacting

The folks who write and maintain NCurses came to a strong realization many years ago that any `move()` function is usually followed by a command to actually stick *text* on the screen. I mean, the following code in any program would be rather silly:

```
move(10,13);           /* move to here */
move(5,6);           /* then to here */
move(17,11);            /* try out this spot */
move(21,0);            /* then put the cursor here */
```

What's the point of all that? No, sir, `move()` functions are followed by some type of text output function or statement. And you already know three of them: `addch()`, `addstr()`, and `printw()`. By prefixing `mv` (for *move*) to each of those commands, you get a combined move-and-print command.

Listing 4-4 shows a modification, do-over to the original `4corner.c` source code:

Listing 4-4: `corners2.c`

```
1    #include <ncurses.h>
2
3    int main(void)
4    {
5        int rows,cols;
6
7        initscr();
8        getmaxyx(stdscr,rows,cols);
9        rows--;
```

(continued)

Listing 4-4 *(continued)*

```
10        cols--;
11
12        mvaddch(0,0,'*');              /* UL corner */
13        refresh();
14        napms(500);                /* pause half a sec. */
15
16        mvaddch(0,cols,'*');         /* UR corner */
17        refresh();
18        napms(500);
19
20        mvaddch(rows,0,'*');         /* LL corner */
21        refresh();
22        napms(500);
23
24        mvaddch(rows,cols,'*');          /* LR corner */
25        refresh();
26
27        getch();
28
29        endwin();
30        return 0;
31    }
```

The output is the same, but you've saved a lot of typing and redundancy. Note the format for the mvaddch() function:

```
mvaddch(y,x,ch)
```

The row and column come first, and the character to punch in that spot goes last. Again, this is just like combining the two functions, move() and addch().

Center that Title!

It's possible to have lots of fun with math and positioning text all over the screen. Don't run away! Remember that the computer does the math. Centering text on the screen is an old and ancient art. It works like this:

1. Figure out how wide the screen is.

2. Figure out how wide your title text is.

3. Subtract the title text length from the screen width. The value left over needs to be shared equally as spaces on either side of the title.

4. Divide the value left over by two. That's the number of characters to space over to center the title.

But don't fret over writing that code yourself. The following program in Listing 4-5 has it all done for you.

Listing 4-5: `ctitle.c`

```
 1    #include <ncurses.h>
 2    #include <string.h>
 3
 4    void center(int row, char *title);
 5
 6    int main(void)
 7    {
 8        initscr();
 9
10        center(1, "Penguin Soccer Finals");
11        center(5, "Cattle Dung Samples from Temecula");
12        center(7, "Catatonic Theater");
13        center(9, "Why Do Ions Hate Each Other?");
14        getch();
15
16        endwin();
17        return 0;
18    }
19
20    void center(int row, char *title)
21    {
22        int len,indent,y,width;
23
24        getmaxyx(stdscr,y,width);          /* get screen width */
25
26        len = strlen(title);        /* get title's length */
27        indent = width - len;       /* subtract it from screen width */
28        indent /= 2;                /* divide result into two */
29
30        mvaddstr(row,indent,title);
31        refresh();
32    }
```

The `center()` function is what centers the title text on a line. You supply the row number and the line of text to center. The `center()` function then centers that text on the given row.

NOTE Remember that the top row on the terminal screen is zero, not 1!

I included several `center()` commands with titles of varying length. Feel free to add more or experiment with the lengths.

The math part is done in the `center()` function. First, the string's length is calculated and returned by the `strlen()` function and stored in the `len` variable. Then that's subtracted from the screen's width, as returned from `getmaxyx()`. Then it's cut in half in line 28.

Some Fun with mvprintw()

Why do the math when the compiler can do it for you? One gem with printf(), and then, of course, NCurses' printw(), is that it can justify strings in its output. For example:

```
printf("%40s", "This is right-justified");
```

The %s normally tells printf() to replace the %s with a string. The %40s, however, tells printf() to set aside 40 spaces in which to stick the string. As with numbers, the string is right-justified:

```
                   This is right-justified
```

Now if you prefix the size of the field with a minus sign, you get left-justified output:

```
printf("%-40s", "This is left-justified");
```

The −40 means to set aside 40 spaces and left-justify the given string. To wit:

```
This is left-justified
```

This calculating feature of printf(), and therefore printw() and therefore mvprintw(), can be put to use to do interesting justification on the screen without a lot of mathematical overhead, as the following program in Listing 4-6 demonstrates:

Listing 4-6: mydata.c

```
 1    #include <ncurses.h>
 2
 3    #define COL1 5
 4    #define COL2 38
 5
 6    int main(void)
 7    {
 8        initscr();
 9
10        mvprintw(5,COL1, "%30s", "Your name:");
11        mvprintw(5,COL2, "%-30s", "Art Grockmeister");
12
13        mvprintw(7,COL1, "%30s", "Your company:");
14        mvprintw(7,COL2, "%-30s", "Sterling/Worbletyme");
15
16        mvprintw(9,COL1, "%30s", "Position:");
```

Listing 4-6 *(continued)*

```
17        mvprintw(9,COL2, "%-30s", "Grand Duke of Finance");
18
19        mvprintw(11,COL1, "%30s", "Date hired:");
20        mvprintw(11,COL2, "%-30s", "October 19, 1993");
21        refresh();
22        getch();
23
24        endwin();
25        return 0;
26    }
```

The move-cursor commands don't seem to be logical until you think of them as placing given 30-character fields on the screen. Remember that the `printw()` function is doing the alignment.

Here's what the output generally looks like:

```
    Your name      : Art Grockmeister

    Your company   : Sterling/Worbletyme

    Position       : Grand Duke of Finance

    Date hired     : October 19, 1993
```

You can adjust the positions of the columns easily by changing the values of the COL1 and COL2 constants. This is why they were declared as constants instead of being hard-coded into the program.

Whither the Cursor?

Knowing where the cursor is doesn't seem as popular or necessary a function as being able to move the cursor. But consider the case where a program involves full-screen user input. In that example, it helps to have a function that tracks down where the booger is.

The `getyx()` function reads the logical cursor location from the window `win` (`stdscr` for the standard screen) and puts its row and column positions into the variables y and x. As with the `move()` function, the home location 0,0 is the upper-left corner of the screen. (See Listing 4-7.)

Listing 4-7: whereami.c

```
1    #include <ncurses.h>
2
3    int main(void)
4    {
5        char ch='\0';              /* initialize ch to NULL */
6        int row,col;
7
8        initscr();
9
10       addstr("Type some text; '~' to end:\n");
11       refresh();
12
13       while( (ch=getch()) != '~')
14           ;
15
16       getyx(stdscr,row,col);
17       printw("\n\nThe cursor was at row %d, column %d\n",row,col);
18       printw("when you stopped typing.");
19       refresh();
20       getch();
21
22       endwin();
23       return 0;
24   }
```

The program lets you type away on the screen, similar to the typewriter.c program shown earlier in this book. When you press the tilde key, ~, the getyx function grabs the location of the cursor, and the printw statement tells you where it was.

Note that the function is named getyx(), not getxy().

Here's a sample of the output you may see:

```
Type some text; '~' to end:
Bill is a jerk!~

The cursor was at row 1, column 16
When you stopped typing.
```

CHAPTER 5

More Text Manipulation

NCurses provides a wealth of text-manipulation functions, which are more than just positioning the cursor. There are functions that can insert and delete characters or lines of text, causing other text on the screen to jump around and make room or to fill in the gaps. This chapter covers those amazing functions.

Inserting and Deleting Functions

Writing a program that spits up text on the screen is a relatively easy task. What becomes a pain in the rear is when you have to *modify* the text you splash on the screen. That becomes the "Oh, no! I now have to rethink how all this is going to work" chore.

Face it. Some dolt somewhere is always going to change his mind. You must learn to be versatile, to plan ahead. And if that's not always possible, you can rely on the following functions in NCurses that insert and delete text:

```
insch(ch)
insertln()
delch()
deleteln()
```

The ins sisters are used to insert a single character or a complete line of text. The insch() inserts a character. The insertln() function scrolls in a blank line of text.

The del brothers have no arguments. They delete a single character or an entire line of text from the screen.

As someone who's struggled to write his own text editor can attest, these routines are blessings in disguise! And they work in the logical manner you would expect them to — yet another wreath to toss on the monument to NCurses' designers.

Editing Shakespeare

The following source code in Listing 5-1 serves as the core for the next several sets of programs.

Listing 5-1: hamlet1.c

```
1     #include <ncurses.h>
2
3     int main(void)
4     {
5         char Ham1[] = "To be, or not to be: that is the question:\n";
6         char Ham2[] = "Whether 'tis nobler in the mind to suffer\n";
7         char Ham3[] = "The slings and arrows of outrageous fortune,\n";
8         char Ham4[] = "Or to take arms against a sea of troubles,\n";
9         char Ham5[] = "And by opposing end them?\n";
10
11        initscr();
12
13        addstr(Ham1);
14        addstr(Ham3);
15        addstr(Ham5);
16        refresh();
17        getch();
18
19        endwin();
20        return 0;
21    }
```

The program dutifully prints every other line of the start of Hamlet's famous soliloquy:

```
To be, or not to be: that is the question:
The slings and arrows of outrageous fortune
And by opposing end them?
```

Doesn't quite sound the same, right? Of course, to the ignorant it still "sounds" like Shakespeare — but I'm not here to argue the merits of the bard's poetry or why people seem so turned off by him.

Inserting Some Lines

The purpose of this lesson is to rebuild the quote properly. The HAMLET1.C code contains all the text so you don't have to retype the entire soliloquy. But just pretend the input was coming from the terminal and you needed to insert a new line of text between lines 1 and 2?

Remember that on the screen, lines 1 and 2 appear on screen rows 0 and 1. Therefore, you would need to insert a blank line at row 1 and shove in the new text there. Further, you would need to scroll the other lines down so that the new line wouldn't overwrite the existing line.

Fortunately, the insertln() function does all that: It inserts a blank line all the way across the screen and scrolls the rest of the text beneath that line down one notch (see Listing 5-2). At that point, you merely need to add the string of text you need.

Listing 5-2: hamlet2.c

```
1    #include <ncurses.h>
2
3    int main(void)
4    {
5        char Ham1[] = "To be, or not to be: that is the question:\n";
6        char Ham2[] = "Whether 'tis nobler in the mind to suffer\n";
7        char Ham3[] = "The slings and arrows of outrageous fortune,\n";
8        char Ham4[] = "Or to take arms against a sea of troubles,\n";
9        char Ham5[] = "And by opposing end them?\n";
10
11       initscr();
12
13       addstr(Ham1);
14       addstr(Ham3);
15       addstr(Ham5);
16       refresh();
17       getch();        /* wait for key press */
18
19       move(1,0);        /* position cursor */
20       insertln();        /* insert a blank line, scroll text down */
21       addstr(Ham2);    /* line to insert */
22       refresh();
23       getch();        /* wait for key press */
24
25       endwin();
26       return 0;
27   }
```

Lines 18 through 22 are the new ones, as shown in the listing, inserting the proper second line of the speech. When the program runs, after the first three lines are displayed, press Enter. That way, getch() has something to eat, and then the rest of the program works.

The new code starts by moving the logical cursor to row 1 (the second row) column 0 (first column).

Next, the insertln() function creates a blank line on the same line where the logical cursor is placed. It always blanks the entire line, even if the cursor is placed on the far left side of the screen.

Finally, the addstr() function inserts a new string of text at the cursor's position, which is still 1,0. The insertln() function does not move the cursor; it uses the cursor's row position as a guide for which line to blank.

The result is that the existing text is scrolled down and the new line is inserted. (Note that insertln() scrolls the entire contents of the standard screen window. If there is text on the last line, that line is scrolled off into oblivion.)

Final Changes to Hamlet

The problem with HAMLET2.C is that it's still missing one line of text. There are multiple ways to add that last line of text and finish the program, any one of which is acceptable as long as the results on the screen look like this:

```
To be, or not to be: that is the question:
Whether 'tis nobler in the mind to suffer
The slings and arrows of outrageous fortune,
Or to take arms against a sea of troubles,
And by opposing end them?
```

Try your own solution before looking at mine in Listing 5-3.

NOTE The most common mistake is forgetting that the first insertln scrolls down the rest of the text; you must move the cursor to row 3, not row 2, to insert the fourth line.

Listing 5-3: hamlet3.c

```
1    #include <ncurses.h>
2
3    int main(void)
4    {
5        char Ham1[] = "To be, or not to be: that is the question:\n";
6        char Ham2[] = "Whether 'tis nobler in the mind to suffer\n";
7        char Ham3[] = "The slings and arrows of outrageous fortune,\n";
8        char Ham4[] = "Or to take arms against a sea of troubles,\n";
```

Listing 5-3 *(continued)*

```
 9         char Ham5[] = "And by opposing end them?\n";
10
11         initscr();
12
13         addstr(Ham1);
14         addstr(Ham3);
15         addstr(Ham5);
16         refresh();
17         getch();
18
19         move(1,0);          /* position cursor */
20         insertln();          /* insert blank line, scroll text down */
21         addstr(Ham2);     /* line to insert */
22         refresh();
23         getch();
24
25         move(3,0);
26         insertln();          /* insert blank line at line 4 */
27         addstr(Ham4);     /* add line 4 */
28         refresh();
29         getch();
30
31         endwin();
32         return 0;
33     }
```

Right

Inserting One Character at a Time

The insch() function inserts only one character into a row of text, shoving all the characters to the left one space to the left. And like insertln(), any character that gets shoved off the left side of the screen is forgotten; no "wrapping" takes place with insch().

The following source code in Listing 5-4 is one of those classic chestnuts, the scrolling marquee. Of course, it's a lot easier to write, thanks to the insch() function.

Listing 5-4: marquee1.c

```
1     #include <ncurses.h>
2     #include <string.h>
3
4     int main(void)
5     {
6         char text[] = "Stock Market Swells! DOW tops 15,000!";
7         char *t;
8         int len;
9
```

(continued)

Listing 5-4 *(continued)*

```
10          initscr();
11
12          len = strlen(text);
13          t = text;                /* initialize pointer */
14          while(len)
15          {
16              move(5,5);            /* always insert at the same spot */
17              insch(*(t+len-1));      /* work through string backwards */
18              refresh();
19              napms(100);           /* .1 sec. delay */
20              len--;
21          }
22          getch();
23
24          endwin();
25          return 0;
26      }
```

Each character in the string is processed backward in the `while` loop (lines 14-21), from the end to the beginning. The `*(t+len-1)` calculation initially points to the last character in the string, based on its length `len` (with the `t` pointer always pointing at the start of the string).

As the `while` loop decrements the value of `len`, the `*(t+len-1)` calculation points to each previous character in the string. The `insch()` function then displays that character at location 5,5, pushing the rest of the text on that line one notch to the left. The result is the scrolling marquee.

A More Visual Example

The following code in Listing 5-5 modifies the original `MARQUEE1.C` source code, filling the screen with text so that you can more graphically see how the `insch()` function affects text on the screen.

Listing 5-5: `marquee2.c`

```
1      #include <ncurses.h>
2      #include <string.h>
3
4      void fill(void);
5
6      int main(void)
7      {
8          char text[] = "Stock Market Swells! DOW tops 15,000!";
9          char *t;
10         int len;
11
12         initscr();
```

Listing 5-5 *(continued)*

```
13
14          fill();
15          refresh();
16          len = strlen(text);
17          t = text;              /* initialize pointer */
18          while(len)
19          {
20              move(5,5);          /* always insert at the same spot */
21              insch(*(t+len-1));    /* work through string backwards */
22              refresh();
23              napms(100);          /* .1 sec. delay */
24              len--;
25          }
26          getch();
27
28          endwin();
29          return 0;
30      }
31
32      void fill(void)
33      {
34          int a,x,y;
35
36          getmaxyx(stdscr,y,x);
37          for(a=0; a<y; a++)
38              addstr("A B C D E F G H I J K L M N O P Q R S T U V W X Y
Z\n");
39      }
```

Less of Hamlet

On the deleting side, NCurses offers the delch() and deleteln() functions. My favorite is delch() because I can pronounce it. Even so, the following source code in Listing 5-6 shows deleteln() first. It's a modification of
the original HAMLET.C source code, which makes typing easier.

Listing 5-6: hamlet4.c

```
1      #include <ncurses.h>
2
3      int main(void)
4      {
5          char Ham1[] = "To be, or not to be: that is the question:\n";
6          char Ham2[] = "Whether 'tis nobler in the mind to suffer\n";
7          char Ham3[] = "The slings and arrows of outrageous fortune,\n";
8          char Ham4[] = "Or to take arms against a sea of troubles,\n";
```

(continued)

Listing 5-6 *(continued)*

```
 9          char Ham5[] = "And by opposing end them?\n";
10
11          initscr();
12
13          addstr(Ham1);
14          addstr(Ham2);
15          addstr(Ham3);
16          addstr(Ham4);
17          addstr(Ham5);
18          refresh();
19          getch();                /* wait for key press */
20
21          move(1,0);                /* move to the line to delete */
22          deleteln();                /* Delete and backscroll */
23          refresh();
24          getch();                /* wait for key press */
25
26          endwin();
27          return 0;
28      }
```

First, the whole chunk of text is displayed. Good.

Press Enter to delete the text. Note how it scrolls up? Yes, the deleteln()
function is nearly the opposite of the insertln() function, complete with
logical reverse scrolling. And the vanished line goes off into bit-hell as well;
don't look for it anywhere.

Do note that deleteln() does not affect the location of the cursor. After
the last refresh() command above, the cursor is still at location 1,0, eagerly
awaiting more text to be added to the screen.

Goodbye, Chunk of Text!

It's time to edit Hamlet's speech. Your job is to display the text, then press a
key to delete the word "outrageous."

The command to use is delch(), which has no arguments. It simply
removes whichever character happens to be lurking at the current cursor position. Any characters to the right on the same line are then shuffled over left one
notch; a blank character is then added to the end of the line.

Hint: "outrageous" is 10 characters long, but you probably also want to
delete the space character immediately after it. So 11.

Here's another hint: Row 2, Column 25.

You should be able to see the text displayed, press a key, and then watch as
the word "outrageous" vanishes. Such tidy editing.

As long as your program worked, everything is fine by me. For comparison purposes only, Listing 5-7 shows my solution to the problem.

Listing 5-7: `hamlet5.c`

```
1    #include <ncurses.h>
2
3    int main(void)
4    {
5        char Ham1[] = "To be, or not to be: that is the question:\n";
6        char Ham2[] = "Whether 'tis nobler in the mind to suffer\n";
7        char Ham3[] = "The slings and arrows of outrageous fortune,\n";
8        char Ham4[] = "Or to take arms against a sea of troubles,\n";
9        char Ham5[] = "And by opposing end them?\n";
10       int c;
11
12       initscr();
13
14       addstr(Ham1);
15       addstr(Ham2);
16       addstr(Ham3);
17       addstr(Ham4);
18       addstr(Ham5);
19       refresh();
20       getch();              /* wait for key press */
21
22       move(2,25);              /* move to the start of "outrageous"  */
23       for(c=0;c<11;c++)
24          delch();           /* gobble! */
25       refresh();
26       getch();              /* wait for key press */
27
28       endwin();
29       return 0;
30   }
```

Gobble! Note that `delch()` does not "backscroll" the screen or "reverse wrap" any text from the following line. You can make such a thing happens, but *you* will have to write the code that does it.

Out It Goes and in It Comes

One more final modification to the Hamlet speech!

On your own, modify the source code so that it displays each character of "`outrageous`" being deleted one at a time. Further, modify the source code so that the word "`obnoxious`" is inserted in place of "`outrageous`," again one character at a time. Hint: Use the `napms()` function to create a delay between inserting and deleting each character.

How did you do? Did you forget to not delete (or reinsert) the space after "outrageous?" Did you use insch() and discover that your new text was inserted backward? Or did you cheat and just use my solution, shown in Listing 5-8?

Listing 5-8: hamlet6.c

```
1    #include <ncurses.h>
2
3    int main(void)
4    {
5        char Ham1[] = "To be, or not to be: that is the question:\n";
6        char Ham2[] = "Whether 'tis nobler in the mind to suffer\n";
7        char Ham3[] = "The slings and arrows of outrageous fortune,\n";
8        char Ham4[] = "Or to take arms against a sea of troubles,\n";
9        char Ham5[] = "And by opposing end them?\n";
10       char *ob = "obnoxious";
11       int c;
12
13       initscr();
14
15       addstr(Ham1);
16       addstr(Ham2);
17       addstr(Ham3);
18       addstr(Ham4);
29       addstr(Ham5);
20       refresh();
21   getch();              /* wait for key press */
22
23   /* First, remove "outrageous" */
24
25       move(2,25);                /* move to the start of "outrageous" */
26       for(c=0;c<10;c++)          /* only loop 2 times */
27       {
28           delch();         /* gobble! */
29           refresh();            /* update screen (cursor doesn't move)
*/
30           napms(100);          /* pause */
31       }
32
33   /* Second, insert "obnoxious" */
34
35       move(2,25);                /* reset cursor */
36       for(c=0;c<9;c++)
37       {
38           insch( *(ob+8-c) );
39           refresh();
40           napms(100);
41       }
42       getch();
```

Listing 5-8 *(continued)*

```
43
44          endwin();
45          return 0;
46     }
```

In this source code, I decided to use a little pointer math to display the "obnoxious" string:

```
insch(*(ob+8-c));
```

Pointer ob is positioned to point at the "s" in obnoxious. That's eight characters into the string minus the value of c, which is zero at the start of the for loop. As the for loop progress, the value of c increases, which backsteps one character at a time through the string.

Remember that insch() inserts text backward because it doesn't move the cursor. So you have to slide "obnoxious" in back to front.

Clearing and Zapping

There is a difference between clearing a chunk of the screen and deleting text in NCurses. That difference is that clearing merely erases, replacing the text with blank characters. Deleting, on the other hand, removes the text and tightens up the hole, which is demonstrated with the delch() and deleteln() functions in Chapter 5.

In this chapter, you're introduced to the handful of NCurses commands that erase text without scrolling or tightening up the holes. I call it "Clearing and Zapping."

Commands to Erase Chunks of the Screen

NCurses sports four functions to clear or erase any chunk of the screen:

    erase()
    clear()
    clrtobot()
    clrtoeol()

The erase() and clear() functions do pretty much the same thing: clear the screen. Between the two, the clear() function is more thorough, though it has more internal overhead.

The clrtobot() function clears from the cursor's current position to the bottom of the screen. And clrtoeol() clears from the cursor's position to the end of the current line. Simple.

The Obligatory Test Program

The best way to demonstrate the erase-chunks commands is to have something on the screen worthy of erasure. For that I present the BLAH1.C program in Listing 6-1.

Listing 6-1: blah1.c

```
1    #include <ncurses.h>
2
3    int main(void)
4    {
5        int c,y,x,cmax;
6
7        initscr();
8
9        getmaxyx(stdscr,y,x);
10       cmax = (x * y) / 5;
11       for(c=0;c<cmax;c++) addstr("blah ");
12       refresh();
13
14       getch();
15
16       endwin();
17       return 0;
18   }
```

The code uses the getmaxyx() function to grab the screen size, given in Y columns and X rows. Then a calculation is made to determine the maximum number of strings, blah+space, that can be put on the terminal screen.

Running the program results in a screen full of blah, as shown in Figure 6-1.

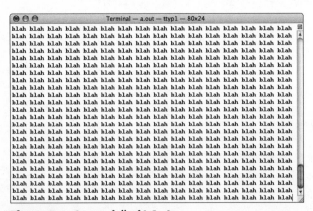

Figure 6-1: Screen full of blah

Now you're ready to experiment with clearing chunks of text on the screen.

Clear the Screen!

The first modification to blah1.c is the BLAH2.C source code shown in Listing 6-2. This code shows how the clear function is used to clear the screen.

Listing 6-2: blah2.c

```
 1    #include <ncurses.h>
 2
 3    int main(void)
 4    {
 5         int c,y,x,cmax;
 6
 7         initscr();
 8
 9         getmaxyx(stdscr,y,x);
10         cmax = (x * y) / 5;
11         for(c=0;c<cmax;c++) addstr("blah ");
12         refresh();
13         getch();
14
15         clear();              /* clear the screen */
16         refresh();               /* don't forget this! */
17         getch();
18
19         endwin();
20         return 0;
21    }
```

The code in Listing 6-2 uses the clear() function in line 15 to clear the standard screen window. But that does nothing visually; remember that a refresh() function is required (line 16) to show what's been done.

Note that this clearing of the screen moves the cursor to "home" after clearing the screen, just as if you issued a move(0,0) function.

Clear or Erase?

The erase() and clear() functions are nearly identical, but the clear() function does a more thorough job, ensuring that the NCurses window is completely redrawn from scratch the next time a refresh() function is issued.

Using the BLAH2.C source code, create a file, BLAH3.C. In that file, replace line 15 with:

```
erase();
```

The output is the same.

Clrto means Clear To

Oftentimes, you don't really want to erase the entire screen but rather only part of it. Because the text screen runs top to bottom, the two nonfull-screen NCurses erasing functions erase text from the cursor's current position to either the end of the current line of text or the end of the screen, depending on which you use.

Less Blah on the End of a Line

The `clrtoeol()` function (see Listing 6-3) is used to erase text from the cursor's position to the end of the current line. If you use the vi/vim editor, this is equivalent to the D command, though, unlike a text editor, `clrtoeol()` erases text on the screen; it's a visual command.

NOTE EOL means *End of Line* in primitive computer-speak. There is no EOL control code, though the Master Computer in the film *Tron* said, "End of line," whenever it was done talking. This trivia tidbit has absolutely nothing to do with NCurses.

Listing 6-3: `blah4.c`

```
1      #include <ncurses.h>
2
3      int main(void)
4      {
5          int c,y,x,cmax;
6
7          initscr();
8
9          getmaxyx(stdscr,y,x);
10         cmax = (x * y) / 5;
11         for(c=0;c<cmax;c++) addstr("blah ");
12         refresh();
13         getch();
14
15         move(5,20);              /* Setup the cursor */
16         clrtoeol();              /* clear to the end of line */
17         refresh();
18         getch();
19
20         endwin();
21         return 0;
22     }
```

The `clrtoeol()` function clears text only from the cursor's position to the end of the line (line 6). No surprises. No shocks. No Taco Bell dog dancing across the screen.

And, yes, the `clrtoeol()` function does not affect the cursor's position, nor does it alter any text on any other row.

Less Blah to the End of the Screen

The `clrtobot()` function (see Listing 6-4) takes all the text from the cursor's position to the last position on the screen and replaces the text with blanks (spaces). After using `clrtobot()`, the screen looks half blank, more or less.

NOTE BOT means *Bottom of Text.*

Listing 6-4: `blah5.c`

```
 1    #include <ncurses.h>
 2
 3    int main(void)
 4    {
 5        int c,y,x,cmax;
 6
 7        initscr();
 8
 9        getmaxyx(stdscr,y,x);
10        cmax = (x * y) / 5;
11        for(c=0;c<cmax;c++) addstr("blah ");
12        refresh();
13        getch();
14
15        move(5,20);              /* Setup the cursor */
16        clrtobot();             /* clear to the end of screen */
17        refresh();
18        getch();
19
20        endwin();
21        return 0;
22    }
```

From the original BLAH4.C source code, only line 16 is changed. Replace the `clrtoeol()` function with `clrtobot()`. That directs NCurses to clear the screen from the cursor's position (5,20) to the end of the screen.

The screen fills with the "blahs" again. Press a key, and the bottom two-thirds is zapped, leaving only four "blahs" on line 6. It looks something like Figure 6-2.

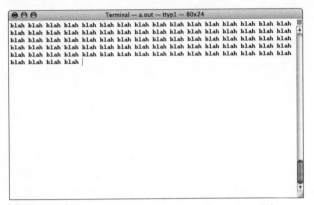

Figure 6-2: Using `clrtobot()` to clear part of the screen

You Mean that's It for My NCurses Erasing Fun and Excitement?

Yep.

There are no NCurses commands to clear the top part of the screen, so no counterpart to `clrtobot()` exists. Likewise, no command exists to erase text from the cursor's position to the *start* of a line. Even so, it's possible to code these commands yourself, should you need them.

CHAPTER 7

Keyboard Madness!

The `getch()` function is one of the immediate blessings that NCurses offers struggling *nix programmers. Unlike the C macro `getchar()`, which is a stream-reading command, `getch()` hops back right away with whatever key was pressed. Such a function helps make your programs more interactive, which can be a huge bonus.

Using `getch()` merely to read the keyboard is grand, but there is far more `getch()` can do. In fact, this lengthy chapter discusses many of the options available to `getch()` and how you can use it to do more than you possibly expected.

Reading from the Keyboard

The `getch()` function normally waits until a key is pressed on the keyboard. This is known as a *blocking* call; program execution is stopped until a key is pressed. But it's possible to change that behavior so that `getch()` does not pause the program. In NCurses, that's done with the `nodelay()` function.

```
nodelay(sdtscr,TRUE)
```

The preceding function directs the getch() function to become nonblocking for the given window, the standard screen (stdscr). To restore getch() to its normal blocking mode, this version of nodelay() is used:

```
nodelay(stdscr,FALSE)
```

When getch() is in nonblocking mode, it will not pause program execution to wait for a key press. Instead, when no key is pressed or a key isn't waiting to be read from the keyboard buffer, getch() returns the value ERR — and the program continues. Likewise, if a key is pressed, getch() returns the key's value, as it usually does — and the program continues.

NOTE TRUE, FALSE, and ERR are defined in NCURSES.H.

Is a Character Waiting?

The following program in Listing 7-1 demonstrates how getch()'s personality can be changed by using the nodelay() function.

Listing 7-1: keywait1.c

```
1    #include <ncurses.h>
2
3    int main(void)
4    {
5        int value = 0;
6
7        initscr();
8
9        addstr("Press any key to begin:\n");
10       refresh();
11       getch();
12
13       nodelay(stdscr,TRUE);              /* turn off getch() wait */
14       addstr("Press any key to stop the insane loop!\n");
15       while(getch() == ERR)
16       {
17           printw("%d\r",value++);
18           refresh();
19       }
20
21       endwin();
22       return 0;
23    }
```

At first, in line 11, getch() carries on its normal blocking function. The program waits for a key to be pressed on the keyboard. (The key's value is unimportant, so it's not saved.)

The nodelay() function in line 13 turns off getch()'s blocking. Therefore, the while loop continues as long as getch() returns the value ERR, which is what it generates when no key has been pressed. During the while loop, values are displayed on the screen so that you're aware of the program continuing.

Note that there is no need to restore getch()'s function with another nodelay() function, at least not in this example.

Testing Waiting Characters

With getch()'s waiting ability turned off, you can use getch() to filter through keys pressed on the keyboard and scan for only those you need, discarding the rest.

For example, suppose you need to modify the KEYWAIT1.C program so that instead of any key stopping the insane loop, only the spacebar works to stop it.

Try it! Modify the KEYWAIT1.C source code on your own. Change the code so that only the spacebar key stops the insane loop. There are many ways to do this, so be creative!

If you've done things properly, the program stops the loop only when the spacebar has been pressed. You can press other keys on the keyboard, and the program continues to loop; only the spacebar stops it.

Listing 7-2 shows my solution, though it is only one of many.

Listing 7-2: keywait2.c

```
1    #include <ncurses.h>
2
3    int main(void)
4    {
5        int value = 0;
6
7        initscr();
8
9        addstr("Press any key to begin:\n");
10       refresh();
11       getch();
12
13       nodelay(stdscr,TRUE);              /* turn off getch() wait */
14       addstr("Press the Spacebar to stop the insane loop!\n");
15       while(1)
16       {
17           printw("%d\r",value++);
```

(continued)

Listing 7-2 *(continued)*

```
18              refresh();
19              if(getch() == ' ') break;
20          }
21
22      endwin();
23      return 0;
24  }
```

How to Implement kbhit()

If you're an ancient DOS programmer or just familiar with the C language on the PC, you might remember (and reminisce about) the old kbhit() function. It was used to determine whether or not characters were waiting to be read from the keyboard buffer. kbhit() returned TRUE if characters were waiting, FALSE otherwise.

You can use nodelay() and getch() in NCurses to emulate this behavior somewhat but not exactly. The problem is that getch() still fetches a key. So what you need is a way to take that key and stuff it back to the keyboard input queue. The function that handles that is called, logically, ungetch(). Here's the format:

```
ungetch(ch)
```

The ungetch() function places the character ch back into the input buffer. You can do this to pre-stuff characters if you like or to toss back characters when creating a kbhit()-like function, as shown in Listing 7-3.

Listing 7-3: kbhit.c

```
1    #include <ncurses.h>
2
3    int kbhit(void)
4    {
5        int ch,r;
6
7    /* turn off getch() blocking and echo */
8        nodelay(stdscr,TRUE);
9        noecho();
10
11   /* check for input */
12        ch = getch();
13        if( ch == ERR)              /* no input */
14            r = FALSE;
15        else                        /* input */
16        {
17            r = TRUE;
18            ungetch(ch);
```

Listing 7-3 *(continued)*

```
19              }
20
21     /* restore block and echo */
22             echo();
23             nodelay(stdscr,FALSE);
24             return(r);
25     }
26
27     int main(void)
28     {
29             initscr();
30
31             addstr("Press any key to end this program:");
32             while(!kbhit())
33                     ;
34
35             endwin();
36             return 0;
37     }
```

And when you press a key, the program ends. *Voílà*, there is your kbhit() function equivalent.

Of course, this function does assume that echo() is set and nodelay() is FALSE for the standard screen. It also assumes that the standard screen is the input screen. Adjust these items as needed for your own use, or just assume that kbhit() makes these assumptions and live with it.

NOTE See the section "Silence, please!" later in this chapter for more information on the echo() function.

Flushing Input

Text typed at the computer keyboard is stored in a buffer. The various text-reading, or keyboard input, functions fetch characters from that buffer as the program needs them, which is a basic description of how keyboard input works.

The reason for the buffer is to allow for keyboard input while the program is doing something else. I can think of two benefits to this:

- First, it allows you to type ahead while the computer can do something else (and the keyboard buffer is often called the *type-ahead buffer*).

- Second, it means that the program doesn't have to constantly scan the keyboard to determine whether you've pressed a key.

There are times, however, when you want to clear or *flush* the keyboard buffer. For example, suppose your program asks a very serious question and requires a Y or N key press. There may just be a rogue Y or N in the keyboard buffer, so when your program pauses to read the keyboard, it may read that older key press instead of the one corresponding to the current question. To prevent that from happening, you can flush input, clearing the keyboard buffer. In NCurses, the `flushinp()` function carries out that task (see Listing 7-4).

Listing 7-4: `flush1.c`

```
1    #include <ncurses.h>
2
3    int main(void)
4    {
5        char buffer[81];
6
7        initscr();
8
9        addstr("Type on the keyboard whilst I wait...\n");
10       refresh();
11       napms(5000);        /* 5 seconds */
12
13       addstr("Here is what you typed:\n");
14       getnstr(buffer,80);
15       refresh();
16
17       endwin();
18       return 0;
19   }
```

The program displays some text:

```
Type on the keyboard whilst I wait...
```

While that's on the screen, type something such as your name or the ever-popular **asdf**. Then, after a five-second pause, you'll see that text displayed.

The FLUSH1.C code demonstrates the type-ahead buffer in action. While the `napms()` function in line 11 is holding up program execution, the keyboard can still be used, and any characters you type are stored in the keyboard's buffer. The `getnstr()` function later picks up, processes, and displays what you typed, what was waiting in the buffer. Pressing Enter ends `getnstr()`'s waiting, also ending the program.

The following modification to FLUSH1.C in Listing 7-5 inserts the `flushinp()` function before `getnstr()`. Because input is flushed, anything you type will be erased from the buffer and `getnstr()` will just have to wait!

Listing 7-5: `flush2.c`

```
1     #include <ncurses.h>
2
3     int main(void)
4     {
5         char buffer[81];
6
7         initscr();
8
9         addstr("Type on the keyboard whilst I wait...\n");
10        refresh();
11        napms(5000);          /* 5 seconds */
12
13        addstr("Here is what you typed:\n");
14        flushinp();
15        getnstr(buffer,80);
16        refresh();
17
18        endwin();
19        return 0;
20    }
```

Line 14 is the new line.
When the code is run, you'll see:

```
Type on the keyboard whilst I wait...
```

Go ahead and type text as you did before. Then wait.

```
Here is what you typed:
```

Because of the `flushinp()` function, no text is displayed.

Silence, Please!

Aside from waiting for your keyboard input, another normal behavior for `getch()` is to echo, or display, the character typed on the screen. It was popular for old C compilers to include a `getch()` function that did not echo the character typed; it was the companion `getche()` function that *echoed* the character typed to the display.

Those old functions are long gone (though I've seen them in some C compilers). Even so, the point is that turning text-echoing off and on is something programmers desire, as shown in Listing 7-6. NCurses is happy to oblige.

Listing 7-6: whoru.c

```
1    #include <ncurses.h>
2
3    int main(void)
4    {
5        char name[46];
6        char password[9];
7
8        initscr();
9
10       mvprintw(3,10,"Enter your name: ");
11       refresh();
12       getnstr(name,45);
13       mvprintw(5,6,"Enter your password: ");
14       refresh();
15
16       getnstr(password,8);
17
18       endwin();
19       return 0;
20   }
```

The program asks for your name and password. Sadly, the password is displayed as it's typed, which is a security risk. It would be nice to turn off the echo of characters while the password is input, right? But not if you insert the following on line 15:

```
noecho();
```

After recompiling and running, the password is typed "in the dark." The noecho() function affected input by not echoing the characters typed. Yes, even though getch() isn't used, internally the getnstr() function does use getch()'s guts, so noecho() turns off the display for *all* input functions.

To turn on the display again (which isn't necessary in this sample program), use the echo() function.

Remember! Even with noecho(), text is being processed by the program. The noecho() function affects only the display, not the keyboard.

Reading Special Keys

The amazing getch() function is so incredibly handy that marketing wizards could do one of those 30-minute, late-night infomercials on the thing. For example, when properly coddled, getch() can be told to interpret nonalphanumeric keys on the keyboard. This includes function keys, arrow keys, cursor control keys, and even a few keys seldom found on the typical PC keyboard.

Keypad On!

All keys on the computer keyboard generate a code when that key is pressed. The code is returned by key-reading functions, either as the raw code itself or as some other special value as "cooked" by the operating system.

In the case of the alphanumeric keys, the key's ASCII character value is returned when you press that key. For other keys, other values are returned, a 16-bit value, a pair of 8-bit values, or perhaps even an escape sequence. Knowing which type of value returned means you can determine exactly which key was pressed, even nonalphanumeric keys. The drawback, of course, is that not every terminal produces the same results or even has the same keys.

NCurses to the rescue!

The NCURSES.H header file defines many of the extra keys found on terminal keyboards. To activate and use those definitions, the keypad() function is used:

```
keypad(stdscr,TRUE)
```

The keypad() function indicates which window it affects, such as stdscr for the standard screen, followed by TRUE to turn the feature on or FALSE to turn it off. Once enabled, your program can use various defined keyboard constants to read those extra keyboard keys, as the following program in Listing 7-7 demonstrates.

Listing 7-7: arrowkeys.c

```
1    #include <ncurses.h>
2
3    int main(void)
4    {
5        int ch;
6
7        initscr();
8
9        keypad(stdscr,TRUE);
10       do
11       {
12           ch = getch();
13           switch(ch)
14           {
15               case KEY_DOWN:
16                   addstr("Down\n");
17                   break;
18               case KEY_UP:
19                   addstr("Up\n");
20                   break;
```

(continued)

Listing 7-7 *(continued)*

```
21              case KEY_LEFT:
22                  addstr("Left\n");
23                  break;
24              case KEY_RIGHT:
25                  addstr("Right\n");
26              default:
27                  break;
28          }
29          refresh();
30      } while(ch != '\n');
31
32      endwin();
33      return 0;
34  }
```

Locate the arrow keys on your computer keyboard. As you press each arrow key, you'll see that key's direction displayed on the screen, as shown in Figure 7-1.

NOTE Note that other keys display as well. That's because `getch()` is in echo mode, and that's the way it behaves.

NOTE You will need to turn the numeric keypad off to use the arrow keys on the 8, 4, 6, and 2 keys on the standard PC keyboard.

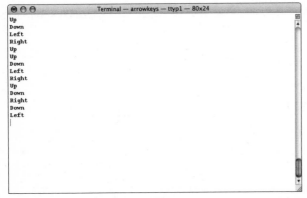

Figure 7-1: Sample output of the ARROWKEYS.C source code

What's Where on the Keyboard

When the keypad() function has activated the keyboard's extra keys, you can use the definitions in NCURSES.H to help your program read the keys.

To determine exactly which keys are available to you, refer to Table 7-1. A more complete list can be found in Appendix D.

You might want to run some tests to assure that NCurses on your computer can access the function keys. For example, to check for Function key 5, you would use:

```
ch == KEY_F(5)
```

as the comparison. Remember that variable ch must be an int, not a char (that's a common mistake).

Also be aware that your operating system may steal the function keys from your program. If so, you can use the raw() function in NCurses to try to get the function keys passed directly to your program. Refer to Appendix A for more information on the raw() function.

The Highlighted Menu Bar

Knowing what you've learned so far in this book, you should now be able to pull off quite a few tricks using NCurses. One of them is a fancy moving menu bar system, similar to what's shown in Figure 7-2.

Table 7-1: Some special key definitions

DEFINITION	KEYBOARD KEY
KEY_UP	Cursor up arrow
KEY_DOWN	Cursor down arrow
KEY_LEFT	Cursor left arrow
KEY_RIGHT	Cursor right arrow
KEY_HOME	Home key
KEY_NPAGE	Page Down or Next Page
KEY_PPAGE	Page Up or Previous Page
KEY_END	End key
KEY_BACKSPACE	Backspace key
KEY_F(n)	Function key n

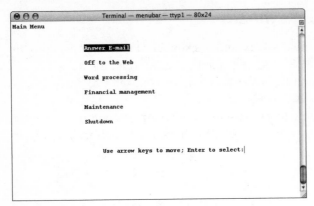

Figure 7-2: A sample menu bar system

Working the menu system involves pressing the up or down arrows on the keyboard. When you do, the highlight bar moves up or down to select an item in the menu. Pressing the Enter key selects that item.

The source code for such a fancy interface isn't really that difficult, given the way NCurses works. Listing 7-8 shows one way to pull it off.

Listing 7-8: menubar.c

```
1    #include <ncurses.h>
2
3    #define MENUMAX 6
4
5    void drawmenu(int item)
6    {
7        int c;
8        char mainmenu[] = "Main Menu";
9        char menu[MENUMAX][21] = {          /* 6 items for MENUMAX
*/
10           "Answer E-mail",
11           "Off to the Web",
12           "Word processing",
13           "Financial management",
14           "Maintenance",
15           "Shutdown"
16           };
17
18       clear();
19       addstr(mainmenu);
20       for(c=0;c<MENUMAX;c++)
21       {
22           if( c==item )
23               attron(A_REVERSE);          /* highlight selection */
24           mvaddstr(3+(c*2),20,menu[c]);
25           attroff(A_REVERSE);             /* remove highlight */
26       }
```

Listing 7-8 *(continued)*

```
27          mvaddstr(17,25,"Use arrow keys to move; Enter to select:");
28          refresh();
29     }
30
31     int main(void)
32     {
33         int key,menuitem;
34
35         menuitem = 0;
36
37         initscr();
38
39         drawmenu(menuitem);
40         keypad(stdscr,TRUE);
41         noecho();                        /* Disable echo */
42         do
43         {
44             key = getch();
45             switch(key)
46             {
47                 case KEY_DOWN:
48                     menuitem++;
49                     if(menuitem > MENUMAX-1) menuitem = 0;
50                     break;
51                 case KEY_UP:
52                     menuitem--;
53                     if(menuitem < 0) menuitem = MENUMAX-1;
54                     break;
55                 default:
56                     break;
57             }
58             drawmenu(menuitem);
59         } while(key != '\n');
60
61         echo();                          /* re-enable echo */
62
63     /* At this point, the value of the selected menu is kept in the
64         menuitem variable. The program can branch off to whatever
subroutine
65         is required to carry out that function
66     */
67
68         endwin();
69         return 0;
70     }
```

It's a long piece of source code, but the actual guts that do the work aren't that complex.

The code required to move the menu bar isn't really that difficult. The program reads the up and down arrow key in the same way as the ARROWKEYS.C source code shown earlier in this chapter. Note, however, that I do turn echo off in line 41 so that extra characters typed at the prompt are not distracting. A complementary echo() command at line 61 turns on echoing for the rest of the code (supposedly).

The menuitem variable keeps track of which menu item is highlighted and selected. Its value is changed by pressing the up or down arrow keys. Those keys merely change the value of menuitem. (The display highlighting is more of an after effect.) The if comparisons in lines 49 and 53 assure that menuitem never gets out of range; if so, the value "wraps."

The core of the program is the drawmenu() function at line 5. It's not really that tough to do; the for loop at line 20 does all the work. It displays each line of the menu one after the other. The math in line 24 assures that a blank line separates each menu command. And the if comparison in line 22 turns on the A_REVERSE attribute for the one menu item that is highlighted.

The advantage of NCurses here is that the refresh() statement in line 28 redraws the entire screen. So the highlight bar doesn't really move; it's merely redrawn. That avoids the work of having to find the previously highlighted text and manually unhighlighting it.

After the fancy display work is done, the program can continue. Branching to the proper menu-routine is simply done by using the value of menuitem and, say, a switch-case structure.

CHAPTER 8

Windows, Windows Everywhere!

From the "And Now He Tells You" Department comes this important tidbit: NCurses is a windowed environment. Nearly all NCurses text output functions are window oriented, either directly or via a macro defined in the NCURSES.H header file.

If you've been plowing through the tutorial part of book front to back, you haven't really noticed this windowed aspect of NCurses. Well, not by much, at least. Those few commands that required a window argument used stdscr, the standard screen. But that really isn't as much the standard screen as it is the default window to which NCurses sends its output.

In the bigger picture, the standard screen is only one of many windows your programs can use in NCurses. So be prepared for some eye-opening looks through various NCurses windows.

Ye Olde Standard Screen

When the initscr() function initializes NCurses, it does various things (performs duties, sets up memory, and so on). One of the many tasks is to create the default window for program output, the standard screen, named stdscr.

Commands that Require a Window Argument

So far in this book, you've experienced commands that use `stdscr` to refer to the terminal window. Here's a sampling:

```
getmaxyx(win,row,col)

getyx(win,y,x)

keypad(win,bf)

nodelay(win,bf)
```

Each of these commands requires a `win` or window argument, so that NCurses knows which window on the screen to refer to. Previous chapters in this book use `stdscr` to represent the standard screen, the only window NCurses creates. But other window names can be used as well, the names of new windows you create yourself. (More on that in a few paragraphs.)

The Pseudo Commands

Nearly all text-output functions in NCurses require a `win` argument, specifying which window to send the output. As a `win` argument, `stdscr` isn't used much, because many of the command text-output functions have been customized for use with `stdscr`; those text-output functions exist as special macros written in the `NCURSES.H` file.

For example, the `addch()` function, which adds a character to the standard screen, is really a macro. The actual function is named `waddch()` and here is its format:

```
waddch(win,ch);
```

The `addch` macro, or pseudo function, looks like this in `NCURSES.H`:

```
#define addch(ch)          waddch(stdscr,ch)
```

So anytime you've used `addch()` in a program, the compiler secretly swaps it out with the proper window-based function, `waddch()`, specifying `stdscr` as the named window.

Pseudo functions have been used for just about all of the character and text-output functions introduced so far in this book's tutorial. There's nothing wrong with using the shorter, nonwindowed version of the function; my purpose here is simply to tell you that NCurses always refers to a specific window for its commands, whether you're using a window version of a function or not. *Surprise!*

The window (real) version of any pseudo function has the same name as the pseudo function, but the real function is prefixed by a w. Also, the function's first argument is the name of the window the function acts upon.

The Other Prefix, mv

NCurses actually sports two prefixes for its text output commands. In addition to w, specifying a window, there is also mv, which was explained in Chapter 4.

When you prefix a command with mv, the first two arguments are the row (y) and column (x) to position the cursor before outputting text. Therefore:

```
addch('Q');
```

The preceding command outputs a Q wherever the cursor currently happens to be.

```
mvaddch(5,10,'Q');
```

The preceding command places a cursor at position 5,10 on the screen. That's the sixth row, 11th column. Remember that the first row and column are numbered zero.

To direct addch() to a specific window *and* a specific location, this format is used:

```
mvwaddch(stdscr,5,10,'Q');
```

The mv prefix always comes first; after all, the *real* command is waddch(), not addch(). *But,* inside the parenthesis, the window's name comes first, as shown above. You'll probably forget that from time to time, but the slew of pointer error messages generated will help remind you.

Making Windows

Creating a new window is simple, thanks to the newwin() function:

```
newwin(rows,cols,y_org,x_org)
```

The newwin() function is told the window's size in rows and cols (vertical by horizontal characters) and where the window is located on the terminal screen, given that the upper-left corner of the terminal is location 0,0.

The range of values for rows, cols, y_org, and x_org depends on your computer's memory and, of course, screen size. The smallest you can go is a one-character window.

When the call to newwin() is successful, a pointer to a window structure is returned. This structure is declared in your program using this format:

```
WINDOW *name;
```

The WINDOW variable is defined in NCURSES.H; you supply the name, which is the name you'll use to refer to the new window. When the call fails, NULL is returned. (The call fails because of a lack of memory or because the window is too large for the screen or doesn't fit entirely on the screen.)

And now: the shortcut!

```
newwin(0,0,0,0);
```

When you use the newwin() function with all zeros, a new window is created that is the exact same size and location as the standard screen. Ta-da!

The Obligatory New Window Sample Program

The following source code directs NCurses to create two windows on the screen. The first, naturally, is the standard screen. But the newwin() function in line 13 creates a second window, named two (line 5), as shown in Listing 8-1.

Listing 8-1: twowin1.c

```
1     #include <ncurses.h>
2
3     int main(void)
4     {
5         WINDOW *two;          /* pointer for new window */
6
7         initscr();
8
9         addstr("This is the original window, stdscr.\n");
10        refresh();
11        getch();
12
13        two = newwin(0,0,0,0);
14        if( two == NULL)
15        {
16            addstr("Unable to allocate memory for new window.");
17            endwin();
18            return(1);
19        }
20        waddstr(two,"This is the new window created!\n");
21
22        getch();
23
```

Listing 8-1 *(continued)*

```
24        endwin();
25        return 0;
26    }
```

When the program runs, you'll see the text:

```
This is the original window, stdscr
```

That's the standard screen. Press Enter to see the new window and its text. And... *nothing!*
Press Enter to end the program.
The program compiled properly, so there must be some other reason why the new window didn't display. Here's a review:

- Line 13: The new window is created.

- Lines 14 through 19: When there is a problem, this chunk of code handles the situation. So the new window most definitely is created and exists in the program. That's not what's wrong.

- Line 20: Could be a problem, but there's no way to find out when you cannot see the text.

Hmmm. You can't see the text. If you recall from your basic knowledge of NCurses, what is required so that you can see text output?
Yep! It's the refresh() function. But for a specific window, you need the wrefresh() function. Here's the format:

```
wrefresh(win)
```

The wrefresh() function is required to update and display the content of a specific window, win. (In fact, the refresh() function itself is merely a macro defined as wrefresh(stdscr).) So all the program is missing is a wrefresh() to update the new window. The following needs to be added at line 23:

```
wrefresh(two);
```

The program now runs as expected, and when you press the Enter key, you'll see the window two and the text displayed:

```
This is the new window created!
```

What you're seeing above and on the screen is text belonging to the window two. Though you cannot see the standard screen window's text, it's still there, in memory somewhere. What's visible on the screen now is only the contents of the new window, two.

If the program continued, you could direct text output to one screen or the other and you can switch between the windows as well, as demonstrated in the following section.

Switching between Windows

There is no advantage of having multiple windows unless you can switch between them. For example, you can have one window (or a set of windows) detailing help information. You can then display those windows when a user hits the Help key or some other key on the keyboard, as the code in Listing 8-2 demonstrates.

Listing 8-2: `helpmenu1.c`

```
1     #include <ncurses.h>
2
3     void showhelp(void);
4
5     WINDOW *help;
6
7     int main(void)
8     {
9         int ch;
10
11        initscr();
12
13    /* build help menu */
14        if((help = newwin(0,0,0,0)) == NULL)
15        {
16            addstr("Unable to allocate window memory\n");
17            endwin();
18            return(1);
19        }
20        mvwaddstr(help,6,32,"Help menu Screen");
21        mvwaddstr(help,9,28,"Press the ~ key to quit");
22        mvwaddstr(help,12,28,"Press ENTER to go back");
23
24    /* now start the program loop */
25
26        addstr("Typer Program\n");
27        addstr("Press + for help:\n\n");
28        refresh();
29        noecho();
30        do
31        {
32            ch = getch();
33            refresh();
34            if(ch == '+')
35                showhelp();
```

Listing 8-2 (continued)

```
36              else
37                  addch(ch);
38          } while (ch != '~');
39
40          endwin();
41          return 0;
42      }
43
44      void showhelp(void)
45      {
46
47          wrefresh(help);
48          getch();                /* wait for key press */
49
50          refresh();
51      }
```

This example is yet another typing program, *la-di-da*! Note, however, that echo is off and, therefore, an addch() function is required (line 37) to display input. But anyway, when you press the + key, a second window help appears displaying the help screen. Pressing Enter then returns you to the standard screen.

The showhelp() function is where the swapping takes place. The function used to display the help screen is wrefresh() function, as shown in line 47. Likewise, a refresh() function in line 50 is used to switch back to the standard screen. That makes sense, so why doesn't it work?

Well, it does work! The wrefresh() function writes only changed text to the screen. Refer to Chapter 2: Only new text written to the screen or text changed — what NCurses refers to as *touched* text — is written to the screen when you wrefresh(). By working in that manner, NCurses is very efficient. But when you want to display an entire window's contents, that behavior isn't very helpful.

The solution is to force NCurses to display the entire window. Without manually going through and rewriting the thing, you can use the touchwin() function:

```
touchwin(win)
```

The touchwin() function leads NCurses to believe that every character location in the window win has been touched or updated since the last refresh. Therefore, on the next refresh() or wrefresh() call, the entire window will be written to the screen.

To fix the code, add the following at line 46:

```
touchwin(help);
```

And add the following at line 49:

```
touchwin(stdscr);
```

After compiling, you can deftly switch between the windows (using + and Enter), with everything working as expected.

Windows of a Smaller Size

There is no reason for the help menu window to be as large as it is. Using the `newwin()` function, you can set the size and location of the new window to be as large as the screen (with all zeros; line 14 of `HELPMENU1.C`) or as tiny as one character. Here is the full format for the `newwin()` function again:

```
newwin(rows,cols,y_org,x_org)
```

Figure 8-1 shows a graphical representation of how those arguments work. The values `rows` and `cols` set the size of the new window. The window's position is relative to the screen, `y_org` and `x_org`, where the *home* position is 0,0. Remember that the `newwin()` function fails either when not enough memory is available or part of the window hangs off the visible screen. I didn't do it in the sample program, but consider using the `getmaxyx()` function to determine screen width and height before you set the new window's size.

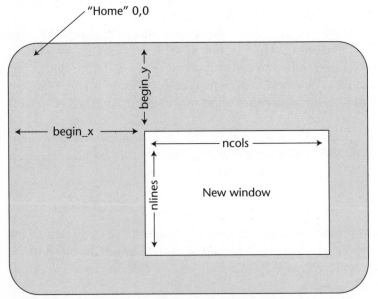

Figure 8-1: Positioning a new window on the screen

Meanwhile, to change the help window's size, edit the `MENUHELP1.C` source code and change line 14 as follows:

```
if((help = newwin(10,30,4,26)) == NULL)
```

Also change lines 20, 21 and 22 to:

```
mvwaddstr(help,1,7,"Help menu Screen");
mvwaddstr(help,5,3,"Press the ~ key to quit");
mvwaddstr(help,8,4,"Press ENTER to go back");
```

The changes are minor; just some positioning and new offsets. But after saving, compiling, and running, you can still see the original window, stdscr, behind the help window.

Removing a Window

To remove a single window, such as a new window you created, the del-win() function is used:

```
delwin(win)
```

The delwin() function removes the window win, a window you created by using the newwin() function sometime earlier in your code. delwin() removes the window's internal structure and memory used by the window, but it does not erase the window's screen image. To do that, you'll have to wrefresh(), and possibly touchwin(), another window on the screen. See Listing 8-3.

Listing 8-3: twowin2.c

```
1    #include <ncurses.h>
2
3    int main(void)
4    {
5        WINDOW *two;        /* pointer for new window */
6
7        initscr();
8
9        addstr("This is the original window, stdscr.\n");
10       refresh();
11       getch();
12
13       two = newwin(0,0,0,0);
```

(continued)

Listing 8-3 *(continued)*

```
14          if( two == NULL)
15          {
16              addstr("Unable to allocate memory for new window.");
17              endwin();
18              return(1);
19          }
20          waddstr(two,"This is the new window created!\n");
21          wrefresh(two);
22          getch();
23
24          delwin(two);
25          addstr("The second window was removed.\n");
26          refresh();
27          getch();
28
29          endwin();
30          return 0;
31      }
```

The preceding source code is a simple update from TWOWIN1.C, wherein the code was added to remove the window created.

When the program is run, after pressing the Enter key, the second window is removed. The screen may look something like this:

```
This is the new window created!

The second window was removed.
```

On some terminals you may need to force NCurses to update the *standard screen*. That's because the delwin() function does not repaint the screen after deleting a window. So to update the screen you need another refresh; insert a new line before the refresh() function in line 26:

```
touchwin(stdscr);
```

That fixes the updating problem.

Dueling Windows

The following series of programs shows you what fun you can have with windows. Each program is based on the code shown in Listing 8-4, which produces four separate windows on the screen.

Listing 8-4: quad1.c

```
1    #include <ncurses.h>
2    #include <stdlib.h>
3
4    void bomb(void);
5
6    int main(void)
7    {
8        WINDOW *a,*b,*c,*d;
9        int maxx,maxy,halfx,halfy;
10
11       initscr();
12
13   /* calculate window sizes and locations */
14       getmaxyx(stdscr,maxy,maxx);
15       halfx = maxx >> 1;
16       halfy = maxy >> 1;
17
18   /* create four windows to fill the screen */
19       if( (a = newwin(halfy,halfx,0,0)) == NULL) bomb();
20       if( (b = newwin(halfy,halfx,0,halfx)) == NULL) bomb();
21       if( (c = newwin(halfy,halfx,halfy,0)) == NULL) bomb();
22       if( (d = newwin(halfy,halfx,halfy,halfx)) == NULL) bomb();
23
24   /* Write to each window */
25       mvwaddstr(a,0,0,"This is window A\n");
26       wrefresh(a);
27       mvwaddstr(b,0,0,"This is window B\n");
28       wrefresh(b);
29       mvwaddstr(c,0,0,"This is window C\n");
30       wrefresh(c);
31       mvwaddstr(d,0,0,"This is window D\n");
32       wrefresh(d);
33       getch();
34
35       endwin();
36       return 0;
37   }
38
39   void bomb(void)
40   {
41       addstr("Unable to allocate memory for new window.\n");
42       refresh();
43       endwin();
44       exit(1);
45   }
```

When run, the program creates four windows: a, b, c, and d. Each window is labeled with a specific `mvwaddstr()` function and a specific `wrefresh()`.

Stained Glass Windows

Is it a window or a hole? In fact, the window itself is really defined by the space around it, the frame and the panes of glass. When I work with windows, I want to see that frame. The best way I think that can happen is with color, as the following improvement to the QUAD1.C program (Listing 8-5) demonstrates.

Listing 8-5: Quad2.c

```
1    #include <ncurses.h>
2    #include <stdlib.h>
3
4    void bomb(void);
5
6    int main(void)
7    {
8        WINDOW *a,*b,*c,*d;
9        int maxx,maxy,halfx,halfy;
10
11        initscr();
12        start_color();
13        init_pair(1,COLOR_BLACK,COLOR_BLUE);
14        init_pair(2,COLOR_BLACK,COLOR_RED);
15        init_pair(3,COLOR_BLACK,COLOR_GREEN);
16        init_pair(4,COLOR_BLACK,COLOR_CYAN);
17
18    /* calculate window sizes and locations */
19        getmaxyx(stdscr,maxy,maxx);
20        halfx = maxx >> 1;
21        halfy = maxy >> 1;
22
23    /* create four windows to fill the screen */
24        if( (a = newwin(halfy,halfx,0,0)) == NULL) bomb();
25        if( (b = newwin(halfy,halfx,0,halfx)) == NULL) bomb();
26        if( (c = newwin(halfy,halfx,halfy,0)) == NULL) bomb();
27        if( (d = newwin(halfy,halfx,halfy,halfx)) == NULL) bomb();
28
29    /* Write to each window */
30        mvwaddstr(a,0,0,"This is window A\n");
31        wbkgd(a,COLOR_PAIR(1));
32        wrefresh(a);
33        mvwaddstr(b,0,0,"This is window B\n");
34        wbkgd(b,COLOR_PAIR(2));
35        wrefresh(b);
36        mvwaddstr(c,0,0,"This is window C\n");
```

Listing 8-5 *(continued)*

```
37        wbkgd(c,COLOR_PAIR(3));
38        wrefresh(c);
49        mvwaddstr(d,0,0,"This is window D\n");
50        wbkgd(d,COLOR_PAIR(4));
41        wrefresh(d);
42        getch();
43
44        endwin();
45        return 0;
46    }
47
48    void bomb(void)
49    {
50        addstr("Unable to allocate memory for new window.\n");
51        refresh();
52        endwin();
53        exit(1);
54    }
```

The `start_color()` function in line 12 initializes color but without error checking: I'm assuming that your terminal can do color and further that `start_color()` will not fail. Remember in your "real" programs to always use `has_colors()` and test to see if `start_color()` returns `OK` before moving on in color.

The program defines four colors pairs, each of which is assigned to a specific window via the `wbkgd()` function.

Sample output is shown in Figure 8-2. As you can see, the four windows appear individually mapped and well delineated (though not in color in this book).

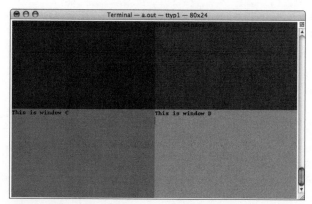

Figure 8-2: Coloring the four windows' separate colors

Stop Repeating Me!

The following, third rendition of the quad series of programs in Listing 8-6 adds a while loop to show you yet another aspect of NCurses and its windows.

Listing 8-6: quad3.c

```
1    #include <ncurses.h>
2    #include <stdlib.h>
3
4    void bomb(void);
5
6    int main(void)
7    {
8        WINDOW *a,*b,*c,*d;
9        int maxx,maxy,halfx,halfy;
10       int ch;
11
12       initscr();
13       start_color();
14       init_pair(1,COLOR_BLACK,COLOR_BLUE);
15       init_pair(2,COLOR_BLACK,COLOR_RED);
16       init_pair(3,COLOR_BLACK,COLOR_GREEN);
17       init_pair(4,COLOR_BLACK,COLOR_CYAN);
18
19   /* calculate window sizes and locations */
20       getmaxyx(stdscr,maxy,maxx);
21       halfx = maxx >> 1;
22       halfy = maxy >> 1;
23
24   /* create four windows to fill the screen */
25       if( (a = newwin(halfy,halfx,0,0)) == NULL) bomb();
26       if( (b = newwin(halfy,halfx,0,halfx)) == NULL) bomb();
27       if( (c = newwin(halfy,halfx,halfy,0)) == NULL) bomb();
28       if( (d = newwin(halfy,halfx,halfy,halfx)) == NULL) bomb();
29
30   /* Write to each window */
31       wbkgd(a,COLOR_PAIR(1));
32       mvwaddstr(a,0,0,"This is window A\n");
33       wrefresh(a);
34       wbkgd(b,COLOR_PAIR(2));
35       mvwaddstr(b,0,0,"This is window B\n");
36       wrefresh(b);
37       wbkgd(c,COLOR_PAIR(3));
38       mvwaddstr(c,0,0,"This is window C\n");
39       wrefresh(c);
```

Listing 8-6 *(continued)*

```
41          wbkgd(d,COLOR_PAIR(4));
40          mvwaddstr(d,0,0,"This is window D\n");
42          wrefresh(d);
43
44    /* Update each window */
45          do
46          {
47              ch = wgetch(a);
48              waddch(b,ch);
49              waddch(c,ch);
50              waddch(d,ch);
51              wrefresh(b);
52              wrefresh(c);
53              wrefresh(d);
54          } while(ch != '~');
55
56          endwin();
57          return 0;
58    }
59
60    void bomb(void)
61    {
62          addstr("Unable to allocate memory for new window.\n");
63          refresh();
64          endwin();
65          exit(1);
66    }
```

In brief:

- Line 10 is added to declare a character input variable; remember that it's an int not a char.

- Lines 45 through 54 are new; creating an input loop. The getch() function automatically displays input, useful here to avoid a flash-peek at the standard screen. The wgetch() function is used in line 47. It reads a character input from window a, which also displays on window a. The remaining functions display the same character on the other three windows.

NOTE Though NCurses uses only one input queue, it's possible to read input from a specific window. This is done mostly for modifying the text, as certain input functions can be filtered through various windows. Refer to the entry for getch() in Appendix A.

On Your Own

Write an NCurses program that creates two side-by-side windows that fill the screen. As you type in the first window, text also appears in the second window but with the rot13 filter applied. (Rot13 is a simple cipher where A and N are swapped, B and O, C and P, and so on for the 26 letters of the alphabet.)

My solution for this problem can be found on this book's companion page on the Web: www.c-for-dummies.com/ncurses/.

Subwindows

Subwindows are strange and interesting creatures in NCurses. From one perspective, they are exactly what you imagine them to be: tiny windows within other windows. But at the same time, because of the way NCurses implements subwindows, they are not what they seem to be.

I once struggled with the concept of subwindows in NCurses. In fact, much of the documentation on the Internet claims that subwindows are buggy and should be avoided. That isn't exactly correct. With proper understanding, subwindows can be time-saving gizmos in NCurses, not to be avoided at all.

The Thing with Subwindows

Subwindows are like real windows in NCurses in that they share the same data structure. You use the same WINDOW variable to create a subwindow as you do a full window. NCurses functions that control or manipulate a window also control and manipulate subwindows (with a few exceptions). But a subwindow is *not* the same thing as a real window.

The main difference between a subwindow and a real window is that subwindows share memory with a parent window. So when you put a character to a subwindow, you're also placing that character into the parent window as well.

For example, in Figure 9-1, it appears that there are two windows on the screen. The smaller window is a subwindow, which has different color attributes from the parent window. The parent window shows the text `Hello, son,` and the subwindow displays `Hello, Dad`. Even so, the text `Hello, Dad` also exists in the parent window. The memory is shared.

If you were to change the text in the subwindow, you would also be changing or adding text to the parent. Likewise, the parent window can change text in the subwindow. This can be confusing and frustrating but only when you assume that a subwindow is like a regular window. It is not.

The best way to think of a subwindow is merely as a convenient way to reference a specific portion of the parent.

Figure 9-2 illustrates an example of using subwindows to reference a region on the screen. The areas boxed at the bottom of the screen in Figure 9-2 contain information that is occasionally rewritten or updated. Rather than have to do a lot of complex cursor-positioning math, simply create a subwindow in the proper spot; then use that window as a reference to position the cursor. This is one example of how subwindows can be used to define regions of the screen instead of separate windows.

As long as you consider the subwindow to be merely a reference to a specific portion of the parent, you'll do well with subwindows. But when you believe the subwindow to be separate and unique, like a real window, you'll get into all sorts of trouble.

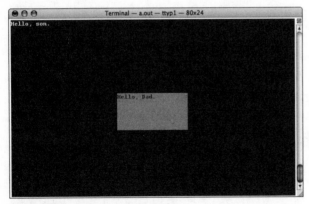

Figure 9-1: A glorious subwindow

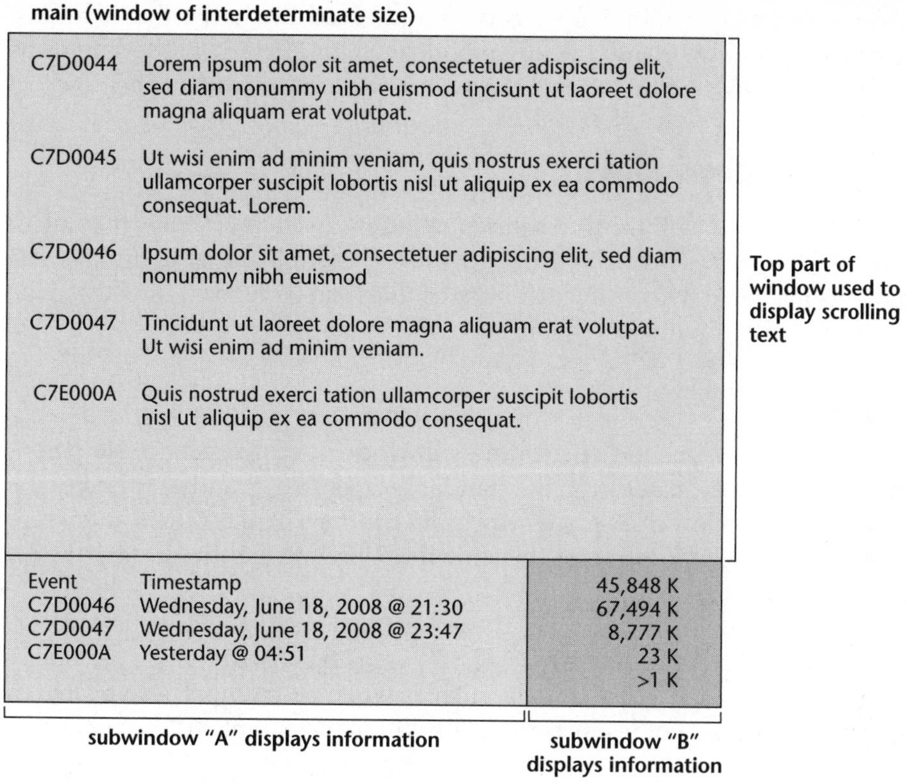

main (window of interderminate size)

C7D0044	Lorem ipsum dolor sit amet, consectetuer adipiscing elit, sed diam nonummy nibh euismod tincisunt ut laoreet dolore magna aliquam erat volutpat.
C7D0045	Ut wisi enim ad minim veniam, quis nostrus exerci tation ullamcorper suscipit lobortis nisl ut aliquip ex ea commodo consequat. Lorem.
C7D0046	Ipsum dolor sit amet, consectetuer adipiscing elit, sed diam nonummy nibh euismod
C7D0047	Tincidunt ut laoreet dolore magna aliquam erat volutpat. Ut wisi enim ad minim veniam.
C7E000A	Quis nostrud exerci tation ullamcorper suscipit lobortis nisl ut aliquip ex ea commodo consequat.

Top part of window used to display scrolling text

Event	Timestamp	
		45,848 K
C7D0046	Wednesday, June 18, 2008 @ 21:30	67,494 K
C7D0047	Wednesday, June 18, 2008 @ 23:47	8,777 K
C7E000A	Yesterday @ 04:51	23 K
		>1 K

subwindow "A" displays information   subwindow "B" displays information

Figure 9-2: An example of a useful subwindow

Making Subwindows

Subwindows have all of the basic attributes of real windows: a name, size, location, unique cursor coordinates, and so on. Because they share memory with the parent, the subwindow must reside completely within the parent window. And, naturally, subwindows are created by using their own unique functions:

```
subwin(win,rows,cols,y,x)
derwin(win,rows,cols,y,x)
```

The only difference between these functions has to do with the final two arguments. With subwin(), y and x are coordinates relative to the screen; in derwin(), y and x are relative to the parent window.

After creation, the subwindow can be addressed like any other window, named in a window-oriented command, deleted, or affected in the same was as regular windows. Subwindows can even have subwindows of their own.

Your First Subwindow

Subwindows exist totally within a parent window. In a way, it helps to think of them more as a *region* of the parent window, though the subwindow still maintains its own cursor and text, and attributes can be written directly to the subwindow just as with other windows in NCurses.

```
subwin(win,rows,cols,y,x)
```

The `subwin()` function creates the subwindow. `win` refers to the parent window, which can be `stdscr`, the standard screen. `rows` and `cols` gives the size of the subwindow in character rows and columns. Finally, the `x` and `y` represent the upper-left location of the subwindow relative to the *screen*, not the parent window org.

When the `subwin()` function is successful, a new window is created, returned as a `WINDOW` pointer by `subwin()` (see line 13 in the `kid1.c` code in Listing 9-1). When the function fails, such as when no memory is available or the subwindow does not reside completely within the parent, `NULL` is returned.

Listing 9-1: kid1.c

```
1      #include <ncurses.h>
2
3      int main(void)
4      {
5          WINDOW *sonny;
6
7          initscr();
8          start_color();           /* remember to check for errors! */
9          init_pair(1,COLOR_WHITE,COLOR_BLUE);
10         init_pair(2,COLOR_RED,COLOR_YELLOW);
11
12     /* create subwindow */
13         sonny = subwin(stdscr,5,20,10,30);
14         if(sonny == NULL)
15         {
16             addstr("Unable to create subwindow\n");
17             endwin();
18             return 1;
19         }
20
21     /* color windows and splash some text */
22         bkgd(COLOR_PAIR(1));
```

Listing 9-1 *(continued)*

```
23        addstr("Hello, son.");
24        wbkgd(sonny,COLOR_PAIR(2));
25        waddstr(sonny,"Hello, Dad.");
26        refresh();
27        getch();
28
29        endwin();
30        return 0;
31    }
```

The code uses color to help you locate the subwindow on the screen. Note that the start_color() function is used in this code without error checking; remember to do error checking, as well as use the has_colors() function for any code you plan on releasing publicly.

(Sample output can be seen in Figure 9-1.)

Your Second Subwindow

The following code in Listing 9-2 is a modification of the original KID1.C source code. This time I've added the derwin() function, which uses coordinates relative to the parent window to create the new subwindow. (Of course, because in both cases the parent is the standard screen, there really is no gross difference shown.)

Listing 9-2: kid2.c

```
1     #include <ncurses.h>
2
3     int main(void)
4     {
5         WINDOW *sonny,*babygirl;
6
7         initscr();
8         start_color();              /* remember to check for errors! */
9         init_pair(1,COLOR_WHITE,COLOR_BLUE);
10        init_pair(2,COLOR_RED,COLOR_YELLOW);
11        init_pair(3,COLOR_CYAN,COLOR_WHITE);
12
13    /* create subwindow and remember to check for errors! */
14        sonny = subwin(stdscr,5,20,10,30);
15        babygirl = derwin(stdscr,5,20,1,50);
16
17    /* color windows and splash some text */
18        bkgd(COLOR_PAIR(1));
19        addstr("Hello, son, hello baby girl.");
20        wbkgd(sonny,COLOR_PAIR(2));
```

(continued)

Listing 9-2 *(continued)*

```
21          waddstr(sonny,"Hello, Dad.");
22          wbkgd(babygirl,COLOR_PAIR(3));
23          waddstr(babygirl,"Hello, Papa.");
24          refresh();
25          getch();
26
27          endwin();
28          return 0;
29      }
```

Sub-subwindows

Because a subwindow is considered a real window in nearly every sense, it's quite possible for a subwindow to have a subwindow of its own. You simply name the subwindow's variable as the `win` in the `subwin()` function, as the code in Listing 9-3 demonstrates.

Listing 9-3: `kid3.c`

```
1    #include <ncurses.h>
2
3    int main(void)
4    {
5        WINDOW *grandpa,*father,*boy;
6        int maxx,maxy;
7
8        initscr();
9
10       start_color();          /* remember to check for errors! */
11       init_pair(1,COLOR_WHITE,COLOR_BLUE);
12       init_pair(2,COLOR_RED,COLOR_YELLOW);
13       init_pair(3,COLOR_CYAN,COLOR_GREEN);
14
15       getmaxyx(stdscr,maxy,maxx);
16
17   /* create windows  - remember to check for errors! */
18       grandpa = newwin(maxy-4,maxx-10,2,5);
19       father = subwin(grandpa,maxy-8,maxx-20,4,10);
20       boy = subwin(father,maxy-16,maxx-40,8,20);
21
22   /* color windows and splash some text */
23       wbkgd(grandpa,COLOR_PAIR(1));
24       waddstr(grandpa, "Grandpa");
25       wbkgd(father,COLOR_PAIR(2));
26       waddstr(father,"Father");
27       wbkgd(boy,COLOR_PAIR(3));
28       waddstr(boy,"Boy");
29       wrefresh(grandpa);
```

Listing 9-3 *(continued)*

```
30        getch();
31
32        endwin();
33        return 0;
34    }
```

The program creates three windows. First comes window `grandpa`, which
is a "real" window. Then `father` is created as a subwindow of `grandpa`.
Finally, `son` is created as a subwindow of `father`. The background colors
make the windows more dramatically visible on the screen.

Removing a Subwindow

Subwindows are killed off just like regular windows, using the same `del-
win()` function. Deleting a subwindow removes the subwindow's internal
structure (the thing `WINDOW` points at) but not the window's data, because that
information is shared with the parent window. Also, to visually remove the
subwindow, the parent window must be touched and refreshed, as the following program in Listing 9-4 demonstrates.

Listing 9-4: `kid4.c`

```
1    #include <ncurses.h>
2
3    int main(void)
4    {
5        WINDOW *grandpa,*father,*boy;
6        int maxx,maxy;
7
8        initscr();
9
10       start_color();        /* remember to check for errors! */
11       init_pair(1,COLOR_WHITE,COLOR_BLUE);
12       init_pair(2,COLOR_RED,COLOR_YELLOW);
13       init_pair(3,COLOR_CYAN,COLOR_GREEN);
14
15       getmaxyx(stdscr,maxy,maxx);
16
17   /* create windows  - remember to check for errors! */
18       grandpa = newwin(maxy-4,maxx-10,2,5);
19       father = subwin(grandpa,maxy-8,maxx-20,4,10);
20       boy = subwin(father,maxy-16,maxx-40,8,20);
21
22   /* color windows and splash some text */
23       wbkgd(grandpa,COLOR_PAIR(1));
```

(continued)

Listing 9-4 *(continued)*

```
24          waddstr(grandpa,"Grandpa\n");
25          wbkgd(father,COLOR_PAIR(2));
26          waddstr(father,"Father\n");
27          wbkgd(boy,COLOR_PAIR(3));
28          waddstr(boy,"Boy\n");
29          wrefresh(grandpa);
30          getch();
31
32      /* remove the subwindow "boy" */
33          delwin(boy);
34          wclear(father);
35          waddstr(father,"Bye, son!\n");
36          wrefresh(father);
37          getch();
38
39          endwin();
40          return 0;
41      }
```

The code is merely a modification to the KID3.C source. Added are lines 32 through 37.

The delwin() function removes window boy in line 33. Then boy's parent window, father, is cleared, a string is added, and the father window is refreshed.

NOTE Merely refreshing the parent window does not remove the subwindow (same data, remember?). The parent window can overwrite the subwindow or remove it entirely with any character-erasing function, including wclear(), as shown in line 34 of the program.

NOTE This is important: You should delete a window's subwindows before you can delete the main window. If you don't, the memory used by the subwindow will not be released in your program, and other, various ugly and unpredictable errors may result.

Subwindows Versus Windows

Subwindows work like real windows in many ways:

- Subwindows use a separate WINDOW data structure in memory.
- Subwindows sport their own cursor, separate from the parent window's cursor.

- Subwindows can have their own color and text attributes.

- Subwindows can be manipulated by all the same functions that manipulate regular windows.

There are a few exceptions to that last point: Some functions do not behave the same way with subwindows as they do with real windows. Those specific functions that don't work with subwindows are documented in Appendix A, as well as in the various man pages and other references.

Internally, a subwindow knows that it's a subwindow. It can reference the parent window, thanks to a pointer stored inside the subwindow's WINDOW structure. Sadly, that doesn't work the other way around: Parent windows have no way of knowing whether they have subwindows. This is the main reason you're not supposed to remove a window unless you first remove its subwindows.

Finally, remember the shared memory deal. Anything you write to a subwindow is also written to the parent. Likewise, the parent has no respect for its subwindow and can effortlessly write text over the subwindow's text. In fact, text written over the subwindow's text becomes part of the subwindow, thanks to the shared memory.

As long as you can keep these points in mind, and put subwindows to use as I've described here, I believe you'll find them useful and handy to have.

CHAPTER 10

More Window Tricks

NCurses has a basket full of windows tricks, more than what one chapter alone can handle. In fact, Chapter 8 just touched on the surface of what you can do with windows. This chapters carries on, offering even more windows tricks, including copying windows, windows that scroll or not, and moving windows.

Copying Window Contents

Copying text between two windows is possible by using one of NCurses window copying functions. They are

```
overlay(swin,dwin)

overwrite(swin,dwin)

copywin(swin,dwin,srow,scol,drow,dcol,dxrow,dxcol,type)

dupwin(win)
```

Of the first three, the `copywin()` function is my favorite and the most powerful. Even so, each one serves a purpose and helps you get text from one window into another.

To overlay or to overwrite?

The overlay() and overwrite() functions work almost identically, taking the contents of source window, the source or scrwin, and plopping that text down into the destination window, or destwin. The difference between the two is subtle, as shown in Listing 10.1.

Listing 10-1: doop1.c

```
1    #include <ncurses.h>
2
3    int main(void)
4    {
5        WINDOW *alpha;
6        char text1[] = "Lorem ipsum dolor sit amet, consectetuer
adipiscing elit, sed diam nonummy nibh euismod tincidunt ut laoreet
dolore magna aliquam erat volutpat. Ut wisi enim ad minim veniam, quis
nostrud exerci tation ullamcorper suscipit lobortis nisl ut aliquip ex
ea commodo consequat.";
7        char text2[]= "Four score and seven years ago our fathers
brought forth on this continent, a new nation, conceived in Liberty, and
dedicated to the proposition that all men are created equal.";
8
9        initscr();
10
11   /* Build windows */
12       alpha = newwin(0,0,0,0);            /* Remember to check for errors! */
13
14       addstr(text1);                /* Add text to stdscr and wait */
15       refresh();
16       getch();
17
18       waddstr(alpha,text2);            /* Show win alpha and wait */
19       wrefresh(alpha);
20       getch();
21
22   /* Copy text from one window to the other, non-destructively */
23       overlay(stdscr,alpha);
24       wrefresh(alpha);
25       getch();
26
27       endwin();
28       return(0);
29   }
```

The source code looks tough, thanks to the two large text strings. The first, text1, is the classic *Lorem ipsum* text. The second, text2, is Lincoln's Gettysburg Address. Honestly, you can replace either string with other text, as long as the text is unique and the two strings are different from each other.

The program doesn't check for an error when the new window, `alpha`, is created in line 12; you would want to do error checking for your "real" programs. The zeros in the `newwin()` function assure that both source and destination windows occupy the full screen, which seems to be how the `overlay()` function (line 23) works best.

First the program displays the *Lorem ipsum* text in the `stdscr` window. Something like this:

```
Lorem ipsum dolor sit amet, consectetuer adipiscing elit, sed diam
nonummy nibh euismod tincidunt ut laoreet dolore magna aliquam erat
volutpat. Ut wisi enim ad minim veniam, quis nostrud exerci tation
ullamcorper suscipit lobortis nisl ut aliquip ex ea commodo consequat.
```

Press the Enter key and the contents of the `alpha` window are displayed, looking something like this:

```
Four score and seven years ago our fathers brought forth on this
continent, a new nation, conceived in Liberty, and dedicated to the
proposition that all men are created equal.
```

Finally, press the Enter key again to overlay the contents of `stdscr` on top of `alpha`. Here's what the mess could look like:

```
Loremsipsumadolorvsityamet,aconsectetuerradipiscingfelit,osedhdiamono
nummy,nibheeuismodntincidunteutilaoreettdolore magnaaaliquamteratrvol
utpat. Utawisilenim ademinimtveniam,lquis nostrud exerci tation
ullamcorper suscipit lobortis nisl ut aliquip ex ea commodo consequat.
```

The *Lorem ipsum* text overlays the original `alpha` window text. The only `alpha` window text that peeks through is whatever was found in the spaces between the `stdscr` text. It's hard to tell which text is which in the output, but Figure 10-1 should help.

```
stdscr:
        Lorem ipsum dolor sit amet, consectetuer adipiscing elit, sed diam nonummy nibh
        euismod tincidunt ut laoreet dolore magna aliquam erat volutpat. Ut wisi enim ad
        minim veniam, quis nostrud exerci tation ullamcorper suscipit lobortis nisl ut
        aliquip ex ea commodo consequat.
alpha:
        Four score and seven years ago our fathers brought forth on this continent, a ne
        w nation, conceived in Liberty, and dedicated to the proposition that all men ar
        e created equal.
overlay(stdscr,alpha):
        Loremsipsumadolorvsityamet,aconsectetuerradipiscingfelit,osedhdiamononummy,nibhe
        euismodntincidunteutilaoreettdolore magnaaaliquamteratrvolutpat. Utawisilenim ad
        eminimtveniam,lquis nostrud exerci tation ullamcorper suscipit lobortis nisl ut
        aliquip ex ea commodo consequat.
```

Figure 10-1: Original text in black, alpha text in gray, overlay showing gray text through black

Sadly, you cannot use color in the program to show how `overlay()` works, similar to what's seen in Figure 10-1. Any text copied from one window to another takes on the attributes of the new window.

The overwrite() difference

To see how `overwrite()` differs from `overlay()` is easy.
Change lines 22 and 23 to read:

```
/* Copy text from one window to the other, destructively */
overwrite(stdscr,alpha);
```

The `overwrite()` function is destructive, so no characters from the original text appear, peeking through *Lorem ipsum* as they did in the `doop1.c` program.

The magic of copywin()

The best of the three basic text-copying functions is `copywin()`, which allows you a great deal of control over which chunk of text is copied from the source window and where it ends up in the destination window. And unlike `overlay()` and `overwrite()`, `copywin()` seems to work on windows of any size. Here's the detailed format:

```
copywin(swin,dwin,srow,scol,drow,dcol,dxrow,dxcol,type)
```

The `srcwin` and `destwin` are the source and destination windows, which can be of any size or position on the screen.
`srow` and `scol` are the starting coordinates of the chunk of text to be copied, as offset within the `srcwin`.
`drow` and `dcol` set the starting coordinates of where the chunk will be copied into the `destwin`. The size of the chunk copied is set by `dxrow` and `dxcol`, which are offsets with `destwin`.
Finally, `type` can be either `TRUE` or `FALSE`. If `TRUE`, then the text copied is non-destructive, as with `overlay()`. If `FALSE`, then the text block replaces the block in the `destwin`, just like `overwrite()`.
I realize that's confusing, so I drew up Figure 10-2 to help you visualize things.

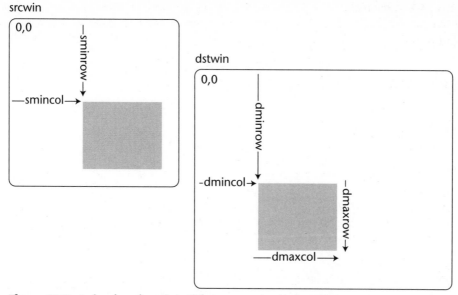

Figure 10-2: A visual explanation of the `copywin()` function

Here's a sample program to toy with (see Listing 10.2).

Listing 10-2: `doop3.c`

```
1     #include <ncurses.h>
2
3     int main(void)
4     {
5         WINDOW *top,*bottom;
6         int maxx, maxy, halfx, halfy, rc;
7         char text1[] = "Lorem ipsum dolor sit amet, consectetuer
adipiscing elit, sed diam nonummy nibh euismod tincidunt ut laoreet
dolore magna aliquam erat volutpat. Ut wisi enim ad minim veniam, quis
nostrud exerci tation ullamcorper suscipit lobortis nisl ut aliquip ex
ea commodo consequat.";
8         char text2[]= "Four score and seven years ago our fathers
brought forth on this continent, a new nation, conceived in Liberty, and
dedicated to the proposition that all men are created equal.";
9
10        initscr();
11
12    /* Get window sizes */
13        getmaxyx(stdscr,maxy,maxx);
14        halfy = maxy >> 1;
15        halfx = maxx >> 1;
16
```

(continued)

Listing 10-2 *(continued)*

```
17    /* Build windows */
18        top = newwin(halfy,maxx,0,0);
19        bottom = newwin(halfy,halfx,halfy,halfx);
20
21        waddstr(top,text1);
22        wrefresh(top);
23        waddstr(bottom,text2);
24        wrefresh(bottom);
25
26    /* Wait for key press */
27        getch();
28
29    /* Copy text from top to bottom */
30        rc = copywin(top,bottom,0,0,0,0,4,12,FALSE);
31        wrefresh(bottom);
32        getch();
33
34        endwin();
35        return 0;
36    }
```

For your "real" programs, remember to check for errors when creating the two windows in lines 19 and 20.

The copywin() function uses the FALSE option, so the rectangle of text from window top overwrites the original contents of window bottom. Figure 10-3 may help you to see the results.

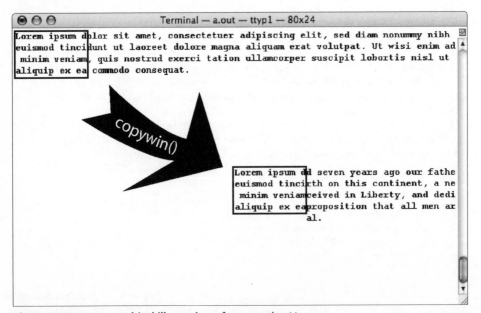

Figure 10-3: Cute graphical illustration of copywin()

Plain old window duplication

The final window copying function is dupwin(), which copies an entire window — size, text and all — to a new window, a duplicate. It's basically the newwin() function, but uses an existing window as a template to create the new window.

```
newwin = dupwin(win)
```

The dupwin() function returns a WINDOW pointer, which is then used to reference and write to the new window (Listing 10.3).

Listing 10-3: dup.c

```
 1    #include <ncurses.h>
 2
 3    int main(void)
 4    {
 5        WINDOW *fred,*barney;
 6
 7        initscr();
 8
 9    /* Build window & wait */
10        fred = newwin(0,0,0,0);
11        waddstr(fred,"This is the original window, Fred.\n");
12        wrefresh(fred);
13        getch();
14
15    /* Create and show barney */
16        barney = dupwin(fred);
17        waddstr(barney,"This is the Barney copy of window Fred.\n");
18        wrefresh(barney);
19        getch();
20
21    /* Go back to fred */
22        waddstr(fred,"Nice to see you again!\n");
23        wrefresh(fred);
24        getch();
25
26    /* One more time to barney */
27        waddstr(barney,"And Barney says 'Hi' as well.\n");
28        touchwin(barney);
29        wrefresh(barney);
30
31        endwin();
32        return 0;
33    }
```

The new window `barney` is created based on `fred` in line 16. The new window inherits `fred`'s text. Then the program bounces back and forth between the windows, displaying information.

Scrolling Around

Scrolling text doesn't seem like a big deal, and it isn't — today! Thirty years ago it *was* a big deal — so much so that a scrolling screen of text was patented (probably by IBM).

The fact that text scrolls on the screen seems to be taken for granted. But it's not something that the terminal does automatically: scrolling must be programmed. After all, the screen is merely a matrix of text. Internally, the screen buffer is only as big as the screen. Whenever you see something larger than the screen displayed (and scrollable), it's programming magic that moves text from a separate buffer to the screen.

Fortunately, scrolling the screen is no big deal, even if you have to program the scroll yourself: a line of text is removed, the remaining text is moved, then a new line of text is added. It's not really that complicated, and you could do it yourself — but you don't have to! NCurses gladly handles any scrolling chores your programs require.

Can it scroll?

In NCurses, scrolling text is a window attribute, just like the window's size, location, cursor location, and other attributes. This attribute is normally turned off, meaning that windows in NCurses doesn't scroll a window by default. Here's proof, as shown in Listing 10-4.

Listing 10-4: `scroller.c`

```
 1     #include <ncurses.h>
 2
 3     #define FILENAME "gettysburg.txt"
 4
 5     int main(void)
 6     {
 7         FILE *text;
 8         WINDOW *lister;
 9         int maxy,maxx,ch;
10
11         initscr();
12         getmaxyx(stdscr,maxy,maxx);
13
14     /* create window lister */
```

Listing 10-4 *(continued)*

```
15          lister = newwin(maxy,maxx/2,0,maxx/4);
16          if( lister == NULL)
17          {
18              addstr("unable to create window\n");
19              refresh(); getch();
20              endwin();
21              return(1);
22          }
23
24      /* open the file */
25          text = fopen(FILENAME,"r");
26          if( text == NULL )
27          {
28              addstr("unable to open file\n");
29              refresh(); getch();
30              endwin();
31              return(2);
32          }
33
34      /* display the file's contents */
35          do
36          {
37              ch = fgetc(text);
38              waddch(lister,ch);
39              wrefresh(lister);
40          } while (ch != EOF);
41          fclose(text);
42          getch();
43
44          endwin();
45          return(0);
46      }
```

This program creates a new window, `lister`. The window is half the width of the standard screen, but just as tall. A file is opened on disk and displayed, character by character, in the window. The notion here is to display enough text that the window needs to scroll to display the whole thing.

Note that the filename is defined in line 3. I'm using the text from Lincoln's Gettysburg Address, which is saved in the same folder as `SCROLLER.C` and in a file named `GETTYSBURG.TXT`. Be sure to specify the name of an existing text file in line 3; the file must contain enough text to require the window to scroll to display it all.

Breaking with tradition here, I'm doing some error-checking in this program, both for creating the new window as well as opening the file.

And... it doesn't scroll. Instead, after the window is filled, remaining text in the file continues to be plugged in to the bottom-most, right character position in window `lister`.

Scroll Away

Enabling scrolling in NCurses is easy, thanks to the `scrollok()` function:

```
scrollok(win,TRUE);
```

The `scrollok()` function sets or resets the ability of a window to scroll. The window is specified as `win`, and the second argument is either `TRUE` or `FALSE` to turn scrolling on or off (respectively) for that window.

Add the following at line 23:

```
scrollok(lister,TRUE);
```

This time the text continues to display as the window scrolls its contents up, allowing for the new text.

If your text file isn't long enough to scroll the window, then choose another file.

Scrolling affects the location of the window's cursor. When a character is placed at the bottom right position in a window, scrolling advances the text up one line (the scroll), then returns the cursor to the start of the bottom line in the window, column zero.

The old manual scroll

Whether a window has its scrolling attribute set or not, you can still manually scroll the text in a window by using the `scroll()` function:

```
scroll(win)
```

The `scroll()` function scrolls text in the window `win` up one line. This works only if the window has its scrolling attribute set. When in doubt, set scrolling on with `scrollok(win,TRUE)`, otherwise the `scroll()` function returns `ERR` (see Listing 10-5).

Listing 10-5: `scrup1.c`

```
1    #include <ncurses.h>
2
3    int main(void)
4    {
5        int maxy,maxx,y;
6        initscr();
7
8        getmaxyx(stdscr,maxy,maxx);
9        scrollok(stdscr,TRUE);
10
```

Listing 10-5 *(continued)*

```
11          for(y=0;y<=maxy;y++)
12              mvprintw(y,0,"This is boring text written to line %d.",y);
13          refresh();
14          getch();
15
16          scroll(stdscr);
17          refresh();
18          getch();
19
20          endwin();
21          return 0;
22      }
```

The code uses the standard screen, `stdscr`, for output, though scrolling works similarly for any window. In line 9, the `scrollok()` function allows the `stdscr` to be scrolled. The `for` loop, lines 11 and 12, fill the screen with text. After pressing Enter (line 14), the `scroll()` function in line 16 scrolls the text on the screen up one notch.

Here are some things to notice when the screen scrolls:

- The top line of the window is scrolled away; it disappears.
- All lines after the top line are each scrolled up one notch.
- A blank line fills the last line of the screen.
- The cursor position *does not* change; it remains at the same coordinates as before the scroll. So if the cursor is at position 10,15, it will not scroll up to line 9,15, but rather remain at 10,15.

Scrolling by leaps and bounds

Say you need to scroll the screen up two lines instead of three? It can happen. One way to make it happen is to just use `scroll()` thrice.

Edit line 16 to read:

```
scroll(stdscr); scroll(stdscr); scroll(stdscr);
```

Did it work? It should have, though I've found some versions of NCurses that require this nonsense:

```
scroll(stdscr);
refresh();
scroll(stdscr);
refresh();
scroll(stdscr);
refresh();
```

Regardless of how you get it to work, you're wasting code. Obviously there must be a better solution than awkwardly re-issuing `scroll()` functions. And that solution is this function:

```
scrl(n)
```

The `scrl()` function scrolls the standard screen n number of lines. So to scroll up three lines, `scrl(3)` would be used. To make `scrl()` imitate `scroll()`, `scrl(1)` would be used (see Listing 10-6).

Listing 10-6: `scrup2.c`

```
1      #include <ncurses.h>
2
3      int main(void)
4      {
5           initscr();
6           int maxy,maxx,y;
7
8           getmaxyx(stdscr,maxy,maxx);
9           scrollok(stdscr,TRUE);
10
11          for(y=0;y<=maxy;y++)
12              mvprintw(y,0,"This is boring text written to line %d.",y);
13          refresh();
14          getch();
15
16          scrl(3);
17          refresh();
18          getch();
19
20          endwin();
21          return(0);
22     }
```

Only line 16 is changed, from the `scroll()` function to `scrl(3)`. The result scrolls the screen up three lines instead of one.

As expected, the `scrl()` function hops text on the screen up by three rows. Blank rows replace the rows scrolled up from the bottom of the window. And, as with the `scroll()` function, the cursor's position on the screen is not affected by the function call.

The window version of the `scroll()` function is `wscrl()`. The format is

```
wscrl(win,n)
```

win is the name of the window being scrolled and n indicates the number of lines to scroll.

Both `wscrl()` and `scrl()` return `OK` upon success and `ERR` when there is problem. The most common problem is that the window does not have its scrolling attribute set.

Negative scrolling

The `scrl()` function is a true scrolling function, one that doesn't assume things always have to scroll *up*. In fact, when you specify a *negative* value for n in `scrl(n)`, text on the screen scrolls *down*. See for yourself; change line 16 to read:

```
scrl(-3)
```

Scrolling down is merely the opposite of scrolling up: lines move *down* on the screen. New, blank lines appear at the top. Text at the bottom of the screen is scrolled into oblivion. The cursor's position does not change.

The Moving Experience

When NCurses creates a window it doesn't really bolt it down on the screen. Just as you can change text within a window, text attributes, the cursor location in the window, you can also change the window's location on the screen. This is thanks to the handy `mvwin()` function:

```
mvwin(win,row,col);
```

The `mvwin()` function moves window `win` to new location `row`, `col`, relative to the standard screen. (So 0,0 is the upper-left corner.) As long as the whole window remains on the screen, you can move it anywhere. See Listing 10-7.

Listing 10-7: `windrop.c`

```
1    #include <ncurses.h>
2
3    #define TSIZE 18
4
5    int main(void)
6    {
7        WINDOW *b;
8        int maxy,maxx,y,x;
9
10       initscr();
11
12       getmaxyx(stdscr,maxy,maxx);
```

(continued)

Listing 10-7 *(continued)*

```
13          x = (maxx-TSIZE) >> 1;
14
15          b = newwin(1,TSIZE,0,x);
16          waddstr(b,"I'm getting sick!");
17
18          for(y=1;y<maxy;y++)
19          {
20              mvwin(b,y,x);
21              wrefresh(b);
22              getch();
23          }
24
25          endwin();
26          return(0);
27      }
```

The code creates a long, thin window b, which barely contains the text I'm getting sick!. The for loop is used to change the window's location on the screen, dropping vertically from the first row down to the last row.

The window drops down on the screen, one line for every press of the Enter key. But because the underlying window isn't updated, window b's old location remains visible. Must fix that!

Insert these two lines after line 21, inside the for loop:

```
touchline(stdscr,y-1,1);
refresh();
```

The touchline() function works like touchwin(), though instead of updating the entire window only a single line of a window is updated — and that saves time. So in this case, the previous line of the background window, stdscr, is updated as window b is moved to the line below.

The window actually does appear to move, now that its previous location is erased. (Actually, the window beneath the moving window is refreshed, which has the effect of erasing the moving window's previous position.)

The only effect you can add now is to populate the background window with something interesting, which further shows that window b is moving over something.

Insert these two lines before line 15:

```
bkgd('.');
refresh();
```

The bkgd() function fills the stdscr window's background with periods. Or if you want to be more creative, just flood the background window with random text or the Gettysburg address — anything that can help prove window b moves (or floats) over the top of that window.

Window b moves as before, but now you can see that the background window's contents do not change.

When using mvwin(), remember these points:

- The window can be moved anywhere on the screen, as long as the entire window remains on the screen. If one or more rows or columns falls off the edge of the screen, then the window is not moved; the mvwin() function returns ERR.

- To complete the move, the window in the background must be updated. The touchline() or touchwin() functions can handle this, followed by a wrefresh() of the background window.

- Do not move subwindows using mvwin(). Subwindows share memory with the parent window, but the parent window is unaware of this. Therefore, when you move the subwindow, NCurses cannot update which text was moved in which window and the results can be disastrous.

- Don't confuse the mvwin() function with wmove(), which is used to move the cursor's location in a window.

CHAPTER 11

Dig My Pad, Man

Welcome to the Brobdingnagian part of your NCurses version of *Gulliver's Travels*. It's the land of the big. If you recall, adventurer Gulliver visits many lands in Jonathan Swift's *Gulliver's Travels*. Nearly everyone remembers Lilliput, land of the little people. But Gulliver also visits a land of giants, called Brobdingnag.

In NCurses, there are windows, but there are also *pads*. A pad is a supersized, Brobdingnagian window (or can be). Unlike regular windows, which can be at least one character in size and at most the same size as the terminal screen, a pad can be any size, up to as much as memory allows. This chapter explores the possibilities of pads.

The Monster Window

Pads are not really the same things as windows in a number of interesting and useful ways. About the most obvious is that a pad can be any size, from one character on up to many columns and rows, far beyond what can be seen on the screen at once.

Making a Pad

Pads are created like windows. The WINDOW type is used to define the variable —
just like a window, though a new command is used to actually create the pad:

```
newpad(rows,cols)
```

rows and cols set the height and width of the pad in characters. Values
range from 1 up to however large a pad memory can handle.

The value returned from newpad() is the address of a WINDOW structure
in memory (see Listing 11-1), which is exactly the same as for a regular
window, though as you'll read in a few paragraphs, pads and windows have
differences.

Listing 11-1: bigpad1.c

```
1     #include <ncurses.h>
2
3     int main(void)
4     {
5         WINDOW *p;
6         int x,c;
7
8         initscr();
9
10    /* create a new pad */
11        p = newpad(50,100);
12        if( p == NULL )
13        {
14            addstr("Unable to create new pad");
15            refresh();
16            endwin();
17            return(1);
18        }
19
20        addstr("New pad created");
21        refresh();
22
23        endwin();
24        return 0;
25    }
```

The pad is created in line 11, assigned to variable p. Line 12 tests to see if
memory can handle a pad of 100 columns by 50 rows (more than four times the
size of the typical terminal screen).

If the pad was created, "New pad created" is displayed on the standard
screen. Why wasn't the text put and displayed from the pad? You'll read why
in the next section!

Viewing a Pad's Contents

Text is put to a pad just like any other window using the standard NCurses text-output commands. Unlike standard windows, however, you just can't refresh a pad, not with `wrefresh()`, at least. Here's proof. Change lines 20 and 21 to read:

```
waddstr(p,"New pad created");
wrefresh(p);
```

Nothing, eh?

True, the `waddstr()` function did indeed add text to the pad. But `wrefresh()` doesn't update or display the pad. Even if it could, consider this: When the pad was created, where was it put on the screen?

Ah-ha!

Pads, unlike windows, lack screen coordinates. In fact, it helps to think of a pad as a virtual screen that's way, way off in memory. There is just no relationship between the pad itself and the visible screen.

To display text written to the pad, you need to know where it is on the pad and copy that chunk from the pad to the screen for display. The `prefresh()` function is what handles the operation:

```
prefresh(pad,pminrow,pmincol,
sminrow,smincol,smaxrow,smaxcol)
```

The `prefresh()` function looks intimidating, but it's not: `pad` is the name of a pad created by using the `newpad()` function. The rest of the arguments define a rectangle of text (and attributes) in the pad and specify where that rectangle will be placed on the standard screen. The remaining arguments of `prefresh()` calculate that rectangle's location:

`pminrow` and `pmincol` represent the Y and X coordinates of the upper-left corner of a chunk of the pad.

`sminrow` and `smincol` are the Y and X coordinates on the standard screen where the chunk of the pad will be displayed. `smaxrow` and `smaxcol` define the size of the rectangle, both relative to the pad and the screen. Figure 11-1 helps illustrate this.

Change line 21 to read:

```
prefresh(p,0,0,0,0,1,15);
```

Now you see the text; `prefresh()` copies a chunk from the pad and displays it on the screen.

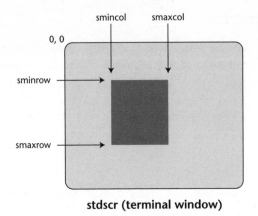

stdscr (terminal window)

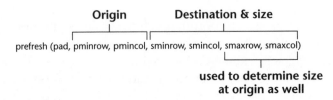

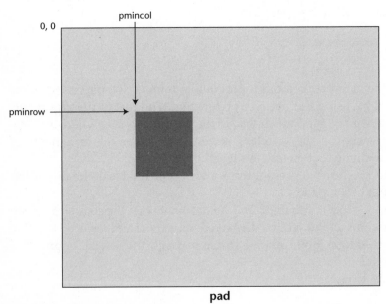

pad

Figure 11-1: Mapping out how `prefresh()` works

More Pad-Viewing Stuff

One key thing to remember about pads is that the pad's size is set starting with one, yet `prefresh()` uses zero as a base. So if a pad were 20 characters wide, you would reference those characters from column 0 through column 19 — not 1 through 20.

Listing 11-2 shows yet another pad program to whet your pad appetite.

Listing 11-2: `paddy1.c`

```
1     #include <ncurses.h>
2     #include <stdlib.h>
3
4     #define FILENAME "gettysburg.txt"
5     #define TALL 24
6     #define WIDE 19
7     #define SPACER 5
8
9     void bomb(char *message);
10
11    int main(void)
12    {
13        WINDOW *p;
14        FILE *f;
15        int ch;
16
17        initscr();
18
19    /* create a new pad */
20        p = newpad(200,WIDE+1);
21        if( p == NULL )
22            bomb("Unable to create new pad\n");
23
24    /* open the file */
25        f = fopen(FILENAME,"r");
26        if( f == NULL)
27            bomb("Unable to open file\n");
28
29    /* display file's contents on the pad */
30        while( (ch=fgetc(f)) != EOF)
31            waddch(p,ch);
32        fclose(f);
33
34    /* display the pad's contents on the screen */
35        prefresh(p,     0, 0, 0,                 0, TALL-1,
WIDE);
36        prefresh(p,   TALL, 0, 0,    WIDE+SPACER, TALL-1,
WIDE*2+SPACER);
```

(continued)

Listing 11-2 (continued)

```
37        prefresh(p, TALL*2, 0, 0,WIDE*2+SPACER*2, TALL-1,
WIDE*3+SPACER*2);
38        wgetch(p);
39
40        endwin();
41        return 0;
42    }
43
44    void bomb(char *message)
45    {
46        addstr(message);
47        refresh(); getch();
48        endwin();
49        exit(1);
50    }
```

The code creates a tall, narrow pad in line 20, 200 lines deep by 20 lines wide. The constant WIDE is defined as 19 because the actual width of the pad goes from zero to 19, not 20. That comes into play later in the code.

The text file defined at line 4 is read in line 25. I've used the GETTYS-BURG.TXT file, which is a text copy of Lincoln's Gettysburg Address. (Ensure that whatever file you specify is in the same directory as the PADDY1.C program.) Each character is read from the program and put to the pad in lines 30 and 31.

Of course, nothing shows up on the screen until prefresh() comes around. This code takes the long, tall pad and displays the first three chunks of the file in the columns on the screen in lines 35, 36, and 37. Constants TALL and WIDE define the height and width of the chunk read; SPACER is used to put some air between the columns.

The output is shown in Figure 11-2, with Figure 11-3 describing how it works.

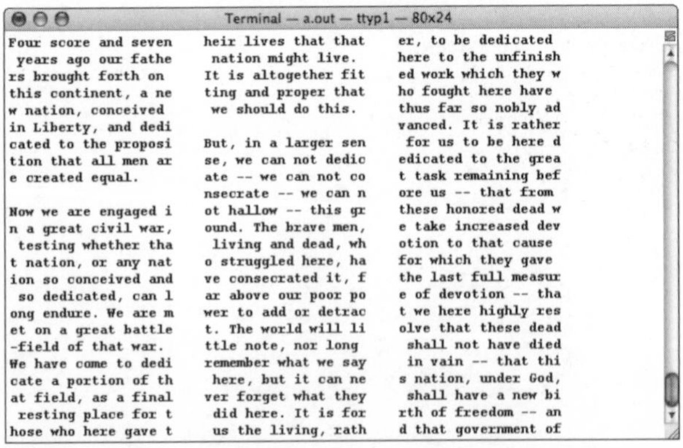

Figure 11-2: Output of the PADDY.C source code

WIDE

TALL

Four score and seven years ago our fathers brought forth on this continent, a new nation, conceived in Liberty, and dedicated to the proposition that all men are created equal.

Now we are engaged in a great civil war, testing whether that nation, or any nation so conceived and so dedicated, can long endure. We are met on a great battle-field of that war. We have come to dedicate a portion of that field, as a final resting place for those who here gave their lives that nation might live. It is altogether fitting and proper that we should do this.

But, in a larger sense, we can not dedicate -- we can not consecrate -- we can not hallow -- this ground. The brave men, living and dead, who struggled here, have consecrated it, far above our poor power to add or detract. The world will little note, nor long remember what we say here, but it can never forget what they did here. It is for us the living, rather, to be dedicated here to the unfinished work which they who fought here have thus far so nobly advanced. It is rather for us to be here dedicated to the great task remaining before us -- that from these honored dead we take increased devotion to that cause for which they gave the last full measure of devotion -- that we here highly resolve that these dead shall not have died in vain -- that this nation, under God, shall have a new birth of freedom -- and that government of the people, by the people, for the people, shall not perish from the earth.

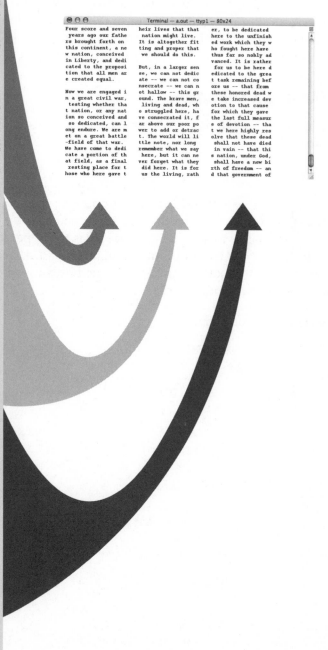

Figure 11-3: What PADDY.C does

Subpads

Just as windows can have subwindows, there is also a beast known as a *subpad*. Yeah, I'm not thrilled about it. Like the subwindow, the subpad shares memory with the parent; changing the contents of a subpad changes the text on a pad.

Making a subpad

Almost without thinking, you can guess that the subpad() function creates a new subpad:

```
subpad(org,rows,cols,y,x)
```

org is the parent pad. rows and cols set the subpad's size, which (logically) must not be greater than the orig pad's size. y and x set the subpad's position relative to the parent, where 0,0 is the upper-left corner.

If the subpad() call is successful, a subpad is created in memory and a pointer to a WINDOW structure is returned by subpad(). If NULL is returned, the subpad was not created. (See Listing 11-3.)

Listing 11-3: sonofpad.c

```
1    #include <ncurses.h>
2    #include <stdlib.h>
3
4    void bomb(char *message);
5
6    int main(void)
7    {
8        WINDOW *pod,*pea;
9
10       initscr();
11
12   /* create a new pad */
13       pod = newpad(50,50);
14       if( pod == NULL )
15           bomb("Unable to create new pad");
16
17       addstr("New pad created\n");
18       refresh();
19
20   /* create a subpad */
21       pea = subpad(pod,20,20,29,29);
```

Listing 11-3 *(continued)*

```
22          if( pea == NULL )
23              bomb("Unable to create subpad");
24
25          addstr("Subpad created\n");
26          refresh(); getch();
27
28          endwin();
29          return 0;
30      }
31
32      void bomb(char *message)
33      {
34          addstr(message);
35          refresh(); getch();
36          endwin();
37          exit(1);
38      }
```

First, the pad is created; if successful, you'll see:

```
New pad created
```

Then a subpad on that pad is created. If the stars are in proper alignment, you'll see:

```
Subpad created
```

Pop the cork on some bubbly.

Working with a Subpad

As with subwindows, I feel that the best way to put a subpad to use is as a quick way to reference specific coordinates within a pad. So if something interesting is happening always at location 20,30 in the pad, consider placing a subpad there so you can use coordinates local to the subpad instead of having to calculate things in the pad.

A perfect example of these local coordinates can be seen in the code for PADDY1.C. Rather than calculate offsets within the pad p, three subpads can be created, each of which represents one of the columns of text displayed on the screen (see Figure 11-2). This greatly helps to clean up the prefresh() statements near the end of the code, as this improvement in Listing 11-4 demonstrates.

Listing 11-4: `paddy2.c`

```
1    #include <ncurses.h>
2    #include <stdlib.h>
3
4    #define FILENAME "gettysburg.txt"
5    #define TALL 24
6    #define WIDE 19
7    #define SPACER 5
8
9    void bomb(char *message);
10
11   int main(void)
12   {
13       WINDOW *p,*s1,*s2,*s3;
14       FILE *f;
15       int ch;
16
17       initscr();
18
19   /* create a new pad */
20       p = newpad(200,WIDE+1);
21       if( p == NULL )
22           bomb("Unable to create new pad\n");
23
24   /* create three subpads */
25       s1 = subpad(p,TALL,WIDE+1,0,0);
26       if( s1 == NULL) bomb("Unable to create subpad 1\n");
27       s2 = subpad(p,TALL,WIDE+1,TALL,0);
28       if( s2 == NULL) bomb("Unable to create subpad 2\n");
29       s3 = subpad(p,TALL,WIDE+1,2*TALL,0);
30       if( s3 == NULL) bomb("Unable to create subpad 3\n");
31
32   /* open the file */
33       f = fopen(FILENAME,"r");
34       if( f == NULL)
35           bomb("Unable to open file\n");
36
37   /* display file's contents on the pad */
38       while( (ch=fgetc(f)) != EOF)
39           waddch(p,ch);
40       fclose(f);
41
42   /* display the pad's contents on the screen */
43       prefresh(s1, 0, 0, 0,              0, TALL-1,              WIDE);
44       prefresh(s2, 0, 0, 0,    WIDE+SPACER, TALL-1,   WIDE*2+SPACER);
45       prefresh(s3, 0, 0, 0, WIDE*2+SPACER*2, TALL-1, WIDE*3+SPACER*2);
46       wgetch(p);
```

Listing 11-4 *(continued)*

```
47
48          endwin();
49          return 0;
50      }
51
52      void bomb(char *message)
53      {
54          addstr(message);
55          refresh(); getch();
56          endwin();
57          exit(1);
58      }
```

The program's output is identical to the original, but some effort was saved by using local references to the subpads in lines 43, 44, and 45.

Some Optimization

Here's a bit of advanced NCurses for you: The code in the previous section uses three `prefresh()` functions in `PADDY2.C` to update pad data to the standard screen:

```
prefresh(s1, 0, 0, 0,                    0, TALL-1,                WIDE);
prefresh(s2, 0, 0, 0,      WIDE+SPACER, TALL-1,    WIDE*2+SPACER);
prefresh(s3, 0, 0, 0, WIDE*2+SPACER*2, TALL-1, WIDE*3+SPACER*2);
```

These three statements work, but they're inefficient. Each `prefresh()` internally calls two lower-level NCurses functions: `pnoutrefresh()` and `doupdate()`.

The `pnoutfresh()` function examines a given rectangle of text in a pad, and notes that the text in that rectangle that has been changed or updated since the last `prefresh()`. That text, referred to as *touched*, is then queued up for display on the standard screen. Then the `doupdate()` function takes care of the task of actually updating the screen. So the three `prefresh()` functions actually work out to be:

```
pnoutrefresh(s1, 0, 0, 0,                    0, TALL-1,                WIDE);
doupdate();
pnoutrefresh(s2, 0, 0, 0,      WIDE+SPACER, TALL-1,    WIDE*2+SPACER);
doupdate();
pnoutrefresh(s3, 0, 0, 0, WIDE*2+SPACER*2, TALL-1, WIDE*3+SPACER*2);
doupdate();
```

That's a lot of work for the processor, so a better way to arrange things is like this:

```
pnoutrefresh(s1, 0, 0, 0,                 0, TALL-1,              WIDE);
pnoutrefresh(s2, 0, 0, 0,       WIDE+SPACER, TALL-1,   WIDE*2+SPACER);
pnoutrefresh(s3, 0, 0, 0, WIDE*2+SPACER*2, TALL-1, WIDE*3+SPACER*2);
doupdate();
```

The original three `prefresh()` functions become `pnoutrefresh()` functions, which is easy to do because both functions have the same exact arguments. Then a single `doupdate()` function is all that's needed to update the standard screen and display information.

Yes, the changes may seem trivial. And it's not like this update to the code results in a peppier program, especially on today's faster computers. But it's a good trick to know.

The `pnoutrefresh()` function is actually a pad-based version of the `wnoutrefresh()` function designed to optimize window updating. For more information on that function, refer to Appendix A.

Removing a Pad

Pads are blown to smithereens just like windows. In fact, the same function, `delwin()`, is used to remove a pad:

```
delwin(pad)
```

The preceding function returns OK when the named pad is successfully removed or it returns ERR when something bad happens.

Just as with removing windows, it's wise to remove subpads (also by using `delwin()`) before removing a pad. When you don't, the memory used by the subpad will not be freed, and bad things will happen: pestilence, darkness, February will get two days back, and other misfortunes may befall you. Listing 11-5 shows an obligatory sample program.

Listing 11-5: `bigpad3.c`

```
1    #include <ncurses.h>
2
3    int main(void)
4    {
5        WINDOW *p;
6        int x,c;
7
8        initscr();
9
```

Chapter 11 ▪ Dig My Pad, Man   143

Listing 11-5 *(continued)*

```
10    /* create a new pad */
11        p = newpad(50,100);
12        if( p == NULL )
13        {
14            addstr("Unable to create new pad");
15            refresh();
16            endwin();
17            return(1);
18        }
19
20        addstr("New pad created");
21        refresh();
22        getch();
23
24        if( delwin(p)==OK )
25            addstr("...and now it's gone!\n");
26        else
27            addstr("...and it's still there!\n");
28        refresh(); getch();
29
30        endwin();
32        return 0;
33    }
```

You should see:

```
New pad created
```

Press Enter and you'll see:

```
New pad created...and now it's gone!
```

Pad Miscellany

Maybe someday one of your NCurses programs will find use for a pad or maybe even a subpad or two. They're handy structures to have, especially if you have a predefined chunk of information you'd like brought into your windows from time to time.

Another Pad Function

The `pechochar()` function both places a character on the pad and displays it on the screen but only after a chunk of the screen has been squared off with `prefresh()`. Listing 11-6 shows a program that makes use of it.

Listing 11-6: oddpad.c

```
1    #include <ncurses.h>
2
3    int main(void)
4    {
5        WINDOW *p;
6        char text[] = "This is interesting";
7        char *t;
8
9        initscr();
10
11   /* create a new pad */
12       p = newpad(50,100);
13       if( p == NULL )
14       {
15           addstr("Unable to create new pad");
16           refresh();
17           endwin();
18           return(1);
19       }
20
21       t = text;
22       prefresh(p,0,0,1,1,1,25);
23       while(*t)
24           pechochar(p,*t++);
25       wgetch(p);
26       endwin();
27       return 0;
28   }
```

The code makes use of prefresh() in line 22 to box off a chunk of the screen, only a line to display the text. The while loop then uses pechochar() to read a string of text that is both sent to the pad and also displayed on the screen.

You should see:

```
This is interesting
```

displayed on the second row, starting at the second column of the screen.

Forbidden Pad Functions

Know that you can use all the standard NCurses functions with a pad except the following:

mvwin()

scroll()

```
scrl()
subwin()
wrefresh()
wnoutrefresh()
```

Additionally, pads are created by using the `newpad()` function, not `newwin()`. (Refer to Appendix A for information on the `wnoutrefresh()` function.)

Forbidden Pad Stuff

Don't bother moving a pad. In fact, the concept seems silly because pads do not exist relative to the screen.

Pads cannot be scrolled.

As with subwindows, do not move a subpad — and for the same reason. The coordination between the parent and the subpad is nonexistent. Because both share memory, moving a subpad results in chaos for the parent and catastrophe for your program.

Also, remember to remove subpads before deleting the pad itself. If you don't, the memory used by the subpads will not be cleared.

CHAPTER 12

The Joy of Soft Labels

Dig down deep into NCurses' bag of tricks and you'll discover a clever and quick instant interface trick called *soft labels*. They really aren't anything amazing, though they can save you time over having to do the programming yourself. So when you want to slap together a quick and friendly interface, soft labels take care of that programming overhead for you.

What Is a Soft Label?

Soft labels are typically associated with a set of function keys found just below the screen on a terminal keyboard. This is something that was more common in the old days of mainframes and their remote terminals than it is today.

For example, the terminal may have keys F1 through F8 just below the built-in screen. Above each key would be a highlighted bit of text on the screen. The text represented the command associated with the key, similar to what you see in Figure 12-1.

Pressing F1, for example, may shift the screen into printing mode. The soft labels might change to reflect the new screen and show the new functions for the keys F1 through F8. Theoretically, the user understands that, by pressing a function key, he or she is issuing the command specified in the soft label. Theoretically.

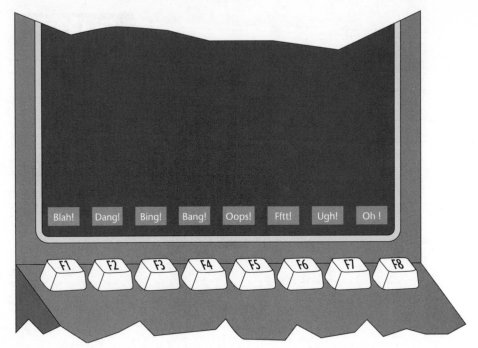

Figure 12-1: How soft labels might have worked on an older terminal

Doing the Soft Label Thing

In NCurses, soft labels are visual elements only. There is no back connection between function keys and soft labels, unless you program one yourself. Otherwise, setting and displaying soft keys is merely a visual part of NCurses.

Stand by for Soft Labels

If you're writing a program that uses soft labels, you'll need to use the `slk_init()` function:

```
slk_init(n)
```

All soft label functions begin with `slk`. I assume that *slk* stands for *soft label keys*, though that's just a guess.

The `slk_init()` function must appear *before* the `initscr()` function in your code. The reason is that `slk_init()` changes the size of the standard screen, reserving the bottom row for the soft keys. All NCurses commands, then, affect only the top several rows of the screen; the bottom row is reserved — and cannot be touched, other than to mess with the soft labels.

The value of n determines how many soft labels there will be, as well as how they're arranged on the screen. Figure 12-2 details the results for valid values of n from 0 through 3.

Gimme Some Soft Labels

The slk_init() function merely announces the presence of soft labels. You must also assign text to the labels, as well as display the labels in their special row on the screen.

Assigning text to the labels is done by using the slk_set() function:

```
slk_set(label,text,pos)
```

The slk_set() function has three arguments.

- label is the label number, ranging from 1 to 12, marching from left to right across the screen. The number of labels you need to set depends on the value used with the slk_init() function.

- text is the text to appear on the label. When there are eight soft labels on the screen, up to eight characters of text appears in the labels. For 12 soft labels on the screen, only five characters of text appear in the labels.

- pos determines the text's orientation within the label. There are three values: 0 for left-justified; 1 for centered; and 2 for right-justified.

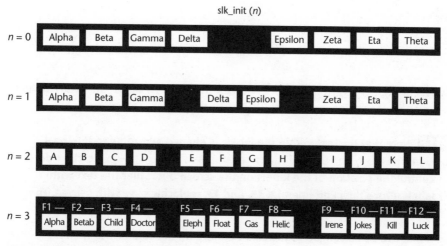

Figure 12-2: Soft key setup options for slk_init(n)

Finally, to make the labels show up, the `slk_refresh()` function is used:

```
slk_refresh()
```

Like other `refresh()` functions in NCurses, this one updates the screen. In this case, only the soft label row on the screen is updated (see Listing 12-1).

Listing 12-1: `softies1.c`

```
 1    #include <ncurses.h>
 2
 3    #define LEFT 0
 4    #define CENTER 1
 5    #define RIGHT 2
 6
 7    int main(void)
 8    {
 9        slk_init(0);
10        initscr();
11
12        slk_set(1,"Help!",LEFT);
13        slk_set(2,"File",LEFT);
14        slk_set(3,"Print",LEFT);
15        slk_set(4,"Text",CENTER);
16        slk_set(5,"Edit",CENTER);
17        slk_set(6,"Quick",RIGHT);
18        slk_set(7,"Conf",RIGHT);
19        slk_set(8,"Change",RIGHT);
20        slk_refresh();
21        getch();
22
23        endwin();
24        return 0;
25    }
```

The code creates eight soft labels across the bottom of the terminal screen: three on the left, two centered, and three on the right.

> **NOTE** Note that the text within the labels is aligned according to the label's position. The LEFT, CENTER, and RIGHT constants in the `slk_set()` function do not control the position of the labels on the screen but rather the text within the labels. Prove this: Edit lines 12, 13, and 13, replacing LEFT with CENTER. Then edit lines 17, 18, and 19, replacing RIGHT with CENTER.
>
> The labels are still arranged in the same pattern on the screen, but the text within the labels is centered.

Making the Index Line

Specifying option 3 for `slk_init()` shows the same layout for soft labels as option 2 but with the addition of an *index line*. In most versions of NCurses I've seen, this index line is a list of function key names right above the soft labels, as shown in Figure 12-2. As with the soft label line, the index line is protected from being overwritten and the standard screen size is decreased by one line accordingly (see listing 12-2).

Listing 12-2: `softies2.c`

```
1    #include <ncurses.h>
2
3    #define LMAX 12
4    #define CENTER 1
5
6    int main(void)
7    {
8        char label_text[LMAX][6] = { "Help", "File", "Edit", "Frmt",
9                            "Find", "Block", "Ins", "Del",
10                           "View", "Switch", "Win", "Help" };
11       int label;
12
13       slk_init(3);
14       initscr();
15
16       for(label=0;label<LMAX;label++)
17           slk_set(label+1,label_text[label],CENTER);
18       slk_refresh();
19
20       getch();
21
22       endwin();
23       return 0;
24   }
```

You'll note that this time a `for` loop is used to load in the labels via `slk_set()` in lines 16 and 17. All the labels will be centered.

Chances are that the index line is there — but blank! That's because NCurses needs a little extra nudge to show that special text.

Insert this new line between lines 15 and 16:

```
slk_restore();
```

This time the index line appears.

The `slk_restore()` function is used primarily in conjunction with `slk_clear()`. The `slk_clear()` function removes the soft labels from the screen and `slk_restore()` puts them back, which is demonstrated later in this chapter. But in SOFTIES2.C, `slk_restore()` somehow supplies NCurses with the extra oomph needed to show the index line. (In fact, you can replace `slk_refresh()` with `slk_restore()` in many instances, though I don't recommend it.)

Soft Labels Here and Gone

The original reason for function keys was variety. The function keys could perform any function assigned to them, depending on the software. Therefore, they were called *function keys* instead of a this-or-that specific key.

Sadly, the role of the function key has changed, thanks to Microsoft Windows. Function keys now do specific things in all programs. That is, F1 is universally the Help key. And I wonder why keyboard manufacturers haven't just relabeled the thing "Help" instead of F1. But I digress.

In the original scheme of things, the role played by the function keys changed from program to program and even within a specific program, depending on what you were doing. Likewise, the soft labels your program might use should be changeable as well. The following sections describe how the soft labels can be manipulated.

Hiding and Restoring the Labels

Two NCurses functions deal with hiding and redisplaying the soft labels:

```
slk_clear()
slk_restore()
```

The `slk_clear()` function hides the soft labels. The `slk_restore()` function unhides them. See Listing 12-3 for examples of this.

Listing 12-3: `lonoff.c`

```
 1    #include <ncurses.h>
 2
 3    #define LMAX 8
 4    #define CENTER 1
 5
 6    int main(void)
 7    {
 8        char label_text[LMAX][8] = { "S", "O", "F", "T",
 9                         "K", "E", "Y", "S" };
10        int label;
11
12        slk_init(1);
```

Listing 12-3 *(continued)*

```
13          initscr();
14
15          for(label=0;label<LMAX;label++)
16              slk_set(label+1,label_text[label],CENTER);
17          slk_refresh();
18          getch();
19
20          slk_clear();
21          getch();
22
23          slk_restore();
24          getch();
25
26          endwin();
27          return 0;
28      }
```

At first the eight labels appear. Press Enter and they're gone. Press Enter again and they're back!

NOTE Note that even while hidden, your programs still cannot access the bottom row(s) of the screen where the soft labels appear.

Changing a Label

When your program needs to change a label, you simply reissue the `slk_set()` function for that label, along with the new text. Add a `slk_refresh()` and you're done (see Listing 12-4).

Listing 12-4: `duck.c`

```
1       #include <ncurses.h>
2
3       #define LMAX 8
4       #define CENTER 1
5
6       int main(void)
7       {
8           char label_text[LMAX][8] = { "Duck", "Duck", "Duck", "Duck",
9                           "Duck", "Duck", "Duck", "Duck" };
10          int label;
11
12          slk_init(1);
13          initscr();
14
```

(continued)

Listing 12-4 *(continued)*

```
15        for(label=0;label<LMAX;label++)
16            slk_set(label+1,label_text[label],CENTER);
17        slk_refresh();
18        getch();
19
20        slk_set(7,"Goose!",CENTER);
21        slk_refresh();
22        getch();
23
24        endwin();
25        return 0;
26    }
```

Pressing the Enter key changes label 7 from Duck to Goose!. Hurry! Run around the monitor and back to your seat before the program catches you!

Removing a Label

To remove a label or, more properly, to remove the text from a label, you simply use the slk_set() function with a null string of text.

Change line 20 to read:

```
slk_set(7,"",CENTER);
```

The seventh label is now blank.

Hooking in the Function Keys

As I write earlier in this chapter, there is no automatic hook in NCurses between soft labels and the function keys. If you want F1 to perform whatever command is listed by soft label 1, you have to do that code yourself.

(Supposedly, on some terminals with built-in soft labels, the connection between the labels and the related key is already made in NCurses. Because I don't have access to those terminals or even emulators, I cannot confirm this.)

Rather than flip back and forth between this chapter and Chapter 7, I decided to offer up a little bit of code in Listing 12-5 that shows how function keys can be linked into soft labels. It may not be much, but it's a start.

Listing 12-5: ham.c

```
1    #include <ncurses.h>
2
3    #define LMAX 12
4    #define CENTER 1
```

Listing 12-5 *(continued)*

```
 5
 6    int main(void)
 7    {
 8        char label_text[LMAX][20] = { "I", "AM", "SAM", "DO",
 9                              "NOT", "LIKE", "THAT", "SAY",
10                              "WOULD", "COULD", "YOU",
11                              "GREEN EGGS AND HAM" };
12        int label,ch;
13
14        slk_init(2);                    /* 12 soft labels */
15        initscr();
16        noecho();                     /* disable key echoing */
17        keypad(stdscr,TRUE);          /* Turn on Fkey reading */
18
19    /* display the labels and instructions */
20        for(label=0;label<LMAX;label++)
21            slk_set(label+1,label_text[label],CENTER);
22        slk_refresh();
23        addstr("Use the Function Keys to type\n");
24        addstr("Press '?' or '!' or '.' to end a line\n");
25        addstr("Press Enter to quit\n\n");
26        refresh();
27
28    /* Process input */
29        while( (ch=getch()) != '\n')
30        {
31            switch(ch)
32            {
33                case '?':
34                case '!':
35                case '.':
36                    addch(ch);
37                    addch('\n');
38                    break;
39                case KEY_F(1):
40                    printw("%s ",label_text[0]);
41                    break;
42                case KEY_F(2):
43                    printw("%s ",label_text[1]);
44                    break;
45                case KEY_F(3):
46                    printw("%s ",label_text[2]);
47                    break;
48                case KEY_F(4):
49                    printw("%s ",label_text[3]);
50                    break;
```

(continued)

Listing 12-5 *(continued)*

```
51                    case KEY_F(5):
52                         printw("%s ",label_text[4]);
53                         break;
54                    case KEY_F(6):
55                         printw("%s ",label_text[5]);
56                         break;
57                    case KEY_F(7):
58                         printw("%s ",label_text[6]);
59                         break;
60                    case KEY_F(8):
61                         printw("%s ",label_text[7]);
62                         break;
63                    case KEY_F(9):
64                         printw("%s ",label_text[8]);
65                         break;
66                    case KEY_F(10):
67                         printw("%s ",label_text[9]);
68                         break;
69                    case KEY_F(11):
70                         printw("%s ",label_text[10]);
71                         break;
72                    case KEY_F(12):
73                         printw("%s ",label_text[11]);
74                         break;
75                    default:
76                         break;
77               }
78          refresh();
79     }
80
81     endwin();
82     return 0;
83  }
```

CHAPTER 13

Messing Mit der Mouse

NCurses has the ability to interface with a mouse or similar pointing device attached to a computer. Information about the mouse can be read and used in your programs in a number of ways, just as mice are used in graphical programs.

All this stuff is optional, of course; NCurses is, after all, a text-based thing and mice are associated with graphical things. But if you want to take advantage of the mouse, you can certainly well do it.

Hello, Mouse

Even though your computer may have a mouse — indeed, the terminal window you use may be an oasis of text floating in a graphical operating system — the sucker may not quite be set up to read the mouse inside the terminal.

For example, some terminals intercept the mouse, using it at the operating system level to select text from the terminal window. If so, any mouse events are probably blocked from your program's view. There is a way to test for this, as covered in the section "Can your terminal deal with the mouse?" later in this chapter. But before that, you should check to see if your version of NCurses supports the mouse in the first place.

Can NCurses Deal with the Mouse?

Mouse programming is specific to NCurses. If your system is using the older Curses or an earlier version of NCurses, mouse functionality might not be available. Before you set out to do mouse programming, first check to see if NCurses is up to the task (see Listing 13-1).

Listing 13-1: mtest.c

```
1     #include <ncurses.h>
2
3     int main(void)
4     {
5         mmask_t mmask;
6
7         initscr();
8
9         if(NCURSES_MOUSE_VERSION > 0)
10            addstr("This version of NCurses supports the mouse.\n");
11        else
12            addstr("This version of NCurses does not support the
mouse.\n");
13        refresh();
14        getch();
15        endwin();
16        return 0;
17    }
```

This program simply reads the value of the NCURSES_MOUSE_VERSION variable, which is defined in the NCURSES.H header file. If the variable exists, the happy message is displayed:

```
This version of NCurses supports the mouse.
```

Otherwise, you end up with:

```
This version of NCurses does not support the mouse.
```

(Refer to the section "To Eek or Not to Eek?" at the end of this chapter for suggestions on how to best use NCURSES_MOUSE_VERSION.)

Can Your Terminal Deal with the Mouse?

Step 1 is to see if you have the latest version of NCurses, complete with mouse support. If so, you need to move on to step 2: Check to see if the terminal you're using properly interprets the mouse. This is done by using the `mousemask()` function:

```
mousemask(newmask,*oldmask)
```

It's the `mousemask()` function's job to make mouse activity visible to your program. To put it another way: `mousemask()` is what turns on mouse monitoring for your program.

The `newmask` argument tells NCurses which mouse events to watch for. The events are defined in `NCURSES.H` and listed in Appendix A. But most of the time you'll probably use the `ALL_MOUSE_EVENTS` value, which tells NCurses to keep an eye on all mouse buttons, up or down, clicked, double- or triple-clicked, or used with Shift, Alt, or Ctrl keys on the keyboard. (In NCurses, only mouse clicks and releases are monitored, not mouse movement.)

Most of the time, the value of `*oldmask` is NULL.

The value returned by `mousemask()` is of the `mmask_t` type (a long integer). The value matches the mask created on a bit-by-bit basis; it also determines whether the mouse is capable of monitoring the particular mouse action. For example:

```
mmask_t mbitmask;

mbitmask = mousemask(BUTTON3_CLICKED,NULL);
if( mbitmask & BUTTON3_CLICKED)
    addstr("I am able to read a button 3 click.");
else
    addstr("I am not able to read the button 3 click.");
refresh();
```

`BUTTON3_CLICKED` is a value defined in `NCURSES.H`. The call above to `mousemask()` tells NCurses to watch for only that value, which is generated when button 3 on the mouse is clicked. If such a thing is possible, the value returned by `mousemask()`, and stored in `mbitmask`, will equal the value of `BUTTON3_CLICKED`. This is checked by the logical comparison in the `if` statement, and `addstr()` displays the happy or unhappy news.

Not every computer mouse has three buttons, so the preceding code is a good way to determine whether or not your program can use button 3. A more useful test of `mousemask()` is with the `ALL_MOUSE_EVENTS` constant, which can be used to determine whether or not the terminal can see anything the mouse does (see Listing 13-2).

Listing 13-2: `mtest.c`

```
1     #include <ncurses.h>
2
3     int main(void)
4     {
5         mmask_t mmask;
6
7         initscr();
8
9         if(NCURSES_MOUSE_VERSION > 0)
10            addstr("This version of NCurses supports the mouse.\n");
11        else
12            addstr("This version of NCurses does not support the
mouse.\n");
13        refresh();
14
15        mmask = mousemask(ALL_MOUSE_EVENTS,NULL);
16        if(mmask == 0)
17            addstr("Unable to access the mouse on this terminal.\n");
18        else
19            addstr("Mouse events can be captured.\n");
20        refresh();
21        getch();
22        endwin();
23        return 0;
24    }
```

The new lines, shown above, are 15 through 21. The code uses the `mousemask()` function call to determine whether or not the terminal can see the mouse. If the value returned in `mmask` is zero, the mouse cannot be read.

Upon running the program, you should hope to see:

```
This version of NCurses supports the mouse.
Mouse events can be captured.
```

The message `Unable to access the mouse on this terminal` may appear, even though you *know* that you computer recognizes the mouse and even uses it to select text in the terminal window. And that's the problem! The operating system is intercepting the mouse before signals can be passed to the terminal. If possible, try to turn off mouse-selection functions for the terminal window or somehow enable mouse actions to pass through to text-based terminal programs.

Reading the Mouse

Once assured that your computer terminal is heavy for some hot mouse action, you'll need some additional tools to snoop out what the mouse is up to.

The "Reading the Mouse" Overview

After `mousemask()` initializes the mouse and tells NCurses which mouse events to scan, you use these two functions to read the mouse:

```
getch()
getmouse(&musevent)
```

First comes the `getch()` function. Just as it can read the keyboard, `getch()` can also detect mouse input. The mouse input is defined in `NCURSES.H` as `KEY_MOUSE`. And to read that *character*, you must activate extended keyboard reading for `getch()` by using the `keypad()` function. Further, many programmers also use `noecho()` so that `getch()` can be read repeatedly.

Don't panic!

Here is a summary so far:

- Issue the `noecho()` and `keypad()` functions to prepare `getch()` for reading mouse events.
- Issue the `mousemask()` function to tell NCurses which mouse events to scan for.
- Compare `getch()` input with `KEY_MOUSE` to see if a mouse event has occurred.

When a mouse event has occurred — the user has clicked one of the mouse buttons somewhere on the terminal screen — you then use the `getmouse()` function to retrieve information about the event:

```
getmouse(&musevent)
```

`musevent` is the address of a pointer variable of the `MEVENT` type:

```
MEVENT musevent;
```

Unlike the `WINDOW` type of pointer, you do not specify a * when declaring a mouse event variable. But you do use the & when specifying the variable name in the `getmouse()` function:

```
getmouse(&musevent);
```

After `getch()` detects a mouse event (`KEY_MOUSE`), a call to `getmouse()` fills the named `MEVENT` structure with information about the mouse event that just occurred. Table 13-1 lists the data you can then read, using `me` as the mouse event variable name (the same that would be used with the `getmouse()` function).

Table 13-1: Events recorded in the mouse event structure

VARIABLE	MOUSE EVENT
me.id	Unique ID number (used to distinguish among multiple mice)
me.x	Screen column coordinate
me.y	Screen row coordinate
me.z	Undefined (though could be used to read wheel button)
me.bstate	Bit pattern representing mouse button action

So, for example, to read the screen coordinates of where a click took place, you would use `musevent.y` and `musevent.x` in your code.

Here is the complete summary of steps needed to take to read a mouse event:

1. Issue the `noecho()` and `keypad()` functions to prepare `getch()` for reading mouse events.

2. Issue the `mousemask()` function to tell NCurses which mouse events to scan for.

3. Compare `getch()` input with `KEY_MOUSE` to see if a mouse event has occurred.

4. After confirming the mouse event (previous step), use `getmouse()` to read the event's information into an `MEVENT` structure.

5. Examine the `MEVENT` structure's data to determine what event took place at which coordinates on the screen.

Once your program has the mouse coordinates, you can do with them whatever you will, depending on the program: Choose an item, draw a block character, beep the speaker, or whatever.

Where Did You Click that Mouse?

The following code in Listing 13-3 reads information about where the mouse was clicked and displays those coordinates on the screen.

Listing 13-3: `mspy.c`

```
1    #include <ncurses.h>
2
3    int main(void)
4    {
5        MEVENT mort;
6        int ch;
```

Listing 13-3 *(continued)*

```
 7
 8          initscr();
 9          noecho();
10          keypad(stdscr,TRUE);
11
12          mousemask(ALL_MOUSE_EVENTS,NULL);
13
14          while(1)
15          {
16              ch = getch();
17              if( ch == KEY_MOUSE )
18              {
19                  getmouse(&mort);
20                  move(0,0);
21                  clrtoeol();
22                  printw("%d\t%d",mort.y,mort.x);
23                  refresh();
24                  continue;
25              }
26              if( ch == '\n' )
27                  break;
28          }
29
30          endwin();
31          return 0;
32      }
```

NOTE This program assumes your terminal has full access to mouse functions! Refer to the program MTEST.C earlier in Listing 13-2 when in doubt.

As you click the mouse about on the terminal screen, the Y (row) and X (column) coordinates are displayed in the upper-left corner.

Press the Enter key to end the program.

On Your Own

Modify the MSPY.C source code so that an asterisk is placed on the screen at the spot where the mouse was clicked. Name this new source code file CLICKPUT.C.

What Clicked?

The following code in Listing 13-4 uses the predefined button constants to display information about which mouse button was pressed.

Listing 13-4: `clicky.c`

```
1    #include <ncurses.h>
2
3    int main(void)
4    {
5        MEVENT mort;
6        int ch;
7
8        initscr();
9        noecho();
10       keypad(stdscr,TRUE);
11
12       mousemask(ALL_MOUSE_EVENTS,NULL);
13
14       while(1)
15       {
16           ch = getch();
17           if( ch == KEY_MOUSE )
18           {
19               clear();
20               getmouse(&mort);
21               switch(mort.bstate)
22               {
23                   case BUTTON1_PRESSED:
24                       mvaddstr(0,0,"Button 1 Pressed!");
25                       break;
26                   case BUTTON1_RELEASED:
27                       mvaddstr(1,0,"Button 1 Released!");
28                       break;
29                   case BUTTON1_CLICKED:
30                       mvaddstr(2,0,"Button 1 Clicked!");
31                       break;
32                   case BUTTON1_DOUBLE_CLICKED:
33                       mvaddstr(3,0,"Button 1 Dbl-Clicked!");
34                       break;
35                   case BUTTON2_PRESSED:
36                       mvaddstr(0,20,"Button 2 Pressed!");
37                       break;
38                   case BUTTON2_RELEASED:
39                       mvaddstr(1,20,"Button 2 Released!");
40                       break;
41                   case BUTTON2_CLICKED:
42                       mvaddstr(2,20,"Button 2 Clicked!");
43                       break;
44                   case BUTTON2_DOUBLE_CLICKED:
45                       mvaddstr(3,40,"Button 2 Dbl-Clicked!");
46                       break;
47                   case BUTTON3_PRESSED:
48                       mvaddstr(0,40,"Button 3 Pressed!");
49                       break;
```

Listing 13-4 (continued)

```
50                  case BUTTON3_RELEASED:
51                      mvaddstr(1,40,"Button 3 Released!");
52                      break;
53                  case BUTTON3_CLICKED:
54                      mvaddstr(2,40,"Button 3 Clicked!");
55                      break;
56                  case BUTTON3_DOUBLE_CLICKED:
57                      mvaddstr(3,40,"Button 3 Dbl-Clicked!");
58                      break;
59                  default:
60                      break;
61              }
62              refresh();
63              continue;
64          }
65          if( ch == '\n' )
66              break;
67      }
68
69      endwin();
70      return 0;
71  }
```

It's long! But you can start with the MSPY.C source as a base and then just use a lot of copy/paste/edit commands to add the bulk of the case statements.

By clicking various mouse buttons — press, release, click, double-click — you'll see appropriate text on the screen. This program may help you determine how NCurses interprets your mouse's buttons.

The code doesn't list every possible constant for the mouse. Refer to Appendix A for the full list.

To Eek or Not to Eek?

If you want to be a good programmer, you may elect to have mouse support optionally compiled into your code, depending on whether or not the version of NCurses on the destination computer supports mouse functions. The idea is to create a program that uses text but can also employ mouse input, should such a thing be available.

Thanks to the presence of the NCURSES_MOUSE_VERSION constant, you can use the #ifdef compiler directive to selectively compile mouse support into your code. For example:

```
#ifdef NCURSES_MOUSE_VERSION
    mousemask(ALL_MOUSE_EVENTS,NULL);
#endif
```

The `mousemask()` function is compiled into the program only when the `NCURSES_MOUSE_VERSION` constant exists. Likewise, the following may appear in the `switch case` structure:

```
#ifdef NCURSES_MOUSE_VERSION
    case KEY_MOUSE:
        getmouse(&event);
        /* mouse stuff here */
        break;
#endif
```

The idea here is to surround the mouse-specific stuff with `#ifdef` and `#endif`. That way, should the target system support the mouse, that support is compiled into your program. If support isn't available, the user will never know.

CHAPTER 14

A Mixture of Stuff

It would be tough to write a book that covers every single last NCurses function. A lot of the functions are internal or used only in specific cases by advanced users who know their operating systems intimately. For most of us programmers, however, the basic smattering of NCurses functions presented in the previous chapters is enough to create more visually interesting programs than by just using the standard C I/O functions.

This chapter contains a mélange of those leftover functions not covered earlier in this book. These functions aren't obscure or unique enough to deserve full banishment into Appendix A, nor are they worthy enough to be put into an earlier chapter. No, they live here. And I love using the word *mélange*.

Adios, Cursor

Sometimes the blinking (or not) cursor is a benefit, and sometimes it just gets in the way. When it gets in the way, NCurses lets you turn it off, hiding the cursor from view. Here's the function:

```
curs_set(n)
```

The `curs_set()` function is how NCursers controls the cursor. The value of n can be 0, 2, or 2: 0 makes the cursor invisible; 1 sets the cursor to normal mode; 2 sets the cursor to a *very* visible mode that must be seen to be believed. See Listing 14-1 for an example.

Listing 14-1: `cursset.c`

```
1    #include <ncurses.h>
2
3    int main(void)
4    {
5        initscr();
6
7    /* first, turn the cursor off */
8        curs_set(0);
9        addstr("  <- The cursor has been turned off");
10       move(0,0);
11       refresh();
12       getch();
13
14   /* second, turn the cursor on */
15       curs_set(1);
16       addstr("\n  <- The cursor now on");
17       move(1,0);
18       refresh();
19       getch();
20
21   /* third, turn the cursor very on */
22       curs_set(2);
23       addstr("\n  <- The cursor is now very on");
24       move(2,0);
25       refresh();
26       getch();
27
28       endwin();
29       return 0;
30   }
```

Note that `curs_set()` works only on terminals that support cursor-visibility options. If your terminal can't reset the cursor, such as when the CURSSET.C program doesn't seem to do anything, check for the availability of the `curs_set()` function:

```
if( curs_set(0) == ERR)
    beep();
```

When you add this snippet of code to your program and you hear the *beep*, know that your terminal doesn't support the `curs_set()` function for the given cursor visibility.

Line Drawing

NCurses has support for a variety of line-drawing and boxing functions, allowing you to spruce up your plain-text screen with some almost-graphical lines.

The quality of the lines depends on the terminal. Sometimes the ASCII text characters such as | – and + are used for drawing. Sometimes the terminal may use extended ASCII or special line-drawing characters that look quite good on the screen. And sometimes you can specify which characters you want to use for drawing.

Boxing Windows

One way to make a window stand out, especially when it's smaller than the screen, is to draw a box around it. NCurses has a handy box() function to help make that possible:

```
box(win,v_char,h_char)
```

win is the window to box. v_char is the character to use when drawing the vertical (up-down) lines around the window; h_char is the character for the horizontal (left-right) lines. If you put zero for v_char or h_char (or both), default characters are chosen as defined in the NCURSES.H header file. (See Listing 14-2.)

Listing 14-2: helpmenu3.c

```
1     #include <ncurses.h>
2
3     void showhelp(void);
4
5     WINDOW *help;
6
7     int main(void)
8     {
9         int ch;
10
11        initscr();
12
13    /* build help menu */
14        if((help = newwin(10,30,4,26)) == NULL)
15        {
16            addstr("Unable to allocate window memory\n");
17            endwin();
18            return(1);
19        }
```

(continued)

Listing 14-2 *(continued)*

```
20          mvwaddstr(help,1,7,"Help menu Screen");
21          mvwaddstr(help,5,3,"Press the ~ key to quit");
22          mvwaddstr(help,8,4,"Press ENTER to go back");
23          box(help,0,0);
24
25      /* now start the program loop */
26          addstr("Typer Program\n");
27          addstr("Press + for help:\n\n");
28          refresh();
29          noecho();
30          do
31          {
32              ch = getch();
33              refresh();
34              if(ch == '+')
35                  showhelp();
36              else
37                  addch(ch);
38          } while (ch != '~');
39
40          endwin();
41          return 0;
42      }
43
44      void showhelp(void)
45      {
46          touchwin(help);                 /* force update */
47          wrefresh(help);
48          getch();                      /* wait for key press */
49          touchwin(stdscr);               /* forces character update */
50          refresh();
51      }
```

NOTE This code is introduced in Chapter 8; the only difference between this and the previous version is the addition of line 23.

The help menu window, when displayed, looks similar to what you see in Figure 14-1, though your terminal may use different characters to create the box.

The box() function doesn't draw a line *around* the window but actually uses the outside rows and columns in which to display its text. There is nothing special protecting the box; text can overwrite it. In fact, if you want to preserve the box, create a subwindow inside the window, a subwindow that is centered and two rows and two columns less than the original window in size. You can then write text to the subwindow directly without having to worry about erasing the box. Figure 14-2 illustrates this.

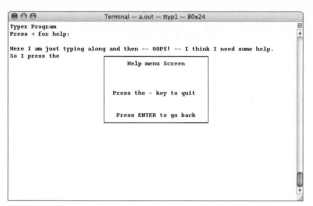

Figure 14-1: The help window is boxed

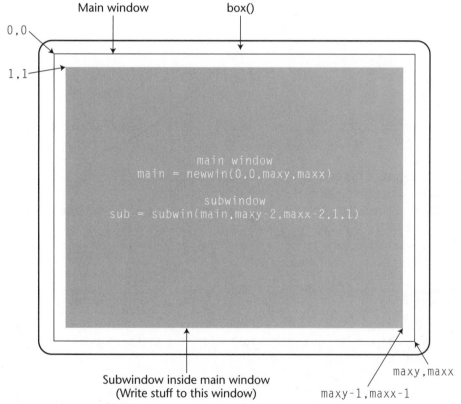

Figure 14-2: Protecting a box from being overwritten

> **NOTE** *Here's a tip*: **If the window is small and the box takes up too much space, consider merely coloring the window instead. Use** `bkgd()` **as described in Chapter 3.**

Building Better Boxes

It's possible to set the characters used to draw the box yourself. The following code in Listing 14-3 demonstrates.

Listing 14-3: `box.c`

```
1     #include <ncurses.h>
2
3     int main(void)
4     {
5         initscr();
6
7         box(stdscr,'*','*');
8         refresh();
9         getch();
10
11        endwin();
12        return 0;
13    }
```

This program draws a box around the standard screen. The asterisk character * is used to draw the horizontal and vertical lines.

Asterisks are used to draw the box. Note that the corners of the box may still be + characters or perhaps specific corner graphics symbols.

If you want to replace the characters in the box's corner, you'll have to use the `border()` function instead:

```
border(left,right,top,bot,uleft,uright,lleft,lright)
```

Note right away that `border()` is specific to the standard screen, `stdscr`. There is a related, `wborder()` function where the first argument is `win`, for the window to be boxed. The arguments in `border()` are characters to place in one of the eight positions of the box: `left`, `right`, `top`, and `bot` are the sides of the box; `uleft`, `uright`, `lleft`, and `lright` are the corners. See Listing 14-4.

Listing 14-4: `border.c`

```
1    #include <ncurses.h>
2
3    int main(void)
4    {
5        initscr();
6
7        border(0x000000ba,0x000000ba,0x000000cd,0x000000cd,
8               0x000000c9,0x000000bb,0x000000c8,0x000000bc);
9        refresh();
10       getch();
11
12       endwin();
13       return 0;
14   }
```

The hex codes supplied for `border()` are the extended ASCII codes to draw a double-line border. Table 14-1 lists them. Note that they only appear as a double border if your computer system's terminal supports the extended ASCII character set. It's found on codepage 437, or it may be included with a special font you can choose for the terminal window.

Lines 7 and 8 in Listing 14-4 use a long `int` hex chunk to display the characters. This is because the characters are NCurses' *chtypes*, not *chars*. Refer to Appendix C for more information on the chtype.

If your terminal window supports codepage 437, you'll see a double-lined border. Otherwise, you'll see various and sundry symbols used, typically letters with diacritical marks, question marks, or other characters various and ugly.

Remember that both `border()` and `box()` wrap around the entire window only, and the box text can be overwritten.

Table 14-1: Extended ASCII/Codepage 437 double-line characters

CHARACTER	DECIMAL	HEX	CHARACTER	DECIMAL	HEX
‖	186	xBA	╗	187	xBB
═	205	xCD	╚	200	xC8
╔	201	xC9	╝	188	xBC

We Control the Horizontal and the Vertical

For plain-on straight lines — lines from here to there but not diagonal or weird angles — NCurses has the following functions:

```
hline(ch,n)
```

```
vline(ch,n)
```

The `hline()` and `vline()` functions draw a horizontal or vertical line from the cursor's current position (right or down, respectively), as shown in Listing 14-5. The line is drawn using character `ch` or using the standard line-drawing character when `ch` is zero. `n` sets the length of the line in characters.

Remember: The line is drawn from the cursor's current position. And neither function, `hline()` nor `vline()`, changes the cursor's position.

Listing 14-5: `steps.c`

```
1     #include <ncurses.h>
2
3     int main(void)
4     {
5          int y,x,maxy,maxx;
6
7          initscr();
8
9          getmaxyx(stdscr,maxy,maxx);
10
11         for(y=x=0;y<maxy;y++,x+=2)
12         {
13             move(y,x);
14             hline(0,maxx-x);
15             vline(0,maxy-y);
16         }
17         refresh();
18         getch();
19
20         endwin();
21         return 0;
22    }
```

When the planets are properly aligned, Figure14-3 should be something like the result you'll see.

As with many other screen-output functions, there are `mv` and `w` prefixes for the `hline()` and `vline()` function (see Listing 14-6).

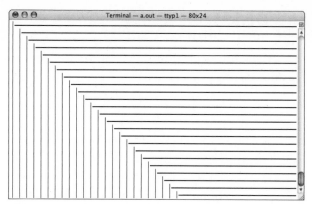

Figure 14-3: The output of STEPS.C

Listing 14-6: plus.c

```
1    #include <ncurses.h>
2
3    #define HLIN 10
4    #define VLIN 5
5
6    int main(void)
7    {
8        int y[] = {  0,  0, 5,  0,  5,  5, 10, 10, 10, 10, 15, 5 };
9        int x[] = { 10, 10, 1, 20, 20, 30,  1, 10, 20, 20, 10, 0 };
10       int c;
11
12       initscr();
13
14       for(c=0;c<12;c+=2)
15       {
16           mvhline(  y[c],   x[c], 0, HLIN);
17           mvvline( y[c+1], x[c+1], 0, VLIN);
18       }
19
20       refresh();
21       getch();
22
23       endwin();
24       return 0;
25   }
```

The result is crude, but I think you'll get the idea.

Between NCurses and Disk

This last quartet of NCurses functions introduced in this chapter are used to save interact between NCurses and disk:

```
scr_dump()

scr_restore()

putwin()

getwin()
```

The `scr_dump()` and `putwin()` functions are used to write information from either the terminal screen or a specific window to a special file on disk. The `scr_restore()` and `getwin()` functions then read that information back from disk, splashing the information up on the screen. The following sections mull over the details.

Functions that Dump the Screen

There are two NCurses functions that "dump the screen," transferring a window's contents from memory disk or disk to memory:

```
scr_dump(filename)

scr_restore(filename)
```

Each function takes `filename`, the name of a file, as an argument. Note that the argument is the file's name itself, not a `FILE` pointer. Both functions open, read, and close the named file. There is no need for `fopen()` or `fclose()` before or after these functions.

The `scr_dump()` function overwrites any existing `filename` already on disk. There is no warning, though you can write your own code to determine whether or not `filename` already exists before using `scr_dump()`.

When the dump or restore is successful, the functions return `OK`; otherwise, `ERR` is returned.

Both functions relate to what is displayed on the `curscr`; these are not window-specific functions.

Taking a Snapshot of the Screen

The `scr_dump()` function performs what old timers refer to as a *screen dump*. The inelegant term *dump* simply means to transfer a chunk of data (often raw data) from one device to another. In the case of a screen dump, the data from the screen is saved to disk. See Listing 14-7 for an example.

Listing 14-7: dump.c

```
1    #include <ncurses.h>
2    #include <stdlib.h>
3    #include <time.h>
4
5    #define FILENAME "windump"
6
7    int main(void)
8    {
9        char word[7];
10       int x,w,r;
11
12       srandom((unsigned)time(NULL));    /* seed randomizer */
13       word[7] = '\0';
14       initscr();
15
16   /* Fill most of the screen with random 6-char words */
17       for(x=0;x<200;x++)
18       {
19           for(w=0;w<6;w++)
20               word[w] = (random() % 26) + 'a';
21           printw("%s\t",word);
22       }
23       addch('\n');
24       addstr("Press Enter to write this screen to disk\n");
25       refresh();
26       getch();
27
28   /* write the window to disk */
29       r = scr_dump(FILENAME);
30       if( r == ERR)
31           addstr("Error writing window to disk\n");
32       else
33           addstr("File written; press Enter to quit\n");
34       refresh();
35       getch();
36
37       endwin();
38       return 0;
39   }
```

Most of the code works to write 200 words to the screen, words composed of six random characters. That's simply to put something unique up on the screen; scr_dump() captures anything and everything.

The actual dump takes place at line 29. If the function fails, ERR is returned. This is evaluated in line 30 and appropriate messages are displayed.

If all goes well, you'll first see the random smattering of text, similar to what is shown in Figure 14-4.

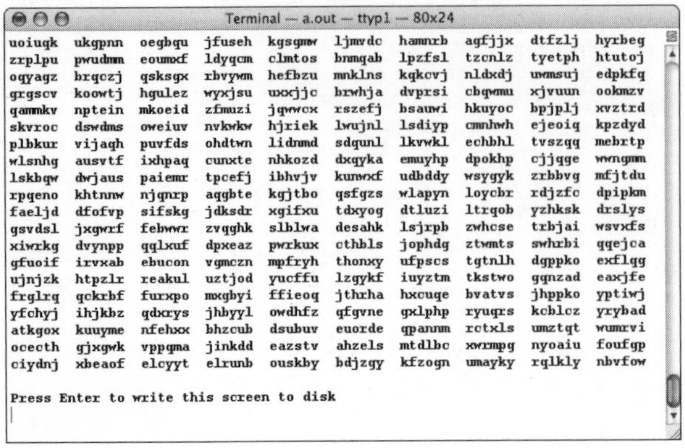

Figure 14-4: The DUMP.C program produces output similar to this.

Press Enter to write that window to disk. Then press Enter again to quit the program.

Examining the Dump File

The code for DUMP.C writes a file to disk named WINDUMP. Using the ls -l command on the windump file shows that it's of quite a substantial size, 45K on my computer:

```
-rw-r--r--   1 dang   dang   46204 Jan 16 13:25 windump
```

The file is a binary representation of an NCurses window data structure. It includes a header followed by the raw data from the window.

The window header is of the structure type _win_st, which is defined in the NCURSES.H header file. It's the same thing as the WINDOW variable used to create a window; _win_st is the structure name. Figure 14-5 lists some of the highlights of a window dump, using the output of the hexdump utility.

The data includes all the screen positions, rows, and columns that show up as the text on the screen. Each screen position is 24 bytes long, which includes the character displayed and any attributes for that screen position. You can see this in how potogav appears in the ASCII column of Figure 14-5 but also as the first "word" of Figure 14-4.

Restoring the Screen

The scr_restore() function is used to read a screen dump back from disk into NCurses. As with scr_dump(), the scr_restore() function merely requires the name of the file (see Listing 14-8).

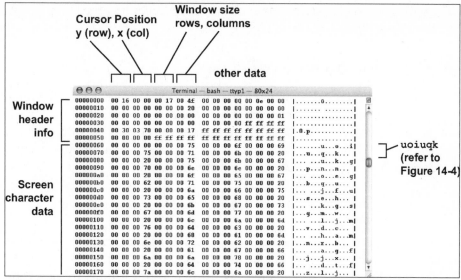

Figure 14-5: Things to see inside a window dump file

Listing 14-8: undump.c

```
1    #include <ncurses.h>
2
3    #define FILENAME "windump"
4
5    int main(void)
6    {
7        int r;
8
9        initscr();
10
11       addstr("Press Enter to restore the screen\n");
12       refresh();
13       getch();
14
15   /* restore the window from disk */
16       r = scr_restore(FILENAME);
17       if( r == ERR)
18           addstr("Error reading window file: press Enter\n");
19       refresh();
20       getch();
21
22       endwin();
23       return 0;
24   }
```

The screen saved to disk by DUMP.C is restored, including the text prompting you to press Enter (shown in Figure 14-4)!

Functions that Dump a Window

When it's only the contents of a window you need to save to disk, pull out the putwin() and getwin() functions. They write the same type of dump to disk, but they use completely different formats from their screen-oriented companions, scr_dump() and scr_restore(), covered in the section "Functions that dump the screen," earlier in this chapter:

```
putwin(win,file)
```

```
win = getwin(file)
```

In both functions, win is the name of a WINDOW pointer, indicated by some window created in NCurses. file is a FILE pointer representing an open file. The file must be successfully opened by fopen() and it must be closed by fclose() (or similar functions). Data is written to the file via putwin() and read by getwin() (see Listing 14-9).

Listing 14-9: windisk.c

```
1    #include <ncurses.h>
2    #include <stdlib.h>
3
4    #define FILENAME "window.dat"
5
6    void bomb(char *message);
7
8    int main(void)
9    {
10       FILE *wfile;
11       WINDOW *win;
12       int r;
13
14       initscr();
15       start_color();
16       init_pair(1,COLOR_WHITE,COLOR_BLUE);
17
18       addstr("Creating new window\n");
19       refresh();
20
21    /* Crete the window */
22       win = newwin(5,20,7,30);
23       if(win == NULL)
24           bomb("Unable to create window\n");
25       wbkgd(win,COLOR_PAIR(1));
26       mvwaddstr(win,1,2,"This program was\n");
```

Listing 14-9 *(continued)*

```
27        mvwaddstr(win,2,5,"created by\n");
28        mvwaddstr(win,3,5,"Dan Gookin\n");          /* put your name
here */
29        wrefresh(win);
30        getch();
31
32    /* open the file */
33        wfile = fopen(FILENAME,"w");
34        if( wfile==NULL)
35            bomb("Error creating file\n");
36
37    /* write the window's data */
38        r = putwin(win,wfile);
39        if( r == ERR)
40            addstr("Error putting window to disk\n");
41        else
42            addstr("Window put to disk\n");
43        fclose(wfile);
44        refresh();
45        getch();
46
47        endwin();
48        return 0;
49    }
50
51    void bomb(char *message)
52    {
53        addstr(message);
54        refresh();
55        getch();
56        endwin();
57        exit(1);
58    }
```

Most of the code is devoted to creating a tiny blue window on the screen and populating that window with text.

In line 33, a file is opened on disk. Line 38 puts the window to the file via the putwin() function. Then the file is closed and the program ends.

NOTE Be sure to use your own name in line 28. Likewise, you may want to adjust the column argument of the mvwaddstr() function so that the name is relatively centered in the window.

The program displays the tiny blue window and then saves that window to disk in the filename WINDOW.DAT. The next program reads that window back in from disk and displays it on the screen, as shown in Listing 14-10.

Listing 14-10: DISKWIN.C

```
1    #include <ncurses.h>
2    #include <stdlib.h>
3
4    #define FILENAME "window.dat"
5
6    void bomb(char *message);
7
8    int main(void)
9    {
10       FILE *wfile;
11       WINDOW *win;
12       int r;
13
14       initscr();
15       start_color();
16       init_pair(1,COLOR_WHITE,COLOR_BLUE);
17
18       addstr("Press Enter to read the window from disk:\n");
19       refresh();
20       getch();
21
22   /* open the file */
23       wfile = fopen(FILENAME,"r");
24       if( wfile==NULL )
25           bomb("Error reading file\n");
26
27   /* write the window's data */
28       win = getwin(wfile);
29       if( win == NULL )
30           bomb("Unable to read/create window\n");
31       fclose(wfile);
32       wrefresh(win);
33       getch();
34
35       endwin();
36       return 0;
37   }
38
39   void bomb(char *message)
40   {
41       addstr(message);
42       refresh();
43       getch();
44       endwin();
45       exit(1);
46   }
```

Note that the getwin() function both reads the window's data from disk *and* initializes the window; there is no need to use newwin() before getwin() to create the window. It does not, however, update the curscr; you still must use a wrefresh() command for that.

The window is restored to the same size, location, and appearance as before. The cursor position is also restored. Any attributes are also restored, though if the specific COLOR_PAIR associated with the window, or the window's text, is redefined as another color, that other color is used. (Attributes include only a COLOR_PAIR value, not the color pairs assigned to that value.)

After being restored, your code can continue to use the window, write to it, manipulate it, and remove it if necessary.

NCurses Library Reference

Some low-level NCurses and terminal functions, as well as some functions listed but not fully implemented, are not documented in this appendix.

A few of the extended NCurses functions are not documented here, including:

```
is_term_resized()
resize_term()
resizeterm()
```

addch()

The addch() functions display a single character to the screen. The character is placed at the cursor's position and overwrites any character already in that spot.

Man Page Formats

```
int addch(const chtype ch);
int waddch(WINDOW *win, const chtype ch);
int mvaddch(int y, int x, const chtype ch);
int mvwaddch(WINDOW *win, int y, int x, const chtype ch);
```

Format Reference

ch is an NCurses chtype variable, which can represent a single character or character and attribute combination. See Appendix C for more information.

Refer to the mv, mvw, and w entries elsewhere in this appendix for information on the win, y, and x arguments.

Return Value

Upon success addch() returns OK, or ERR upon failure.

Notes

Characters placed at the last column cause the cursor's location to drop to the next row. Characters placed at the last column of the last row do not advance the cursor unless scrolling is enabled for the window, in which case the window will scroll up one line. See scrollok().

The addch() function interprets some characters specially:

- \t. the tab character advances the cursor to the next *tab stop*, which is set every eight columns in a window. This value can be reset by using the TABSIZE variable; see TABSIZE.

- \n. the newline character erases all text from the cursor's position to the end of the line (see clrtoeol()), then drops the cursor down to the next line. If the cursor is on the last line of the screen, then the window's contents are scrolled, but only if scrolling is enabled for that window; see scrollok().

- \r. the carriage return moves the cursor to the start of the current line (column zero). It will not erase to the end of the line.

- \b. the backspace character moves the cursor back one notch. It does not erase. When the cursor is at the start of a line (column zero), the backspace does nothing.

Control characters other than \t (^I), \n (^J), \r (^M), or \b (^H) are displayed using the ^c notation by addch(). This effectively puts *two* characters to the screen, both the ^ and the control character's corresponding key value, such as G for ^G. See unctrl() for more information.

You can also use addch() to place ACS (Alternate Character Set) characters to the screen. Refer to Appendix B for more information on those characters.

Examples

```
addch('A');
```

This statement puts the character A to the standard screen at the cursor's current position.

```
addch('1' | A_BOLD);
```

This statement displays at the cursor's current position the character 1 with the bold text attribute applied.

```
waddch(zippy,'\t');
```

This statement places a tab a the cursor's current position in window zippy. The tab character advances the cursor to the next tab stop.

```
mvaddch(y,x,ACS_PI);
```

This statement places at the row and column represented by int variables y and x the character constant ACS_PI, the character π. (See Appendix B for a list of the ACS constants.)

```
mvwaddch(main,0,0,bullet);
```

This statement moves the cursor to home position 0,0 in window main and places there the chtype character represented by the variable bullet.

Sample Program

```
1    #include <ncurses.h>
2
3    int main(void)
4    {
5        initscr();
6
7        addch('H');
8        addch('i');
9        addch('!');
10       refresh();
11       getch();
12
13       endwin();
14       return 0;
15   }
```

Sample output:

```
Hi!
```

Also See

Chapter 2, addstr(), clrtoeol(), scroll(), TABSIZE

addchstr()

The addchstr() functions place a *formatted* string of text at the cursor's position. The string of formatted text is not a char array, but an array of NCurses chtype characters, which includes both the character and its formatting information.

Man Page Formats

```
int addchstr(const chtype *chstr);
int addchnstr(const chtype *chstr, int n);
int waddchstr(WINDOW *win, const chtype *chstr);
int waddchnstr(WINDOW *win, const chtype *chstr, int n);
int mvaddchstr(int y, int x, const chtype *chstr);
int mvaddchnstr(int y, int x, const chtype *chstr, int n);
int mvwaddchstr(WINDOW *win, int y, int x, const chtype *chstr);
int mvwaddchnstr(WINDOW  *win,  int y, int x, const chtype *chstr, int n);
```

Format Reference

chstr is an array of formatted text to be displayed on the screen. The array is composed of chtype characters, which are not char but long int values. (The chtype character consists of a character plus attribute information.)

n is used only in the addchnstr() functions. It is an int value, a variable or constant, that represents the maximum number of characters to write to the screen. When n is less than the string's length, then only n characters are displayed. When n is equal to -1, the entire string is displayed. (Also see Notes, below.) When n is greater than the string's length, garbage may be displayed on the screen.

Refer to the mv, mvw, and w prefix entries elsewhere in this appendix for information on the win, y, and x arguments.

Return Value

Upon success the addchstr() family of functions return integer constants OK or ERR upon success or failure, respectively.

Normally, returns values are not checked with addchstr(); however, if you use the mv- or mvw- prefix versions of the functions, then be sure to check the return value should the function accidentally try to move the cursor to an off-screen location.

Notes

It helps if you understand this function as add-chstr: add a chtype string to the screen. For displaying a standard character string to the screen, use addstr() instead.

Unlike other output functions, text displayed by addchstr() does not wrap from one line to another. Any excess text displayed beyond the last column in the window just doesn't appear.

addchstr() does not interpret the control characters \t, \n, or \b, nor will it display control characters prefixed with a ^, as other NCurses output functions do.

Placing chtype characters on the screen with the addchstr() function is faster than using the addstr() function.

The chtype array is terminated with a \0 value, just as char arrays, or strings, are terminated.

Try not to use values of n larger than the string. Doing so results in random data being displayed.

Examples

```
addchnstr(fline,25);
```

This statement puts the first 25 characters of the chtype string fline to the screen at the current cursor position.

```
mvaddchstr(0,xc,title);
```

This statement puts the chtype string title at row zero and the column represented by variable xc.

Sample Program

```
1    #include <ncurses.h>
2
3    int main(void)
4    {
5        chtype text[6] = { 'H' | A_BOLD, 'e', 'l', 'l', 'o', '\0' };
6
7        initscr();
8
9        addchstr(text);
10       refresh();
11       getch();
12
13       endwin();
14       return 0;
15   }
```

Sample output:

`Hello`

Also See

Appendix C, `inchstr()`

addstr()

The `addstr()` function displays a string of text on the screen. The text is displayed at the cursor's current position and each character displayed advances the cursor.

Man Page Formats

```
int addstr(const char *str);
int addnstr(const char *str, int n);
int waddstr(WINDOW *win, const char *str);
int waddnstr(WINDOW *win, const char *str, int n);
int mvaddstr(int y, int x, const char *str);
int mvaddnstr(int y, int x, const char *str, int n);
int mvwaddstr(WINDOW *win, int y, int x, const char *str);
int mvwaddnstr(WINDOW *win, int y, int x, const char *str, int n);
```

Format Reference

`str` is text, either a literal string or text stored in a string variable (`char` array). The string is terminated with a `\0` (null) character.

n is an `int` value or variable used to limit output to only n characters of the `string`. The value of n ranges from 0 through the length of the `string`. When n is -1, the entire `string` is written.

Refer to the `mv`, `mvw`, and `w` prefix entries elsewhere in this appendix for information on the `win`, `y`, and `x` arguments.

Return Value

The `addstr()` function returns the integer constant `OK`, or `ERR` upon failure.

Notes

`addstr()` features the same type of output as `addch()`: control codes `\t`, `\n`, `\r`, and `\b` are interpreted as tab, newline, return, and backspace. Other control codes are displayed using the ^ followed by the code's text character equivalent. Refer to the addch() entry for more information.

When string is longer than the screen or window's width, then it continues to the following line on the screen. If scrolling is enabled for the window, then text displayed on the last line causes the screen to scroll.

The addstr() function does *not* automatically append a \n to the text it displays.

Remember that in addition to performing a carriage return/line feed, the \n will erase any existing text to the end of the line.

Setting the value of n greater than the length of the string does not appear to affect output, unlike addchstr(). In this case, setting n to a value greater than the string's length merely outputs the entire string and nothing extra.

Examples

```
addstr(first_name);
```

This statement displays text stored in the string variable first_name on the screen at the cursor's current position.

```
waddstr(status,"Results:\n");
```

This statement displays the text Results, plus a new line, in the window named status. The newline drops the cursor down to the following line on the screen.

```
mvaddstr(y,x,"Copyright 2006, Grockmeister Studios.");
```

This statement displays the string Copyright 2006, Grockmeister Studios. at the position represented by int variables y and x on the screen.

Sample Program

```
1    #include <ncurses.h>
2
3    int main(void)
4    {
5        initscr();
6
7        addnstr("The password is 'Zeppelin.'\n",17);
8        refresh();
9        getch();
10
11       endwin();
12       return 0;
13   }
```

Sample output:

```
The password is '
```

Only the first 17 characters are displayed.

Also See

Chapter 2, addch(), printw()

assume_default_colors()

assume_default_colors() is an extended NCurses function that allows you to set which foreground and background colors to use as the default after start_color() initializes NCurses for color.

Explanation

After start_color() turns on NCurses text color support, the text background color is set to black and the foreground color set to white. Black and white, or COLOR_BLACK and COLOR_WHITE, are the defaults, defined as COLOR_PAIR(0). By using the assume_default_colors() function, you can change the values of COLOR_PAIR(0) to something else or to whichever colors the terminal program otherwise uses to display text.

Man Page Format

```
int assume_default_colors(int fg, int bg);
```

Format Reference

fg is an int value representing the color for text, the foreground color.

bg is an int value represent the background color.

Values for both fg and bg range from 0 through the value of COLORS-1.

A special value of -1 sets the foreground and background colors equal to the same color as used by terminal when not running NCurses. See the Notes for more information.

Return Value

When all goes well, the function returns OK, ERR otherwise.

Notes

The color constants defined in NCURSES.H can also be used as values for fg and bg. Refer to init_pair() for the list.

The assume_default_colors() (or use_default_colors()) function is the only way to set COLOR_PAIR(0).

Using -1 for fg and bg tells NCurses to use the same foreground and background colors as the terminal. For example, if you've configured your xterm window to use blue text on a white background, then specifying assume_default_colors(-1,-1) directs NCurses to use those same two colors as the foreground and background for COLOR_PAIR(0), the color pair used when start_color() first initializes NCurses color.

Note that by using -1 it's possible on some terminals to use colors not normally available to NCurses. For example, on xterm in OS X it's possible to set text color to gray text on a pink background. Sadly, these colors are not available to the other NCurses color functions.

It's not wise to set both the bg and fg values to the same thing. You can; but nothing shows up on the screen.

assume_default_colors() is a an extended NCurses function. See "Extended Functions" later in this appendix.

Examples

```
assume_default_colors(COLOR_WHITE,COLOR_BLUE);
```

The colors used for text output after start_color() initializes NCurses color will be white text on a blue background. White on blue becomes the values for COLOR_PAIR(0).

```
assume_default_colors(-1,-1);
```

The colors set by start_color() for COLOR_PAIR(0) will be the same as used in the terminal window.

Sample Program

```
1    #include <ncurses.h>
2
3    int main(void)
4    {
5        int r;
6
7        initscr();
8        start_color();
9
10       assume_default_colors(COLOR_RED,COLOR_CYAN);
11       addstr("The default colors have been set to\n");
```

```
12          addstr("Red text on a cyan background.\n");
13          refresh();
14          getch();
15
16          endwin();
17          return 0;
18     }
```

Sample output:

```
The default colors have been set to
Red text on a cyan background.
The text above appears as red on a cyan background.
```

Also See

COLORS, init_pair(), use_default_colors()

attr_get()

The attr_get() function is used to read which text attributes are being used in a window. The values returned are compared (by logical OR) with known attributes. The function also determines whether the window uses color and if so which color pair is being used.

Man Page Formats

```
int attr_get(attr_t *attrs, short *pair, void *opts);
int wattr_get(WINDOW *win, attr_t *attrs, short *pair,void *opts);
```

Format Reference

attrs is the location of a variable of the NCurses type attr_t, a long int (the same as a chtype). It is used to store the attribute information read from window. Essentially attrs is a bit field and the bits in the field are set according to which attributes are active in the window. Appendix C describes the chtype bit field.

pair is the memory location of a short int value used to store the color pair number used to color the window.

The NULL placeholder represents the opts argument. opts is not defined presently but reserved for future use.

Refer to the w prefix entry later in this appendix for information on the win argument.

Return Value

The functions return OK or ERR upon success or failure.

Notes

The attrs argument is declared by using NCurses' attr_t variable type:

```
attr_t ats;
```

Here in this line of code, the variable ats is created from the attr_t type.

Both the attrib and pair argument are memory locations. They can be represented by pointer variables or regular variables prefixed with the & unary operator.

It's possible to replace either attrib or pair with NULL, in which case that particular chunk of information will not be returned by attr_get().

The pair value returns only the color pair number. It does not tell you which colors are assigned to that color pair number. For that tidbit you need to use the pair_content() function.

In my experiments I've been unable to get attr_get() to return both text and color attributes from a given window. The function seems to prioritize text attributes, such as A_BOLD, A_BLINK, and so on. But when those attributes are present along with color information, only the attribute values are returned. When the attributes are removed from the window, the color information is returned. (This is probably an effect of NCurses' handling the ncv (no_color_video) capability of the terminal. When the terminal description says (with this capability) that colors do not mix with the given video attributes, it only uses the colors.)

To specifically retrieve a window's background attributes, use the getbkgd() function. See getbkgd().

Example

```
attr_get(&a,&cp,NULL);
```

This statement returns the attributes used in the stdscr, saving them in the a variable. Color pairs, if used, are saved in the cp variable.

Sample Program

```
1    #include <ncurses.h>
2
3    int main(void)
4    {
5        attr_t attributes;
6        short cpair;
```

```
 7
 8          initscr();
 9          attrset(A_BOLD | A_REVERSE | A_BLINK);
10
11          attr_get(&attributes,&cpair,NULL);
12          addstr("Attributes active in this window:\n");
13          if( attributes & A_COLOR)      printw("Color w/ pair ⏎
%d\n",cpair);
14          if( attributes & A_STANDOUT)     addstr("Standout\n");
15          if( attributes & A_REVERSE)      addstr("Reverse\n");
16          if( attributes & A_BLINK)      addstr("Blink\n");
17          if( attributes & A_DIM)      addstr("Dim\n");
18            if( attributes & A_BOLD)      addstr("Bold\n");
19          refresh();
20          getch();
21
22          endwin();
23          return 0;
24     }
```

Sample output:

Also See

Appendix C, `attrset()`, `COLOR_PAIR()`, `getbkgd()`

attroff()

The `attroff()` function is used to turn off one or more text attributes. The attributes have previously been applied by either the `attron()`, `attrset()`, or similar attribute functions.

Man Page Formats

```
int wattroff(WINDOW *win, int attrs);
int wattroff(WINDOW *win, int attrs);
int attr_off(attr_t attrs, void *opts);
int wattr_off(WINDOW *win, attr_t attrs, void *opts);
```

Format Reference

`attrs` is an `int` value in one set of calls, and **attr_t** in the others. But it is really the same thing in NCurses. It is typically one or more attribute constants as defined in `NCURSES.H`, and listed in under `attrset()` later in this appendix. The named attribute is removed from any text displayed after the `attroff()` function is used; other attributes are not affected.

Multiple attributes can be specified in a single `attroff()` function by separating each with a | (logical OR).

`COLOR_PAIR(n)` is also considered a text attribute, where `n` is a color pair number defined by an `init_pair()` function earlier in the program.

`NULL` is used as a placeholder for the as-yet-to-be-defined `opts` value found in the `attr_off()` and `wattr_off()` functions. (Honestly, it's been ten years, so it's doubtful that X/Open is going to define it!)

Refer to the `w` prefix entry later in this appendix for information on the `win` argument.

Return Value

The return value is stated as "not important" according to the documentation.

Notes

`attroff()` affects only the text displayed after the `attroff()` function is issued. It does not affect all text on the screen at once.

To turn off all attributes with `attroff()`, each attribute must be specified individually; you cannot use `A_NORMAL` with `attroff()` to reset all text attributes back to normal. (See `attrset()`.)

Removing a `COLOR_PAIR` attribute with `attroff()` restores the text to "normal" (white on black) text. So if you set one `COLOR_PAIR` attribute, then apply a second `COLOR_PAIR` attribute, removing the second `COLOR_PAIR` *does not* restore the first `COLOR_PAIR`. You must re-apply the `COLOR_PAIR` using an `attron()` function.

Apparently removing a `COLOR_PAIR` attribute with `attroff()` also removes all other text attributes.

`attroff()` and `attr_off()` are pretty much identical, save for the `NULL` argument required in `attr_off()`. (In NCurses, you'll mostly find underscores used by functions that manipulate wide characters.) Attributes are set by either the `attrset()` or `attron()` functions.

Attributes affect the output of the `addch()`, `addstr()`, and `printw()` functions.

Also refer to the Notes for `attrset()`.

Examples

```
attroff(A_BOLD);
```

This statement removes the bold text attribute from any new text displayed.

```
wattroff(help,COLOR_PAIR(1));
```

This statement removes the text color assigned to COLOR_PAIR 1 from any new text displayed in the window help.

```
attroff(A_BOLD | A_REVERSE);
```

This statement removes both the bold and reverse attributes from any new text displayed.

Sample Program

Refer to the entry for attrset() for a sample program.

Also See

Chapter 3, Appendix C, attrset()

attron()

The attron() function enables specified text attributes for any text put to the screen or a specific window.

Man Page Formats

```
int attron(int attrs);
int wattron(WINDOW *win, int attrs);
int attr_on(attr_t attrs, void *opts);
int wattr_on(WINDOW *win, attr_t attrs, void *opts);
```

Format Reference

attrs is usually one or more attribute constants as defined in NCURSES.H, each an long int. The named attribute is applied to any text displayed after the attron() function is used. Setting a new attribute does not affect previous attributes applied to the text.

Refer to the entry for attrset() for a list of attribute values.

Multiple attributes can be specified in a single `attron()` function by separating each with a | (logical OR).

`COLOR_PAIR(n)` is also considered a text attribute, where `n` is a color pair number defined by an `init_pair()` function earlier in the program.

`NULL` is used in the `attr_on()` functions as a placeholder for the undefined `opts` value.

Refer to the `w` prefix entry later in this appendix for information on the `win` argument.

Return Value

The return value is stated as "not important" according to the documentation.

Notes

The new attributes are applied only to new text displayed after the `attron()` function. These attributes are in addition to any set by previous `attron()` or `attrset()` functions.

Applying a new `COLOR_PAIR` value with `attron()` replaces any previously defined text colors with the new colors.

Only one `COLOR_PAIR` can be used at a time; `COLOR_PAIR` attributes cannot be combined, as other attributes can.

Attributes affect the output of the `addch()`, `addstr()`, and `printw()` functions.

Also refer to the Notes for `attrset()`.

Examples

```
attron(A_REVERSE);
```

This statement applies the reverse text attribute from any new text displayed. This attribute is applied in addition to any previously-applied text attributes.

```
wattron(warning,A_BOLD | A_BLINK);
```

This statement sets both the bold and blink attributes from any new text displayed in the `warning` window.

```
attron(COLOR_PAIR(3));
```

This statement set the text displayed to the color assigned to `COLOR_PAIR` 3.

Sample Program

Refer to the entry for `attrset()` for a sample program.

Also See

Chapter 3, Appendix C, `attrset()`, `chgat()`

attrset()

The `attrset()` function sets attributes for all text output functions that follow. The text displayed after using `attrset()` ignores any attributes previously assigned by an `attrset()` or `attron()` function and instead uses the new attributes specified by `attrset()`.

Man Page Formats

```
int attrset(int attrs);
int wattrset(WINDOW *win, int attrs);
int attr_set(attr_t attrs, short pair, void *opts);
int wattr_set(WINDOW *win, attr_t attrs, short pair, void *opts);
```

Format Reference

`attrs` is a `long int` value representing one or more attribute constants. The attribute(s) affect text put to the screen after the `attrset()` command is used. The attributes defined in NCURSES.H are as follows:

A_ALTCHARSET	A_UNDERLINE
A_BLINK	A_PROTECT
A_BOLD	A_HORIZONTAL
A_DIM	A_LEFT
A_INVIS	A_LOW
A_NORMAL	A_RIGHT
A_REVERSE	A_TOP
A_STANDOUT	A_VERTICAL

`pair` is a `short int` value representing a color pair number, similar to the `n` used in COLOR_PAIR(n).

NULL is used in the `attr_set()` functions as a placeholder the undefined `opts` value.

Refer to the w prefix entry later in this appendix for information on the win argument.

Return Value

The return value is stated as "not important" according to the documentation.

Notes

Attributes set by `attrset()` can be removed by using the `attroff()` function. New attributes can be added by using the `attron()` function.

`attrset()` is an in-line function; it affects only text displayed after `attrset()` is used. `attrset()` does not reset all text in a window at once.

Attributes affect the output of the `addch()`, `addstr()`, and `printw()` functions.

All text attributes can be turned off by using this statement:

```
attrset(A_NORMAL);
```

Both `attron()` and the `attrset()` functions are used to set text attributes. `attron()` always adds the text attribute(s) specified to whatever attributes exist already. `attrset()`, on the other hand, resets all text attributes to only those listed by the `attrset()` function.

In NCurses, text attributes are combined with a character to produce the NCurses `chtype`. The attributes and character stay together; move or copy the character, and the attributes go with it. This is unlike other text attribute systems where the attribute is applied to the character's location on the screen and characters at that location take on the attributes of the location. In NCurses, characters and attributes are often the same thing. (Also see Appendix C.)

Multiple attributes are applied by specifying each in the `attrset()` function, separated by a | (logical OR). This also includes using the `COLOR_PAIR(n)` attribute.

It is technically possible that using a logical OR to combine attributes may not work. For example, if more than the maximum number of color pairs are defined (which can happen on some terminals, such as xterm-88color or xterm-256color), then using the logical OR may result in nonexistent attributes being assigned. (NCurses 5.5 can be compiled to support 32768 color pairs.)

The attributes listed in this entry can also be combined with `COLOR_PAIR(n)` values, where n indicates a foreground (text) and background color combination, as defined by `init_pair()`.

Not all the attributes listed in this entry are implemented on every terminal. For example, NCurses doesn't implement the `A_TOP`, `A_LEFT`, `A_RIGHT`, `A_VERTICAL`, or `A_HORIZTIONAL` attributes because there is no terminal that uses those features. Refer to the "Format Reference" section earlier to see which are available for you to use.

`attrset(A_NORMAL)` turns off all attributes.

To determine which attributes are available for the terminal, use the `termattrs()` function.

Also refer to the Notes for `attron` and `attroff()`.

Examples

```
attrset(A_BOLD);
```

This statement sets text attributes to bold. Any attributes previously assigned to the text are removed.

```
wattrset(new,A_NORMAL | COLOR_PAIR(1));
```

This statement resets all text attributes for the window `new` to use the colors specified by `COLOR_PAIR(1)`.

Sample Program

```
1     #include <ncurses.h>
2
3     int main(void)
4     {
5         initscr();
6         start_color();
7         init_pair(1,COLOR_WHITE,COLOR_BLUE);
8
9         attrset(A_BOLD);
10        addstr("Attributes set for the screen to BOLD.\n");
11        attroff(A_BOLD);
12        addstr("Bold attribute has been removed.\n");
13        attron(COLOR_PAIR(1));
14        addstr("Color pair 1 has been added.\n");
15        attrset(A_REVERSE);
16        addstr("Attrset just reset things to reverse.\n");
17        attroff(A_REVERSE);
18        addstr("And now things are back to normal.\n");
19        refresh();
20        getch();
21
22        endwin();
23        return 0;
24    }
```

Sample output:

```
Attributes set for the screen to BOLD.
Bold attribute has been removed.
Color pair 1 has been added.
Attrset just reset things to reverse.
And now things are back to normal.
```

Also See

Chapter 3, Appendix C, `attroff()`, `attron()`, `chgat()`, `init_pair()`

baudrate()

The `baudrate()` function returns the terminal's speed in bits per second (bps).

Man Page Format

```
int baudrate(void);
```

Format Reference

The function has no arguments.

Return Value

`baudrate()` returns an `int` value representing the terminal's speed value in bps. Values returned depend on the terminal.

Notes

A *baud* is a measurement of signal modulation. The term is a holdover from the early days of modems when a 300 baud modem communicated at roughly 300 bps. As modem technology advanced, the bps rating was used while many incorrectly used the term "baud" instead. The value returned by `baudrate()` is really a bps value.

Virtual terminals return whichever value is defined for the terminal. This value probably will not reflect reality but merely the speed defined for the tty. Use the `stty` command to see which speed is set for a virtual terminal; the same value is returned by NCurses `baudrate()` function.

Knowing the speed of a terminal becomes relative when using some NCurses functions that update an entire screen of information. At 9600 bps, a full re-write of a screen by `touchwin()`/`refresh()` becomes noticeable. Therefore, the `baudrate()` function can be used to avoid redundant text writing to slower terminals. But given that some terminal windows don't properly report bps values, this may end up being a futile exercise.

Example

```
speed = baudrate();
```

This statement sets the value of int variable speed equal to the terminal's speed in bps.

Sample Program

```
1    #include <ncurses.h>
2
3    int main(void)
4    {
5        int b;
6
7        initscr();
8
9        b = baudrate();
10       printw("This terminal's baud rate is %d.\n",b);
11       refresh();
12       getch();
13
14       endwin();
15       return 0;
16   }
```

Sample output:

```
This terminal's baud rate is 9600.
```

beep()

The beep() function plays a tone over the computer's speaker. beep() literally causes the computer to go *beep*!

Man Page Format

```
int beep(void);
```

Format Reference

The function takes no arguments.

Return Value

If the computer beeps, beep() returns OK. It returns ERR otherwise.

Notes

The standard C output functions can make a *beep* by displaying the Ctrl-G character, the ASCII Bell. NCurses' output functions, however, are not passed through standard output. Displaying a Ctrl-G (0x07) character with NCurses output functions displays ^G on the screen. Silently.

This function doesn't work if the terminal has been configured not to beep.

The beep produced is whatever sound is set up as the default computer sound. For text-based systems, this is just a tone over the speaker. For graphical interfaces, the sound used is the default sound, which can be any tone, sound file, or whatever.

It is not possible to change the beep sound from within NCurses.

I would not rely on this function's return of ERR to determine whether or not a terminal can produce sound.

Example

```
beep();
```

This entry makes the computer go *beep*!

Sample Program

```
1    #include <ncurses.h>
2
3    int main(void)
4    {
5        initscr();
6
7        addstr("Press any key to beep:\n");
8        refresh();
9        getch();
10       beep();
11       addstr("Thanks!\n");
12       refresh();
13       getch();
14
15       endwin();
16       return 0;
17   }
```

Sample output:

```
Press any key to beep:
```

(Press Enter .)
BEEP!

```
Thanks!
```

Also See

Chapter 3, `flash()`

bkgd()

The `bkgd()` functions set the background attributes for the `stdscr` or a specific window. It writes new attributes to every character position on the window and even fills in blanks (spaces) with characters, if a character is specified as part of the attribute. `bkgd()` does not overwrite any existing text.

Man Page Formats

```
int bkgd(chtype ch);
int wbkgd(WINDOW *win, chtype ch);
```

Format Reference

`ch` is an NCurses `chtype` variable, a `long int`. It typically consists of formatting attributes, which are constants declared in `NCURSES.H`. It can also consist of regular text characters. Multiple attributes are combined by using the | (logical OR).

Refer to `attrset()`, as well as Appendix C, for a list of the `chtype` formatting attributes.

Refer to the `w` prefix entry later in this appendix for information on the `win` argument.

Return Value

The `bkgd()` function returns `ERR` on failure.

Notes

bkgd() over-writes any existing text attributes applied by attrset() or attron(). For example, if a word is highlighted in bold text and then bkgd() is used to color the screen yellow-on-white, the bold text attribute is removed and the text takes on the yellow-on-white attribute.

Characters fill the background, or nontext locations on the screen, when applied by bkgd(). Any text output function overwrites those "background" characters. And a further use of bkgd() with a text character as part of the attribute also erases those background characters.

bkgd() differs from bkgdset() in that the latter affects only new text written to the window. So if you want to change a window's background all at once, use bkgd().

It's a common typo to transpose the g and d in bkgd().

Examples

```
bkgd(A_BOLD);
```

This function sets all text attributes on the screen to bold. This replaces any existing applied attributes, including color.

```
bkgd(COLOR_PAIR(1) | '+');
```

Here, the screen is colored according to COLOR_PAIR 1 and all the non-text places are filled with + as a background character. Additional text written to the screen overwrites the + background characters. Space characters will not overwrite the + background, however, and space characters used to overwrite text also let the + background "shine through."

```
wbkgd(summary,A_NORMAL);
```

This statement removes all attributes from the window summary.

Sample Program

```
1     #include <ncurses.h>
2
3     int main(void)
4     {
5         initscr();
6         start_color();
7         init_pair(1,COLOR_WHITE,COLOR_BLUE);
8         init_pair(2,COLOR_YELLOW,COLOR_RED);
9
```

```
10          bkgd(COLOR_PAIR(1) | '.');
11          refresh();
12          getch();
13
14          addstr("bkgd() has preset the background.\n");
15          addstr("Press Enter to change it again.\n");
16          refresh();
17          getch();
18
19          bkgd(COLOR_PAIR(2));
20          addstr("All done!\n");
21          refresh();
22          getch();
23
24          endwin();
25          return 0;
26      }
```

Sample output:

At first, the screen is filled with white periods on a blue background.

Press the Enter key to see text displayed over the background, as shown in Figure A-1.

Press Enter again and the window background is changed to yellow text on a red background with the periods gone.

Also See

Chapter 3, Appendix C, attrset(), bkgdset()

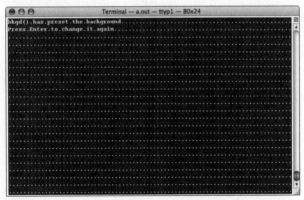

Figure A-1: A white dot on blue background

bkgdset()

The bkgdset() function sets the background attributes for a window, affecting only the text put to the screen after the bkgdset() function is issued.

Man Page Formats

```
int bkgdset(chtype ch);
void wbkgdset(WINDOW *win, chtype ch);
```

Format Reference

ch is an NCurses chtype variable, a long int, which represents formatting attributes for the screen. It can also include a text character to be used as the screen background character. Multiple attributes can be combined by using a | (logical OR).

Refer to attrset(), as well as Appendix C, for a list of the chtype formatting attributes.

Refer to the w prefix entry later in this appendix for information on the win argument.

Return Value

Nothing; bkgdset() is a void function.

Notes

Issuing a bkgdset() function by itself does not affect the screen at all. Only after text is written to the screen, or a portion of the screen is erased, do the affects of bkgdset() show up.

Unlike bkgd(), the bkgdset() function does not override any attributes previously set on the screen.

Text attributes set by attrset(), as well as other text-attribute-setting functions, are different from the background attributes.

Examples

```
bkgdset(A_BOLD);
```

This function sets text attributes for any text displayed afterwards to include bold.

```
wbkgd(fireworks,COLOR_PAIR(4));
```

This statement sets the text color to COLOR_PAIR 4 for any text to be displayed in the window fireworks.

Sample Program

```
1     #include <ncurses.h>
2
3     int main(void)
4     {
5         initscr();
6         start_color();
7         init_pair(1,COLOR_YELLOW,COLOR_RED);
8
9         bkgdset(A_BOLD);
10        addstr("bkgd() has set the background attributes to bold.\n");
11        addstr("Press Enter to change it.\n");
12        refresh();
13        getch();
14
15        bkgdset(COLOR_PAIR(1));
16        addstr("All done!\n");
17        refresh();
18        getch();
19
20        endwin();
21        return 0;
22    }
```

Sample output:
The following is displayed in bold:

```
bkgd() has set the background attributes to bold.
Press Enter to change it.
```

Press Enter and the attributes change to yellow text on a red background; the following is displayed:

```
All done!
```

Also See

Chapter 3, Appendix C, attrset(), bkgd()

border()

The border() function is used to draw a line or box around a window. The line can use default line drawing characters or you can chosse specific characters, and the line occupies the outside character positions (rows and columns) of the window.

Man Page Formats

```
int border(chtype ls, chtype rs, chtype ts, chtype bs,
        chtype tl, chtype tr, chtype bl, chtype br);
int wborder(WINDOW *win, chtype ls, chtype rs,
        chtype ts, chtype bs, chtype tl, chtype tr,
        chtype bl, chtype br);
```

Format Reference

All arguments to border (save for win) represent characters to be used to draw the border. The eight arguments represent the four edges and four corners:

- ls represents the character used to draw the border's left side
- rs, the right side
- ts, the top side
- bs, the bottom side
- tl represents the character used to draw the top left corner
- tr, the top right corner
- bl, the bottom left corner
- br, the bottom right corner

Each of these arguments are a chtype character, i.e., a long int representing both a character and an attribute. (See Appendix C.)

When any argument is zero, default characters are used, as shown in Table A-1.

Refer to Appendix B for more information about Alternative Character Set (ACS) characters.

Refer to the w prefix entry later in this appendix for information on the win argument.

Table A-1: ACS line drawing characters

Argument	ACS default	Argument	ACS default
ls	ACS_VLINE	tl	ACS_ULCORNER
rs	ACS_VLINE	tr	ACS_URCORNER
ts	ACS_HLINE	bl	ACS_LLCORNER
bs	ACS_HLINE	br	ACS_LRCORNER

Return Value

OK is returned.

Notes

Remember: You do not set the border's size or origin; the border follows the outline of the stdscr or named window. So if you want a border of a specific size, create a new window or subwindow and place the border in there.

The border occupies the top and bottom rows and the far left and right columns of the window.

The border is not protected and can easily be erased or replaced by putting characters to the window at the border's position.

Text placed inside a window with a border must reside within the border to avoid over-writing the border. For example, the first line of text in such a window should be placed at position 1, 1, not position 0, 0.

You can apply a border to the smallest window possible, which is one character in size. In that case, the only part of the border visible is the lower-right corner.

The smallest window where the full border is visible is a 3-by-3 character window. The borders four corners are used to box a 2-by-2 window, though no window content can be displayed without erasing the border.

Examples

```
border(0,0,0,0, 0,0,0,0);
```

This statement draws a border around the outside edge of the standard screen. The ACS line drawing characters are used to create the border.

```
wborder(menu, '|', '|', '-', '-', '+', '+', '+', '+');
```

This statement places a border around the window menu. The characters used to draw the border are specified: | for the vertical lines, – for the horizontal lines, and + for the four corners.

Sample Program

```
1    #include <ncurses.h>
2
3    int main(void)
4    {
5        WINDOW *newman;
6
7        initscr();
8        start_color();
```

```
 9          init_pair(1,COLOR_YELLOW,COLOR_RED);
10
11          newman = newwin(5,30,5,10);
12          if( newman == NULL)
13          {
14              endwin();
15              puts("Error creating window");
16              return(1);
17          }
18
19          wbkgd(newman,COLOR_PAIR(1));
20          wborder(newman,0,0,0,0,0,0,0,0);
21          mvwaddstr(newman,1,1,"Ta-da!");
22          wrefresh(newman);
23          wgetch(newman);
24
25          endwin();
26          return 0;
27      }
```

Sample output:
The program creates a window on the screen 30 characters wide by 5 characters tall.
The window is colored red with yellow text. A border is drawn around the window, and
text inside the border says Ta-da!.

Also See

Chapter 14, Appendix B, box(), hline(), vline()

box()

The box() function draws a simple box around the outside edges of a window. The function uses the ACS characters to draw the box, though the characters used to draw the horizontal and vertical lines can be specified inside the box() function.

Man Page Format

```
int box(WINDOW *win, chtype verch, chtype horch);
```

Format Reference

win refers to a specific window or stdscr for the standard screen.

verch is a chtype character used to create the left and right (vertical) lines of the box. The chtype combines both a character and an attribute, though typically only a character (constant or variable) is used. See Appendix C for more information on chtypes.

horch is a chtype character used to create the top and bottom (horizontal) lines of the box.

When zero is specified for either verch or horch the default ACS character is used: ACS_VLINE for verch and ACS_HLINE for horch. See Appendix B for more information on these characters.

Return Value

box() always returns int 0 or OK.

Notes

The characters used to draw the corners of the box are shown in Table A-2.

The box() function is equivalent to the following border() function:

```
wborder(win,verch,verch,horch,horch,0,0,0,0)
```

There is no wbox() function.

Also refer to the Notes for border() as the same information applies to both functions.

Examples

```
box(stdscr,0,0);
```

This function draws a box around the standard screen window using the default line drawing characters.

```
box(table1, '*', '*');
```

This function draws a box around the window table1, using asterisks for both the horizontal and vertical lines.

Table A-2: ACS line drawing characters used in box()

POSITION	ACS CHARACTER	POSITION	ACS CHARACTER
Top left	ACS_ULCORNER	Bottom left	ACS_LLCORNER
Top right	ACS_URCORNER	Bottom right	ACS_LRCORNER

Sample Program

```
1    #include <ncurses.h>
2
3    int main(void)
4    {
5        initscr();
6
7        box(stdscr,0,0);
8        mvaddstr(1,1,"Ta-da!");
9        refresh();
10       getch();
11
12       endwin();
13       return 0;
14   }
```

Sample output:
The program draws a box around the entire screen, placing the words Ta-da! *inside the box at row 1, column 1.*

Also See

Chapter 14, Appendix B, border(), hline(), vline()

can_change_color()

The can_change_color() function determines whether or not a terminal can re-define its color set. If so, then the color_content() function can be used to create new color values for use with NCurses various text color attribute functions.

Man Page Format

```
bool can_change_color(void);
```

Format Reference

The function has no arguments.

Return Value

can_change_color() returns a Boolean value, TRUE or FALSE, depending on whether the terminal can redefine its colors.

Notes

Terminals where this command returns TRUE include the Linux console, xterm-88color, xterm-256color, PuTTY, or anything with "ccc" in the terminal description.

Examples

```
r = can_change_color();
```

In this statement, the value of r equals TRUE if color values can be changed on the terminal, FALSE otherwise.

```
if(can_change_color())
```

This if condition evaluates true if the color values can be changed.

Sample Program

```
1    #include <ncurses.h>
2
3    int main(void)
4    {
5        bool tf;
6        initscr();
7
8        tf =  can_change_color();
9        if( tf == TRUE)
10           addstr("This terminal can change the standard colors.\n");
11       else
12           addstr("This terminal cannot change the colors.\n");
13       refresh();
14       getch();
15
16       endwin();
17       return 0;
18   }
```

Sample output:

```
This terminal can change the standard colors.
```

Or:

```
This terminal cannot change the colors.
```

Also See

start_color(), color_content(), TRUE

cbreak()

The cbreak() function modifies input, activating what's called *cbreak mode*. This increases the number of characters available to your program, as well as speeds up input somewhat.

Explanation

NCurses reads keyboard input through the terminal. This is known as *cooked* input mode as text input is buffered by the terminal and certain characters typed at the keyboard are intercepted and used for certain things. This all happens before the text is passed through to your NCurses program.

Buffering refers to how text is read. The terminal uses line buffering, which stores a line of text and sends it to NCurses after \n is encountered.

The special characters include, for example, the Killchar key used at the command prompt to erase a line of text or the Erasechar key used to delete text.

The cbreak mode disables the line buffering and the trapping of keys such as Killchar and Erasechar.

Man Page Format

```
int cbreak(void);
int nocbreak(void);
```

Format Reference

The cbreak() command activates cbreak mode.

The nocbreak() command restores cooked input mode (normal).

Return Value

OK upon success, ERR upon failure.

Notes

The settings that cbreak() and nocbreak() affect are *inherited*. That is, the settings may be on or off when your program starts. The only way to ensure that your program uses cbreak() mode input is to issue the cbreak() function in your code. Ditto for nocbreak().

The cbreak() setting overrides raw(). Even so, try to use either cbreak() or raw() functions, not both at the same time. See raw().

The `nocbreak()` function also disables (or undoes) any delay set by the `halfdelay()` function. See `halfdelay()`.

Examples

```
cbreak()
```

Here, cbreak mode is set for the program.

```
nocbreak()
```

Here, the cbreak mode is cancelled.

Sample Program

```
1     #include <ncurses.h>
2
3     int main(void)
4     {
5         int ch;
6         initscr();
7
8         cbreak();
9         mvaddstr(0,0,"Type away, cbreak mode is on:");
10        while( getch() != '\n')
11            ;
12
13        nocbreak();
14        mvaddstr(3,0,"Type away, cbreak mode is off:");
15        while( getch() != '\n')
16            ;
17
18        endwin();
19        return 0;
20    }
```

Sample output:

```
Type away, cbreak mode is on:
```

You can't really determine the change in the line buffering, but try typing the kill/erase character. On my terminal, Ctrl-U is the Killchar key and typing it with cbreak mode on merely displays ^U on the screen. Similarly, pressing Delete displays ^?.

```
Type away, cbreak mode is off:
```

Try typing `Killchar` *or* `Delete` *and the results are the same as if you typed them at the command prompt.*

Also See

raw(),halfdelay()

chgat()

The chgat() function changes text attributes on the screen. New attributes specified replace any existing attributes without overwriting text. In fact, the advantage of using chgat() is that it lets you change text attributes without having to rewrite that bit of text.

Man Page Formats

```
int chgat(int n, attr_t attr, short color,
    const void *opts);
int wchgat(WINDOW *win, int n, attr_t attr,short color,
    const void *opts)
int mvchgat(int y, int x, int n, attr_t attr,short color,
    const void *opts)
int mvwchgat(WINDOW *win, int y, int x, int n,attr_t attr, short color,
    const void *opts)
```

Format Reference

n is the number of characters chgat() affects. When n is -1, then all characters from the cursor's current position to the end of the line are affected. When 0 is specified, no text is changed. Otherwise, the new attributes are applied to n number of characters from the cursor's current position and to the right. When n is greater than the window width, the window width is assumed.

attr is an NCurses attr_t type (long int) value representing text attributes to be applied. Refer to attrset() for a list of attr_t constants as defined in NCURSES.H.

color is short int representing the number of a COLOR_PAIR defined by the init_pair function. Note that color is the pair number itself, not the COLOR_PAIR(n) thing.

NULL is required for the opts argument, which is currently not defined in NCurses.

Refer to the mv, mvw, and w prefix entries elsewhere in this appendix for information on the win, row, and col arguments.

Return Value

The return value is stated as "not important" according to the documentation.

Notes

chgat() affects text attributes from the current cursor's position *right*.

The most common mistake you'll make is specifying COLOR_PAIR(1), for example, for the color argument. Instead you should just specify the pair number, 1.

A simple refresh() will not update the new attributes put to the screen. Therefore a touchline() function applied to the same line, or a touchwin() function for the entire window, is necessary to see the effects of chgat().

Examples

```
chgat(-1,A_BOLD,0,NULL);
```

This statement applies the bold text attribute to all text from the cursor's current position to the end of the line. Color isn't changed.

```
mvchgat(4,28,5,0,3,NULL);
```

Here, the mvchgat() function moves the cursor to row 4, column 28 on the screen. The color attributes for the five characters at that location (and to the right) are changed to COLOR_PAIR(3). (It's assumed that color has been started and COLOR_PAIR(3) defined elsewhere in the code.)

```
wchgat(popup,20,A_UNDERLINE,1,NULL);
```

The statement here changes attributes for 20 characters starting at the cursor's current position in window popup. Both the underline text attribute and COLOR_PAIR(1) are applied to the 20 characters.

Sample Program

```
1    #include <ncurses.h>
2
3    int main(void)
4    {
5        initscr();
6        start_color();
7        init_pair(1,COLOR_RED,COLOR_WHITE);
8        init_pair(2,COLOR_WHITE,COLOR_BLUE);
9
10       addstr("This is the incredibly boring first line\n");
11       addstr("This is the incredibly boring second line\n");
12       addstr("This is the incredibly boring third line\n");
13       addstr("This is the incredibly boring fourth line\n");
14       refresh();
15       getch();
16
```

```
17          mvchgat(0,0,4,0,1,NULL);
18          mvchgat(1,12,10,0,2,NULL);
19          mvchgat(2,23,6,A_UNDERLINE,0,NULL);
20          mvchgat(3,30,6,A_BOLD,0,NULL);
21          touchwin(stdscr);
22          refresh();
23          getch();
24
25          endwin();
26          return 0;
27      }
```

Sample output:

```
This is the incredibly boring first line
This is the incredibly boring second line
This is the incredibly boring third line
This is the incredibly boring fourth line
```

Press Enter and new attributes are applied to the text: In the first line, the word This *appears with red text on a white background; the second line shows the word* incredibly *with white text on a blue background; in the third row, the word* boring *is underlined; in the last row, the word* fourth *appears in bold text.*

Also See

attrset(), attron()

clear()

The clear() function clears the screen or named window, writing blanks, or space characters, to every screen position. Additionally, the clear() function calls clearok(), to ensure that the screen is erased and completely rewritten with the next call to a refresh() function. (See clearok().)

Man Page Formats

```
int clear(void);
int wclear(WINDOW *win);
```

Format Reference

The clear() function takes no arguments. It's a pseudo function that affects only the standard screen.

Refer to the w prefix entry later in this appendix for information on the win argument.

Return Value

Always returns OK.

Notes

clear() is the same as wclear(stdscr).

Clearing the screen also homes the cursor; after the clear() function, the cursor is placed at location 0, 0.

The clear() function removes only characters and their attributes. It does not affect the background attributes. If a background character is set via bkgd() or bkgdset(),that character will show up in the blanks clear() fills the screen with.

The clear() function is the same as the erase() function, though erase() does not also call clearok().

Examples

```
clear();
```

The statement clears the standard screen, erasing all the text.

```
wclear(sidebar);
```

The statement erases the contents of the window sidebar.

Sample Program

```
1     #include <ncurses.h>
2
3     int main(void)
4     {
5         int c,y,x,cmax;
6
7         initscr();
8
9         getmaxyx(stdscr,y,x);
10        cmax = (x * y) / 5;
11        for(c=0;c<cmax;c++) addstr("blah ");
12        refresh();
13        getch();
14
15        clear();         /* clear the screen */
16        refresh();        /* don't forget this! */
```

```
17        getch();
18
19        endwin();
20        return 0;
21   }
```

Sample output:

The screen is filled with the text blah blah blah. *Pressing the Enter key erases the screen.*

Also See

Chapter 6, erase(), clearok(), refresh()

clearok()

The clearok() function modifies window behavior in NCurses. When switched on, clearok() forces the next call to refresh() to entirely erase the window and redraw it from scratch.

Explanation

Normally, the refresh() function merely updates those parts of the window that have been changed. But by switching on clearok(), a complete erasure and rewrite of the window is possible.

Man Page Format

```
int clearok(WINDOW *win, bool bf);
```

Format Reference

win is the name of the window to erase and redraw. stdscr can be used for win to update the standard screen.

bf is a Boolean value, either TRUE or FALSE. TRUE is used to activate erasing/redrawing for the named window; FALSE turns it off.

Return Value

The function always returns OK.

Notes

The screen isn't actually erased and redrawn until a refresh() or wrefresh() function is used.

When the current screen, curscr, is used as the win argument, NCurses erases and redraws the entire screen from scratch at the next refresh().

Apparently erasing and redrawing the entire screen is visually distracting, but this must only be so with slower terminal speeds. (Refer to baudrate().)

Examples

```
clearok(stdscr,TRUE);
```

The statement causes the next call to refresh() to erase and redraw the standard screen, ensuring that what's shown in the screen matches memory.

```
clearok(menu,FALSE);
```

Here, clearok() updating is disabled for the window menu. Any subsequent calls to refresh() update only changed parts of the screen.

```
clearok(curscr,TRUE);
```

After executing this statement, the next call to wrefresh() forces the standard screen to be cleared and then redrawn from scratch.

Sample Program

```
1    #include <ncurses.h>
2
3    int main(void)
4    {
5        int x;
6
7        initscr();
8
9        for(x=0;x<350;x++)          /* fills screen with junk */
10           printw("-0- ");
11       refresh();
12       getch();
13
14       mvaddstr(5,20,"Holy updates, Batman!");
15       clearok(stdscr,TRUE);
16       refresh();
17       getch();
18
19       endwin();
20       return 0;
21   }
```

Sample output:

The screen is partially filled with a pattern. Press Enter and a new string of text is written to the screen, the screen is then erased and redrawn. (This can happen so fast that the visual effect isn't noticed.)

Also See

```
clear(), TRUE, refresh(), touchwin()
```

clrtobot()

The `clrtobot()` function clears the screen from the cursor's current position to the end of the line (right) and to the bottom of the screen.

Man Page Formats

```
int clrtobot(void);
int wclrtobot(WINDOW *win);
```

Format Reference

The `clrtobot()` function has no arguments.

Refer to the `w` prefix entry later in this appendix for information on the `win` argument.

Return Value

The function returns `OK`.

Notes

The function does not move the cursor.

Any text attributes are erased by this function.

Remember that the text doesn't visually go away until you `refresh()` the window.

Example

```
clrtobot();
```

After this statement, text is cleared from the cursor's position to the right, all the way to the end of the line, and then all rows below to the bottom of the window.

Sample Program

```
1      #include <ncurses.h>
2
3      int main(void)
4      {
5          int c,y,x,cmax;
6
7          initscr();
8
9          getmaxyx(stdscr,y,x);
10         cmax = (x * y) / 5;
11         for(c=0;c<cmax;c++) addstr("blah ");
12         refresh();
13         getch();
14
15         move(5,20);          /* Setup the cursor */
16         clrtobot();          /* Clear to end of screen */
17         refresh();
18         getch();
19
20         endwin();
21         return 0;
22     }
```

Sample output:

The screen is filled with the text blah blah blah. *Pressing the Enter key clears the screen from cursor location 5,20 to the end of the screen.*

Also See

Chapter 6, clear(), clrtoeol(), refresh()

clrtoeol()

The clrtoeol() function clears text from the cursor's current position to the end of the line.

Man Page Formats

```
int clrtoeol(void);
int wclrtoeol(WINDOW *win);
```

Format Reference

The clrtoeol() function has no arguments.

Refer to the w prefix entry later in this appendix for information on the win argument.

Return Value

The function returns OK.

Notes

Refer to the Notes for clrtobot().

Example

```
wclrtoeol(inputwin);
```

After this statement, text is cleared from the cursor's position to the right, all the way to the end of the line, in the window inputwin.

Sample Program

```
1    #include <ncurses.h>
2
3    int main(void)
4    {
5        int c,y,x,cmax;
6
7        initscr();
8
9        getmaxyx(stdscr,y,x);
10       cmax = (x * y) / 5;
11       for(c=0;c<cmax;c++) addstr("blah ");
12       refresh();
13       getch();
14
15       move(5,20);          /* Setup the cursor */
16       clrtoeol();          /* Clear to end of line */
17       refresh();
18       getch();
19
20       endwin();
21       return 0;
22   }
```

Sample output:

The screen is filled with the text blah blah blah. *Pressing the Enter key clears the screen from cursor location 5,20 to the end of the line.*

Also See

Chapter 6, `clear()`, `clrtobot()`, `refresh()`

color_content()

The `color_content()` function reads the individual red, green, and blue intensity values for each one of NCurses color values.

Man Page Format

```
int color_content(short color, short *r, short *g, short *b);
```

Format Reference

c is a `short int` representing a color number. Values for c range from 0 through the value of COLOR. (See COLOR.)

r, g, and b are the addresses of `short int` variables that will store the red, green, and blue intensity values, respectively. Note that these arguments are pointers, either pointer variables or the address of `short int` variables. Refer to the Examples section.

Return Value

The function returns OK on success, ERR otherwise.

Notes

This function is useless unless the `start_color()` function has first been issued to set up NCurses for using color.

Values for the color intensity can range from 0 up to 1000.

This function works on any NCurses colors, whether they are the default NCurses colors or custom colors you created yourself by using the `init_color()` function.

Examples

```
color_content(3,rd,gr,bl);
```

Here, the statement reads intensity values for color 3 and stores them at the addresses indicated by pointer variables rd, gr, and bl. (It is assumed that these pointer variables are initialized and actually point to the address of some short ints.)

```
color_content(6,&red,&green,&blue);
```

Here, the intensity values are stored in short int variables red, green, and blue. Note that they are simply short int variables; the & is used to get the address of those variables, which is what the color_content() function craves for those arguments.

Sample Program

```
1    #include <ncurses.h>
2
3    int main(void)
4    {
5         short x,r,b,g;
6
7         initscr();
8         start_color();
9
10        for(x=0;x<COLORS;x++)
11        {
12             color_content(x,&r,&g,&b);
13             printw("Color %d = Red: %4d\tGreen: %4d\tBlue: %4d\n",
14                 x,r,g,b);
15        }
16        refresh();
17        getch();
18
19        endwin();
20        return 0;
21   }
```

Sample output:

```
Color 0 = Red:    0    Green:    0    Blue:    0
Color 1 = Red:  680    Green:    0    Blue:    0
Color 2 = Red:    0    Green:  680    Blue:    0
Color 3 = Red:  680    Green:  680    Blue:    0
Color 4 = Red:    0    Green:    0    Blue:  680
Color 5 = Red:  680    Green:    0    Blue:  680
Color 6 = Red:    0    Green:  680    Blue:  680
Color 7 = Red:  680    Green:  680    Blue:  680
```

Also See

start_color(), COLORS, init_color()

color_set()

The `color_set()` function sets the foreground and background text color attributes to a specific color pair.

Man Page Format

```
int color_set(short color_pair_number, void* opts);
```

Format Reference

`color_pair_number` is a `short int` representing a color pair number, a foreground/background text color combination as previously defined by an `init_pair()` function.

The `opts` value is currently set to `NULL`. It's reserved for use in a future version of NCurses.

Return Value

`color_set()` returns an `int` value when the color pair argument is outside the range 0 to COLOR_PAIRS-1.

Notes

The `color_set()` function affects only text put to the window. To color the entire window, use the `bkgd()` function.

Argument p is a number representing the value n from a `COLOR_PAIR(n)` number. It is not the constant `COLOR_PAIR(n)` itself.

`color_set(2,NULL)` is equivalent to `attrset(COLOR_PAIR(2))`.

Example

```
color_set(2,NULL);
```

This statement causes any text displayed afterward to use the foreground and background color combination defined in the color pair 2.

Sample Program

```
1    #include <ncurses.h>
2
3    int main(void)
4    {
5        initscr();
```

```
 6          start_color();
 7
 8          init_pair(1,COLOR_RED,COLOR_YELLOW);
 9          color_set(1,NULL);
10          addstr("The color of this window is now\n");
11          addstr("Red on Yellow.\n");
12          refresh();
13          getch();
14
15          endwin();
16          return 0;
17      }
```

Sample output:

```
The color of this window is no
Red on Yellow
```

The text above appears in red on a yellow background.

Also See

```
init_pair(),attrset(),bkgd()
```

COLORS

COLORS is an `int` constant set internally by NCurses. It represents the number of colors available for use by the various color functions.

The value COLORS holds is correct only after the `start_color()` function has initialized NCurses color functions.

Man Page Format

Not applicable.

Format Reference

COLORS works like any constant value in C. It can be used as an immediate value, a comparison, or in combination with other values.

Return Value

The value of COLORS depends on the number of colors available to the terminal. If the `start_color()` function has not yet been used, then COLORS equals zero.

Notes

Because the first color number is zero, the highest valid color value is really COLORS-1.

The typical PC uses eight basic colors — black, red, green, brown, blue, magenta, cyan, and white — so the value of COLORS is set to 8. Also see the entry for init_pair().

For some reason, NCurses refers to the PC color "brown" as being yellow. It's brown.

Though only 8 colors are available, 16 text colors are possible on the PC. By applying the A_BOLD attribute to color text, the "bright" version of each text color can be used. (So "bright brown" is finally the "yellow" NCurses desires to see.) See attrset(). (Note that the A_BOLD attribute actually uses a specific bold font on certain terminals, not just brightly colored text.)

The basic eight colors are based upon setting bits for the RGB (red, green, and blue) values on the standard PC monitor, where R is the first bit, G is the second, and B the third. Table A-3 illustrates the colors, constants, and bit values.

Examples

```
if(COLORS)
```

Here, when the value of COLORS is greater than zero, the if test passes.

```
printw("This terminal can use %d colors.\n",COLORS);
```

This statement displays the number of colors available for the terminal.

Table A-3: NCurses color values, Bits, and Constants

COLOR	BITS B-G-R	COLOR CONSTANT
0	0 0 0	COLOR_BLACK
1	0 0 1	COLOR_RED
2	0 1 0	COLOR_GREEN
3	0 1 1	COLOR_YELLOW
4	1 0 0	COLOR_BLUE
5	1 0 1	COLOR_MAGENTA
6	1 1 0	COLOR_CYAN
7	1 1 1	COLOR_WHITE

Sample Program

Refer to the entry for start_color() for a sample program and output.

Also See

Chapter 3, COLOR_PAIRS, attrset(), start_color()

COLOR_PAIRS

The COLOR_PAIRS constant is an int value set internally by NCurses. It represents the number of COLOR_PAIR(n) color pairs available for use when you apply foreground and background text colors.

Man Page Format

Not applicable.

Format Reference

COLOR_PAIRS works like any C language constant. You can use COLOR_PAIRS as an immediate value, a comparison, or in combination with other values.

Return Value

The value of COLOR_PAIRS depends on the number of colors available to the terminal. If the start_color() function has not yet been used, then COLORS equals zero.

Notes

You must first use the start_color() function to initialize NCurses color functions before the COLOR_PAIRS constant can hold a meaningful value.

There is a difference between the COLOR_PAIRS constant and the text attribute COLOR_PAIR(n). The first is a constant value created by NCurses. The second is a text attribute representing a color pair combination created by the init_pair() function.

Yes, the COLOR_PAIRS constant is plural, while the COLOR_PAIR(n) attribute is singular. But it makes sense when you think that COLOR_PAIRS is a quantity whereas COLOR_PAIR(n) is a single pair.

A common value for COLOR_PAIRS is 64, though do not consider that to be true for all terminals or implementations of NCurses.

Examples

```
printw("This terminal can use %d color pairs.\n",COLOR_PAIRS);
```

This statement displays the number of color pairs available for the terminal.

```
if(COLOR_PAIRS)
```

Here, when the value of COLOR_PAIRS is greater than zero, the if test passes.

Sample Program

Refer to the entry for start_color() for a sample program and output.

Also See

Chapter 3, COLORS, init_pair(), attrset(), start_color()

COLS

The COLS constant is an int value set internally by NCurses to represent the number of columns available on the standard screen.

Man Page Format

Not applicable.

Format Reference

COLS works like any C language constant. It can be used as an immediate value, in a comparison, or in combination with other values.

Return Value

The value of COLS depends on the number of columns in the terminal or standard screen, stdscr.

COLS is an int.

Notes

Most standard terminal windows use 80 columns.

Do note that with terminal windows in graphical environments, terminals can be just about any size. Some text screens also have the ability to display more than 80 columns of text on the screen.

COLS is a variable, not a constant. Note that changing the value of COLS does not re-size the standard screen or terminal window.

Normally, NCurses sets COLS equal to the COLUMNS environment variable. This can be changed by using the use_env() function. See use_env().

Use the getmaxyx() function to determine the number of columns in any NCurses window.

Example

```
step = COLS/10;
```

Here, the value of variable step is equal to COLS divided by 10.

Sample Program

```
1    #include <ncurses.h>
2
3    int main(void)
4    {
5        initscr();
6
7        printw("This window is %d lines by %d columns.\n",\
8            LINES,COLS);
9        refresh();
10       getch();
11
12       endwin();
13       return 0;
14   }
```

Sample output:

```
This window is 24 lines by 80 columns.
```

Also See

LINES, getmaxyx(), use_env()

copywin()

The copywin() function copies a rectangle of text and attributes from one window to another window, either destructively or nondestructively.

Man Page Format

```
int copywin(const WINDOW *srcwin, WINDOW *dstwin, int sminrow,
            int smincol, int dminrow, int dmincol, int dmaxrow,
            int dmaxcol, int overlay);
```

Format Reference

srcwin is a WINDOW pointer to the window from which text and attributes will be copied, the source window.

dstwin is a WINDOW pointer to the window into which text will be copied, the destination window.

sminrow and smincol are int values representing the row and column from which text is copied in the source window (srcwin).

dminrow, dmincol, dmaxrow, and dmaxcol, represent a rectangle in the destination window (dstwin) where the copied text is pasted. dminrow and dmincol form the upper-left corner of the rectangle as row and column values; dmaxrow and dmaxcol form the lower-right corner of the rectangle as row and column values.

overlay is a Boolean value, either TRUE or FALSE. If TRUE, the text copied is nondestructive, and only blanks in the destination window are overwritten with text from the source window. If FALSE, the text copied is destructive, replacing all text in the destination window's rectangle with text and attributes from the source window.

Return Value

OK or ERR, based on the function's success or failure.

Notes

A visual example of how copywin() works can be found in Figure 10-2.

NCurses uses the difference between dminrow and dmaxrow, as well as the difference between dmincol and dmaxcol, to help calculate the size of both the source and destination rectangles.

When overlay is TRUE only text is copied from srcwin to dstwin. The text appears only in the "blank" portions of the window. Text will not overwrite any existing text.

When `overlay` is `FALSE`, the entire rectangle of text and attributes is copied from `srcwin` to `dstwin`. Any existing text and any attributes applied to that text in `dstwin` is replaced with text and attributes from `srcwin`.

Example

```
copywin(top,bottom,0,0,0,20,10,30,FALSE);
```

Here, `copywin()` copies a chunk of text from window `top` to window `bottom`. The chunk starts at location 0,0 in window `top`. It is pasted to location 0,20 in window `bottom`. The text chunk measures 10 rows by 10 columns (10-0 and 30-20).

Sample Program

```
1     #include <ncurses.h>
2
3     int main(void)
4     {
5         WINDOW *alpha,*beta;
6         int half,size,x;
7
8         initscr();
9         start_color();
10        init_pair(1,COLOR_WHITE,COLOR_BLUE);
11        init_pair(2,COLOR_WHITE,COLOR_RED);
12
13     /* create and color two side-by-side windows */
14        half = COLS >> 1;
15        size = half * COLS;
16        size >>= 1;
17        alpha = newwin(LINES,half-1,0,0);
18        wbkgd(alpha,COLOR_PAIR(1));
19        beta = newwin(LINES,half-1,0,half);
20        wbkgd(beta,COLOR_PAIR(2));
21
22     /* populate the windows with text */
23        for(x=0;x<size;x++)
24        {
25            wprintw(alpha,"O ");
26            wprintw(beta," X");
27        }
28        wrefresh(alpha);
29        wrefresh(beta);
30        wgetch(beta);
31
32     /* copy from window beta to window alpha */
33        copywin(beta,alpha,10,5,10,5,15,30,TRUE);
34        wrefresh(alpha);
35        wgetch(alpha);
```

```
36
37        endwin();
38        return 0;
39   }
```

> **NOTE** Error checking is not being done for the two newwin() functions; be sure to check errors for this function in your own code.

Sample output:

Two windows are created, side-by-side. On the left is window alpha, colored blue with white O's. On the right is window beta, colored red with white X's. Pressing Enter copies a chunk of text from beta to alpha. With TRUE in line 33, only the X's are copied. When you edit line 33 to change TRUE to FALSE, a red rectangle with only X's and spaces is copied, clobbering all underlying text already in window alpha.

Also See

Chapter 10, overlay(), overwrite(), dupwin()

curs_set()

The curs_set() function controls the cursor's visibility.

Man Page Format

```
int curs_set(int visibility);
```

Format Reference

The value of visibility can be 0, 1, or 2:

- 0 makes the cursor invisible
- 1 sets the cursor to normal mode
- 2 sets the cursor to a *very* visible mode

Return Value

The function returns a value, 0, 1, 2, representing the previous cursor state, defined above. ERR is returned if the cursor state cannot be changed.

Notes

Not all terminals support the curs_set() function.

By returning the cursor's previous state, it's possible to restore the cursor later. But note that the endwin() function restores the terminal's cursor to a visible state if curs_set() has altered it. However, the cursor may not be restored to the same state it was in before the NCurses program was started, meaning that if the cursor was invisible when your program started, that state will not be restored when your program ends.

Examples

```
curs_set(0);
```

This command makes the cursor invisible.

```
curs_set(1);
```

Here, the cursor is restored to normal, visible mode.

Sample Program

```
1     #include <ncurses.h>
2
3     int main(void)
4     {
5          int r;
6          initscr();
7
8     /* first, turn the cursor off */
9          r = curs_set(0);
10         if(r == ERR)
11         {
12              endwin();
13              puts("This terminal cannot change the cursor.");
14              return(1);
15         }
16         addstr("The cursor has been turned off: ");
17         refresh();
18         getch();
19
20    /* second, turn the cursor on */
21         curs_set(1);
22         move(1,0);
23         addstr("The cursor now on: ");
24         refresh();
25         getch();
26
27    /* third, turn the cursor very on */
```

```
28          curs_set(2);
29          move(2,0);
30          addstr("The cursor is now very on: ");
31          refresh();
32          getch();
33
34          curs_set(r);            /* restore cursor */
35          endwin();
36          return 0;
37      }
```

Sample output:

```
This terminal cannot change the cursor.
```

Or:

```
The cursor has been turned off:
The cursor now on:
The cursor is now very on:
```

Each line is followed by the cursor in the indicated state.

Also See

Chapter 14, move()

curses_version()

The curses_version() function returns a string that describes the name, version, release, and patch information for the version of NCurses being run. This is an extended NCurses function.

Man Page Format

```
const char * curses_version(void);
```

Format Reference

The function has no arguments.

Return Value

The function returns a string in the format:

```
ncurses major.minor.patch
```

The text `ncurses` begins the string. It stands for NCurses or New Curses, the version of the NCurses library used to compile the program.

`major` is the major release number.

`minor` is the minor release number.

`patch` is the number of the most recent patch.

Notes

Several constants defined in `NCURSES.H` contain similar information for determining NCurses version, as listed in Table A-4.

The `NCURSES_VERSION` string is simply the `NCURSES_VERSION_MAJOR` and `NCURSES_VERSION_MINOR` values, separated by a dot.

Example

```
vernum = curses_version();
```

Here, the string returned by `curses_version()` is stored in the char array (string variable) `vernum`.

Sample Program

```
1    #include <ncurses.h>
2
3    int main(void)
4    {
5        initscr();
6
7    #ifdef NCURSES_VERSION
8        printw("This is %s.\n",curses_version());
9    #else
10       printw("You are apparently not using NCurses.\n");
11   #endif
12       refresh();
13       getch();
14
15       endwin();
16       return 0;
17   }
```

Sample output:
Hopefully, something like:

```
This is ncurses 5.4.20040208.
```

Table A-4: NCurses version constants

CONSTANT	DEFINES
NCURSES_VERSION	String containing NCurses major and minor versions
NCURSES_VERSION_MAJOR	Major version number
NCURSES_VERSION_MINOR	Minor version number
NCURSES_VERSION_PATCH	Patch number

Also See

NCURSES_VERSION

delch()

The delch() function deletes the character at the cursor's position. Any characters to the right on the same line are then slid one place to the left. Blanks are used to fill in the end of the line.

Man Page Formats

```
int delch(void);
int wdelch(WINDOW *win);
int mvdelch(int y, int x);
int mvwdelch(WINDOW *win, int y, int x);
```

Format Reference

The base function has no arguments; refer to the mv, mvw, and w prefix entries elsewhere in this appendix for information on the win, y, and x arguments.

Return Value

OK on success, or ERR on failure.

Notes

This function does not change the cursor's position.

To delete a line of text, use the deleteln() function.

To insert a single character, the insch() function is used.

Example

```
mvdelch(5,0);
```

After this statement, the character at location 5,0 is removed, and all remaining text on that line is slid over to the left one notch.

Sample Program

```
1    #include <ncurses.h>
2
3    #define Y 5
4    #define X1 10
5    #define X2 60
6    #define DELAY 250
7
8    int main(void)
9    {
10       char text[] = "Elvis found alive *** Stock market tops 20,000 ***↺
     Rocky XII big box office hit *** Congressman indicted *** ";
11       char *t;
12
13       initscr();
14       noecho();
15       nodelay(stdscr,TRUE);
16
17       t = text;
18       while( getch() == ERR )
19       {
20           if( *t == '\0') t = text;
21           mvinsch(Y,X2,*t);
22           mvdelch(Y,X1);
23           refresh();
24           napms(DELAY);
25           t++;
26       }
27
28       endwin();
29       return 0;
30    }
```

Sample output:

A scrolling marquee appears on line 5 between columns 10 and 60. The text (line 10) is repeatedly scrolled right to left.

Also See

Chapter 5, deleteln(), insch()

deleteln()

The deleteln() function removes a line of text from the screen. The line removed is based on the cursor's position, the Y or row value. All lines below are then scrolled up one line, with a blank line of text appearing at the bottom of the screen.

Man Page Formats

```
int deleteln(void);
int wdeleteln(WINDOW *win);
```

Format Reference

The function takes no arguments; refer to the entry for w elsewhere in this appendix for information on the win argument.

Return Value

OK upon success, ERR on failure.

Notes

The line that is deleted is the line the cursor is on, specifically the cursor's row.

Unlike clrtoeol(), the entire line is erased regardless of the cursor's position.

The lines below the current line are scrolled up one notch regardless of the window's scroll setting. See scrollok().

Example

```
deleteln();
```

After this statement, all text on the same line as the cursor is erased. The rows below the line erased are scrolled up one row, with a new blank row appearing at the bottom of the window.

Sample Program

```
1    #include <ncurses.h>
2
3    int main(void)
4    {
5        int x;
```

```
 6
 7          initscr();
 8          noecho();
 9          addstr("To be, or not to be: that is the question:\n");
10          addstr("Whether 'tis nobler in the mind to suffer\n");
11          addstr("The slings and arrows of outrageous fortune,\n");
12          addstr("Or to take arms against a sea of troubles,\n");
13          addstr("And by opposing end them?\n");
14
15          move(0,0);
16          for(x=0;x<5;x++)
17          {
18              refresh();
19              getch();
20              deleteln();
21          }
22
23          endwin();
24          return 0;
25      }
```

Sample output:

```
To be, or not to be: that is the question:
Whether 'tis nobler in the mind to suffer
The slings and arrows of outrageous fortune,
Or to take arms against a sea of troubles,
And by opposing end them?
```

Each time Enter is pressed, a line is removed from the screen.

Also See

Chapter 5, delch(), insertln(), clrtoeol(), insdelln()

delscreen()

The delscreen() function deletes a SCREEN structure, freeing memory and undoing the things done when the structure was created. It's a clean-up routine.

Man Page Format

```
void delscreen(SCREEN* sp);
```

Format Reference

sp is the address of a SCREEN pointer, returned/created by the newterm() function.

Return Value

The function returns nothing.

Notes

The newterm() function creates SCREEN pointers. See newterm().

The endwin() function does not release the space referenced by a SCREEN pointer. Therefore delscreen() can be used to free up that space.

The SCREEN pointer is not reset to NULL by delscreen().

The SCREEN pointer returned by a program's first set_term() call, which represents the default terminal, should not be removed by delscreen().

Example

```
delscreen(newsp);
```

Memory associated with the SCREEN structure referenced by the pointer newsp is freed by the delscreen() function.

Sample Program

```
1     #include <ncurses.h>
2
3     int main(void)
4     {
5         SCREEN *s;
6
7         s = newterm(NULL, stdout, stdin);
8         set_term(s);
9
10        addstr("Hello!");
11
12        refresh();
13        getch();
14
15        endwin();
16        delscreen(s);
17        return 0;
18    }
```

Sample output:

```
Hello!
```

Also See

`newterm()`, `set_term()`, `endwin()`

delwin()

The `delwin()` function removes a window, releasing the memory used by both the `WINDOW` structure and the window itself.

Man Page Format

```
int delwin(WINDOW *win);
```

Format Reference

`win` refers to a `WINDOW` variable, a window created earlier in the program by the `newwin()`, `subwin()`, `derwin()`, `dupwin()`, or `newpad()` function.

Return Value

`OK` upon success, or `ERR` on failure.

Notes

The `delwin()` function removes the window's information from memory. It does not remove the window from the current screen. For that, the underlying window should be touched and refreshed. See `touchwin()` and `refresh()`.

`delwin()` can delete both subwindows and parent windows. It can also be used to remove pads. See `newpad()`.

You must delete subwindows before deleting their parents. Because subwindows share memory with the parent window, the end result of removing the parent would be memory violations by the subwindow.

Example

```
delwin(menu);
```

Here, the window `menu` and its `WINDOW` structure are removed from memory.

Sample Program

```
1    #include <ncurses.h>
2
3    #define ALPHA_W 30
4    #define ALPHA_H 5
5
6    int main(void)
7    {
8        WINDOW *alpha;
9        int x,y;
10
11       initscr(); noecho();
12       start_color();
13       init_pair(1,COLOR_WHITE,COLOR_BLUE);
14
15       x = (COLS - ALPHA_W) >> 1;
16       y = (LINES - ALPHA_H) >> 1;
17
18       addstr("Creating new window....\n");
19       refresh();
20       alpha = newwin(ALPHA_H,ALPHA_W,y,x);
21       if( alpha == NULL)
22       {
23           endwin();
24           puts("Problem creating window");
25           return(1);
26       }
27
28       addstr("Displaying window:\n");
29       addstr("Press Enter to remove the window:\n");
30       refresh();
31       wbkgd(alpha,COLOR_PAIR(1));
32       mvwaddstr(alpha,2,12,"Hello!");
33       wrefresh(alpha);
34       wgetch(alpha);
35
36       delwin(alpha);
37       addstr("Window removed: press Enter to clear it:\n");
38       refresh();
39       getch();
40
41       touchwin(stdscr);
42       addstr("Done!\n");
43       refresh();
44       getch();
45
46       endwin();
47       return 0;
48   }
```

Sample output:

```
Creating new window....
Displaying window:
```

A blue window appears in the center of the screen with the text (in white) Hello!

```
Press Enter to remove the window:
```

Press Enter.

```
Window removed: press Enter to clear it:
```

The window has been removed from memory, but the screen still needs to be updated. Press Enter:

```
Done!
```

Also See

Chapter 8, newwin(), subwin(), touchwin()

derwin()

The derwin() function is used to create a subwindow, similar to the subwin() function though derwin() places the subwindow relative to the parent window, not the screen.

Man Page Format

```
WINDOW *derwin(WINDOW *orig, int nlines, int ncols,
          int begin_y, int begin_x);
```

Format Reference

orig is a pointer to a window. That window then becomes the parent of the subwindow derwin() creates.

nlines and ncols are int values that set the subwindow's size in rows and columns, respectively. Values range from 1 on up, though the window created cannot be taller or wider than the screen or its parent. When 0 is specified for nlines or ncols, then the subwindow extends to the bottom or right edge of the window, respectively.

begin_y and begin_x give the subwindow's origin relative to the parent window. Values for begin_y and begin_x are ints, ranging from 0, 0 (the upper-left corner of the parent window) to the maximum number of rows and columns for the parent window minus the size of the subwindow.

Return Value

Upon success, a WINDOW pointer is returned, used to reference the subwindow. On failure, NULL is returned. (See NULL.)

Notes

The main difference between derwin() and subwin() is in the arguments that set the window's original. In the derwin() call, the coordinates are relative to the parent window; in subwin() the coordinates are relative to the standard screen.

Aside from the one difference in the origin coordinates, subwin() and derwin() are pretty much the same. Refer to the entry for subwin() for a host of notes that also apply to derwin().

Example

```
subby = derwin(main,MAXY-2,MAXX-2,1,1);
```

This statement creates a subwindow subby within the parent window main. The size of subby is equal to MAXY-2 rows by MAXX-2 columns, and subby's upper-left corner is set down at row 1, column 1 of the window main.

Sample Program

```
1    #include <ncurses.h>
2
3    int main(void)
4    {
5        WINDOW *pops,*sonny;
6        int x2,y2,x4,y4;
7
8        initscr();
9        start_color();
10       init_pair(1,COLOR_WHITE,COLOR_BLUE);
11       init_pair(2,COLOR_RED,COLOR_YELLOW);
12       x2 = COLS >> 1;
13       y2 = LINES >> 1;
```

```
14          x4 = (COLS - x2) >> 1;
15          y4 = (LINES - y2)  >> 1;
16
17    /* create parent and subwindow */
18          pops = newwin(y2,x2,y4,x4);
19          sonny = derwin(pops,y4,x4,2,2);
20          if(sonny == NULL)
21          {
22              endwin();
23              puts("Unable to create subwindow\n");
24              return(1);
25          }
26
27    /* color windows and splash some text */
28          wbkgd(pops,COLOR_PAIR(1));
29          waddstr(pops,"Hello, son.");
30          wbkgd(sonny,COLOR_PAIR(2));
31          waddstr(sonny,"Hello, Dad.");
32          wrefresh(pops);
33          wgetch(pops);
34
35          endwin();
36          return 0;
37    }
```

Sample output:
See Figure A-2 to view the sample output.

Also See

subwin()

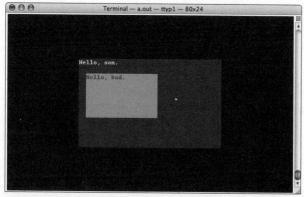

Figure A-2: The derived window (subwindow), says hello to its parent.

doupdate()

The `doupdate()` function directs NCurses to write text stored internally, from the virtual screen to the terminal. It's the latter half of what takes place during a `refresh()` operation.

Explanation

Refer to the entry for `wnoutrefresh()` for an explanation of how `doupdate()` works in the refresh process.

Man Page Format

```
int doupdate(void);
```

Format Reference

The function has no arguments.

Return Value

Always OK.

Notes

`wnoutrefresh()` is a direct companion to the `doupdate()` function.

   `doupdate()` can also be used to update the screen for a `pnoutrefresh()` function, as well as the `slk_noutrefresh()` function.

Example

```
doupdate();
```

After this statement, any text waiting to be updated on the screen will be displayed on the terminal.

Sample Program

```
1     #include <ncurses.h>
2
3     int main(void)
4     {
5         initscr();
6
```

```
 7            addstr("The screen has been updated thanks to the\n");
 8            addstr("wnoutrefresh() and doupdate() functions.\n");
 9            wnoutrefresh(stdscr);
10            doupdate();
11            getch();
12
13            endwin();
14            return 0;
15    }
```

Sample output:

```
The screen has been updated thanks to the

wnoutrefresh() and doupdate() functions.
```

Also See

`wnoutrefresh(), refresh()`

dupwin(win)

The `dupwin()` function creates an exact duplicate of a window. The new window is of the same size and at the same location as the original window.

Man Page Format

```
WINDOW *dupwin(WINDOW *win);
```

Format Reference

`win` is a `WINDOW` pointer variable, indicating a window previously created in the program.

Return Value

The function returns a pointer to a `WINDOW` variable, which is the exact duplicate of the original `win`. If there is a problem, `NULL` is returned.

Notes

Unlike a window created by using the `newwin()` function, a window created using `dupwin()` inherits the text and attributes from the original window, as well as input modes and filters, such as `keypad()`.

Example

```
doppelganger = dupwin(original);
```

This statement creates a new window, doppelganger, an exact duplicate of window original. If the operation is a success, then doppelganger is of the same size and at the same location as original, and it has the same contents. If the operation fails, doppelganger is NULL.

Sample Program

```
1    #include <ncurses.h>
2
3    int main(void)
4    {
5        WINDOW *alpha,*beta;
6        int x;
7
8        initscr();
9        start_color();
10       init_pair(1,COLOR_WHITE,COLOR_BLUE);
11       init_pair(2,COLOR_WHITE,COLOR_RED);
12
13       /* create and populate the original window */
14       alpha = newwin(5,30,0,0);
15       wbkgd(alpha,COLOR_PAIR(1));
16       for(x=0;x<75;x++)
17           wprintw(alpha,"O ");
18       wrefresh(alpha);
19       wgetch(alpha);
20
21       /* duplicate window alpha to window beta */
22       beta = dupwin(alpha);
23       if( beta == NULL)
24       {
25           endwin();
26           puts("Error creating duplicate window");
27           return 1;
28       }
29
30       /* move new window and change color */
31       mvwin(beta,10,40);
32       wbkgd(beta,COLOR_PAIR(2));
33       mvwaddstr(alpha,0,0,"This is window Alpha!");
34       mvwaddstr(beta,0,0,"This is window Beta!");
35       wrefresh(alpha);
36       wrefresh(beta);
37       wgetch(beta);
38
```

```
39      endwin();
40      return 0;
41   }
```

The sample output is shown in Figure A-3.

Also See

Chapter 10, `newwin()`, `copywin()`

echo()

The `echo()` and `noecho()` functions control the behavior of NCurses text input functions, `getch()` and `getstr()`. When `echo()` is set, the `getch()` function displays (echoes) characters typed to the screen. When `noecho()` is set, `getch()` does not display the text typed.

Man Page Formats

```
int echo(void);
int noecho(void);
```

Format Reference

`echo()` enables echoing of input text.
　　`noecho()` directs NCurses to suppress the local echo of input text.
　　Both functions lack an argument.

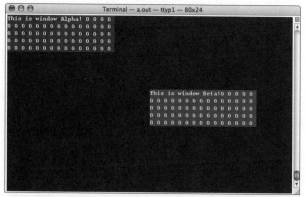

Figure A-3: Window Alpha and its duplicate, Beta

Return Value

OK upon success, ERR on failure.

Notes

Echo mode is initially set on in a new window.

It's useful to use noecho() when your program processes its own input (such as in an editor) or when the display of text isn't needed, as in a game.

noecho() does not hide the cursor. Refer to curs_set().

Examples

```
echo();
```

This statement directs NCurses to turn on the echo of text to the screen for input during the getch(), getstr() and related functions.

```
noecho();
```

This statement disables the display of text to the screen for the getch(), getstr(), and related text input functions.

Sample Program

```
1    #include <ncurses.h>
2    #include <ctype.h>
3
4    int main(void)
5    {
6        int ch;
7 87    initscr();
9
10       addstr("Normally echo is on. Type your name and press ⏎
Enter:\n");
11       refresh();
12       while( getch() != '\n')
13           ;
14
15       mvaddstr(2,0,"Now echo is off. Type your name and press ⏎
Enter:\n");
16       refresh();
17       noecho();
18       while( getch() != '\n')
19           ;
20
21       mvaddstr(4,0,"Echo is still off, but input is being ⏎
displayed\n");
```

```
22        addstr("and manipulated manually. Type your name and press ⏎
Enter:\n");
23        do
24        {
25            ch = getch();
26            addch(toupper(ch));
27            refresh();
28        } while( ch != '\n');
29
30        addstr("Press Enter to quit:");
31        refresh();
32        getch();
33
34        endwin();
35        return 0;
36   }
```

Sample output:

```
Normally echo is on. Type your name and press Enter:
Joe Bazooka
```

With echo() *set, text displays as it normally does.*

```
Now echo is off. Type your name and press Enter:
```

When noecho() *is set, nothing appears during input.*

```
Echo is still off, but input is being displayed
and manipulated manually. Type your name and press Enter:
JOE BAZOOKA
```

The noecho() *mode is still active, but above the program provides its own, modified output.*

```
Press Enter to quit:
```

Also See

getch(), getstr()

echochar()

The echochar() function provides improved performance in displaying single characters.

Explanation

echochar() is basically a combined version of the addch() and refresh() functions, yet it's more efficient than using those two functions separately. For output of multiple single characters to a window, echochar() is best.

Man Page Formats

```
int echochar(const chtype ch);
int wechochar(WINDOW *win, const chtype ch);
```

Format Reference

ch is an NCurses chtype character — a long int value that combines a single character with optional attributes. Refer to Appendix C.

Refer to the w entry elsewhere in this appendix for information on the win argument.

Return Value

ERR upon failure, or OK on success.

Notes

While echochar() is more efficient for placing text on the screen on character at a time, it is not as efficient when it comes to placing control characters.

The notes for addch() also apply to echochar(). See addch() for more information.

Examples

```
echochar(vch);
```

This statement places the character and formatting saved in the chtype variable vch on the screen.

```
echochar('H' | A_BOLD);
```

Here, a bold H is placed on the screen.

Sample Program

```
1    #include <ncurses.h>
2
3    int main(void)
```

```
 4    {
 5          char text[] = "Hello there, handsome!";
 6          char *t;
 7
 8          t = text;
 9          initscr();
10
11          while(*t)
12              echochar(*t++);
13          getch();
14
15          endwin();
16          return 0;
17    }
```

Sample output:

```
Hello there, handsome!
```

Also See

```
addch(), refresh()
```

endwin()

The endwin() function is used to end a NCurses program, returning terminal operation to normal.

Man Page Format

```
int endwin(void);
```

Format Reference

The function has no arguments.

Return Value

OK upon success, ERR on not success.

Notes

endwin() is required at the end of a NCurses program to undo what was done by either initscr() or newterm(), and to restore terminal behavior.

The `endwin()` function does not remove windows or other data structures from memory.

It's possible to use `endwin()` merely as a way to escape from NCurses visual mode and briefly return to tty mode. To restore NCurses operations, merely call `refresh()` or `doupdate()`. But you must still call `endwin()` again when the NCurses program is done. (See the Sample Programs.)

This function does move the cursor. After calling `endwin()`, the cursor is placed on the lower-left corner of the screen.

Example

```
endwin();
```

This statement restores normal terminal operation.

Sample Program #1

```
1    #include <ncurses.h>
2
3    int main(void)
4    {
5        initscr();
6
7        addstr("Now you're in NCurses.\n");
8        refresh();
9        getch();
10
11       endwin();
12
13       fputs("Now you're not in NCurses.\n",stdout);
14       fflush(stdout);
15       getch();
16
17       addstr("Now you're back in NCurses again.\n");
18       refresh();
19       getch();
20
21       endwin();
22       return 0;
23   }
```

Sample output:

```
Now you're in NCurses.
```

Press Enter and you'll see the tty screen:

```
Now you're not in NCurses.
```

Press Enter and you're returned to NCurses:

```
Now you're in NCurses
Now you're back in NCurses again.
```

Sample Program #2

```
1      #include <ncurses.h>
2      #include <stdlib.h>
.3
4      int main(void)
5      {
6          initscr();
7
8          addstr("Press Enter to go to the shell....:\n");
9          refresh();
10         getch();
11
12         endwin();
13         system("`echo $SHELL`");
14
15         addstr("Back safe and sound....\n");
16         refresh();
17         getch();
18
19         endwin();
20         return 0;
21     }
```

Sample output:

```
Press Enter to go to the shell....:
```

*Press Enter and you'll see your shell prompt displayed. Type **exit** to return to the NCurses program, and:*

```
Press Enter to go to the shell....:
Back safe and sound....
```

Also See

```
initscr(),newterm(),isendwin()
```

erase()

The clear() function clears the screen or named window, writing blanks, or space characters, to every screen position.

Man Page Formats

```
int erase(void);
int werase(WINDOW *win);
```

Format Reference

The `erase()` function has no arguments. It's a pseudo function that affects only the standard screen.

Refer to the `w` prefix entry later in this appendix for information on the `win` argument.

Return Value

Always returns `OK`.

Notes

You don't see the window erased until a call to `refresh()` updates the window.

Clearing the screen also homes the cursor; after the `erase()` function, the cursor is placed at location 0, 0.

The `erase()` function removes only characters and their attributes. It does not affect the background character and its attributes. If a background character is set via `bkgd()` or `bkgdset()`, then that character will show up in the blanks `erase()` fills the screen with.

`erase()` is the same as `werase(stdscr)`.

The `erase()` function is visually the same as the `clear()` function; however, `clear()` also calls the `clearok()` function to enforce the erasure and redisplay of the screen.

Because of the overhead involved with `clear()`, `erase()` is the quicker of the two functions, though on many terminals the speed difference is negligible.

Examples

```
erase();
```

The statement erases the standard screen.

```
werase(sidebar);
```

The statement clears away the text in the window `sidebar`.

Sample Program

```
1    #include <ncurses.h>
2
3    int main(void)
4    {
5        int c,y,x,cmax;
6
7        initscr();
8
9        getmaxyx(stdscr,y,x);
10       cmax = (x * y) / 5;
11       for(c=0;c<cmax;c++) addstr("blah ");
12       refresh();
13       getch();
14
15       erase();          /* clear the screen */
16       refresh();           /* don't forget this! */
17       getch();
18
19       endwin();
20       return 0;
21   }
```

Sample output:
The screen is filled with the text blah blah blah. *Pressing the Enter key clears the screen.*

Also See

Chapter 6, clear(), refresh()

erasechar()

The erasechar() function returns whatever character or character code currently serves as the terminal's Erasechar, or ERASE, key.

Man Page Format

```
char erasechar(void);
```

Format Reference

The function has no arguments.

Return Value

A `char` value is returned, indicating the terminal's currently set Erasechar.

Notes

The Erasechar is the key or key combination you press to back up and erase text at the command prompt. On the keyboard it could be Del, Backspace, Rubout, Ctrl+H or ^H, code 0x7F or ^?, or what have you.

The `getstr()` functions properly interpret the Erasechar. Other input functions can use the `erasechar()` function to determine which character is the Erasechar and then programming can be used to adjust behavior appropriately. (Or just use `getstr()` instead.)

The `cbreak()` and `raw()` modes modify NCurses input functions to ignore the Erasechar key's function. When Erasechar is input, it's treated just like any other character, typically displayed on the screen in the ^c format.

The `unctrl()` function can be used to translate a control code, such as the code used for Erasechar, into the displayable ^c format.

Example

```
if( ch == echochar())
```

The `if` condition tests true when the value of variable `ch` is the same as the terminal's Erasechar.

Sample Program

```
1    #include <ncurses.h>
2
3    int main(void)
4    {
5        char ch;
6
7        initscr();
8
9        ch = erasechar();
10       printw("The Erasechar is 0x%02x or %s\n",ch,unctrl(ch));
11       refresh();
12       getch();
13
14       endwin();
15       return 0;
16   }
```

Sample output:

```
The Erasechar is 0x7f or ^?
```

Also See

`killchar(), cbreak(), raw(), unctrl()`

ERR

NCurses uses the `int` value `ERR` as a return value for functions that have not or are unable to complete their tasks.

Man Page Format

Not applicable.

Format Reference

`ERR` can be used like any other constant, though it is most often found in a comparison:

```
if( function() == ERR)
```

Or if the return value from a function is saved in a variable, r:

```
if( r == ERR)
```

Or:

```
while( function() == ERR)
```

Return Value

The value of `ERR` is set in `NCURSES.H` to -1.

Notes

Not every function returns `ERR` on failure. Some don't return anything; others may return `NULL` or have some other factor used to determine the function's failure.

`ERR`'s counterpart is the `OK` constant. See `OK`.

Examples

```
if( touchwin(menu) == ERR)
```

The statement works out to be true when the `touchwin()` function fails.

```
nodelay(stdscr,TRUE);
while( getch() == ERR)
```

Here, the `while` loop continues to spin as long as no key is touched on the keyboard.

Sample Program

```
1     #include <ncurses.h>
2
3     int main(void)
4     {
5         int y = 0,x = 0, r;
6
7         initscr();
8
9         addstr("You Move The Cursor!\n");
10        addstr("Enter the Y (row) coordinate: ");
11        refresh();
12        scanw("%d",&y);
13        addstr("Enter the X (column) coordinate: ");
14        refresh();
15        scanw("%d",&x);
16
17        r = move(y,x);
18        if(r == ERR)
19            mvaddstr(3,0,"You cannot move the cursor there!");
20        else
21        {
22            mvaddstr(3,0,"You have moved the cursor!");
23            move(y,x);
24        }
25        refresh();
26        getch();
27
28        endwin();
29        return 0;
30    }
```

Sample output:

```
You Move The Cursor!
Enter the Y (row) coordinate: 12
Enter the X (column) coordinate: 40
You have moved the cursor!
```

Also See

OK

FALSE

NCurses uses the Boolean value FALSE for comparisons, for setting options, as a value returned from specific functions.

Man Page Format

Not applicable.

Format Reference

FALSE is used in one of many ways:

```
function([arg(s)],FALSE)
```

Some functions use FALSE as shown above to reset an option in a NCurses function.

```
var = function([arg(s)])
```

The value FALSE may be returned by some NCurses functions. Above, the value of var could be either TRUE or FALSE. var is a bool variable type.

```
if( eval == FALSE)
while([eval ==] FALSE)
```

The value FALSE can be used in comparisons, as shown above.

Functions that return FALSE can also be used immediately inside comparisons:

```
if( function([arg(s)] )
while( function([arg(s)] )
```

Here, when the function returns a FALSE value, the program responds accordingly.

Return Value

The value of FALSE is set in NCURSES.H to zero.

Notes

The logical opposite of FALSE is TRUE. Functions that use or return FALSE can equally use or return TRUE, depending on the situation. Refer to the Notes under the TRUE entry later in this Appendix, for a list of NCurses functions that use the value FALSE.

Examples

```
if(can_change_color())
```

Here, `if` evaluates the results of the `can_change_color()` function. If `FALSE` is returned, then the terminal cannot use custom colors for text attributes.

```
meta(stdscr,FALSE);
```

This function truncates text input from the standard screen to 7-bits wide instead of 8. (See `meta()`.)

Sample Program

```
1     #include <ncurses.h>
2
3     int main(void)
4     {
5         bool tf;
6         initscr();
7
8         tf =  has_colors();
9         if( tf == FALSE)
10            addstr("This terminal cannot do colors.\n");
11        else
12            addstr("This terminal can do colors.\n");
13        refresh();
14        getch();
15
16        endwin();
17        return 0;
18    }
```

Sample output:

```
This terminal can do colors.
```

Or:

```
This terminal cannot do colors.
```

Also See

TRUE

filter()

The filter() function restricts all of NCurses output to only one line on the screen.

Man Page Format

```
void filter(void);
```

Format Reference

Nothing ventured.

Return Value

Nothing gained.

Notes

filter() must be used before the initscr() or newterm() function that initializes NCurses.

The filter() function disables some of the terminal's cursor movement commands, specifically those that move the cursor up or down or to the home position. In fact, the terminal command to home the cursor is reinterpreted as a simple carriage return when the filter() is active.

The documentation describes filter() as disabling the cursor movement commands described in Table A-5.

Table A-5: Cursor movements disabled by filter()

NAME	TERMCAP	DESCRIPTION
clear	cl	Clears the screen.
cud	DO	Moves the cursor down a given number of lines.
cud1	do	Moves the cursor down one line.
cup	cm	Moves the cursor to a specific row/column location or to Home.
cuu	UP	Moves the cursor up a given number of lines.
cuu1	up	Moves the cursor up one line.
vpa	cv	Moves the cursor to row 1.

The `filter()` function sets the value of the `LINES` constant to 1.

The cursor can be moved to specific locations on the first line (row zero), but attempts to move the cursor to other lines when `filter()` is on results in no text being displayed.

The `bkgd()` functions affect only the current line of the screen when `filter()` is on.

There is no `nofilter()` function to reverse this function. To undo the `filter()` effects, open the terminal again with `newterm()`.

Example

```
filter();
initscr();
```

These statements direct NCurses to limit its output to only the top line of the screen, or to format the output for a terminal that can display or print only one line of text at a time.

Sample Program

```
1     #include <ncurses.h>
2
3     int main(void)
4     {
5         char name[80];
6
7         filter();
8         initscr();
9
10        addstr("With the filter on, all of NCurses fits on only\n");
11        addstr("one line of the screen.\n");
12        refresh();
13        getch();
14
15        mvaddstr(0,0,"Enter your name: ");
16        refresh();
17        getnstr(name,79);
18        mvprintw(0,0,"Pleased to meet you, %s!\n",name);
19        refresh();
20        getch();
21
22        endwin();
23        return 0;
24    }
```

Sample output:

```
With the filter on, all of NCurses fits on only one line of the screen.
```

Note how both lines of text appear on the same screen line? Press Enter:

```
Enter your name: n, all of NCurses fits on only one line of the screen.
```

The cursor is "homed," but the line isn't erased.
Input your name, press Enter and the line will be erased:

```
Pleased to meet you, Joe Bazooka!
```

Also See

LINES, initscr(), newterm()

flash()

The flash() function causes the screen to *blink,* or quickly display a solid color, then return to normal. This is done as an attention-getting move, similar to playing a tone over the computer's speaker.

Man Page Format

```
int flash(void);
```

Format Reference

The function takes no arguments.

Return Value

Supposedly, if the screen flashes, OK is returned. flash() returns ERR otherwise. Both OK and ERR are defined in NCURSES.H.

Do not rely upon the ERR return value to determine whether or not the terminal really did flash.

Notes

flash() is used mostly an alternative to the beep() function, specifically designed for situations where noise is undesirable or for the hearing impaired.

This function doesn't work if the terminal has been configured not to flash.

On most monitors, the flash is made of the current text foreground color.

Some terminals may both beep and flash the screen when the flash() function is used.

Example

```
flash();
```

And the screen winks at you.

Sample Program

```
1      #include <ncurses.h>
2
3      int main(void)
4      {
5          initscr();
6
7          addstr("Press any key to flash:\n");
8          refresh();
9          getch();
10         flash();
11         addstr("Thanks!\n");
12         refresh();
13         getch();
14
15         endwin();
16         return 0;
17     }
```

Sample output:

```
Press any key to flash:
```

(Press Enter.)
The screen winks at you!

```
Thanks!
```

Also See

Chapter 3, beep()

flushinp()

The flushinp() function clears the keyboard input buffer, or queue, ensuring that no characters are waiting to be read.

Man Page Format

```
int flushinp(void);
```

Format Reference

The function takes no arguments.

Return Value

Always OK.

Notes

Flushing input is recommended for situations where the user is posed a vital question. By using `flushinp()` you ensure that no stray keys will be read, for example, as input to a critical yes/no question.

You can use the `intrflush()` function to have keyboard input flushed when the user presses an interrupt key. See `interflush()`.

Example

```
flushinp();
```

This statement removes all characters typed and waiting in the keyboard input queue.

Sample Program

```
1     #include <ncurses.h>
2
3     int main(void)
4     {
5         char buffer[81];
6
7         initscr();
8
9         addstr("Type on the keyboard whilst I wait...\n");
10        refresh();
11        napms(5000);              /* 5 seconds */
12
13        addstr("Here is what you typed:\n");
14        flushinp();
15        getnstr(buffer,80);
16        refresh();
17
18        endwin();
```

```
19        return 0;
20    }
```

Sample output:

```
Type on the keyboard whilst I wait...
```

There is a pause of 5 seconds while you type.

```
Here is what you typed:
```

Nothing is displayed, because the input was flushed. Press Enter.

Also See

Chapter 7, `intrflush()`, `quiflush()`, `typeahead()`

getbegyx()

The `getbegyx()` function returns the upper-left coordinates, the top-left corner, of the named window.

Man Page Format

```
void getbegyx(WINDOW *win, int y, int x);
```

Format Reference

`win` refers to a specific window. It's a `WINDOW` variable representing a window or subwindow. (Pads do not have an origin coordinate.)

   `y` and `x` are `int` variables that will hold the starting row and column number of the `win` window. Row 0, column 0 represents the upper-left corner of the screen. Note that these are not pointer variables.

Return Value

This function is really a macro and as such its return value doesn't exist and shouldn't be used.

Notes

The `y` and `x` values for the standard screen, `stdscr`, are always 0, 0.

   The `y` and `x` arguments are not pointers; do not prefix them with the & operator!

The coordinates returned are relative to the standard screen.

The other coordinates of the window's right side and bottom can be calculated by using the getmaxyx() function, the getbegyx() function, and a modicum of math.

To discover the beginning coordinates of a subwindow within a parent window, use the getparyx() function; see getparyx().

A window's location can be changed. See mvwin().

Pads are not created on the terminal screen, and therefore they do not have a beginning coordinate or origin.

Example

```
getbegyx(menu,mrow,mcol);
```

This statement fetches the beginning location of the window menu and places the row and column coordinates into the mrow and mcol variables, respectively.

Sample Program

```
1    #include <ncurses.h>
2
3    int main(void)
4    {
5        int row,col;
6        WINDOW *peri;
7
8        initscr(); noecho();
9        start_color();
10       init_pair(1,COLOR_WHITE,COLOR_BLUE);
11
12       peri = newwin(5,30,2,30);
13       wbkgd(peri,COLOR_PAIR(1));
14       waddstr(peri,"I am the peripatetic window");
15
16       getbegyx(peri,row,col);
17       printw("The origin for window %s is row %d, column %d.\n",\
18           "peri",row,col);
19       refresh();
20       wrefresh(peri);
21       getch();
22
23       wtouchln(stdscr,2,5,1);
24       mvwin(peri,12,40);
25       wrefresh(peri);
26       getbegyx(peri,row,col);
27       printw("The origin for window %s is now row %d, column ⏎
%d.\n",\
28           "peri",row,col);
```

```
29        refresh();
30        getch();
31
32        endwin();
33        return 0;
34    }
```

The sample output is shown in Figure A-4.
Press Enter, and you will see what appears in Figure A-5.

Also See

```
getparyx(),getmaxyx(),mvwin()
```

Figure A-4: Window *peri*'s original location

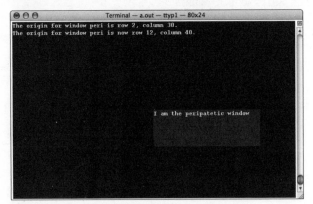

Figure A-5: Window *peri*'s final resting place

getbkgd()

The getbkgd() function returns the current background attribute for the name window.

Man Page Format

```
chtype getbkgd(WINDOW *win);
```

Format Reference

win is a WINDOW variable representing a window in NCurses.

Return Value

A chtype variable is returned, which includes any characters, attributes, or color pair applied as the background for the named window.

If the background has not been set, either by bkgd() or bkgdset(), then getbkgd() returns zero.

Notes

Refer to attrset() earlier in this appendix for a list of NCurses attribute constants. Also refer to Appendix C for more information on the chtype variable.

It is up to your code to extract information about the specific formats used from the chtype variable getbkgd() returns.

The chtype merely lists the color pair being used for the background. You can, however, use the pair_content() function to determine which two colors have been assigned to the color pair.

Example

```
bkgdattrib = getbkgd(main);
```

Here, a chtype character holding the attributes for the background of window main is saved in the bkgdattrib variable.

Sample Program

```
1    #include <ncurses.h>
2
3    int main(void)
4    {
5        chtype ch,a;
```

```
 6          char bgchar;
 7          int bgcolor,x;
 8          short fore,back;
 9          char colors[8][8] = { "Black", "Red", "Green", "Yellow",
10                          "Blue", "Magenta", "Cyan", "White" };
11          char attribs[15][11] = { "Standout", "Underline", "Reverse",
12                          "Blink", "Dim", "Bold",
13                          "AltChar", "Invis", "Protect",
14                          "Horizontal", "Left", "Low",
15                          "Right", "Top", "Vertical" };
16
17          a = 0x10000;
18
19          initscr();
20          start_color();
21          init_pair(1,COLOR_WHITE,COLOR_BLUE);
22          bkgd(COLOR_PAIR(1) | A_BOLD);
23
24          ch = getbkgd(stdscr);
25
26          bgchar = (ch & A_CHARTEXT);          /* Read character */
27          bgcolor = (ch & A_COLOR) >> 8;        /* Read color pair */
28          pair_content(bgcolor,&fore,&back);       /* Read colors */
29
30          printw("Background chtype is 0x%04x\n",(unsigned)ch);
31          printw("Background character is 0x%02x or '%c'\n",\
32              bgchar,bgchar);
33          printw("Background color pair is %d\n",bgcolor);
34          printw("\tForeground color is %s\n",colors[fore]);
35          printw("\tBackground color is %s\n",colors[back]);
36          addstr("Other attributes found:\n");
37          for(x=0;x<15;x++)
38          {
39              if(a & ch)
40                  printw("%s\n",attribs[x]);
41              a <<= 1;
42          }
43          refresh();
44          getch();
45
46          endwin();
47          return 0;
48      }
```

Sample output:

```
Background chtype is 0x200120
Background character is 0x20 or ' '
Background color pair is 1
        Foreground color is White
        Background color is Blue
```

```
Other attributes found:
Bold
```

Also See

`bkgd()`, `attr_get()`, `pair_content()`, Appendix C

getch()

The `getch()` function reads a single character input from the keyboard.

Man Page Formats

```
int getch(void);
int wgetch(WINDOW *win);
int mvgetch(int y, int x);
int mvwgetch(WINDOW *win, int y, int x);
```

Format Reference

The function has no arguments; refer to the entries for *w*, *mv*, and *mvw* elsewhere in this appendix for more information on the `win`, `y`, and `x` arguments.

Return Value

Under typical operation, `getch()` returns an `int` value equal to the key pressed, such as a specific character, symbol, control code, and so on.

When the `keypad()` function is set `TRUE` for a specific window, then a `getch()` call referencing that window can also return special keys on the keyboard. Refer to Appendix D for a list of these keys.

When the `nodelay()` function is `TRUE` for a specific window, then `getch()` calls referencing that window return `ERR` when a key is not waiting in the input queue. Otherwise the `int` key value is returned as normal.

Notes

It is not necessary to call `refresh()` after the `getch()` function as `getch()` naturally echoes its input to the screen. Also see `echo()`.

The functions listed in Table A-6 affect the behavior and return value of `getch()`. (Refer to each entry elsewhere in this appendix for details.)

NCurses has only one input queue; therefore, it may seem bizarre that wgetch() has a win argument. This argument isn't used to direct input *from* a particular window, but rather for the selective application of specific input filters that can be assigned to a window. The functions that apply such filtering are: intrflush(), keypad(), meta(), nodelay(), and notimeout(), as listed in Table A-6.

The wgetch() function also determines which window is checked for changes and that window is then refreshed For example, by specifying wgetch(two), you get a character from the keyboard *and* refresh the window two.

To apply a window-specific input modification to wgetch(), use stdscr, the standard screen.

Table A-6: NCurses functions that affect input

FUNCTION ON/OFF	DESCRIPTION
cbreak() nocbreak()	Disables text input line buffering and erase/kill character processing
echo() noecho()	Controls display (echo) of text as its input
halfdelay()	Similar to cbreak mode, though with a timeout value
intrflush(win,TRUE) intrflush(win,FALSE)	Activates text buffer flush on interrupt key input
keypad(win,TRUE) keypad(win,FALSE)	Allows special keyboard keys to be input; refer to Appendix D
meta(win,TRUE) meta(win,FALSE)	Determines whether 7 or 8 bits of keyboard input are read
nodelay(win,TRUE) nodelay(win,FALSE)	Transforms getch() into a nonblocking call
notimeout(win,TRUE) notimeout(win,FALSE)	Controls a delay after Esc key press
raw() noraw()	Disables all keyboard buffering and key traps; enters *raw mode* text processing
qiflush() noqiflush()	Flushes input on the SUSP, QUIT, and INTR keys
timeout(delay)	Similar to cbreak (and halfdelay) mode but with a variable timeout value
typeahead()	Enables/disables typeahead interrupt on refresh

The echo()/noecho() functions control whether or not getch() displays its input on the screen. Normally, getch() displays each character typed as its input; no refresh() is required.

To turn getch() into a non-blocking call (meaning getch() does not wait for a key to be pressed), use nodelay(). See nodelay().

To read non-alphanumeric keys on the keyboard, the keypad() function is used. See keypad().

Input modification functions that are not window-specific apply to all input for getch(), as well as getstr().

To read a character at a specific location on the screen, the inch() function is used.

To insert a character, pushing text to the right, use the insch() function.

Remember that getch() returns an int value, not a char. There are still a few old fogies such as myself who will mistakenly use char variables with getch(). Nope! Use int variables.

Examples

```
c = getch();
```

Here, the int variable c receives the value of the next key typed at the keyboard.

```
key = mvgetch(5,30);
```

Here, the cursor is moved to row 5, column 3, where the program waits for a key to be pressed and its value stored in the key variable.

```
while( (ch=getch()) != '\n')
```

The while loop continues to turn, once for each key pressed at the keyboard, but it will stop when the newline character is input (pressing Enter).

```
keypad(editor,TRUE);
ch = wgetch(editor);
```

Above, the keypad() function is applied to the window editor, meaning that special keys can be read. Those keys are then read using the wgetch() function, and stored in the ch variable, along with any alphanumeric keys read.

Sample Program

```
1    #include <ncurses.h>
2
3    int main(void)
```

```
4    {
5        int key;
6
7        initscr();
8
9        noecho();              /* turn input echo off */
10       addstr("Type your name: ");
11       while( (key=getch()) != '\n')
12       {
13           switch(key)
14           {
15               case 'a':
16                   addch('A');
17                   break;
18               case 'e':
19                   addch('E');
20                   break;
21               case 'i':
22                   addch('I');
23                   break;
24               case 'o':
25                   addch('O');
26                   break;
27               case 'u':
28                   addch('U');
29                   break;
30               default:
31                   addch(key);
32                   break;
33           }
34           refresh();
35       }
36       getch();
37
38       endwin();
39       return 0;
40   }
```

Sample output:

```
Type your name:
```

As you type, any vowels typed appear in uppercase.

Also See

Chapter 2, Chapter 7, Appendix D, ungetch(), getstr(), insch()

getmaxyx()

getmaxyx() fetches the height and width of a named window in rows and columns. Technically, this is not a function but a macro defined in NCURSES.H.

Man Page Format

```
void getmaxyx(WINDOW *win, int y, int x);
```

Format Reference

win is the name of a WINDOW pointer representing a window created earlier in the code. stdscr can be used for the standard screen.

y is an int variable. After the call to getmaxyx(), that variable holds the number of rows found in win. Values returned by y range from 1 on up to the window's height.

x is an int variable. After the call to getmaxyx() it holds the number of columns found in win. Values returned by x range from 1 on up to the window's width.

Return Value

getmaxyx() is a macro and its return value is undefined.

Notes

Rows go left and right across the screen and may also be called *lines*. They're counted from the top of the screen to the bottom. In the Cartesian coordinate system, rows represent Y values.

Columns go up and down. They're counted from the left of the screen to the right. In the Cartesian coordinate system, columns represent X values.

The key to remembering the order of the arguments is in the name of the getmaxyx() function itself: *Get Max Y X*, the y or row value comes first.

The arguments y and x are int variables, not pointers. Even though it seems like they should be prefixed with the & (address) operator, do not do this.

The values returned by y and x measure screen height and width starting with the number 1. But note that when placing the cursor on the screen, the first row and first column are numbered zero. So while getmaxyx() may return 25 and 80 for the number of row and col, the bottom right location on the window is 24, 79.

As a pseudo function, getmaxyx() merely reads the window's size values from the WINDOW structure. See WINDOW for more information.

The size of the standard screen is stored in the COLS and LINES variables defined by NCurses when the initscr() function is run.

A macro getmaxy() exists in NCURSES.H. It returns the maximum row value for a named window. The format is getmaxy(win), and it returns the maximum row value for window win, or ERR upon failure.

Example

```
getmaxyx(menu,menurow,menucol);
```

This statement reads the height and width of the window menu, storing the total number of rows in menurow, and the number of columns in menucol.

Sample Program

```
1    #include <ncurses.h>
2
3    int main(void)
4    {
5        int x,y;
6
7        initscr();
8
9        getmaxyx(stdscr,y,x);
10       printw("Window size is %d rows, %d columns.\n",y,x);
11       refresh();
12       getch();
13
14       endwin();
15       return 0;
16   }
```

Sample output:

```
Window size is 24 rows by 80 columns.
```

Also See

Chapter 4, newwin(), COLS, LINES, WINDOW

getmouse() → 287

getnstr()

See getstr().

getparyx()

The `getparyx()` function returns a subwindow's origin relative to its parent window.

Man Page Format

```
void getparyx(WINDOW *win, int y, int x);
```

Format Reference

`win` is the name of a `WINDOW` variable representing a subwindow.

`y` and `x` are `int` variables that will hold the subwindow's origin relative to the parent window. These are not pointers! `y` and `x` are relative to the parent window, where row 0 and column 0 are the upper-left corner of the parent window.

Return Value

`getparyx()` is a macro and as such it has no return value.

Notes

When `win` is not a subwindow, the values -1 and -1 are returned for `y` and `x`.

Remember that the coordinates returned are relative to the parent window, not the screen.

The `getbegyx()` function is used to return a window's coordinates relative to the screen. `getbegyx()` can be used on any window.

Example

```
getparyx(footer,y,x);
```

Here, the origin of subwindow `footer` relative to its parent window is saved in `int` variables `y` (row) and `x` (column).

Sample Program

```
1    #include <ncurses.h>
2
3    int main(void)
4    {
5        WINDOW *subby,*sonny;
```

```
 6          int row,col;
 7
 8          initscr();
 9          start_color();
10          init_pair(1,COLOR_WHITE,COLOR_BLUE);
11          init_pair(2,COLOR_YELLOW,COLOR_RED);
12
13          subby = newwin(10,30,10,40);
14          wbkgd(subby,COLOR_PAIR(1));
15          getparyx(subby,row,col);
16          wprintw(subby,"This subwin's org: %d, %d.",row,col);
17          wrefresh(subby);
18
19          sonny = subwin(subby,7,30,13,40);
20          wbkgd(sonny,COLOR_PAIR(2));
21          getparyx(sonny,row,col);
22          wprintw(sonny,"This subwin's org: %d, %d.",row,col);
23          wrefresh(sonny);
24
25          wgetch(sonny);
26
27          endwin();
28          return 0;
29      }
```

The sample output is shown in Figure A-6.

Also See

```
subwin(), getmaxyx()
```

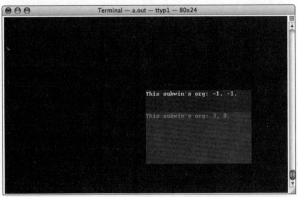

Figure A-6: The `getbegyx()` function reads the windows' origin.

getmouse()   *Should be on Page 284*

The getmouse() function is used to retrieve a mouse event, storing information about the event — button state, coordinates — in a special MEVENT structure.

Man Page Format

```
int getmouse(MEVENT *event);
```

Format Reference

event is the address of a MEVENT structure, which will be used to store information about a mouse event. See MEVENT for the details.

Return Value

OK when an event was captured or ERR if no event was visible.

Notes

The types of events getmouse() monitors are determined in advance by the mousemask() function. See mousemask().

It's actually the getch() function that reads when a mouse event has occurred. The getmouse() function is used to place information about that event into the MEVENT structure, which the program can then act upon.

Example

```
getmouse(&me);
```

This statement reads a recent mouse event, storing information about the event in the MEVENT structure referenced by variable me.

Sample Program

```
1    #include <ncurses.h>
2
3    int main(void)
4    {
5        MEVENT mort;
6        int ch;
```

```
 7
 8          initscr();
 9          noecho();
10          keypad(stdscr,TRUE);
11
12          mousemask(BUTTON1_CLICKED,NULL);
13          while(1)
14          {
15              ch = getch();
16              if( ch == KEY_MOUSE )
17              {
18                  getmouse(&mort);
19                  move(0,0);
20                  clrtoeol();
21                  printw("Mouse clicked at %d, %d",mort.y,mort.x);
22                  refresh();
23                  continue;
24              }
25              if( ch == '\n' )
26                  break;
27          }
28
29          endwin();
30          return 0;
31      }
```

Sample output:
Clicking mouse button one results in its position being displayed:

```
Mouse clicked at 10, 14
```

Also See

Chapter 13, NCURSES_MOUSE_VERSION, MEVENT, mousemask(), unget mouse()

getstr()

The getstr() function reads a line of text from the terminal, with a newline or a carriage return (Enter/Return) character marking the end of input.

Man Page Formats

```
int getstr(char *str);
int getnstr(char *str, int n);
int wgetstr(WINDOW *win, char *str);
int wgetnstr(WINDOW *win, char *str, int n);
```

```
int mvgetstr(int y, int x, char *str);
int mvwgetstr(WINDOW *win, int y, int x, char *str);
int mvgetnstr(int y, int x, char *str, int n);
int mvwgetnstr(WINDOW *, int y, int x, char *str, int n);
```

Format Reference

str represents string variable (char array) storage, either an array declared or a buffer allocated via malloc() or a similar function.

For those functions where n is specified, n is an int value representing the maximum number of characters that can be input. The value of n should be one less than the size of the buffer to account for the \0 (null) character getstr() appends to the end of the string.

Refer to the entries for *w, mv,* and *mvw* elsewhere in this appendix for information on the w, mv, and mvw variations to this function.

Return Value

OK on success; ERR upon failure.

Notes

I highly recommend using the getnstr() variation of the functions, which helps limit input and avoids the potential for a nasty buffer overflow.

Attempting to input more characters than n has specified results in the terminal beeping at the user, once for each character over the n limit.

When input is longer than the length of the current line, getstr() wraps text to the following line.

Text input by getstr() overwrites any existing text in the row. To insert a string of text, use the insstr() function instead, though note that insstr() does not read text from the keyboard. See insstr().

The \n or \r that ends input is not included with the string returned by getstr().

getstr() is essentially a series of calls to the getch() function, and therefore the input modification functions that change getch()'s behavior also apply to getstr(). See getch() for the details.

The Killchar and Erasechar keys function appropriately for the getstr() function. Refer to killchar() and erasechar() for details. When keypad() is set true for a window, the wgetstr() functions interpret both the KEY_BACKSPACE and KEY_LEFT keys as the Killchar key.

Using the Killchar key does not count as an input character when n is specified in the getnstr() functions. The same holds for Erasechar. getnstr() properly maintains the number of characters input, resetting input characters to zero when Erasechar is pressed and decrementing input characters by 1 when Killchar is pressed.

Using the Erasechar key returns the cursor to its original location. This holds true even when input text has wrapped to the following line.

Examples

```
mvgetnstr(5,12,command,64);
```

This statement moves the cursor to row 5, column 12 and accepts up to 64 characters of input to be stored in the buffer referenced by the command variable.

```
wgetnstr(main,input[y],len);
```

This statement reads input as filtered through the window main. Text is stored in the input[y] variable, and only len characters may be input.

Sample Program

```
1     #include <ncurses.h>
2
3     int main(void)
4     {
5         char first[50],last[4];
6
7         initscr();
8         addstr("Enter the first 3 letters of your first name? ");
9         refresh();
10        getnstr(first,3);
11
12        addstr("Enter the first 3 letters of your last name? ");
13        refresh();
14        getnstr(last,3);
15
16        printw("Your secret agent name is %s%s!",first,last);
17        refresh();
18        getch();
19
20        endwin();
21        return 0;
22    }
```

Sample output:

```
Enter the first 3 letters of your first name? Con
Enter the first 3 letters of your last name? Dor
Your secret agent name is ConDor!
```

Also See

Chapter 2, `getch()`, `scanw()`

getsyx()

The `getsyx()` reads the virtual screen's cursor location.

Explanation

NCurses is a window-oriented environment. The cursor's position is normally read relative to a window, such as the standard screen. Yet the cursor also has a location in the real world on the terminal. It's the `getsyx()` function that returns that real world location.

Man Page Format

```
void getsyx(int y, int x);
```

Format Reference

`y` and `x` are `int` variables, not pointers. After the function call, `y` holds the value of the cursor's row and `x` holds the column value.

Return Value

This function is a macro, and as such its return value is unimportant.

Notes

Values returned in `y` and `x` range from 0, for the upper-left corner of the window, though the maximum row and column values for the standard screen.

When -1, -1 is returned it means that `leaveok()` has been set `TRUE` for a window.

To read the cursor's location in a window use the `getyx()` function.

When using the `ripoffline()` function you should limit the use of the values returned by `getsyx()` only as arguments for the `setsyx()` function.

I get the hint from the man pages that `getsyx()` is really meant as an internal NCurses function to be used in conjunction with `setsyx()`.

Example

```
getsyx(row,col);
```

This statement reads the cursor's location on the virtual screen, saving it into the row and col variables.

Sample Program

```
1    #include <ncurses.h>
2
3    int main(void)
4    {
5        WINDOW *win;
6        int vy,vx,stdy,stdx,winy,winx;
7
8        initscr();
9        noecho();
10       win = newwin(5,20,10,30);
11       box(win,0,0);
12       waddstr(win,"This is 'win'");
13       wrefresh(win);
14
15       getyx(win,winy,winx);
16       getyx(stdscr,stdy,stdx);
17       getsyx(vy,vx);
18       printw("In Window win, the cursor is at %d,%d.\n",winy,winx);
19       printw("On the standard screen, the cursor is at ⊃
%d,%d.\n",stdy,stdx);
20       printw("On the virtual screen, the cursor is at ⊃
%d,%d.\n",vy,vx);
21       refresh();
22       getch();
23
24       getsyx(vy,vx);
25       printw("Now on the virtual screen, the cursor is at ⊃
%d,%d.\n",vy,vx);
26       refresh();
27       getch();
28
29       leaveok(win,TRUE);
30       wrefresh(win);
31       getyx(win,winy,winx);
32       getsyx(vy,vx);
33       printw("In Window win, the cursor is now at ⊃
%d,%d.\n",winy,winx);
34       printw("On the virtual screen, the cursor is ⊃
now at %d,%d.\n",vy,vx);
35       refresh();
36       getch();
37
38       endwin();
39       return 0;
40   }
```

Sample output:

```
In Window win, the cursor is at 0,13.
On the standard screen, the cursor is at 0,0.
On the virtual screen, the cursor is at 10,43.
```

Press Enter.

```
Now on the virtual screen, the cursor is at 3,0.
```

Press Enter again.

```
In Window win, the cursor is now at 0,13.
On the virtual screen, the cursor is now at -1,-1.
```

Also See

`leaveok()`, `getyx()`, `setsyx()`

getwin()

The `getwin()` function reads a window from disk, one previously saved via the `putwin()` function.

Man Page Format

```
WINDOW *getwin(FILE *filep);
```

Format Reference

`filep` is a `FILE` variable representing a file opened for reading on disk. The file should be a window previously saved by using the `putwin()` function.

Return Value

On success, a window is created and a `WINDOW` pointer returned representing that window. On failure, `NULL` is returned.

Notes

`getwin()` is the companion function to `putwin()`, which saves `WINDOW` data to disk.

The window is restored in the same position and size on the screen. Even the cursor is placed in the same position from which it was saved.

All text attributes are restored when the saved window is loaded via getwin(). The same color pairs, if specified, are assigned as attributes though the color values of each pair are not retained (unless the program is using the same color pair values).

Example

```
nextwin = getwin(wfp);
```

The statement creates a new window named footnote based on data previously saved to disk and referenced by the wfp file pointer.

Sample Program

This program assumes a file named WINDOW.DAT has previously been saved to disk. See putwin().

```
1    #include <ncurses.h>
2    #include <stdlib.h>
3
4    #define FILENAME "window.dat"
5
6    void bomb(char *message);
7
8    int main(void)
9    {
10       FILE *wfile;
11       WINDOW *win;
12       int r;
13
14       initscr();
15       start_color();
16       init_pair(1,COLOR_WHITE,COLOR_RED);
17
18       addstr("Press Enter to read the window from disk:\n");
19       refresh();
20       getch();
21
22   /* open the file */
23       wfile = fopen(FILENAME,"r");
24       if( wfile==NULL)
25           bomb("Error reading file\n");
26
27   /* write the window's data */
28       win = getwin(wfile);
29       if( win == NULL )
```

```
30                bomb("Unable to read/create window\n");
31           fclose(wfile);
32           wrefresh(win);
33           getch();
34
35           endwin();
36           return 0;
37      }
38
39    void bomb(char *message)
40      {
41           endwin();
42           puts(message);
43           exit(1);
44      }
```

Sample output:
Refer to putwin() *for what the output looks like (well, similar to).*

Also See

Chapter 14, putwin(), scr_dump(), scr_restore()

getyx()

The getyx() function reads the cursor location from a specific window and saves it in two int variables.

Man Page Format

```
void getyx(WINDOW *win, int y, int x);
```

Format Reference

win is the name of a WINDOW pointer, indicating a window created earlier in the code. It can also be stdscr for the standard screen.

y is an int variable to hold a value indicating which row the cursor is blinking on.

x is an int variable to hold a value indicating which column the cursor blinks in.

Return Value

getyx() is a macro and as such its return value should not be used.

Notes

Note that it's always getyx(), not getxy().

The yx part of getyx() also helps you to remember that the row, or Y, component comes first.

Both y and x are int variables, not pointers. Do *not* prefix them with & though it would seem like you need to do this.

Location 0, 0 is the *home* position, the upper-left corner of the screen.

Maximum values for y and x depend on the size of the screen.

In a way, getyx() is the opposite of the wmove() function.

Example

```
getyx(stdscr,y,x);
```

This statement reads the cursor's current position on the standard screen and stores it in the y and x variable.

Sample Program

```
1     #include <ncurses.h>
2     #include <time.h>
3     #include <stdlib.h>
4
5     int main(void)
6     {
7         int r,x,row,col;
8
9         initscr();
10         srandom((unsigned)time(NULL));
11
12         r = random();
13         r %= 300;
14         for(x=0;x<r;x++)
15             addch('*');
16         getyx(stdscr,row,col);
17         printw("\nThe cursor ended up at location %d, %d.\n",\
18             row,col);
19         refresh();
20         getch();
21
22         endwin();
23         return 0;
24     }
```

Sample output:

```
**********************************************
The cursor ended up at location 0, 43.
```

Also See

Chapter 4, move()

halfdelay()

The halfdelay() function directs NCurses input functions to enter half delay mode.

Explanation

Half delay mode is similar to cbreak mode with regard to characters being made available immediately to the program as they're typed. Unlike cbreak mode, however, halfdelay() sets the blocking delay duration. After a given number of tenths of a second, the input function returns ERR when nothing has been typed.

Man Page Format

```
int halfdelay(int tenths);
```

Format Reference

tenths is an int value ranging from 1 to 255, indicating the number of tenths of a second getch() (and related functions) to wait for character input.

Return Value

ERR on failure, OK or a value other than ERR on success.

Notes

halfdelay() covers all NCurses input. If you want to vary the delay associated with a specific window, use the wtimeout() function instead: See timeout().

Small values of tenths require quite a fast typist to keep up!

Remember that it's the input function, such as getch(), that returns ERR when half delay mode times out. The halfdelay() function returns ERR only when there is an error setting that function.

The nodelay() function essentially is like setting halfdelay(0), though zero is an invalid argument for halfdelay().

Your program can leave half delay mode by using the nocbreak() function. See cbreak().

Examples

```
halfdelay(20);
```

This statement sets the half delay pause to 2 full seconds.

```
halfdelay(1);
```

This statement sets the pause to 1/10th of a second, demanding fast input!

Sample Program

```
1      #include <ncurses.h>
2
3      #define DELAY 10
4
5      int main(void)
6      {
7          int ch;
8
9          initscr();
10
11         halfdelay(DELAY);
12         printw("Half delay has been set to %d/10 seconds.\n",DELAY);
13         addstr("Try to type in your name fast enough:\n");
14         refresh();
15
16         do
17         {
18             ch = getch();
19             if(ch == '\n')
20                 break;
21         } while(ch != ERR);
22
23         mvaddstr(5,0,"Hope you got it all in!");
24         refresh();
25         getch();
26
27         endwin();
28         return 0;
29     }
```

Sample output:

```
Half delay has been set to 10/10 seconds.
Try to type in your name fast enough:
```

Try to type quickly; if you pause longer than 1 second, either at first or between any keys, the program is over.

Also See

```
nodelay(), timeout(), cbreak(), getch()
```

has_colors()

The has_colors() function is used to determine whether or not the terminal has the ability to display color text attributes.

This function is used before start_color(). Obviously there's no point in doing colors in a program for a terminal that cannot display them.

Man Page Format

```
bool has_colors(void);
```

Format Reference

The function has no arguments.

Return Value

has_colors() returns a Boolean value, either TRUE or FALSE, the former when the terminal can do color and the latter when it cannot.

Notes

This is one of the rare text color function in NCurses that uses the plural *colors*. The other two are assume_default_colors() and use_default_colors().

Examples

```
r = has_colors();
```

After this statement, the value of r will equal TRUE if the terminal can produce color text, FALSE otherwise.

```
if(has_colors)
```

The above if condition evaluates true if the console has the ability to use color text.

Sample Program

```
1     #include <ncurses.h>
2
3     int main(void)
4     {
5         bool tf;
6         initscr();
7
8         tf =  has_colors();
9         if( tf == TRUE)
10            addstr("This terminal can do colors.\n");
11        else
12            addstr("This terminal cannot do colors.\n");
13        refresh();
14        getch();
15
16        endwin();
17        return 0;
18    }
```

Sample output:

```
This terminal can do colors.
```

Or:

```
This terminal cannot do colors.
```

Also See

```
start_color(),TRUE
```

has_ic()

The has_ic() function determines whether the terminal has the ability to insert and delete characters.

Man Page Format

```
bool has_ic(void);
```

Format Reference

The function has no arguments.

Return Value

A Boolean value is returned: TRUE if the terminal has insert and delete character capabilities, FALSE if not.

Notes

If the terminal does not have the ability to insert and delete characters, then it will be provided by NCurses in software.

The insch() function is used to insert a character on the screen. The delch() function deletes a character.

The idcok() function is used to switch between hardware and software modes for inserting and deleting characters. See idcok().

This is one of several NCurses functions that report back information on the terminal. The others include baudrate(), erasechar(), killchar(), has_il(), longname(), termattrs(), and termname().

Example

```
if(has_ic())
```

The if condition passes when the terminal has the ability to insert and delete characters.

Sample Program

```
1    #include <ncurses.h>
2
3    int main(void)
4    {
5        initscr();
6
7        addstr("This terminal ");
8        if(has_ic())
9            addstr("has ");
10       else
11           addstr("does not have ");
12       addstr("insert/delete character abilities");
13       refresh();
14       getch();
15
16       endwin();
17       return 0;
18   }
```

Sample output:

```
This terminal has insert/delete character abilities
```

Also See

has_il(),insch(),delch(),idcok()

has_il()

The has_il() function determines whether the terminal has the ability to insert and delete lines or can perform that ability to affect a scrolling region of text.

Man Page Format

```
bool has_il(void);
```

Format Reference

The function has no arguments.

Return Value

A Boolean value is returned: TRUE if the terminal has insert and delete line capabilities, FALSE if not.

Notes

The insdelln() function is used to insert or delete lines of text on the screen.

The idlok() function is used to switch between hardware and software modes for inserting and deleting lines of text. See idlok().

When the terminal has the ability to insert and remove lines, then it can use those abilities to scroll text. Also see scrollok() and scrl().

Example

```
if(has_il())
```

The if condition passes when the terminal has the ability to insert and delete lines of text.

Sample Program

```
1    #include <ncurses.h>
2
3    int main(void)
4    {
5        initscr();
6
7        addstr("This terminal ");
8        if(has_il())
9            addstr("has ");
10       else
11           addstr("does not have ");
12       addstr("insert/delete line abilities");
13       refresh();
14       getch();
15
16       endwin();
17       return 0;
18   }
```

Sample output:

```
This terminal has insert/delete character abilities
```

Also See

has_ic(), insdelln(), scrollok(), scrl(), idcok()

hline()

The hline() function draws a horizontal (left-right) line from the cursor's current location to the right a given number of character places.

Man Page Format

```
int hline(chtype ch, int n);
```

Format Reference

ch is a chtype character used to draw the line. Though typically only a single character, such as –, is used, you can combine characters, text attributes and colors with the `chtype` variable. See Appendix C. When zero is specified for `ch`, the default `ASC_HLINE` character is used. See Appendix B for more information on ACS characters.

n is an `int` value that sets the length of the line in characters. Valid values for n range from 0 on up to whatever an integer can hold. If n is zero, then no line is displayed. When n is greater than the distance between the current cursor position and the left edge of the window, then only as many `ch` characters as can be displayed on a line are shown. (The line does not wrap.)

Refer to the *mv*, *mvw*, and *w* prefix entries elsewhere in this appendix for information on the `win`, `row`, and `col` arguments.

Return Value

`hline()` always returns `OK`.

Notes

The line always goes from the cursor's current position to the right.

Drawing the line does not affect the cursor's location. The cursor remains at its previous location, or whichever location was set by the `mvhline()` or `mvwhline()` functions.

The line drawn is not protected against erasure by other NCurses text output functions; the line can be overwritten at any time.

Examples

```
hline(0,10);
```

This function draws a line 10 characters long (wide) from the cursor's current position. The default line drawing character is used.

```
mvhline(y,10,'*',len);
```

Here, the function draws a line using asterisks. The line is `len` characters long from location row `y`, column `10`.

```
mvwhline(tasks,0,0,0,100);
```

Here, a line is drawn across the top of window `tasks` using the default line drawing character. If the window is narrower than `100` characters, the excess line is ignored.

Sample Program

```
1    #include <ncurses.h>
2
3    int main(void)
4    {
5        int maxy,maxx,halfx,y,len;
6        initscr();
7
8        getmaxyx(stdscr,maxy,maxx);
9        halfx = maxx >> 1;                    /* x/2 */
10       len = 1;
11
12       for(y=0;y<maxy;y++,len++)
13       {
14           mvhline(y,halfx-len,0,len+len);
15       }
16       refresh();
17       getch();
18
19       endwin();
20       return 0;
21   }
```

The sample output is shown in Figure A-7.

Also See

Chapter 14, Appendix B, box(), vline()

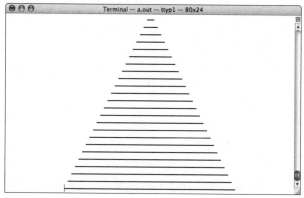

Figure A-7: The hline() festive tree

idcok()

The idcok() function directs whether NCurses uses the terminal (hardware) ability to insert or delete characters, or whether software routines are used instead.

Man Page Format

```
void idcok(WINDOW *win, bool bf);
```

Format Reference

win is the name of a WINDOW variable representing a window on the screen or stdscr for the standard screen.

bf is a Boolean value, either TRUE or FALSE. When set TRUE, the terminal's insert/delete character routines are used. When set FALSE, software routines are used instead.

Return Value

This function always returns OK.

Notes

Normally, the software insert/delete character routines are used, as in idcok(win, TRUE). Therefore it is unnecessary to use idcok(win, TRUE) in a window unless the terminal routines have been previously disabled and you want to re-enable them.

The has_ic() function determines whether or not the terminal has the ability to insert and delete characters.

NCurses uses the insch() function to insert a character on the screen; the delch() function is used to delete a character.

Example

```
idcok(w,FALSE);
```

The statement directs NCurses to use software routines for inserting and deleting characters in the window w.

Sample Program

```
1    #include <ncurses.h>
2
3    #define LENA 8
```

```
 4     #define LENF 11
 5     #define LENS 7
 6     #define DELAY 150
 7     #define ROW 10
 8
 9     int main(void)
10     {
11         char first[] = "The terminal";
12         char second[] = "Software";
13         int x;
14
15         initscr();
16
17         mvaddstr(ROW,0,"Something is doing the inserting ⏎
and deleting.");
18         refresh();
19         getch();
20
21         move(ROW,0);
22         for(x=0;x<=LENA;x++)
23         {
24             delch();
25             refresh();
26             napms(DELAY);
27         }
28         for(x=LENF;x>=0;x--)
29         {
30             insch(first[x]);
31             refresh();
32             napms(DELAY);
33         }
34         getch();
35
36         idcok(stdscr,FALSE);
37
38         for(x=0;x<=LENF;x++)
39         {
40             delch();
41             refresh();
42             napms(DELAY);
43         }
44         for(x=LENS;x>=0;x--)
45         {
46             insch(second[x]);
47             refresh();
48             napms(DELAY);
49         }
50         getch();
51
52         endwin();
53         return 0;
54     }
```

Sample output:

```
Something is doing the inserting and deleting.
```

Press Enter and Something *is gobbled up and replaced by* The terminal.

```
The terminal is doing the inserting and deleting.
```

Press Enter and The terminal *is gobbled up and replaced by* Software.

```
Software is doing the inserting and deleting.
```

Also See

has_ic(), insch(), delch(), idlok()

idlok()

The idlok() function directs whether NCurses uses the terminal (hardware) ability to insert or delete characters or whether software routines are used instead.

Man Page Format

```
void idcok(WINDOW *win, bool bf);
```

Format Reference

win is the name of a WINDOW variable representing a window on the screen, such ass stdscr for the standard screen.

bf is a Boolean value, either TRUE or FALSE. When set TRUE, the terminal's (hardware) insert/delete line routines are used. When set FALSE, software routines are used instead.

Return Value

idlok() always returns OK.

Notes

The has_il() function determines whether or not the terminal has the ability to insert and delete lines of text.

NCurses uses the `insdelln()` function to insert or delete lines of text on the screen.

Example

```
idcok(w,FALSE);
```

The statement directs NCurses to use software routines for inserting and deleting characters in the window w.

Sample Program

```
1    #include <ncurses.h>
2
3    #define DELAY 150
4    #define ROW 10
5    #define REPEAT 5
6
7    static void fancy(char *text)
8    {
9        int x;
10
11       for(x=0;x<REPEAT;x++)
12       {
13           mvaddstr(ROW+1,0,text);
14           refresh();
15           napms(DELAY);
16           insdelln(1);
17       }
18       for(x=0;x<=REPEAT;x++)
19       {
20           insdelln(-1);
21           refresh();
22           napms(DELAY);
23       }
24   }
25
26   int main(void)
27   {
28       initscr();
29
30       mvaddstr(ROW,0,"What is inserting and deleting the text?");
31       refresh();
32       getch();
33
34       idlok(stdscr,TRUE);
35       fancy("Hardware is!");
36       getch();
37
```

```
38          idlok(stdscr,FALSE);
39          fancy("Software is!");
40          getch();
41
42          endwin();
43          return 0;
44     }
```

Sample output:

The program inserts and deletes rows of text, first with idlok() *set to* TRUE, *then with it set to* FALSE.

Also See

has_il(),insdelln(),idcok()

immedok()

The immedok() function provides for automatic update (refreshing) in a window any time that window's information is changed.

Man Page Format

```
void immedok(WINDOW *win, bool bf);
```

Format Reference

win is the name of a WINDOW variable representing a window on the screen, such as stdscr for the standard screen.

bf is a Boolean value, either TRUE to enable the immedok() function or FALSE to disable it. NCurses normally sets immedok() to the FALSE state for new windows and the standard screen.

Return Value

The function has no return value.

Notes

getch(), and related input functions such as getstr(), automatically update a window. Pretty much all NCurses text output functions, however, require a refresh() to update the screen. immedok() set TRUE removes that requirement and the updating is done automatically.

Yes, it's true: By setting `immedok()` to `TRUE`, you greatly increase the overhead required to update the screen. Refer to `wnoutrefresh()` for information on optimizing window and text output.

Example

```
immedok(menu,TRUE);
```

Here, the statement sets immediate refreshing for all output to the window menu.

Sample Program

```
1    #include <ncurses.h>
2
3    #define DELAY 500
4    #define TEXT "Lookee Here!"
5
6    static void show(void)
7    {
8        mvaddstr(1,10,TEXT);
9        napms(DELAY);
10       mvaddstr(2,50,TEXT);
11       napms(DELAY);
12       mvaddstr(10,1,TEXT);
13       napms(DELAY);
14       mvaddstr(20,30,TEXT);
15       napms(DELAY);
16   }
17
18   int main(void)
19   {
20       initscr();
21
22       addstr("First round: immedok() is OFF! (Press Enter ⤶
and wait!)");
23       refresh();
24       getch();
25       show();
26       mvaddstr(LINES-1,0,"Press Enter:");
27       refresh();
28       getch();
29
30       immedok(stdscr,TRUE);
31       clear();
32       addstr("Second round: immedok() is ON! (Press Enter ⤶
and watch!)");
33       getch();
34       show();
35       mvaddstr(LINES-1,0,"Press Enter:");
```

```
36          getch();
37
38          endwin();
39          return 0;
40    }
```

Sample output:

```
First round: immedok() is OFF! (Press Enter and wait!)
```

Press Enter. Nothing happens until the `refresh()` *in line 27.*

```
Second round: immedok() is ON! (Press Enter and watch!)
```

Press Enter. Note that text is updated on the screen with nary a `refresh()` *in sight!*

Also See

`refresh()`, `clearok()`

inch()

The `inch()` function returns the character and text attribute at the cursor's position.

Man Page Format

```
chtype inch(void);
chtype winch(WINDOW *win);
chtype mvinch(int y, int x);
chtype mvwinch(WINDOW *win, int y, int x);
```

Format Reference

The base function has no arguments; refer to the *mv*, *mvw*, and *w* prefix entries elsewhere in this appendix for information on the `win`, `y`, and `x` arguments.

Return Value

A `chtype` variable is returned, indicating the character and text attribute(s) found at the cursor's location.

Notes

Reading the text and attribute with inch() does not advance the cursor.

The chtype variable returned can be stored or used in any NCurses function that swallows chtype variables. If you want to extract something specific from that variable, then a logical AND operation is in order. For example, to extract the character from the value returned:

```
char_var = ( inch() & A_CHARTEXT);
```

The A_CHARTEXT constant helps mask off the non-character attributes of the chtype. Likewise, to extract the text formatting attributes only:

```
attrib = ( inch() & A_ATTRIBUTES);
```

A_ATTRIBUTES helps mask off color and text information, saving the attributes value into the long int attrib, above. And to extract the color pair value:

```
cpair = ( inch() & A_COLOR);
```

The cpair int variable holds the color pair value returned by the inch() function.

There is another NCurses function, insch(), which inserts characters on the screen. Do not confuse that with inch().

Examples

```
v = inch();
```

Here, the text character and attributes at the cursor's location on the standard screen are saved in chtype variable v.

```
attr = winch(menu) & A_ATTRIBUTES;
```

The long int variable attr (or type attr_t) saves the attributes only from the cursor's current position in window menu.

```
ch = mvwinch(help,0,0) & A_CHARTEXT;
```

Here, int variable ch saves the text character from position 0, 0 in window help.

Sample Program

```
1    #include <ncurses.h>
2
3    int main(void)
4    {
5        WINDOW *other;
6        int x;
7        chtype ch;
8
9        initscr();
10       start_color();
11       init_pair(1,COLOR_WHITE,COLOR_BLUE);
12
13       addstr("Creating and filling other window...");
14       other = newwin(0,0,0,0);
15       if( other==NULL)
16       {
17           endwin();
18           puts("Error creating window");
19           return(1);
20       }
21       wbkgd(other,COLOR_PAIR(1));
22       waddch(other,'\"');
23       wattron(other,A_BOLD);
24       waddstr(other,"Hello!");
25       wattroff(other,A_BOLD);
26       waddstr(other,"\" from the other window!");
27       addstr("Done!\n");
28       addstr("Press Enter to evaluate the other window's text:\n");
29       refresh();
30       getch();
31
32       addstr("Other window's text:\n");
33       for(x=0;x<31;x++)
34       {
35           ch = mvwinch(other,0,x);
36           addch(ch & A_CHARTEXT);
37       }
38       refresh();
39       getch();
40
41       addstr("\nAnd here are the other window's text ⏎
     and attributes:\n");
42       for(x=0;x<31;x++)
43       {
44           ch = mvwinch(other,0,x);
45           addch(ch);
46       }
47       refresh();
```

```
48        getch();
49
50        endwin();
51        return 0;
52    }
```

Sample output:

```
Creating and filling other window...Done!
Press Enter to evaluate the other window's text:
```

Press Enter.

```
Other window's text:
"Hello!" from the other window!
```

Press Enter.

```
And here are the other window's text and attributes:
"Hello!" from the other window!
```

The text displayed is lifted from the other window thanks to the inch() *function.*

Also See

inchstr(), insch()

inchstr()

The inchstr() function reads an array of chtype characters from a window, found at the cursor's position and for a given length of characters or until the end of the line. The chtype characters are returned in an array, and each chtype character contains text, attribute, and color information.

Man Page Formats

```
int inchstr(chtype *chstr);
int inchnstr(chtype *chstr, int n);
int winchstr(WINDOW *win, chtype *chstr);
int winchnstr(WINDOW *win, chtype *chstr, int n);
int mvinchstr(int y, int x, chtype *chstr);
int mvinchnstr(int y, int x, chtype *chstr, int n);
int mvwinchstr(WINDOW *win, int y, int x, chtype *chstr);
int mvwinchnstr(WINDOW *win, int y, int x, chtype *chstr, int n);
```

Format Reference

chstr is an array of the NCurses chtype, a long int containing character and formatting information read from a window. The array contains chtype characters read from the cursor's current position to the right a given number of characters or to the right edge of the window. The array is saved with \0 as the final element.

When n is specified (in the inchnstr() functions) n characters are read from the cursor's current position. The value of n ranges from 0 through the width of the window, though when 0 is specified nothing is read. A value of -1 reads all characters from the cursor's position to the end of the row. Values larger than the length of the row are read only to the end of the row, not beyond.

When n is not specified, as with the inchstr() functions, then characters are read from the cursor's location to the end of the row. (This is the same as when -1 is specified for n.)

Refer to the *mv*, *mvw*, and *w* prefix entries elsewhere in this appendix for information on the win, y, and x arguments.

Return Value

ERR is returned when the function fails. Otherwise, an int value other than ERR is returned.

Notes

Do not assume the width of the window being read! It's possible by using inchstr() to overflow the chtype array. Buffer overflows are a Bad Thing and must be avoided.

I recommend using getmaxy() to determine a window's row width, then use malloc() to properly allocate a chtype array, and finally use inchnstr() to read in the proper number of chtype characters from the window. Refer to the Sample Program.

Each chtype character can be masked using the logical & (AND) to extract specific information: character, attribute, or color pair. Refer to the entry for inch() for the details.

This function does not move the cursor.

Examples

```
inchstr(chstr)
```

Here, inchstr() reads text from the cursor's current position on the standard screen to the end of the row. The text and attributes are stored in the chtype array, chstr.

```
mvinchstr(0,0,title)
```

Here, the cursor is moved to location 0,0 on the standard screen. Text and attributes from the entire top row are read into `chtype` array `title`.

```
mvwinchnstr(menu,5,31,option,12)
```

In this statement, text and attributes are read from cursor location row 5, column 31 in window `menu`. Twelve characters are read and stored in the `chtype` array `option`.

Sample Program

```
1    #include <ncurses.h>
2    #include <stdlib.h>
3
4    int main(void)
5    {
6        int y,x;
7        chtype *c;
8
9        initscr();
10       start_color();
11       init_pair(1,COLOR_RED,COLOR_WHITE);
12
13   /* set aside memory for chtype array */
14       getmaxyx(stdscr,y,x);
15       c = calloc((x+1), sizeof(chtype));
16       if( c == NULL)
17       {
18           endwin();
19           puts("Unable to allocate memory.");
20           return(1);
21       }
22
23   /* write something interesting to the screen */
24       attron(COLOR_PAIR(1));
25       addstr("This is a bit of text!");
26       attroff(COLOR_PAIR(1));
27       refresh();
28       getch();
29
30   /* copy the text using inchstr */
31       mvinchstr(0,0,c);
32       mvaddstr(10,0,"Here is the chtype string read:\n");
33       addchstr(c);
34       refresh();
35       getch();
36
37       endwin();
38       return 0;
39   }
```

Sample output:
In red on white text:

```
This is a bit of text!
```

Press Enter, and appearing mid-screen:

```
Here is the chtype string read:
This is a bit of text!
```

Also See

Appendix C, inch(), addchstr()

init_color()

The init_color() function allows you to redefine colors NCurses can use for text attributes. For those terminals on which this function works, you can create interesting colors by adjusting individual red, green, and blue values, theoretically creating a billion possible colors.

Man Page Format

```
int init_color(short color, short r, short g, short b);
```

Format Reference

c is a short int representing a color number to change. The range of valid values for c is from 0 through the value of COLOR. (See COLOR.)

r, g, and b are short int values representing the intensity of the red, green and blue hues of the color created. Values range from 0 through 1000, where 0 is black and 1000 is full intensity for red, green, or blue.

Return Value

ERR upon failure, OK otherwise.

Notes

Use the can_change_color() function to determine whether or not the terminal has the ability to redefine its colors set. When can_change_color() returns TRUE, then the init_color() function can be used.

When all three color arguments, red, green, and blue, are set to the same value the result is a gray tone. The lower the value, the darker the gray; the higher the value, the lighter the gray.

The default colors used by NCurses relate to the init_color() statements shown in Table A-7.

The color_content() function is used to determine the red, green, and blue color values of colors in NCurses, kind of the opposite of the init_color() function. See color_content() elsewhere in this appendix.

Examples

```
init_color(5,1000,500,0);
```

The statement defines color 5 in NCurses to be a flavor of orange. Full intensity red and half intensity green equals orange.

```
init_color(6,1000,500,0);
```

The statement defines color 6 to be purple.

Sample Program

```
1     #include <ncurses.h>
2
3     #define NEW_COLOR 1
4     #define RED 1000
5     #define GREEN 750
6     #define BLUE 750
7
8     int main(void)
9     {
10        initscr();
11        start_color();
12        if(!can_change_color())
13            addstr("This probably won't work, but anyway:\n");
14
15        init_color(NEW_COLOR,RED,GREEN,BLUE);
16
17        init_pair(1,NEW_COLOR,COLOR_BLACK);
18        attrset(COLOR_PAIR(1));
19        printw("This is the new color %d.\n",NEW_COLOR);
20        refresh();
21        getch();
22
23        endwin();
24        return 0;
25    }
```

Table A-7: Values for NCurses colors

COLOR	INIT_COLOR() FUNCTION	CONSTANT NAME
0	`init_color(0,0,0,0);`	COLOR_BLACK
1	`init_color(0,1000,0,0);`	COLOR_RED
2	`init_color(0,0,1000,0);`	COLOR_GREEN
3	`init_color(0,1000,1000,0);`	COLOR_YELLOW
4	`init_color(0,0,0,1000);`	COLOR_BLUE
5	`init_color(0,1000,0,1000);`	COLOR_MAGENTA
6	`init_color(0,0,1000,1000);`	COLOR_CYAN
7	`init_color(0,1000,1000,1000);`	COLOR_WHITE

Sample output:

```
This is the new color 1
```

The text is displayed in pink on a black background.

Also See

Chapter 3, `can_change_color()`, `COLORS`, `color_content()`

init_pair()

The `init_pair()` function assigns a foreground and background text color to a color pair value. The color pair value is then used with the `COLOR_PAIR(n)` attribute to apply those foreground and background colors to text or a window as a whole.

Man Page Format

```
int init_pair(short pair, short f, short b);
```

Format Reference

`pair` is a `short int` value representing a color pair number. Values range from 0 through the value of the `COLOR_PAIR` constant, minus 1. The color pair number is used to reference the foreground/background text color combination, specifically with the `COLOR_PAIR(n)` attribute. The n in `COLOR_PAIR(n)` is the same as `pair`, representing the color pair created.

f and b are a short int values representing the text foreground and text background colors, respectively. Values range from 0 through the value of COLOR, minus 1. Refer to COLOR elsewhere in this appendix for the list of colors and color constants commonly available.

Return Value

The function returns OK when the pair has been created successfully; otherwise, ERR is returned.

Notes

The start_color() function must be used before this function. start_color() initializes NCurses to do color. See start_color().

Table A-8 lists NCurses color numbers, hues, and constants.

Values for the color pair number, pair, range from 1 through COLOR_PAIR-1. This is because pair number 0 is reserved as the default text color, typically white on black. Also see the assume_default_colors() function elsewhere in this appendix.

Examples

```
init_pair(1,COLOR_WHITE,COLOR_BLUE);
```

The statement creates a new color pair attribute, COLOR_PAIR(1), which colors text white on a blue background.

```
init_pair(13,4,2);
```

Here, COLOR_PAIR(13) is created. The colors used correspond to color 4 and 2, for blue text on a green background. (See COLORS.)

Table A-8: NCurses color constants

COLOR	CONSTANT NAME
0	COLOR_BLACK
1	COLOR_RED
2	COLOR_GREEN
3	COLOR_YELLOW
4	COLOR_BLUE
5	COLOR_MAGENTA
6	COLOR_CYAN
7	COLOR_WHITE

Sample Program

```
1    #include <ncurses.h>
2
3    int main(void)
4    {
5        int pair,fg,bg;
6
7        initscr();
8        start_color();
9
10       pair = 1;
11       for(fg=0;fg<COLORS;fg++)
12           for(bg=0;bg<COLORS;bg++)
13           {
14               init_pair(pair,fg,bg);
15               pair++;
16           }
17
18       for(pair=0;pair<COLOR_PAIRS;pair++)
19       {
20           attrset(COLOR_PAIR(pair));
21               addstr("Color! ");
22           if( !(pair % COLORS))
23               addch('\n');
24       }
25       refresh();
26       getch();
27
28       endwin();
29       return 0;
30   }
```

The sample output is shown in Figure A-8.

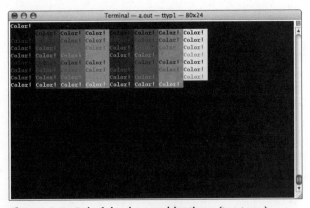

Figure A-8: Colorful color combinations (trust me)

Also See

`start_color()`, `attrset()`, `COLOR`, `COLOR_PAIR`, `pair_content()`

initscr()

The `initscr()` function initializes NCurses functions. It sets up various internal memory structures, creates the standard screen window, and displays the virtual screen on the terminal.

Man Page Format

```
WINDOW *initscr(void);
```

Format Reference

The function has no arguments.

Return Value

`initscr()` returns a pointer to a `WINDOW` variable, which ends up being the standard screen, `stdscr`.

Notes

The `newterm()` function can also be used to initialize NCurses, specifically for special input and output needs.

There are a few special NCurses functions that must be called before `initscr()` (or `newterm()`) is used to initialize NCurses. These are `filter()`, `ripoffline()`, `slk_init()`, and `use_env()`.

It is not necessary to save the `WINDOW` pointer returned by `initscr()`, as NCurses creates the `stdscr` variable automatically.

The `endwin()` function is required to end NCurses programming and return the terminal to normal behavior. See `endwin()`.

When `initscr()` cannot initialize the terminal, it exits the program.

Example

```
initscr();
```

This statement is found near the top of just about every NCurses program.

Sample Program

```
1    #include <ncurses.h>
2
3    int main(void)
4    {
5        initscr();
6        addstr("Goodbye, cruel C programming!");
7        refresh();
8        getch();
9
10       endwin();
11       return 0;
12   }
```

Sample output:

```
Goodbye, cruel C programming!
```

Also See

Chapter 1, newterm(), endwin()

innstr()

See instr().

insch()

The insch() function inserts only one character into a row of text, shoving all the characters to the right one space to the right. The character is inserted at the cursor's current position.

Man Page Format

```
int insch(chtype ch);
int winsch(WINDOW *win, chtype ch);
int mvinsch(int y, int x, chtype ch);
int mvwinsch(WINDOW *win, int y, int x, chtype ch);
```

Format Reference

ch is a chtype character, which can be a single character, a text attribute, a color pair, or a combination of each. (See Appendix C.)

Refer to the *mv*, *mvw*, and *w* prefix entries elsewhere in this appendix for information on the win, y, and x arguments.

Return Value

ERR on failure, or OK if everything ends up happily ever after.

Notes

The insch() function *inserts* a character at the cursor's position. It does not delete any character already at that position, nor does it move the cursor's location.

Any characters shoved off the right edge of the window by insch() are not wrapped to the next line. Those characters pushed off are lost.

When you merely want to put a character at a location without rearranging the rest of the text, use the addch() function instead.

To insert a string of characters use the insstr() function. See insstr().

When inserting multiple characters remember to insert them *backwards*. That is, insert the last characters first; otherwise, the string inserted (one character at a time) appears sdrawkcab.

There is another NCurses function, inch(), which *reads* a character from a window (kind of the opposite of addch()). Do not confuse inch() with insch()!

Examples

```
mvinsch(5,10,'A');
```

After this statement, an A is placed on the screen at row 5, column 10. Any text from column 10 to the right edge of the window is scooted one notch to the right to make room for the A.

```
winsch(tally,c);
```

Here, the character stored in variable c is placed at the cursor's current position in window tally. Existing text on that row is moved over one notch to the right to make room.

```
insch('*' | A_BOLD);
```

Here, a bold * is inserted at the cursor's current position in the standard screen.

Sample Program

Refer to the entry for delch() for a sample program and output.

Also See

Chapter 5, `insstr()`, `addch()`, `insertln()`, `delch()`

insdelln()

The `insdelln()` function either inserts or deletes a given number of lines in a window.

Man Page Format

```
int insdelln(int n);
int winsdelln(WINDOW *win, int n);
```

Format Reference

n is an `int` value that indicates the number of lines to insert or delete. When n is positive, then that number of lines are inserted at the row the cursor is on. When n is negative, that number of lines are removed from the row the cursor is on.

Refer to the entry for *w* later in this appendix for information on the `win` argument.

Return Value

ERR on failure or OK when things are all sunny and okay.

Notes

The `insdelln()` function does not change the cursor's location.

Lines inserted cause text below to scroll down. The bottom n line(s) are then removed from the window.

Lines removed cause the text below to scroll up; n blank lines are inserted at the bottom of the window.

`insdelln(1)` is equivalent to `insertln()`.

`insdelln(-1)` is equivalent to `deleteln()`.

When n is zero, obviously, nothing happens.

Examples

```
insdelln(2);
```

Two new, blank rows of text are inserted at the line the cursor is on. The two blank lines will be on the cursor line and below that line. Any text already on those two lines is scrolled down, with the bottom two rows on the window scrolled off.

```
winsdelln(editor,-12);
```

Here, 12 lines of text are deleted from the window, editor. The lines start on the cursor's line and extend down 11 lines. Any lines below are then scrolled up, with blank lines inserted at the bottom of the window.

Sample Program

```
1    #include <ncurses.h>
2
3    int main(void)
4    {
5        int y,x,c,halfy;
6
7        initscr();
8
9        getmaxyx(stdscr,y,x);
10       halfy = y >> 1;
11
12       for(c=0;c<y;c++)
13           mvprintw(c,15,"This is amazing row %d!\n",c);
14       refresh();
15       getch();
16
17       move(halfy,0);
18       for(c=0;c<halfy;c++)
19       {
20           insdelln(1);
21           refresh();
22           napms(100);
23       }
24
25       move(0,0);
26       for(c=0;c<halfy;c++)
27       {
28           insdelln(-1);
29           refresh();
30           napms(100);
31       }
32
33       endwin();
34       return 0;
35   }
```

Sample output:

The screen is filled with text on each line. Pressing Enter clears the screen by scrolling the bottom half down and then the top half up.

Also See

```
insertln(),deleteln()
```

insertln()

The `insertln()` function inserts a fresh, blank line of text on the screen above the cursor's current line. All lines from the cursor's current line to the bottom of the window are scrolled down one row. The last row of the screen is removed.

Man Page Format

```
int insertln(void);
int winsdelln(WINDOW *win, int n);
```

Format Reference

The function takes no arguments; refer to the entry for w elsewhere in this appendix for information on the `win` argument.

Return Value

OK upon success, ERR on failure.

Notes

The cursor's row position determines which row the new blank line appears on. Text already on that row is scrolled down to the row beneath, as is all text below that line.

    `insertln()` scrolls text on the screen down even when scrolling is not active for the window. See `scrollok()`.

    This function does not move the cursor.

Example

```
insertln();
```

After the statement, all text in the window from the line the cursor is on to the bottom is scrolled down one row. A new blank row then appears on the cursor's line.

Sample Program

```
1    #include <ncurses.h>
2
3    int main(void)
4    {
5        int x;
6        char hamlet[5][46] = { "And by opposing end them?",
7                        "Or to take arms against a sea of troubles,",
8                        "The slings and arrows of outrageous fortune,",
9                        "Whether 'tis nobler in the mind to suffer",
10                          "To be, or not to be: that is the question:" };
11
12       initscr();
13
14       for(x=0;x<5;x++)
15       {
16           move(0,0);
17           insertln();
18           addstr(hamlet[x]);
19           refresh();
20           getch();
21       }
22
23       endwin();
24       return 0;
25   }
```

Sample output:

```
And by opposing end them?
```

Press Enter.

```
Or to take arms against a sea of troubles,
And by opposing end them?
```

Press Enter.

```
The slings and arrows of outrageous fortune,
Or to take arms against a sea of troubles,
And by opposing end them?
```

Press Enter.

```
Whether 'tis nobler in the mind to suffer
The slings and arrows of outrageous fortune,
Or to take arms against a sea of troubles,
And by opposing end them?
```

Press Enter.

```
To be, or not to be: that is the question:
Whether 'tis nobler in the mind to suffer
The slings and arrows of outrageous fortune,
Or to take arms against a sea of troubles,
And by opposing end them?
```

Also See

Chapter 5, deleteln(), insch(), insdelln()

insstr()

The insstr() function inserts a string of characters at the cursor's position, shoving remaining text on that line to the right. It's equivalent to multiple calls to the insch() function.

Man Page Formats

```
int insstr(const char *str);
int insnstr(const char *str, int n);
int winsstr(WINDOW *win, const char *str);
int winsnstr(WINDOW *win, const char *str, int n);
int mvinsstr(int y, int x, const char *str);
int mvinsnstr(int y, int x, const char *str, int n);
int mvwinsstr(WINDOW *win, int y, int x, const char *str);
int mvwinsnstr(WINDOW *win, int y, int x, const char *str, int n);
```

Format Reference

str is a string of text characters (a char array) inserted at the cursor's position. These are plain text characters, not chtype characters.

Those functions that use n specify how many characters of str to display. Values for n range from 0 on up to the length of the str. If n is greater than the length of the str, or when n is 0 (or less than 0), then the entire str is displayed.

Refer to the *mv*, *mvw*, and *w* prefix entries elsewhere in this appendix for information on the win, y, and x arguments.

Return Value

OK upon success, ERR upon not-success.

Notes

The insstr() function does not change the cursor's location. (Contrast this with addstr(), which does move the cursor.)

Characters moved beyond the right edge of the screen are lost; the insstr() function does not wrap text or scroll the screen.

Specifying values of n longer than the actual length of the string does not cause blanks to be displayed. Instead, the entire string is displayed, just as if the insstr() (non-n) version of the function were used.

Just as with addstr() and addch(), this function interprets the control characters for Tab, Newline, and Backspace. For example, a tab advances text to the next tab stop; newline erases the rest of the line and causes insstr() to continue to insert text on the following line (column 0), and backspace moves the cursor backward one notch.

When inserting only one character, use the insch() function instead.

Examples

```
insstr("ERROR ->");
```

Here, the string ERROR-> is inserted into the standard screen at the cursor's position.

```
mvinsnstr(found_y,found_x,patch,5);
```

Here, the first five characters from the string patch are inserted into the standard screen at the locations specified in the found_y and found_x variables.

```
winsstr(tally,result[x]);
```

Here, the text represented by result[x] is inserted at the cursor's current position in the window tally.

Sample Program

```
1    #include <ncurses.h>
2
3    int main(void)
4    {
5        int y,x,a,b;
6        char ch;
7        char s[] = "Excuse me while I squeeze in here!";
8
9        initscr();
```

```
10
11          getmaxyx(stdscr,y,x);
12          x >>= 1;                   /* cut x in half*/
13          for(a=0;a<y;a++)
14          {
15              for(b=0;b<x;b++)
16                  addch('.');
17              addch('\n');
18          }
19          refresh();
20          getch();
21
22          mvinsstr(5,10,s);
23          refresh();
24          getch();
25
26          endwin();
27          return 0;
28      }
```

Sample output:

The left side of the screen is populated with dots. Pressing Enter causes text to be inserted, visually showing the dots previously there pushed off to the right.

Also See

insch(), addstr()

instr()

The instr() function reads text characters from a window and stores them in a char array. Text is read from the cursor's current position to the end of the line or for the length specified, depending on the version of the function.

Man Page Formats

```
int instr(char *str);
int innstr(char *str, int n);
int winstr(WINDOW *win, char *str);
int winnstr(WINDOW *win, char *str, int n);
int mvinstr(int y, int x, char *str);
int mvinnstr(int y, int x, char *str, int n);
int mvwinstr(WINDOW *win, int y, int x, char *str);
int mvwinnstr(WINDOW *win, int y, int x, char *str, int n);
```

Format Reference

str indicates a char array big enough to hold text from the window, plus the terminating \0 character NCurses appends to the end of the string. The text is read from the cursor's position to the end of the row.

For the n functions, n represents the maximum number of characters to read and place into the str. When n is 0, less than 0, longer than the width of the window, or longer than the distance from the cursor to the end of the row, then the whole line is read — just like the instr() version of the function.

Refer to the *w*, *mv*, and *mvw* entries elsewhere in this appendix for information on the win, y, and x arguments.

Return Value

OK on success, ERR on failure. Refer to OK and ERR elsewhere in this appendix for additional and vital information.

Notes

The instr() function does not move the cursor.

instr() reads the entire line of text, saving blanks as the space character (\x20). The last character of the array is \0, not \n.

This function reads only text characters from the window. To read chtype characters, which include both text and formatting attributes, use the inchstr() function instead. See inchstr().

When control characters are put to the screen, NCurses displays them as two characters, ^ followed by the control character's key code. When a function such as instr() reads the screen, it returns the ^ and character code values, not the control code that was originally put to the screen.

Examples

```
winnstr(beta,first_name,32);
```

In the statement, 32 characters of text are read from the cursor's current location (to the right) in the window beta. The characters are stored in the string first_name.

```
mvinstr(0,0,row[0]);
```

The entire top row of the standard screen is read and stored into the string array row[0].

Sample Program

```
1    #include <ncurses.h>
2    #include <stdlib.h>
3
4    int main(void)
5    {
6        int y,x;
7        char *c;
8
9        initscr();
10       start_color();
11       init_pair(1,COLOR_RED,COLOR_WHITE);
12
13   /* set aside memory for chtype array */
14       getmaxyx(stdscr,y,x);
15       c = (char *)malloc((x+1));
16       if( c == NULL)
17       {
18           endwin();
19           puts("Unable to allocate memory.");
20           return(1);
21       }
22
23   /* write something interesting to the screen */
24       attron(COLOR_PAIR(1));
25       addstr("This is a bit of text!");
26       attroff(COLOR_PAIR(1));
27       refresh();
28       getch();
29
30   /* copy the text only using instr */
31       mvinstr(0,0,c);
32       mvaddstr(10,0,"Here is the text read:\n");
33       addstr(c);
34       refresh();
35       getch();
36
37       endwin();
38       return 0;
39   }
```

Sample output:

This is a bit of text *appears at the top of the screen in red-on-white text. Only the text is read by* mvinstr() *in line 31, and displayed on line 11 after the Enter key is pressed.*

Also See

inchstr()

intrflush()

The `intrflush()` function controls whether the keyboard input queue is flushed when an interrupt key is typed at the keyboard.

Man Page Format

```
int intrflush(WINDOW *win, bool bf);
```

Format Reference

`win` is ignored.

`bf` is a Boolean value, either `TRUE` or `FALSE`. `TRUE` turns on interrupt flushing on keyboard input. `FALSE` disables interrupt flushing.

Return Value

`ERR` upon failure, `OK` or some value other than `ERR` upon success.

Notes

When `intrflush()` is `TRUE`, pressing a break key results in an instant flush of the input queue, and immediate action upon the break key. When it is `FALSE`, then the interrupt is still acted upon, but any text in the buffer may appear later, such as at the command prompt.

The interrupt keys `intrflush()` monitors are listed in Table A-9.

The behavior of the Break key on your keyboard (if one exists) depends on how its mapped in the terminal.

When `intrflush()` is turned on, pressing an interrupt key results in a faster response than would otherwise be experienced.

On the downside, having `intrflush()` turned on may result in disconnect between what NCurses believes to be displayed on the screen versus what's actually there.

Table A-9: Interrupt keys monitored by *intrflush()*

KEY FUNCTION	NAME	KEY(S)	ASCII	SIGNAL
Break	BREAK	Break?	n/a	BRKINT
Interrupt	INTR	^C	0x03	SIGINT
Quit	QUIT	^\	0x1c	SIGQUIT

The default state for interrupt flushing is set by the terminal and inherited by your NCurses program.

Examples

```
intrflush(NULL,TRUE);
```

Here, the `intrflush()` state is set `TRUE`, meaning that the input buffer is flushed when an interrupt key is pressed.

```
intrflush(NULL,TRUE);
```

The `intrflush()` state is set above to `FALSE`, meaning that the input is not flushed when an interrupt key is pressed but may be flushed afterwards.

Sample Program

```
1    #include <ncurses.h>
2
3    int main(void)
4    {
5        char buffer[81];
6
7        initscr();
8        intrflush(NULL,FALSE);
9
10       addstr("Type on the keyboard whilst I wait...\n");
11       refresh();
12       napms(5000);                /* 5 seconds */
13
14       addstr("Here is what you typed:\n");
15       getnstr(buffer,80);
16       refresh();
17
18       endwin();
19       return 0;
20   }
```

Sample output:

```
Type on the keyboard whilst I wait...
```

Type something; then press Ctrl+C. The Ctrl+C quits the program, and then you'll see the text you typed appear at the prompt.

Also See

```
flushinp(),qiflush(),typeahead()
```

isendwin()

The `isendwin()` function is used to determine whether NCurses visual mode has not been reactivated after a call to the `endwin()` function has been made.

Explanation

Though `endwin()` is officially the "End of NCurses Program" function, it's still possible to use NCurses functions after the `endwin()` call has been made.

For example, `endwin()` can be used to suspend NCurses visual mode and return to tty mode. Afterwards, any subsequent calls to `refresh()` or `doupdate()` restore NCurses visual mode, meaning that though `endwin()` has been called, NCurses functions are still being used. (The `endwin()` function still needs to be called when the program really does quit.)

The `isendwin()` function returns TRUE if `endwin()` has been called and the program has not re-activated NCurses visual mode. `isendwin()` returns FALSE if `endwin()` has been called *and* followed by a `refresh()` or `doupdate()` function to once again activate NCurses visual mode.

Man Page Format

```
bool isendwin(void);
```

Format Reference

The function has no arguments.

Return Value

A Boolean value, either TRUE or FALSE, both of which are defined in NCURSES.H.

TRUE is returned when the `endwin()` function has been called and NCurses visual mode has been restarted by a `refresh()` or `doupdate()` function.

FALSE is returned when `endwin()` has been called and NCurses has not returned to visual mode.

Notes

Do not use this function to determine whether or not NCurses is in visual mode.

FALSE is returned when `isendwin()` is called before `endwin()` has been issued.

Calling isendwin() before initscr() or newterm() has initialized
NCurses isn't necessarily a Bad Thing; like other NCurses functions used outside of initialization it will merely return FALSE.

I refer to this as the "Is it really over?" function.

Examples

```
endwin();
if(isendwin())
```

The if condition evaluates to TRUE because the endwin() function was
just issued.

```
endwin();
refresh();
if(isendwin())
```

The if condition evaluates to FALSE because although the endwin() function has been issued, the refresh() function has restarted NCurses visual
mode.

Sample Program

```
1    #include <ncurses.h>
2
3    int main(void)
4    {
5        initscr();
6
7        addstr("Press Enter to temporarily suspend this program:\n");
8        refresh();
9        getch();
10
11       endwin();
12
13       fputs("Program suspended...",stdout);
14       if(isendwin())
15           fputs("isendwin() returns TRUE...",stdout);
16       else
17           fputs("isendwin() returns FALSE...",stdout);
18       puts("Press Enter:");
19       fflush(stdout);
20       getch();
21
22       addstr("Now NCurses visual mode has been restarted ⊃
after endwin().\n");
23       if(isendwin())
```

```
24              addstr("isendwin() returns TRUE.\n");
25          else
26              addstr("isendwin() returns FALSE.\n");
27          refresh();
28          getch();
29
30          endwin();
31          return 0;
32      }
```

Sample output:

```
Press Enter to temporarily suspend this program:
```

Press Enter and the program ends. You see:

```
Program suspended...isendwin() returns TRUE...Press Enter:
```

Press Enter:

```
Press Enter to temporarily suspend this program:
Now NCurses visual mode has been restarted after endwin().
isendwin() returns TRUE.
```

Also See

```
endwin()
```

is_linetouched()

The is_linetouched() function determines whether a line of text in a window has been altered since the last screen update.

Explanation

NCurses keeps track of which portions of a window have been changed since the last refresh(). The is_linetouched() function determines whether or not any text on a given line (row) of text has been modified since that refresh(). If so, the function returns TRUE, FALSE otherwise.

Man Page Format

```
bool is_linetouched(WINDOW *win, int line);
```

Format Reference

win is an NCurses window, either stdscr for the standard screen or the name of a WINDOW variable returned from a function that creates new windows.

line is an int value indicating which row (line) to check for updates. Values range from 0 for the top row to the maximum rows in a window.

Return Value

The value returned by is_linetouched() is one of the following constants declared in NCURSES.H:

- TRUE, indicating that the line has been modified since the last refresh()
- FALSE, indicating that the line and the current screen match up (or should match up as far as NCurses is concerned)
- ERR, which happens when an invalid line number is specified

Notes

The is_linetouched() function is merely a tool you can use to determine whether or not a row of text has been updated since the last refresh(). Using the is_linetouched() function does not force NCurses to update the screen but rather indicates which line will be updated on the next refresh.

is_linetouched() works best after a recent refresh. For example, when a window is just created, or initscr() has created the standard screen, then effectively all lines in the window are *touched*. Only after issuing a recent refresh() does the is_linetouched() function become truly useful.

The is_linetouched() function always returns TRUE after the touchline() function is used. See touchline().

Example

```
if(is_linetouched(alpha,0));
```

Here, the if test passes when modifications have been made to line 0 in window alpha.

Sample Program

```
1    #include <ncurses.h>
2
3    int main(void)
4    {
```

```
 5          WINDOW *hide;
 6          int row;
 7
 8          initscr();
 9          hide = newwin(0,0,0,0);
10
11          refresh();              /* Initial write of the standard ⏎
screen */
12          waddstr(hide,"Changes are being made to the standard ⏎
screen\n");
13          mvaddstr(3,5,"Change!");
14          mvaddstr(10,60,"Change!");
15          mvaddstr(20,40,"Change!");
16          waddstr(hide,"Press Enter to see which rows have been ⏎
changed:\n");
17          wrefresh(hide);
18          getch();
19
20          for(row=0;row<LINES;row++)
21          {
22              if(is_linetouched(stdscr,row))
23                  wprintw(hide,"Line %d has been updated.\n",row);
24          }
25          wrefresh(hide);
26          getch();
27
28          endwin();
29          return 0;
30      }
```

Sample output:

```
Changes are being made to the standard screen
Press Enter to see which rows have been changed:
Line 3 has been updated.
Line 10 has been updated.
Line 20 has been updated.
```

Also See

touchline(),wtouchln(),is_wintouched(),refresh()

is_wintouched()

The is_wintouched() function helps determine whether any part of a window has been changed or updated since the last refresh().

Man Page Format

```
bool is_wintouched(WINDOW *win);
```

Format Reference

win is the name of the window to examine.

Return Value

The function returns TRUE when the window has been changed, FALSE otherwise. TRUE and FALSE are defined in NCURSES.H.

Notes

A window is considered touched immediately after it's created or, in the case of stdscr, immediately after the initscr() function. On such a new window, the is_wintouched() function always returns TRUE. Therefore, it's best to use is_wintouched() after a refresh() or wrefresh() call is made for a specific window.

is_wintouched() always returns TRUE after the touchwin() function is used. See touchwin().

The is_wintouched() function does not force NCurses to update a window on the next call to refresh(). Instead, is_wintouched() is merely a tool you can use to determine whether or not a window has been modified since the last refresh or whether a refresh for a particular window is really necessary.

Example

```
if(is_wintouched(stdscr));
```

This if test is true when the standard screen has been updated since the last call to refresh().

Sample Program

```
1    #include <ncurses.h>
2
3    int main(void)
4    {
5        WINDOW *fred;
6
7        initscr();
8        fred = newwin(0,0,0,0);
9
```

```
10          wrefresh(fred);              /* Initial write of fred */
11          waddstr(fred,"Hello?");
12          addstr("The window 'fred' ");
13          if(is_wintouched(fred))
14              addstr("has");
15          else
16              addstr("has not");
17          addstr(" been changed since the last refresh().\n");
18          refresh();
19          getch();
20
21          endwin();
22          return 0;
23      }
```

Sample output:

```
The window 'fred' has been changed since the last refresh().
```

Also See

`touchwin(), untouchwin(), is_linetouched(), refresh()`

keyname()

The `keyname()` function returns a string representing the character or key code associated with a specific value.

Man Page Format

```
char *keyname(int c);
char *key_name(wchar_t w);
```

Format Reference

c is an `int` value representing a specific character code.

wchar_t w is used to represent wide character formats with the `key_name()` variation of this function.

Return Value

A string, char pointer, representing the character, control code, meta code, or keyboard constant for the key code specified. NULL is returned on error.

Notes

Codes corresponding to ASCII control codes are displayed using their corresponding alphabetic or punctuation symbol, prefixed by the ^ symbol.

Extended ASCII codes are displayed prefixed by M- (for *meta*), followed by their corresponding ASCII code characters.

keyname() also returns the constant name defined for special keys on the keyboard, such as KEY_UP. While KEY_UP is defined in NCURSES.H as a specific value, when that value (the KEY_UP constant) is used with keyname(), the string "KEY_UP" is returned, and similarly for other special keyboard keys and constants.

Example

```
ckey = keyname(v);
```

Here, the string returned by keyname() for the key code in variable v is saved in the char pointer variable ckey.

Sample Program

```
1    #include <ncurses.h>
2
3    int main(void)
4    {
5        int c;
6
7        initscr();
8
9        for(c=0;c<255;c++)
10            printw("%-5s",keyname(c));
11
12       refresh();
13       getch();
14
15       endwin();
16       return 0;
17   }
```

Sample output:

^@	^A	^B	^C	^D	^E	^F	^G	^H	^I	^J	^K	^L
^M	^N	^O										
^P	^Q	^R	^S	^T	^U	^V	^W	^X	^Y	^Z	^[	^\
^]	^^	^_										
	!	"	#	$	%	&	'	(	)	*	+	,
	.	/										
0	1	2	3	4	5	6	7	8	9	:	;	<
	>	?										

```
@   A   B   C   D   E   F   G   H   I   J   K   L   M↵
    N   O
P   Q   R   S   T   U   V   W   X   Y   Z   [   \   ]↵
        ^   _
`   a   b   c   d   e   f   g   h   i   j   k   l   m↵
    n   o
p   q   r   s   t   u   v   w   x   y   z   {   |   }↵
    ~   ^?
M-^@ M-^A M-^B M-^C M-^D M-^E M-^F M-^G M-^H M-^I M-^J M-^K M-^L M-↵
^M M-^N M-^O
M-^P M-^Q M-^R M-^S M-^T M-^U M-^V M-^W M-^X M-^Y M-^Z M-^[ M-^\ ↵
M-^] M-^^ M-^_
M-   M-!  M-"  M-#  M-$  M-%  M-&  M-'  M-(  M-)  M-*  M-+  M-,  M↵
--   M-.  M-/
M-0  M-1  M-2  M-3  M-4  M-5  M-6  M-7  M-8  M-9  M-:  M-;  M-<  ↵
M-=  M->  M-?
M-@  M-A  M-B  M-C  M-D  M-E  M-F  M-G  M-H  M-I  M-J  M-K  M-L  M-M↵
  M-N  M-O
M-P  M-Q  M-R  M-S  M-T  M-U  M-V  M-W  M-X  M-Y  M-Z  M-[  M-\  M-]↵
   M-^  M-_
M-`  M-a  M-b  M-c  M-d  M-e  M-f  M-g  M-h  M-i  M-j  M-k  M-l  M-m↵
  M-n  M-o
M-p  M-q  M-r  M-s  M-t  M-u  M-v  M-w  M-x  M-y  M-z  M-{  M-|  M-}↵
  M-~
```

Also See

`unctrl()`, `addch()`

keypad()

The `keypad()` function allows special keys (nonalphanumeric), function keys, and cursor control keys to be read by NCurses programs.

Man Page Format

```
int keypad(WINDOW *win, bool bf);
```

Format Reference

`win` is the name of a `WINDOW` variable, indicating the window through which special keys can be read, or `stdscr` for the standard screen. (See `getch()` for more information on how the `win` argument plays out with NCurses input.)

`bf` is a Boolean value, either `TRUE` to turn on the read of special keys or `FALSE` to disable that feature.

Return Value

ERR on failure, OK or some value other than ERR on success.

Notes

Many of the special keys keypad() allows your code to monitor are defined in NCURSES.H and listed in Appendix D.

The operating system may steal special function keys from your program, intercepting them before your code has a chance to process the key process. When that's the case, you can try to use the raw() function in NCurses to get the function keys passed directly to your program.

On PCs, the Num Lock state must be off for the keys on the numeric keypad to be read as cursor movement keys, not numbers. Note, however, that xterm looks to see what's going on and overlays its own configuration, which may override this.

Example

```
keypad(menu,TRUE);
```

Here, reading of special keys from the keyboard is possible by wgetch() functions reading input from the window menu.

Sample Program

```
1     #include <ncurses.h>
2
3     int main(void)
4     {
5         int ch;
6
7         initscr();
8
9         keypad(stdscr,TRUE);
10        do
11        {
12            ch = getch();
13            switch(ch)
14            {
15                case KEY_DOWN:
16                    addstr("Down\n");
17                    break;
18                case KEY_UP:
19                    addstr("Up\n");
20                    break;
21                case KEY_LEFT:
22                    addstr("Left\n");
```

```
23                   break;
24              case KEY_RIGHT:
25                   addstr("Right\n");
26              default:
27                   break;
28          }
29          refresh();
30      } while(ch != '\n');
31
32      endwin();
33      return 0;
34  }
```

Sample output:

```
Up
Down
Left
Right
Up
Up
Down
Left
Right
Left
Right
Up
Down
Down
```

Also See

Chapter 7, Appendix D, getch()

killchar()

The killchar() function returns the character that currently serves as the terminal's Killchar, or KILL, key.

Man Page Format

```
char killchar(void);
```

Format Reference

The function has no arguments.

Return Value

A `char` value is returned, indicating the terminal's currently set Killchar.

Notes

The Killchar is the key or key combination you press to back up and erase an entire line of text at the command prompt, resetting the cursor back to the start of input.

The `getstr()` functions properly interpret the Killchar.

The `cbreak()` and `raw()` modes modify NCurses input functions to ignore the Killchar's keys function. When Killchar is input, it's treated just like any other character, typically displayed on the screen in the ^c format.

The `unctrl()` function can be used to translate a control code, such as the code used for Killchar, into the displayable ^c format.

Example

```
if( ch == killchar())
```

The `if` condition tests true when the value of variable `ch` is the same as the terminal's Killchar.

Sample Program

```
1     #include <ncurses.h>
2
3     int main(void)
4     {
5         char ch = '\0';
6
7         initscr();
8
9         ch = killchar();
10        printw("The Killchar is 0x%02x or %s\n",ch,unctrl(ch));
11        refresh();
12        getch();
13
14        endwin();
15        return 0;
16    }
```

Sample output:

```
The Killchar is 0x15 or ^U
```

Also See

erasechar(), cbreak(), raw(), unctrl()

leaveok()

The leaveok() function directs NCurses not to update a window's virtual cursor location to the hardware cursor location during a refresh() operation.

Explanation

As part of the refresh operation, NCurses synchronizes a window's virtual cursor location with the hardware location on the screen. When the leaveok() function is activated for a window (set TRUE), then NCurses does not synchronize the cursor's position for the window; the hardware cursor's position then remains where it was or ends up in some other location.

Man Page Format

```
int leaveok(WINDOW *win, bool bf);
```

Format Reference

win is a WINDOW variable indicating which window leaveok() is to monitor. The cursor's location for win will not be updated when win is refreshed.

   bf is a Boolean value, either TRUE to have the cursor position not updated during a refresh, or FALSE to have the cursor position updated. Most windows are preset to FALSE.

Return Value

The function always returns OK.

Notes

The location where the cursor ends up cannot be predicted in advance. In fact, in my experience you should not rely on the cursor being or staying anywhere when leaveok() is TRUE.

   The cursor's location on one window does not affect the cursor's location on another window.

The leaveok() function can be issued any time after a window has been created and before it's refreshed.

leaveok() can save overhead for those programs that don't rely upon the cursor or need a cursor blinking on the screen in any particular spot.

leaveok() does not hide the cursor. For that you need to use the curs_set() function (and hope that your terminal supports it).

Examples

```
leaveok(stdscr,TRUE);
```

Here, the statement directs NCurses not to synchronize the hardware cursor with the virtual cursor location on the standard screen.

```
leaveok(help,FALSE);
```

This statement isn't needed, as FALSE is the normal condition for a window. However, if a previous leaveok() function set leaveok() to TRUE for the window help, then the statement restores the window's cursor back to normal updating.

Sample Program

```
1     #include <ncurses.h>
2
3     int main(void)
4     {
5         initscr();
6         start_color();
7         init_pair(1,COLOR_WHITE,COLOR_BLUE);
8
9         addstr("This is the standard screen as it normally ⏎
appears.\n");
10        addstr("The cursor is synchronized ->");
11        refresh();
12        getch();
13
14        leaveok(stdscr,TRUE);
15        bkgd(COLOR_PAIR(1));
16        addstr("\n\nThe cursor is now not being updated.\n");
17        addstr("This means that its position could be anywhere.\n");
18        refresh();
19        getch();
20
21        endwin();
22        return 0;
23    }
```

Sample output:

```
This is the standard screen as it normally appears.
The cursor is synchronized ->
```

The cursor appears after the >. Press Enter and the screen is painted white-on-blue, and the cursor blinks in the lower-right corner (well, on my screen).

```
The cursor is now not being updated.
This means that its position could be anywhere.
```

Also See

`refresh(), curs_set(), getsyx()`

LINES

The `LINES` constant is an `int` value set internally by NCurses to represent the number of rows, or lines, available on the standard screen.

Man Page Format

Not applicable.

Format Reference

`LINES` works like any C language constant. It can be used as an immediate value, in a comparison, or in combination with other values.

Return Value

The value of `LINES` depends on the number of rows in the terminal or standard screen, `stdscr`.

`LINES` is an `int`.

Notes

Most standard terminal windows have either 24 or 25 rows.

Do note that with terminal windows in graphical environments, terminals can be just about any size. Also, some text screens have the ability to show 30, 40, 50, or even more rows.

LINES   *LINES*

~~ROWS~~ is a variable, not a constant. Note that changing the value of ~~ROWS~~ does not re-size the standard screen or terminal window.

Normally NCurses sets LINES equal to the LINES environment variable. This can be changed by using the use_env() function. See use_env().

Use the getmaxyx() function to determine the number of rows in any NCurses window.

Yeah, this should really be ROWS, but who am I?

Examples

```
printw("This screen has only %d rows.\n",LINES);
```

Here, the printw() function displays the value of LINES in a string of text put to the screen.

```
if(LINES<25)
```

This statement tests to see if the value of LINES is less than 25. If so, then the next block of statements are executed.

Sample Program

Refer to the entry for COLS for a sample program and output.

Also See

COLS, getmaxyx(), use_env()

longname()

The longname() function returns a string describing the current terminal.

Man Page Format

```
char *termname(void);
```

Format Reference

The function has no arguments.

Return Value

A string representing information about the terminal. On error, NULL is returned.

Notes

It's best to call longname() after the initscr() or newterm() function has been used.

The termname() function returns only the terminal's name, which may be part of the string returned by longname().

The string longname() returns is the *verbose* terminal description — but not that verbose! The maximum number of characters returned by longname() is 128, which includes the trailing \0.

Other functions that return information about the terminal include baudrate(), erasechar(), killchar(), has_il(), has_ic(), termattrs(), and termname().

Example

```
tp = longname();
```

Here, the memory location of the string returned by the longname() function is saved in the tp pointer.

Sample Program

```
1    #include <ncurses.h>
2
3    int main(void)
4    {
5        initscr();
6
7        addstr("Here is the longname() information:\n");
8        addstr(longname());
9        refresh();
10       getch();
11
12       endwin();
13       return 0;
14   }
```

Sample output:

```
Here is the longname() information:
generic color xterm
```

Also See

termname()

meta()

The meta() function controls whether the keyboard is read in 7-bit or 8-bit mode.

Explanation

Meta comes from old terminal keyboards that had a Meta key, similar to the Alt key on a PC or the Command key on a Mac. The Meta key was a special shift key used in combination with other keys to allow for extended input of keyboard commands. In many cases, the Meta key merely added the 8th bit on input of standard keys. So the U key, which has a 7-bit value of 1010101 would have the 8-bit value 11010101 when input with the Meta key pressed.

Man Page Format

```
int meta(WINDOW *win, bool bf);
```

Format Reference

win is the name of a WINDOW variable representing a window on the screen. The man page says that this argument, however, is ignored.

bf is a Boolean value, TRUE to enable the reading of the 8th bit on input, FALSE to restrict character input to 7 bits.

Return Value

ERR on failure, or OK or a value other than ERR on success.

Notes

Setting meta() TRUE is the same as setting the CS8 flag for the terminal in POSIX.

When the meta_off/rmm and meta_on/smm abilities are defined for the terminal, NCurses sends those signals to the terminal when you call meta(): smm is sent for meta() TRUE, and rmm is sent for meta() FALSE.

Eight-bit characters can be input on the PC by using the Alt key pad. Pressing and holding the Alt key, type a meta key value between 128 and 255 on the keypad. Release the Alt key to generate that key value.

Example

```
meta(win,TRUE);
```

The statement allows for 8-bit character input in the window win.

Sample Program

```
1      #include <ncurses.h>
2
3      int main(void)
4      {
5          int c;
6
7          initscr();
8
9          meta(stdscr,TRUE);
10         addstr("Input is now 8 bits wide.\n");
11         refresh();
12         c = getch();
13         printw("\nAnd getch() reads the value %d.\n",c);
14         meta(stdscr,FALSE);
15         addstr("Input is now 7 bits wide.\n");
16         refresh();
17         c = getch();
18         printw("\nAnd getch() reads the value %d.\n",c);
19
20         refresh();
21         getch();
22
23         endwin();
24         return 0;
25     }
```

Sample output:

```
Input is now 8 bits wide.
?
And getch() reads the value 197.
Input is now 7 bits wide.
~S
And getch() reads the value 19.
```

Also See

getch()

MEVENT

NCurses uses the MEVENT structure to store information about a specific mouse event. The getch() function is used to determine when a mouse event has taken place. After that, getmouse() reads information about the mouse event and stores that data into a MEVENT structure. The program can then read data from the MEVENT structure to see what happened and act accordingly.

Man Page Format

Not applicable.

Format Reference

MEVENT is a structure defined in NCURSES.H. It has the following components:

```
short id;
int x, y, z;
mmask_t bstate;
```

id is a short int value used to make a distinction between multiple pointing devices, for example on a laptop with both a mouse pad and external mouse.

x is an int value representing the column in which the mouse pointer was at during the event. Values start at 0 for the leftmost column.

y is an int value representing the row in which the mouse pointer was at during the event. Values start at 0 for the top row.

z is an int value reserved for future use, though it might be for reading the wheel button.

bstate is a mmask_t (long int) value representing the mouse's button state at the time of the event. mmask_t values and their defined constants are listed in Table A-10.

Return Value

Not applicable.

Table A-10: Mouse action constant values

MOUSE ACTION CONSTANT	VALUE
BUTTON1_RELEASED	0x1
BUTTON1_PRESSED	0x2
BUTTON1_CLICKED	0x4
BUTTON1_DOUBLE_CLICKED	0x8
BUTTON1_TRIPLE_CLICKED	0x10
BUTTON1_RESERVED_EVENT	0x20
BUTTON2_RELEASED	0x40
BUTTON2_PRESSED	0x80
BUTTON2_CLICKED	0x100
BUTTON2_DOUBLE_CLICKED	0x200
BUTTON2_TRIPLE_CLICKED	0x400
BUTTON2_RESERVED_EVENT	0x800
BUTTON3_RELEASED	0x1000
BUTTON3_PRESSED	0x2000
BUTTON3_CLICKED	0x4000
BUTTON3_DOUBLE_CLICKED	0x8000
BUTTON3_TRIPLE_CLICKED	0x10000
BUTTON3_RESERVED_EVENT	0x20000
BUTTON4_RELEASED	0x40000
BUTTON4_PRESSED	0x80000
BUTTON4_CLICKED	0x100000
BUTTON4_DOUBLE_CLICKED	0x200000
BUTTON4_TRIPLE_CLICKED	0x400000
BUTTON4_RESERVED_EVENT	0x800000
BUTTON_CTRL	0x1000000
BUTTON_SHIFT	0x2000000
BUTTON_ALT	0x4000000
ALL_MOUSE_EVENTS	0x7ffffff
REPORT_MOUSE_POSITION	0x8000000

Notes

The actions the mouse can perform are defined as constants in NCURSES.H. Table A-10 lists them, along with their long int values. Please do note that these values may change in the future as more mouse abilities come to be monitored in NCurses.

Examples

```
MEVENT me;
```

The statement creates a MEVENT structure named me.

```
getmouse(&me)
```

The getmouse() function above reads information about the most recent mouse event and stores it in the MEVENT structure me.

```
row = me.y;
col = me.x;
```

The two statements read the values of the mouse's row and column locations from the MEVENT structure me. The row location is saved in the variable row; the column location is saved in the variable col.

Sample Program

Refer to the entry for getmouse() for a sample program and output.

Also See

Chapter 13, getmouse(), mousemask()

mouse_trafo()

The mouse_trafo() function helps translate mouse coordinates between the screen and the standard screen.

Man Page Format

```
bool mouse_trafo(int* pY, int* pX, bool to_screen);
bool wmouse_trafo(const WINDOW* win, int* pY, int* pX, bool to_screen);
```

Format Reference

pY and pX are the addresses of int variables. pY holds the row value of a screen coordinate, pX holds the column value.

to_screen is a Boolean value, either TRUE or FALSE. When to_screen is TRUE, the coordinates pY and pX are converted from the window's coordinates to the screen's coordinates. When to_screen is FALSE, the coordinates are converted from the screen's coordinates into the window's coordinates.

Refer to the *w* entry later in this appendix for information on the win argument.

Return Value

The function returns a Boolean value, either TRUE upon success or FALSE when one of the coordinates is NULL or the coordinates are outside the window.

Notes

This isn't an easy one to figure out, but the Sample Program should help.

The function is called with pY and pX already filled with a set of coordinates. When the function is successful, new coordinates are put into those variables. Otherwise, when the function fails, the coordinate pair is unchanged.

Functions such as ripoffline() and slk_init() affect the size of the standard screen, meaning that mouse_trafo() might be necessary to check the mouse event coordinates for such a reduced-size standard screen.

Example

```
if (mouse_trafo(&ry,&rx,FALSE))
```

Here, the ry and rx variables contain the coordinates of a mouse click obtained from the MEVENT structure, read by getmouse(). The mouse_trafo() function translates those coordinates from screen-relative to window-relative. When the translation is successful, the condition passes and the if statement(s) are then executed.

Sample Program

```
1    #include <ncurses.h>
2
3    int main(void)
4    {
5        WINDOW *tinkie;
6        MEVENT mwhat;
```

```
 7        int ch,row,col;
 8
 9        initscr();
10        noecho();
11        mousemask(ALL_MOUSE_EVENTS,NULL);
12
13        tinkie = newwin(LINES-4,COLS-4,2,1);
14        keypad(tinkie,TRUE);
15
16        while(1)
17        {
18            ch = wgetch(tinkie);
19            if( ch == KEY_MOUSE )
20            {
21                getmouse(&mwhat);
22                row = mwhat.y;
23                col = mwhat.x;
24                wmouse_trafo(tinkie,&row,&col,FALSE);
25                mvwaddch(tinkie,row,col,'*');
26                refresh();
27                continue;
28            }
29            if( ch == '\n' )
30                break;
31        }
32
33        endwin();
34        return 0;
35    }
```

Sample output:

The mouse clicks produce an asterisk, ∗, in the window tinkie. *The* mouse_trafo() *function helps translate the coordinates from screen-relative to relative to the window, meaning that the asterisks show up where the mouse is clicked. (Recompile with* FALSE *in line 24 to see the difference.)*

Also See

getmouse()

mousemask()

The mousemask() function determines which mouse events are to be monitored for those programs that use the mouse.

Explanation

A mouse event is some type of action done with the mouse. It includes pressing, releasing, clicking, double-clicking, and triple-clicking for up to four mouse buttons, as well as using the Ctrl, Shift, or Alt keys while clicking. Refer to Table A-10 for the full list.

The `mousemask()` function merely determines which or how many of the various mouse events a program is to monitor. The actual reading of the mouse events is done through a combination of the `getch()` and `getmouse()` functions. See `getmouse()`.

Additionally, the `mousemask()` function can be used to determine whether or not a given terminal can read the mouse. Refer to the Sample Program.

Man Page Format

```
mmask_t mousemask(mmask_t newmask, mmask_t *oldmask);
```

Format Reference

`newmask` is a `mmask_t` variable (`long int`), representing the mouse actions your program monitors. Mouse action constants are defined in the `NCURSES.H` file and listed in the Notes section. Multiple actions are specified in the `newmask` argument by using a | (logical OR) between the constants. Or the `ALL_MOUSE_EVENTS` value can be used to monitor all mouse actions.

`oldmask`, also an `mmask_t` variable, can be a previous value returned from the `mousemask()` function, but mostly `NULL` is specified in its place.

Return Value

The value returned by `mousemask()` is an `mmask_t` variable representing the mouse actions `mousemask()` will be monitoring, specifically those actions your terminal is capable of monitoring. Therefore it's important to check this value to determine that your program is using those mouse actions you need.

Notes

Setting the value of `newmask` to zero has the effect of turning off the mouse pointer.

Mouse button constants are listed in Table A-11. In Table A-12 you'll find a list of multi-click functions. Finally, Table A-13 lists keyboard shift states that can be logically OR'd with other mouse states.

Table A-11: Mouse action constant values

BUTTON	UP/RELEASED	DOWN/PRESSED	DOWN-UP/CLICKED
1	BUTTON1_RELEASED	BUTTON1_PRESSED	BUTTON1_CLICKED
2	BUTTON2_RELEASED	BUTTON2_PRESSED	BUTTON2_CLICKED
3	BUTTON3_RELEASED	BUTTON3_PRESSED	BUTTON3_CLICKED
4	BUTTON4_RELEASED	BUTTON4_PRESSED	BUTTON4_CLICKED

Table A-12: Mouse action constants

BUTTON	DOUBLE-CLICKED	TRIPLE-CLICKED	RESERVED EVENT
1	BUTTON1_DOUBLE_CLICKED	BUTTON1_TRIPLE_CLICKED	BUTTON1_RESERVED_EVENT
2	BUTTON2_DOUBLE_CLICKED	BUTTON2_TRIPLE_CLICKED	BUTTON2_RESERVED_EVENT
3	BUTTON3_DOUBLE_CLICKED	BUTTON3_TRIPLE_CLICKED	BUTTON3_RESERVED_EVENT
4	BUTTON4_DOUBLE_CLICKED	BUTTON4_TRIPLE_CLICKED	BUTTON4_RESERVED_EVENT

Table A-13: Mouse action constants (continued)

ACTION	CONSTANT
Control key pressed during button up/down	BUTTON_CTRL
Shift key pressed during button up/down	BUTTON_SHIFT
Alt key pressed during button up/down	BUTTON_ALT
All events	ALL_MOUSE_EVENTS

Examples

```
mousemask(ALL_MOUSE_EVENTS);
```

The statement directs NCurses to scan for all available mouse events.

```
mmask = mousemask(ALL_MOUSE_EVENTS);
```

Here, the statement saves the return value of mousemask() to the mmask_t variable mmask. Then mmask can be used later to check for which mouse events are available.

```
mousemask(BUTTON1_CLICKED | BUTTON_CTRL);
```

The statement directs NCurses to monitor both the button 1 click as well as the button 1 click with the keyboard's Ctrl (control) key pressed.

Sample Program

Refer to the entry for getmouse() for a sample program and output.

Also See

Chapter 13, getmouse(), MEVENT

move()

The move() function relocates the cursor to the given row and column coordinates.

Man Page Format

```
int move(int y, int x);
int wmove(WINDOW *win, int y, int x);
```

Format Reference

y is an int value representing the number of the row to which to move the cursor. Values range from 0 for the top row, to whatever the size of the window.

x is an int value representing the number of the column to which the cursor is moved. Values range from 0 for the left-most column, to the width of the window.

Refer to the entry for *w* later in this appendix for more information on the win argument.

Return Value

ERR upon failure, or OK on success, though values other than ERR may also be returned upon success.

Notes

move() is a pseudo function, representing wmove(stdscr, row, col).

The row, or y, argument comes first.

Location 0, 0 is the *home* position, the upper-left corner of a window.

The function fails when it attempts to place the cursor outside the bounds of the window.

Use the `getmaxyx()` function to determine the size of the window and, therefore, the bounds for `row` and `col` in the `move()` function. But remember that the first row and column in a window are numbered 0 (zero), not 1.

Most functions that place text to the screen also advance the cursor.

The `mv` and `mvw` prefix functions both more the cursor as well as place text.

Examples

```
move(0,0);
```

The statement homes the cursor on the standard screen.

```
wmove(menu,xmax/2,ymax/2);
```

After the statement, the cursor is placed at the center of the window `menu`, assuming the `xmax` and `ymax` represent the maximum values for the rows and columns for that window.

Sample Program

```
1     #include <ncurses.h>
2
3     int main(void)
4     {
5         initscr();
6
7         addstr("Putting an asterisk at location 10,50:");
8         move(10,50);
9         addch('*');
10        refresh();
11        getch();
12
13        endwin();
14        return 0;
15    }
```

Sample output:

```
Putting an asterisk at location 10, 50:
```

And an asterisk appears at that position on the standard screen.

Also See

Chapter 4, mv prefix, curs_set(), mvcur(), getyx(), getmaxyx()

mv prefix functions

Nearly all NCurses text output functions come with a variation prefixed by mv. The mv means that the function includes a new cursor location. This saves typing over having to use a move() function before using a standard text output function; both functions are combined into one.

Format

The mv prefix functions feature y and x as their first arguments.

y is the vertical or row position at which to place the character. Zero represents the top row. The maximum value for y depends on the window's height.

x is the horizontal or column position at which to place the character. Zero represents the far left column. The maximum value for x depends on the window's width.

Refer to the individual functions elsewhere in this appendix for information on other arguments listed.

Return Value

All the mv-prefixed functions shown earlier return either OK or ERR. Normally, these values aren't checked; however, it's a good idea to check them with the mv-prefixed functions — especially when there is a possibility that a character would be placed outside a window's boundary.

OK and ERR are defined in NCURSES.H.

Notes

The functions mvwin() and mvderwin() are not mv-prefix functions.

While the mv prefix functions save typing, using them is not more efficient nor saves any time over using the separate move() function before an output function.

Also See

addch(), addchstr(), addstr(), and so on

mvderwin()

The mvderwin() function uses a subwindow to display a different portion of the parent window. It does not really move anything other than data.

Explanation

Subwindows share memory with their parent. Therefore, moving a subwindow doesn't really do anything. Instead, what this function does is allow you to display a different portion of the parent window in the subwindow rectangle.

Man Page Format

```
int mvderwin(WINDOW *win, int par_y, int par_x);
```

Format Reference

win is the name of a WINDOW variable representing a subwindow.

par_y is an int value representing the row value of a coordinate in the parent window.

par_x is an int value representing the column value of a coordinate in the parent window.

Return Value

OK on success or ERR upon failure.

Notes

The mvderwin() function takes a rectangle of text from the parent window at location par_y, par_x, with the same width and depth as the subwindow, as copies that text into the subwindow's location.

This function also copies any text attributes from the source location in the parent window to the subwindow, overwriting any attributes already in the subwindow.

mvderwin() updates a window inside a subwindow in much the same manner as prefresh() updates a portion of a pad inside a window. See prefresh().

This function works on all subwindows, whether they were created by the subwin() or derwin() functions.

The mvwin() function is used to move a window. It should not be used on a subwindow.

According to popular lore on the Internet, "The subwindow functions are flaky, incompletely implemented, and not well tested."

Example

```
mvderwin(sub,5,10);
```

Here, the statement copies text from location row 5, column 10 in the parent window and places it into the subwindow sub. The width and depth of the information copied is equal in size to the subwindow.

Sample Program

```
1      #include <ncurses.h>
2
3      int main(void)
4      {
5          WINDOW *sonny;
6
7          initscr();
8          start_color();
9          init_pair(1,COLOR_WHITE,COLOR_BLUE);
10         init_pair(2,COLOR_RED,COLOR_YELLOW);
11
12         sonny = subwin(stdscr,5,20,10,30);
13
14         bkgd(COLOR_PAIR(1));
15         addstr("Hello, son.");
16         wbkgd(sonny,COLOR_PAIR(2));
17         waddstr(sonny,"Hello, Dad!");
18         refresh();
19         getch();
20
21         mvderwin(sonny,0,0);
22         wbkgd(sonny,COLOR_PAIR(2));
23         wrefresh(sonny);
24         getch(sonny);
25
26         endwin();
27         return 0;
28     }
```

Sample output:

A yellow subwindow is created with the text Hello, Dad! *Press Enter and the text* Hello, son. *is copied from the upper-right corner of the parent into the subwindow via* mvderwin()*.*

Also See

mvwin(),prefresh(),subwin(),derwin()

mvw prefix functions

A host of NCurses text output functions come prefixed by mvw. This combines the mv and w prefixes, allowing text to be placed at a specific position within a specific window.

Format

The mvw prefix functions feature win, y, and x as their first arguments.

win is a WINDOW variable, representing a window created earlier in the program. Refer to the W Prefix entry later in this appendix for more details.

y and x represent the cursor's position on the screen. They are int values for the row and column, ranging from 0 to the height and width of the window, respectively.

Refer to the individual functions elsewhere in this appendix for information on the other arguments in the various *mvw* prefix functions.

Notes

Note that win always comes first, even though mv comes first in the mvw prefix.

The mvwin() function is not an mvw-prefix function.

Also See

addch(),addchstr(),addstr(),and so on

mvwin()

The mvwin() function is used to move a window on the screen, changing its origin to the coordinates given.

Man Page Format

```
int mvwin(WINDOW *win, int y, int x);
```

Format Reference

```
mvwin(win,row,col)
```

win is a WINDOW variable referring to the window you want moved.

row is the new starting row for the window's left edge.

col is the new starting column for the window's top.

Values for row and col are ints, ranging from 0 for the left/top edge of the standard screen, on through the dimensions of the standard screen, minus the size of window win. See LINES and COLS.

Return Value

OK upon success, or ERR on failure. Failure most often occurs when the move results in part of the window being off-screen. In that case, ERR is returned and the window remains at its original location.

Notes

The original window is not erased by the move, leading to a "Picard maneuver" type situation where the moved window appears twice on the screen. To remove the old window, use a touchline() or touchwin() function on the background window. Refer to the Sample Program.

According to the man page, "moving subwindows is allowed, but should be avoided." I'll go one step further: *do not use this function on a subwindow!* Also see mvderwin().

The wmove() function is used to relocate the cursor in a window. See move().

Example

```
mvwin(help,ybase+dy,xbase+dx);
```

The function moves the window help to the new location specified by the ybase+dy (row) and xbase+dx (column) arguments.

Sample Program

```
1    #include <ncurses.h>
2
3    int main(void)
4    {
5        int row,col;
6        WINDOW *peri;
7
8        initscr();
9        start_color();
10       init_pair(1,COLOR_WHITE,COLOR_BLUE);
11
12       peri = newwin(5,30,2,30);
```

```
13          wbkgd(peri,COLOR_PAIR(1));
14          waddstr(peri,"I am the peripatetic window");
15          wrefresh(peri);
16          getch(peri);
17
18          wtouchln(stdscr,2,5,1);
19          mvwin(peri,12,40);
20          wnoutrefresh(stdscr);
21          wnoutrefresh(peri);
22          doupdate();
23          getch();
24
25          endwin();
26          return 0;
27     }
```

Sample output:
A blue subwindow appears on the screen. Press Enter and it moves to a new location.

Also See

Chapter 10, `touchline()`

napms(ms)

The `napms()` function pauses program execution for a given number of microseconds (millionth of a second).

Man Page Format

```
int napms(int ms);
```

Format Reference

```
napms(ms)
```

`ms` is the number of milliseconds program execution pauses. It's an `int` value, therefore the maximum pause for any computer system depends on the size of an `int`. Negative values and 0 result in no pause, but do not produce an error.

Return Value

Always returns `OK`.

Notes

Yeah, the name is cute: nap ms. Get it? Still, *namps* is a popular typo.

1000 milliseconds equals 1 second.

napms() is defined as a low-level NCurses function, one of the few documented in this appendix.

Examples

```
napms(500);
```

The statement causes program execution to pause for half a second.

```
napms(60000);
```

The statement delays program execution for one minute.

Sample Program

```
1    #include <ncurses.h>
2
3    int main(void)
4    {
5        initscr();
6
7        addstr("Give me a second...");
8        refresh();
9        napms(1000);
10        addstr("...Thanks!\n");
11        refresh();
12        getch();
13
14        endwin();
15        return 0;
16    }
```

Sample output:

```
Give me a second...
```

A second passes . . .

```
...Thanks!
```

Also See

Chapter 2

NCURSES_MOUSE_VERSION

The NCURSES_MOUSE_VERSION constant is defined in NCURSES.H and set equal to the NCurses mouse support release version.

Man Page Format

Not applicable.

Format Reference

The NCURSES_MOUSE_VERSION constant returns an int value equal to the current version of the mouse support software.

Return Value

NCURSES_MOUSE_VERSION is set equal to 2 for the current release of NCurses as this book goes to press.

Notes

The NCURSES_MOUSE_VERSION constant is used to help programmers determine mouse support as well as integrate mouse support into their code.

Examples

```
#ifdef NCURSES_MOUSE_VERSION
   /*
    * Mouse functions go here
    */
#endif
```

Here, NCURSES_MOUSE_VERSION is used in a macro to allow mouse access in a program where NCurses mouse support is available.

```
printw("This is NCurses  mouse version %d.\n",NCURSES_MOUSE_VERSION);
```

The printw() function displays the text This is NCurses mouse version followed by the current version value.

Sample Program

```
1    #include <ncurses.h>
2
3    int main(void)
```

```
 4    {
 5        initscr();
 6
 7        if(NCURSES_MOUSE_VERSION > 0)
 8            addstr("This version of NCurses supports the mouse.\n");
 9        else
10            addstr("This version of NCurses does not support ⤵
the mouse.\n");
11        refresh();
12        getch();
13
14        endwin();
15        return 0;
16    }
```

Sample output:

```
This version of NCurses supports the mouse.
```

Also See

Chapter 13, `NCURSES_VERSION`, `mousemask()`, `getmouse()`

NCURSES_VERSION

`NCURSES_VERSION` is one of a series of constants defined in `NCURSES.H` that describe which version of NCurses is being used.

Explanation

NCurses version constants are employed in programs that rely upon version-specific NCurses commands, typically used with various preprocessor directives to selectively compile code, though they can also be used as immediate values.

Man Page Format

Not applicable.

Format Reference

```
NCURSES_VERSION
NCURSES_VERSION_MAJOR
NCURSES_VERSION_MINOR
NCURSES_VERSION_PATCH
```

The NCURSES_VERSION constant contains a string specifying NCurses major and minor versions.

The NCURSES_VERSION_MAJOR constant contains NCurses major version number.

The NCURSES_VERSION_MINOR constant contains NCurses minor version number.

The NCURSES_VERSION_PATCH constant contains NCurses most recent patch number.

Return Value

The values the constants contain depend on the release of NCurses, obviously. Otherwise:

- NCURSES_VERSION is a string value, such as 5.4.
- NCURSES_VERSION_MAJOR is a numeric value, such as 5.
- NCURSES_VERSION_MINOR is a numeric value, such as 4.
- NCURSES_VERSION_PATCH is a numeric value combining the year, month and day of the most recent NCurses patch release, such as 20040208. (This value is also defined for release versions of NCurses.)

Notes

You can find newer versions of Curses (well, NCurses) at:

```
http://ftp.gnu.org/pub/gnu/ncurses/
```

A constant CURSES also exists, which is set to 1. Your programs should use the NCURSES_VERSION... constants instead.

Examples

```
printw("This is NCurses version %s.\n",NCURSES_VERSION);
```

Here, the printw() function displays the text This is NCurses version followed by the current version string.

```
if(NCURSES_VERSION_MAJOR<5)
```

The if test checks to ensure that the user's version of NCurses is at least major release 5.

Sample Program

```
1    #include <ncurses.h>
2
3    int main(void)
4    {
5        initscr();
6
7    #ifdef NCURSES_VERSION
8        printw("This is NCurses version %s.%d.\n",\
9            NCURSES_VERSION,NCURSES_VERSION_PATCH);
10   #else
11       printw("You are apparently not using NCurses.\n");
12   #endif
13       refresh();
14       getch();
15
16       endwin();
17       return 0;
18   }
```

Sample output:

```
This is NCurses version 5.4.20040208.
```

Also See

```
curses_version()
```

newpad()

The newpad() function is used to create a special type of window storage area called a *pad*.

Explanation

Pads work a lot like windows, though they're not displayed on the screen as such. Instead, the pad exists in memory and only chunks of it at a time are written to an actual window on the screen. The main advantage of this arrangement is that pads can be of any size, even a size greater than the screen.

Man Page Format

```
WINDOW *newpad(int nlines, int ncols);
```

Format Reference

`nlines` is an int value indicating the number of rows the pad will have. Values for `nlines` range from 1 on up to 32767, or the value of NCURSES_SIZE_T (normally defined as a `short`)..

ncols is an int value indicating the number columns for the new pad. Values range from 1 on up to 327676, or the value of NCURSES_SIZE_T.

The maximum value for ncols is 32767, the same as for nlines and is set by NCURSES_SIZE_T

Return Value

Upon successful creation of a new pad, a WINDOW pointer is returned. NULL is returned when there is a problem.

Notes

It's the `prefresh()` function that determines which part of a pad appears on a window. See `prefresh()`.

The symbol NCURSES_SIZE_T can be modified, though not casually. By doing so you can change the maximum size of a pad. Do keep in mind that NCurses applications are limited to short integers.

All text output and formatting commands work with a pad just as they do any window.

The `getch()` and `getch()` functions can be used with a pad, but unlike a window the input will not be displayed. Pads are not automatically updated with those functions, whereas regular windows are.

Pads cannot be scrolled. Do not use `scrollok()`, `scroll()` or `scrl()` with a pad.

Pads cannot be moved. Do not use `mvwin()` with a pad.

Do not use `wrefresh()` or `wnoutrefresh()` with a pad.

Pads cannot have subwindows; do not use `subwin()` with a pad. Instead, use `subpad()` to create a subpad. See `subpad()` for additional information and warnings.

Pads are removed by using the `delwin()` function, just as windows are removed. See `delwin()`.

Examples

```
p = newpad(200,WIDE+1);
```

The statement creates a pad with 200 rows and WIDE+1 columns. If successfully created, variable p is used like any other WINDOW variable to reference the pad in the code.

```
tinypad = newpad(2,10);
```

Here, a pad with 2 rows and 10 columns is created. Such a small pad could be used as off-screen storage.

```
doc = newpad(LINES,COLS+40);
```

The doc pad created here is as tall as the standard screen, but 40 characters wider. This type of pad could be used to facilitate sideways scrolling — coupled with adept programming and use of the prefresh() function.

Sample Program

```
1     #include <ncurses.h>
2
3     int main(void)
4     {
5         WINDOW *p;
6
7         initscr();
8
9         p = newpad(50,100);          /* create a new pad */
10        if( p == NULL )
11        {
12            endwin();
13            puts("Unable to create new pad");
14            return(1);
15        }
16
17        addstr("New pad created\n");
18        refresh();
19        getch();
20
21        endwin();
22        return 0;
23    }
```

Sample output:

```
New pad created
```

Also See

Chapter 11, prefresh(), pechochar(), delwin(), subpad()

newterm()

The `newterm()` function initializes NCurses for use on a specific terminal, with a specific terminal configuration, for a one-line terminal, or for multiple terminals. `newterm()` is used in place of `initscr()` when your code needs to access terminals in a special way.

Man Page Format

```
SCREEN *newterm(char *type, FILE *outfd, FILE *infd);
```

Format Reference

`type` is a string of text representing a terminal type, such as `ansi` or `xterm`, which is what helps facilitate placing stuff on the screen. When `NULL` is specified, the value of environmental variable `$TERM` is used.

`outfd` is a `FILE` pointer representing a file opened for output to the terminal.

`infd` is a `FILE` pointer representing a file opened for input from the terminal.

Return Value

The function returns a `SCREEN` pointer, which identifies a screen structure in memory. It's through that pointer that NCurses accesses the terminal named by `newterm()`.

Notes

Use the `set_term()` function after initializing NCurses with `newterm()` to set the output terminal. See `set_term()`.

After everything is set up, you can use NCurses input and output functions with the new terminal just as you did when `initscr()` set things up for one terminal only.

The `termname()` function can be used to obtain the current terminal name (the `termtype` argument), though using `NULL` seems simple enough. See `termname()`.

Example

```
term_a = newterm("ansi",fileout,filein);
```

Here, a new `ansi` terminal is created using open file handles `fileout` for output and `filein` for input. The resulting NCurses terminal is saved in the

SCREEN pointer `term_a`. (Also refer to the Sample Program for more of the setup involved before `newterm()` can be called.)

Sample Program

```
1    #include <ncurses.h>
2
3    #define INTERM "/dev/ttyp1"
4    #define OUTTERM "/dev/ttyp2"
5
6    int main(void)
7    {
8        FILE *termin,*termout;
9        SCREEN *tp1,*tp2;
10       char name[81];
11
12   /* Open terminal one for reading
13      Open terminal two for writing */
14       termin = fopen(INTERM,"r");
15       termout = fopen(OUTTERM,"w");
16       if( termin==NULL || termout==NULL )
17       {
18           puts("Unable to open terminal.");
19           return(1);
20       }
21
22   /* set up the new terminal in NCurses */
23       tp2 = newterm(NULL,termout,termin);
24       if( tp2 == NULL)
25       {
26           puts("Unable to open terminal window.");
27           return(2);
28       }
29
30   /* NCurses is now started for the new terminal */
31       tp1 = set_term(tp2);
32       printw("Welcome to NCurses output on terminal %s.\n",OUTTERM);
33       printw("You can type on terminal %s, and see it ⊃
here.\n",INTERM);
34       addstr("What is your name: ");
35       refresh();
36       getnstr(name,80);
37       printw("%s, glad to have you aboard!",name);
38       refresh();
39       getch();
40
41       endwin();
42       return 0;
43   }
```

> **NOTE** Specify the proper terminal device names and types in lines 3 and 4. I used the names of the virtual terminals on the screen in Mac OS X. The terminal names you use should be two screens you can access and see on your console.

Sample output:

If possible, configure the two terminal windows so that you can see both at once. Make sure no programs are running on the second terminal. On the second terminal, you'll see:

```
Welcome to NCurses output on terminal /dev/ttyp2.
You can type on terminal /dev/ttyp1, and see it here.
What is your name:
```

Type your name on the first terminal window and press Enter.

```
Dan Gookin, glad to have you aboard!
```

Press Enter to quit the program and restore both windows.

Also See

```
set_term(), initscr()
```

newwin()

The newwin() function creates a new window within NCurses.

Man Page Format

```
WINDOW *newwin(int nlines, int ncols, int begin_y, int begin_x);
```

Format Reference

nlines is an int value that sets the height of the window in rows. Values for nlines range from 1 through the height of the standard screen. When 0 is specified for nlines, the new window's height will be the same as the standard screen's height.

ncols is an int value setting the width of the window in columns. Values range from 1 through the width of the standard screen. Specifying 0 for ncols sets the new window's width to the same as the standard screen's width.

begin_y is an int value indicating the location of the new window's top row relative to the standard screen. Values range from 0 for the top row to the maximum number of rows on the standard screen *minus* the new window's height.

begin_x is an int value indicating the location of the new window's leftmost column. Values range from 0 for the far left column to the maximum number of columns on the standard screen *minus* the new window's width.

Together, begin_y and begin_x plot the coordinates of the new window's upper-left corner. The window's lower-right corner is calculated by adding the nlines and ncols values to that coordinate.

Return Value

Upon success, the function returns a pointer referencing a WINDOW structure in memory. The pointer is used to reference the window in other NCurses commands.

Upon failure, the pointer is equal to NULL. Failure occurs when the window is larger than the screen, part of the window does not fit on the screen, or not enough memory is available to allocate space for the window.

Notes

Refer to Figure 8-1 for a visual representation of how the newwin() function's arguments map out onto the screen.

The smallest window possible is a 1-by-1 character window, big enough for only one character.

The window cannot be larger than the standard screen, nor can the window be positioned so that part of it extends beyond the edge of the screen's rectangle. Either condition causes an error (NULL pointer) to be returned by newwin().

When you need a window larger than the screen, you need a *pad*. See newpad().

Refer to the entries for COLS and LINES to get the size of the standard screen.

The function newwin(0,0,0,0) creates a new window the same size and position as the standard screen.

newwin() merely creates the new window's structure and the pointer reference. It does not display the window's contents. Use wrefresh() for that task.

The w prefix commands direct output or detect input associated with a particular window.

Windows can be splashed with color, text attributes, or even a "background" text character. Refer to the bkgd() function for more info.

To place a box or border around a window, refer to the box() and border() functions.

Examples

```
if((help = newwin(10,30,4,26)) == NULL)
```

Here, a new window named `help` is created, being 10 rows high and 30 rows wide and located at position 4, 26 on the standard screen. But the statement is also a comparison, and if that `newwin()` function fails, then the `if` test passes and the next few statements are executed.

```
a = newwin(halfy,halfx,0,0);
b = newwin(halfy,halfx,0,halfx);
c = newwin(halfy,halfx,halfy,0);
d = newwin(halfy,halfx,halfy,halfx);
```

These four statements create four windows, a, b, c, and d. Assuming that `halfy` and `halfx` are half the row height and column width of the standard screen, then the four windows occupy four equal sections of the standard screen: a in the upper left; b in the upper right; c in the lower left; and d in the lower right.

Sample Program

```
1    #include <ncurses.h>
2
3    #define ALPHA_W 30
4    #define ALPHA_H 5
5
6    int main(void)
7    {
8        WINDOW *alpha;
9        int x,y;
10
11   /* set things up */
12       initscr();
13       start_color();
14       init_pair(1,COLOR_WHITE,COLOR_BLUE);
15
16   /* Calculate the window origin coordinates that will place
17      the window at the center of the standard screen */
18       x = (COLS - ALPHA_W) >> 1;
19       y = (LINES - ALPHA_H) >> 1;
20
21       addstr("Creating new window....\n");
22       refresh();
23       alpha = newwin(ALPHA_H,ALPHA_W,y,x);
24       if( alpha == NULL)
25       {
26           endwin();
27           puts("Problem creating window");
```

```
28              return(1);
29         }
30
31         addstr("Displaying window:\n");
32         refresh();
33         wbkgd(alpha,COLOR_PAIR(1));
34         mvwaddstr(alpha,2,12,"Hello!");
35         wrefresh(alpha);
36
37         getch();
38
39         endwin();
40         return 0;
41     }
```

Sample output:

```
Creating new window....
Displaying window:
```

And a blue window appears in the center of the screen, with the word Hello! *displayed in its center.*

Also See

Chapter 8, WINDOW, dupwin(), refresh(), delwin(), *w* prefix commands

nl()

nl() is an input modification function that allows your program to distinguish between the line feed and carriage return codes.

Explanation

The newline \n actually generates two separate cursor movement commands. The first is the carriage return (CR), which moves the cursor to the start of a line — just like the carriage return bar on the old manual typewriters. The second cursor movement command is the line feed (LF), which advances the cursor down one row on the screen.

Code-wise, ASCII defines CR as code 13 or ^M, and LF as code 10 or ^J. On the PC keyboard, the Enter key is traditionally mapped to ^M, which is why you often find text files imported from a PC (Windows) to UNIX as lacking linefeeds. Similarly, PC users often find imported UNIX text files to lack carriage returns. The reason is that the Enter key in UNIX, the \n, is mapped to code 10, which provides both carriage return and line feed functions.

The terminal normally interprets both code 13 or ^M and code 10 or ^J as the \n, which is code 10. So whether you type Enter, Ctrl+J, or Ctrl+M on the keyboard, the nl() mode translates that key press into code 10. When nonl() is specified, your program can properly interpret the Ctrl+M key combination as code 13, a carriage return or \r. NCurses uses the nl() mode by default.

Man Page Format

```
int nl(void);
int nonl(void);
```

Format Reference

The function takes no arguments.

Return Value

Always OK.

Notes

Regardless of the nl() or *nonl()* modes, NCurses always displays the \n character as both a carriage return/line feed. (The \r character always returns to the beginning of the line.)

Supposedly NCurses is able to more efficiently move the cursor in nonl() mode.

Example

```
nonl();
```

The statement allows the program to distinguish between the line feed and carriage return characters.

Sample Program

```
1    #include <ncurses.h>
2
3    int main(void)
4    {
5        int ch = '\0';
6
7        initscr();
8
```

```
 9          nonl();
10          while(ch != 'z')
11              ch = getch();
12
13          endwin();
14          return 0;
15      }
```

Sample output:

As you type, experiment with the Ctrl+M and Ctrl+J keys to see how they perform differently. Recompiling the program after commenting out line 9 shows how NCurses interprets both Ctrl+M and Ctrl+J the same.

Also See

`getch()`

nocbreak()

See `cbreak()`.

nodelay()

The `nodelay()` function transforms the `getch()` function from a blocking call to nonblocking.

Explanation

Normally the `getch()` function waits for a key to be pressed. Waiting, waiting. `nodelay()` turns off the delay for a window, causing `wgetch()` to return `ERR` when a character isn't waiting or the character's value when a key has been pressed and its character is waiting in the input queue.

Man Page Format

```
int nodelay(WINDOW *win, bool bf);
```

Format Reference

`win` is the name of a window. Only `wgetch()` commands referencing `win` (or `getch()` for `stdscr`) are affected by `nodelay()`.

bf is a Boolean value, either TRUE or FALSE. TRUE turns on nodelay for the named window, causing calls to getch() not to pause. FALSE sets the normal mode, where getch() pauses to wait for a key.

Return Value

OK upon success, ERR on failure.

Notes

Normally, nodelay is set equal to FALSE.

There is no delay() function, but two other NCurses functions control input delay. Check out timeout() and halfdelay().

NCurses uses only one input queue from the keyboard, but by assigning a window value, it's possible to manipulate the input stream differently by associating wgetch() with a specific window. See getch() for more information.

Example

```
nodelay(stdscr,TRUE);
```

The statement turns getch() into a non-blocking call for the standard screen.

Sample Program

```
1     #include <ncurses.h>
2
3     int main(void)
4     {
5         int value = 0;
6
7         initscr();
8
9         nodelay(stdscr,TRUE);        /* turn off getch() wait */
10        addstr("Press the Spacebar to stop the insane loop!\n");
11        while(1)
12        {
13            printw("%d\r",value++);
14            refresh();
15            if(getch() == ' ') break;
16        }
17        getch();
18
19        endwin();
20        return 0;
21    }
```

Sample output:

```
Press the Spacebar to stop the insane loop!
```

Press the Spacebar to stop the counter.

Also See

Chapter 7, getch(), timeout(), halfdelay()

noecho()

See echo().

nonl()

See nl().

noqiflush()

See qiflush().

noraw()

See raw().

notimeout()

The notimeout() function determines whether or not NCurses input functions pause after the user presses the Esc key.

Explanation

An escape sequence can be generated either by the keyboard, such as when a specialty or function key is pressed, or manually input by the user. A one-second timeout is used to help determine whether the escape sequence is generated by the keyboard or the user, seeing how user input is slower than the escape sequence produced by the keyboard.

When `notimeout()` is set TRUE for a window, then `getch()` calls to that window will not wait one second to determine whether an escape sequence comes from the keyboard or user. The end effect is that input is greatly sped up for those programs where it's unlikely that the user will be manually inputting escape sequences or when keyboard escape sequences are not used. (Also see `keypad()`.)

Man Page Format

```
int notimeout(WINDOW *win, bool bf);
```

Format Reference

`win` is a `WINDOW` variable representing a window on the screen.

`bf` if a Boolean value, either `TRUE` or `FALSE`, both of which are defined in `NCURSES.H`.

Return Value

`ERR` upon failure or an `int` value other than `ERR` upon success.

Notes

There are three delays the `getch()` function checks when it is first called: `notimeout()`, `nodelay()`, and `halfdelay()`.

Don't confuse this function with `timeout()`, which adjusts the delay associated with blocking text input, not just the delay associated with Escape character input.

The delay doesn't seem to be present one way or the other when `keypad()` is set `FALSE` for the window.

Internally, NCurses uses the `ESCDELAY` constant to set the Esc key delay in increments of a millisecond. The value of 1000 sets a 1 second Esc key delay, which is the default on many systems.

The `notimeout()` state is only used in one special case: deciding whether to continue reading after a character was read. It's done independently of the `keypad()` logic.

I have not been able to get this function to work. As a workaround, I recommend setting the value of the `ESCDELAY` variable to zero when `notimeout(win, TRUE)` fails to behave:

```
ESCDELAY = 0;
```

Example

```
notimeout(stdscr,TRUE);
```

The statement disables the Esc key delay for the standard screen window.

Sample Program

```
1     #include <ncurses.h>
2
3     int main(void)
4     {
5         int ch = '\0';
6
7         initscr();
8
9         keypad(stdscr,TRUE);
10        notimeout(stdscr,FALSE);
11        addstr("Press the Esc key and note the delay:\n");
12        refresh();
13        while( ch != '\n')
14            ch = getch();
15
16        ch = '\0';
17        notimeout(stdscr,TRUE);
18        mvaddstr(3,0,"Now with notimeout TRUE, press Esc:\n");
19        refresh();
20        while( ch != '\n')
21            ch = getch();
22
23        endwin();
24        return 0;
25    }
```

Sample output:

```
Press the Esc key and note the delay:
^[
Now with notimeout TRUE, press Esc:
^[
```

Also See

```
getch(),timeout(),notimeout(),nodelay(),halfdelay()
```

OK

The int constant OK is used to indicate successful completion of a function.

Man Page Format

Not applicable.

Format Reference

OK can be used like any other constant, though it is most often found in a comparison:

```
if( function() == OK)
```

Or if the return value from a function is saved in a variable, r:

```
if( r == OK)
```

Or:

```
while( function() == OK)
```

Return Value

The value of OK is set in NCURSES.H to 0.

Notes

Not every function returns OK upon success.

Some functions are documented as returning ERR upon failure, but any value other than ERR — not specifically OK — upon success.

Note that OK might be defined as being zero, therefore something like:

```
while( function() )
```

cannot work based upon the function's success if the success returned is OK and OK is defined as zero.

OK's counterpart is the ERR constant. See ERR.

Example

```
if( putwin(menu,mfile) != OK)
```

The statement checks to see if the `putwin()` function has not returned `OK`, meaning that the operation has failed.

Sample Program

```
1     #include <ncurses.h>
2
3     int main(void)
4     {
5         int y = 0,x = 0, r;
6
7         initscr();
8
9         addstr("You Move The Cursor!\n");
10        addstr("Enter the Y (row) coordinate: ");
11        refresh();
12        scanw("%d",&y);
13        addstr("Enter the X (column) coordinate: ");
14        refresh();
15        scanw("%d",&x);
16
17        r = move(y,x);
18        if(r == ERR)
19        {
20            mvaddstr(3,0,"You have moved the cursor!");
21            move(y,x);
22        }
23        else
24            mvaddstr(3,0,"You cannot move the cursor there!");
25        refresh();
26        getch();
27
28        endwin();
29        return 0;
30    }
```

Sample output:

```
You Move The Cursor!
Enter the Y (row) coordinate: 50
Enter the X (column) coordinate: 5
You cannot move the cursor there!
```

Also See

ERR

overlay()

The `overlay()` function takes text from one window and places that text into the blank portions of another window.

Man Page Format

```
int overlay(const WINDOW *srcwin, WINDOW *dstwin);
```

Format Reference

`srcwin` is a `WINDOW` pointer representing the source window, from which text is copied.

`dstwin` is a `WINDOW` pointer representing the destination, the window where text from `srcwin` is pasted.

Return Value

The function returns `OK` upon success, or `ERR` when there is a problem.

Notes

With the `overlay()` function, only the blank parts of the destination window are over-written with text from the source window. Text from `srcwin` will not replace text in `dstwin`, neither will text attributes be copied to the `dstwin`.

`srcwin` and `dstwin` do not need to be the same size. However:

- The two windows *must* overlap. It is only the overlapping portion of the windows that is overlaid.

- When the two windows do not overlap, `overlay()` returns `ERR`.

The `overlay()` function behaves the same as the `copywin()` function with the `TRUE` argument.

Example

```
overlay(first,second);
```

After the statement, locations where window `first` overlaps window `second` will be changed; any blank spots in window `second` will be filled by overlapping text from window `first`.

Sample Program

```
1    #include <ncurses.h>
2
3    int main(void)
4    {
5        WINDOW *alpha,*beta;
6        int x;
7
8        initscr();
9        start_color();
10        init_pair(1,COLOR_WHITE,COLOR_BLUE);
11        init_pair(2,COLOR_WHITE,COLOR_RED);
12
13    /* create and color two side-by-side windows */
14        alpha = newwin(5,30,0,0);
15        wbkgd(alpha,COLOR_PAIR(1));
16        beta = newwin(5,30,1,2);
17        wbkgd(beta,COLOR_PAIR(2));
18
19    /* populate the windows with text */
20        for(x=0;x<75;x++)
21        {
22            wprintw(alpha,"O ");
23            wprintw(beta," X");
24        }
25        wrefresh(alpha);
26        wrefresh(beta);
27        getch(beta);
28
29    /* copy from window beta to window alpha */
30        overlay(beta,alpha);
31        wrefresh(alpha);
32        wrefresh(beta);
33        wgetch(beta);
34
35        endwin();
36        return 0;
37    }
```

Sample output:

Two windows appear, one blue with Os and another red with Xs. The two windows overlap for all but one row and column. Pressing Enter copies the Xs from the red window to the blue.

Also See

Chapter 10, copywin(), overwrite(), dupwin()

overwrite()

The `overwrite()` function takes text from one window and pastes it into another window, replacing the second window's text contents and attributes.

Man Page Format

```
int overwrite(const WINDOW *srcwin, WINDOW *dstwin);
```

Format Reference

`srcwin` is a `WINDOW` pointer representing the source window, from which text is copied.

`dstwin` is a `WINDOW` pointer representing the destination, the window where text from `srcwin` is pasted.

Return Value

The function returns `OK` or `ERR` upon success or failure, respectively.

Notes

The `overwrite()` function literally overwrites the contents of `srcwin` with `dstwin`; both text and attributes from `srcwin` replace text in `dstwin`.

`srcwin` and `dstwin` do not need to be the same size, but the two windows *must* overlap. Only the overlapping portion of the windows is affected by the `overwrite()` function.

When the two windows do not overlap, `overlay()` returns `ERR`.

The `overwrite()` function behaves the same as the `copywin()` function with the `FALSE` argument.

Example

```
overwrite(top, bottom);
```

The statement causes text from window `top` to overwrite and replace text from window `bottom` at those locations where the two windows overlap.

Sample Program

```
1    #include <ncurses.h>
2
3    int main(void)
4    {
```

```
 5          WINDOW *alpha,*beta;
 6          int x;
 7
 8          initscr();
 9          start_color();
10          init_pair(1,COLOR_WHITE,COLOR_BLUE);
11          init_pair(2,COLOR_WHITE,COLOR_RED);
12
13   /* create and color two side-by-side windows */
14          alpha = newwin(5,30,0,0);
15          wbkgd(alpha,COLOR_PAIR(1));
16          beta = newwin(5,30,1,2);
17          wbkgd(beta,COLOR_PAIR(2));
18
19   /* populate the windows with text */
20          for(x=0;x<75;x++)
21          {
22              wprintw(alpha,"O ");
23              wprintw(beta," X");
24          }
25          wrefresh(beta);
26          wrefresh(alpha);
27          wgetch(alpha);
28
29   /* copy from window beta to window alpha */
30          overwrite(beta,alpha);
31          wrefresh(beta);
32          wrefresh(alpha);
33          wgetch(alpha);
34
35          endwin();
36          return 0;
37   }
```

Sample output:

Two windows appear, one blue with Os overlapping another red with Xs. Pressing Enter copies the Xs from the red window to the blue, replacing any existing text and attributes. In fact, it appears as if the red window is on top, but it is not.

Also See

Chapter 10, copywin(), overlay(), dupwin()

pair_content()

The pair_content() function is used to determine which two colors have been assigned to a color pair.

Man Page Format

```
int pair_content(short pair, short *f, short *b);
```

Format Reference

pair is a short int value representing a color pair number. Values range from 0 through the value of the COLOR_PAIRS constant, minus 1.

f and b are addresses of short int variables to hold the color value of the text foreground and text background colors for pair, respectively. Values returned for foreground or background range from 0 through the value returned by COLORS, minus 1.

Return Value

The function returns OK for success or ERR for failure.

Notes

The start_color() function must be issued first in a program, or the pair_content() function will return ERR.

It is not necessary that pair represent a defined color pair. When called with an undefined color pair value, pair_content() returns zero for both foreground and background colors.

Colors 0 through 7 are defined as constants in NCURSES.H. See COLORS elsewhere in this appendix for the values.

Examples

```
pair_content(3,fg,bg);
```

This statement reads the color attributes assigned to color pair 3. The foreground value is stored in the location indicated by pointer variable fg, and the background value is stored in the location indicated by pointer variable bg. It's assumed that the pointer variables are initialized earlier in the code.

```
pair_content(pair,&fore,&back);
```

Here, the color values for color pair indicated by variable pair are stored in the locations for variables fore and back.

Sample Program

```
1    #include <ncurses.h>
2
3    char *ncolor(int color);
4
5    int main(void)
6    {
7        short pair,f,b;
8
9        initscr();
10       start_color();
11
12   /* Create color pairs */
13       init_pair(1,COLOR_WHITE,COLOR_BLUE);
14       init_pair(2,COLOR_BLACK,COLOR_RED);
15       init_pair(3,COLOR_YELLOW,COLOR_RED);
16       init_pair(4,COLOR_BLUE,COLOR_GREEN);
17       init_pair(5,COLOR_CYAN,COLOR_MAGENTA);
18
19   /* display pair colors */
20       for(pair=1;pair<=5;pair++)
21       {
22           attrset(COLOR_PAIR(pair));
23           pair_content(pair,&f,&b);
24           printw("Pair %d: %s foreground, %s background.\n",\
25               pair,ncolor(f),ncolor(b));
26       }
27       refresh();
28       getch();
29
30       endwin();
31       return 0;
32   }
33
34   char *ncolor(int color)
35   {
36       switch(color)
37       {
38           case COLOR_BLACK:
39               return("Black");
40           case COLOR_RED:
41               return("Red");
42           case COLOR_GREEN:
43               return("Green");
44           case COLOR_YELLOW:
45               return("Yellow");
```

```
46              case COLOR_BLUE:
47                  return("Blue");
48              case COLOR_MAGENTA:
49                  return("Magenta");
50              case COLOR_CYAN:
51                  return("Cyan");
52              case COLOR_WHITE:
53                  return("White");
54          }
55          return("?");
56      }
```

Sample output:

```
Pair 1: White foreground, Blue background.
Pair 2: Black foreground, Red background.
Pair 3: Yellow foreground, Red background.
Pair 4: Blue foreground, Green background.
Pair 5: Cyan foreground, Magenta background.
```

And the code here appears formatted with the colors indicated.

Also See

start_color(), init_pair(), COLOR_PAIRS

PAIR_NUMBER()

The PAIR_NUMBER() pseudo function is used to return which color pair is being used to format text.

Man Page Format

Not applicable.

Format Reference

```
PAIR_NUMBER(attr)
```

attr is the value produced by the COLOR_PAIR(n) attribute. It's the value used internally when NCurses builds attribute information to be stored on the screen in the chtype variable. (See Appendix C.)

Return Value

The value returned by PAIR_NUMBER() is an int is equal to whichever color pair number has been used to format the text and background colors. Its range is between 0 and the value of COLOR_PAIRS, minus 1.

Notes

In reality, COLOR_PAIR(n) is simply a cluster of bits used in the chtype value to define how a character in an NCurses window is formatted. The PAIR_NUMBER() pseudo function simply extracts the COLOR_PAIR(n) value, n itself, from that chtype value. This is why it's often written that PAIR_NUMBER() is the "opposite" of the COLOR_PAIR(n) function.

Examples

```
n = PAIR_NUMBER(a)
```

The value of variable a is equal to the value of a specific COLOR_PAIR(n). The value returned in variable n will be the same as a from COLOR_PAIR(a).

```
x = PAIR_NUMBER(COLOR_PAIR(n));
```

This statement is basically the same as x = n.

Sample Program

```
1    #include <ncurses.h>
2
3    int main(void)
4    {
5        int c,p;
6
7        initscr();
8        start_color();
9
10       init_pair(1,COLOR_RED,COLOR_WHITE);
11
12       c = COLOR_PAIR(1);
13       p = PAIR_NUMBER(c);
14       printw("COLOR_PAIR(1) = %d\n",c);
15       printw("PAIR_NUMBER(%d) = %d\n",c,p);
16       refresh();
17       getch();
```

```
18
19        endwin();
20        return 0;
21    }
```

Sample output:

```
COLOR_PAIR(1) = 256
PAIR_NUMBER(256) = 1
```

Also See

```
init_pair(),COLOR_PAIR
```

pechochar()

The pechochar() function is used to both put single characters to a pad and display those characters on the standard screen.

Man Page Format

```
int pechochar(WINDOW *pad, chtype ch);
```

Format Reference

pad is the name of a WINDOW pointer, referencing a pad created by the newpad() function.

ch is a chtype variable, a long int value. It can be a single character or a combination character and formatting attributes. See Appendix C for more information on chtype characters.

Return Value

OK on success, ERR on utter failure.

Notes

For the pechochar() function to work, a prefresh() function must first be used. prefresh() defines both the area on the standard screen where text appears as well as the part of the pad to which text is written. See the "Sample Program" for more information.

After `prefresh()` has been issued, then `pechochar()` can be used to simultaneously put text to the pad and display that text on the screen; no further calls to `prefresh()` are needed.

`pechochar()` advances the cursor's location on both the pad and standard screen. It behaves exactly like the `addch()` function in that respect.

The wide character version of this command is `pecho_wchar()`. Here is the man page format:

```
int pecho_wchar(WINDOW *pad, const cchar_t *wch);
```

Examples

```
pechochar(p,c);
```

The statement places the character represented by c onto pad p, displaying that character on the standard screen.

```
pechochar(xpad,'A' | A_BOLD);
```

Here, the statement places a bold letter A on pad xpad as well as on the standard screen.

Sample Program

```
1    #include <ncurses.h>
2
3    int main(void)
4    {
5        WINDOW *p;
6        char text[] = "Greetings from pad p.";
7        char *t;
8
9        initscr();
10
11       p = newpad(50,100);           /* create a new pad */
12       if( p == NULL )
13       {
14           endwin();
15           puts("Unable to create new pad");
16           return(1);
17       }
18
19       t = text;
20       prefresh(p,0,0,0,0,1,25);
21       while(*t)
22       {
```

```
23              pechochar(p,*t);
24              t++;
25              napms(50);
26          }
27          wgetch(p);
28
29          endwin();
30          return 0;
31      }
```

Sample output:

```
Greetings from pad p.
```

Also See

```
addch(), newpad(), prefresh()
```

pnoutrefresh()

The pnoutrefresh() function is analogous to the wnoutrefresh() function, but for a pad instead of a window. It's used to optimize the updating of multiple pads to the standard screen.

Explanation

pnoutrefresh() can best be used when updating several pads on the standard screen. Rather than using prefresh() on each pad, you can use pnoutrefresh() on each pad, then a single doupate() function to perform all the updates at once.

Man Page Format

```
int pnoutrefresh(WINDOW *pad, int pminrow, int pmincol,
int sminrow, int smincol, int smaxrow, int smaxcol);
```

Format Reference

Refer to the entry for prefresh() as the arguments are the same for both.

Return Value

OK on success; ERR when things get fouled up.

Notes

Internally, the prefresh() function is composed of a pnoutfresh() function followed by a call to doupdate().

Example

```
pnoutrefresh(p,0, 0, 0, 0, 23,19);
pnoutrefresh(p,24, 0, 0,24,23,43);
pnoutrefresh(p,48, 0, 0,48,23, 67);
doupdate();
```

The pnoutrefresh() functions update portions of the pad p to various locations on the standard screen. The final doupdate() function updates the screen with the information.

Sample Program

```
1      #include <ncurses.h>
2
3      int main(void)
4      {
5          WINDOW *pad;
6          int a;
7
8          initscr();
9
10         pad = newpad(40,100);
11         if(pad == NULL)
12         {
13             endwin();
14             puts("Problem creating pad");
15             return(1);
16         }
17
18         for(a=0;a<4000;a++)
19         {
20             waddch(pad,'A' + (a % 26));
21         }
22
23         prefresh(pad,0,0,7,30,17,50);
24         wgetch(pad);
```

```
25
26          mvwaddstr(pad,1,0,"Hello, there!");
27          pnoutrefresh(pad,0,0,7,30,17,50);
28          doupdate();
29          wgetch(pad);
30
31          endwin();
32          return 0;
33    }
```

Sample output:

The output is the same as shown for prefresh() *below, though after pressing the Enter key, the text* Hello, there! *appears on the second line.*

Also See

newpad(),prefresh(),doupdate(),wnoutrefresh()

prefresh()

The prefresh() function is used to display information stored in a pad structure to a window.

Explanation

Pads work like windows, though they're not displayed on the screen. To see the information put to a pad, the prefresh() function is used. Unlike the refresh() function, prefresh() takes a rectangle of text (and attributes) from the pad and places it in a window. This is how information from a pad is displayed.

Man Page Format

```
int prefresh(WINDOW *pad, int pminrow, int pmincol,
         int sminrow, int smincol, int smaxrow, int smaxcol);
```

Format Reference

pad is the name of a pad, a WINDOW pointer returned from the newpad() function.

pminrow and pmincol are int values represents the upper-left (Y and X) coordinates of a rectangle of text on the pad.

sminrow and smincol are int values representing the upper-left (Y and X) coordinates of a rectangle of text on the standard screen. This location is where the text from the pad will be placed.

smaxrow and smaxcol represent the lower-right (Y and X) coordinate of the rectangle on the standard screen. These are int values and they are relative to the home location, not to sminrow and smincol. The differences between the upper-left and lower-right coordinates on the screen are also used to calculate the size of the rectangle copied from the pad.

Return Value

OK or ERR depending on success or failure of the call.

Notes

prefresh() always outputs text to the standard screen.

The prefresh() function updates the standard screen; there is no need to call refresh() after prefresh() to see the text.

You cannot prefresh() a rectangle from the pad that is larger than the standard screen (or larger than the pad, for that matter).

Examples

```
prefresh(p,0,0,0,0,10,35);
```

The statement here places part of the pad p on the standard screen. The text from the pad starts at location 0, 0. The rectangle on the standard screen starts at location 0, 0, and it is 10 rows deep by 35 columns wide.

```
prefresh(psto,py,px,10,5,11,75);
```

Here, text from the pad psto is read from starting location py, px, and placed on the screen at location 10, 5. The rectangle is 1 row high and 70 characters wide.

Sample Program

```
1    #include <ncurses.h>
2
3    int main(void)
```

```
 4      {
 5          WINDOW *pad;
 6          int a;
 7
 8          initscr();
 9
10          pad = newpad(40,100);
11          if(pad == NULL)
12          {
13              endwin();
14              puts("Problem creating pad");
15              return(1);
16          }
17
18          for(a=0;a<4000;a++)
19          {
20              waddch(pad,'A' + (a % 26));
21          }
22
23          prefresh(pad,0,0,7,30,17,50);
24          wgetch(pad);
25
26          endwin();
27          return 0;
28      }
```

The sample output is shown in Figure A-9.

Also See

Chapter 11, newpad()

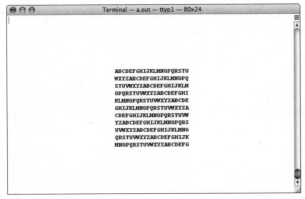

Figure A-9: A square chunk of the pad appears on the terminal screen.

printw()

The `printw()` function is the NCurses equivalent to the standard C `printf()` function. Use `printw()` in your NCurses programs when you need `printf()`.

Man Page Format

```
int printw(const char *fmt, ...);
int wprintw(WINDOW *win, const char *fmt, ...);
int mvprintw(int y, int x, const char *fmt, ...);
int mvwprintw(WINDOW *win, int y, int x, const char *fmt, ...);
int vw_printw(WINDOW *win, const char *fmt, va_list varglist);
int vwprintw(WINDOW *win, const char *fmt, va_list varglist);
```

Format Reference

The format for `printw()` is identical to `printf()`. `fmt` is a formatting string that defines text to be output. The string can contain text, escape characters, and replaceable parameters. `fmt` is followed by a list of variables that are displayed by the replaceable parameters.

Refer to the entries for *w*, *mv*, and *mvw* elsewhere in this appendix for information on the w, mv, and mvw variations to this function.

The `vwprintw()` functions are the NCurses versions of the `vprintf()` function, where `varglist` is a `va_list` (for example, a pointer) representing variable arguments. Refer to the man page for `vprintf()`.

Return Value

ERR on failure, OK or any `int` value other than ERR on success.

Notes

Internally, NCurses calls the `sprintf()` or vsprintf() functions to do the evaluation and text formatting for `printw()`. The output is done through the `addstr()` function and therefore all the notes for `addstr()` also apply to `printw()`.

A variable argument version of `printw()`, analogous to vsprintf(), is `vw_printw()`. Here is the man page format:

```
int vw_printw(WINDOW *win, const char *fmt, va_list varglist);
```

The older version of `vw_printw()` was `vwprintw()`. It carries the same format as `vw_printw()` but has been deprecated.

Examples

```
printw("Pleased to meet you, %s %s!",first,last);
```

Here, the statement displays on the standard·screen the text Pleased to meet you followed by the strings represented by first and last.

```
wprintw(test,"_maxx = %d, _maxy = %d\n",test->_maxx,test->_maxy);
```

The statement displays the values of _maxx and _maxy for the window test on the window test.

```
mvprintw(11,COL2, "%-30s", "October 19, 1993");
```

Here, the statement displays at row 11 and the column indicated by COL2, the text October 19, 1993 right-justified in a column 30 characters wide.

Sample Program

```
1    #include <ncurses.h>
2
3    int main(void)
4    {
5        int yoda = 874,ss = 65;
6
7        initscr();
8
9        printw("Yoda is %d years old\n",yoda);
10       printw("He has collected %d years\n",yoda-ss);
11       printw("of Social Security.");
12       refresh();
13       getch();
14
15       endwin();
16       return 0;
17   }
```

Sample output:

```
Yoda is 874 years old
He has collected 809 years
of Social Security.
```

Also See

Chapter 2, addstr(), scanw()

putwin()

The putwin() function saves a window's data to a formatted file on disk. All window information is saved: size, text, attributes, and so forth.

Man Page Format

```
int putwin(WINDOW *win, FILE *filep);
```

Format Reference

win is the name of a WINDOW variable representing the window to save to disk.
   filep is a FILE pointer representing a file open for writing.

Return Value

ERR on failure, or OK (or a value other than ERR) on success.

Notes

The getwin() function is used to read a window data file previously saved to disk by putwin(). See getwin().

   The file saved to disk starts with a WINDOW structure header and then contains chtype-like data for each character in the window. As saved to disk, each character in the window occupies 16 bytes.

Example

```
putwin(help,hfile);
```

   The statement saves information about and contents of the window help to a file referenced by hfile.

Sample Program

```
1      #include <ncurses.h>
2      #include <stdlib.h>
3
4      #define FILENAME "window.dat"
5
6      void bomb(char *message);
7
8      int main(void)
9      {
```

```
10        FILE *wfile;
11        WINDOW *win;
12        int r;
13
14        initscr();
15        start_color();
16        init_pair(1,COLOR_WHITE,COLOR_BLUE);
17
18        addstr("Creating new window\n");
19        refresh();
20
21    /* Crete the window */
22        win = newwin(5,20,7,30);
23        if(win == NULL)
24            bomb("Unable to create window\n");
25        wbkgd(win,COLOR_PAIR(1));
26        mvwaddstr(win,1,2,"This program was\n");
27        mvwaddstr(win,2,5,"created by\n");
28        mvwaddstr(win,3,5,"Dan Gookin\n");          ⏎
/* put your name here */
29        wrefresh(win);
30        getch();
31
32    /* open the file */
33        wfile = fopen(FILENAME,"w");
34        if( wfile==NULL)
35            bomb("Error creating file\n");
36
37    /* write the window's data */
38        r = putwin(win,wfile);
39        if( r == ERR)
40            addstr("Error putting window to disk\n");
41        else
42            addstr("Window put to disk\n");
43        fclose(wfile);
44        refresh();
45        getch();
46
47        endwin();
48        return 0;
49    }
50
51    void bomb(char *message)
52    {
53        endwin();
54        puts(message);
55        exit(1);
56    }
```

The sample output is shown in Figure A-10.

Figure A-10: This window is saved to disk.

Refer to the entry for getwin() *for a sample program that loads in the window image.*

Also See

Chapter 14, getwin(), scr_dump(), scr_restore()

qiflush()

The qiflush() and noqiflush() function control whether or not the keyboard input buffer is flushed when the Interrupt, Quit, or Suspend keys are used.

Man Page Format

```
void qiflush(void);
void noqiflush(void);
```

Format Reference

The functions take no arguments.

The qiflush() function directs NCurses to flush any text waiting in the input queue whenever the Interrupt, Quit, or Suspend keys are pressed.

The noqiflush() function directs NCurses to retain whatever text is in the buffer, which is typically flushed out at the next command prompt.

Return Value

OK upon success; ERR on failure.

Notes

Table A-14 explains the Interrupt, Quit, and Suspend keys.

The terminal's initial state determines whether `qiflush()` or `noqiflush()` is the norm for NCurses. You can use the `stty -a` command to check for your terminal: the `noflsh` and `-noflush` lflags disable or enable flush after `INTR`, `QUIT`, `SUSP`, respectively.

Examples

```
qiflush();
```

The statement causes any text left in the input queue to be flushed when the Interrupt, Quit, or Suspend keys are pressed.

```
noqiflush();
```

If the Interrupt, Quit, or Suspend keys are pressed after this command is issued, then any text remaining in the input queue stays there, only to be dumped out at the next opportunity.

Sample Program

```
1    #include <ncurses.h>
2
3    int main(void)
4    {
5        char buffer[81];
6
7        initscr();
8        noqiflush();
9
10       addstr("Type on the keyboard whilst I wait...\n");
11       refresh();
12       napms(5000);              /* 5 seconds */
13
14       addstr("Here is what you typed:\n");
15       getnstr(buffer,80);
16       refresh();
17
18       endwin();
19       return 0;
20   }
```

Table A-14: Interrupt, Quit, and Suspend Explained

KEY FUNCTION	NAME	KEY(S)	ASCII	FUNCTION
Interrupt	INTR	^C	0x03	Halt the program (SIGINT)
Quit	QUIT	^\	0x1c	Halts the program (SIGQUIT)
Suspend	SUSP	^Z	0x1a	Immediately stops program and sends it into the background (SIGTSTP)

Sample output:

```
Type on the keyboard whilst I wait...
```

Type something, then press Ctrl+Z. The Ctrl+Z suspends the program, placing it into the background. Any text you typed appears on the command prompt because noqiflsh() *prevented it from being flushed. Type* fg *to return to the program.*

Also See

flushinp(), intrflush(), typeahead()

raw()

The raw() function removes any modifications done by the terminal to input, allowing your program to read input in the *un-cooked* or *raw* mode. The companion noraw() function ensures that cooked mode, not raw, is enforced in NCurses.

Explanation

Normally the terminal has some control over input that's passed to your program. For example, your terminal's Killchar, Erase, Interrupt, and other special keys can also be used in your program. By using the raw() function, you can disable all that interception, allowing your program to receive all keyboard input.

Man Page Format

```
int raw(void);
int noraw(void);
```

Format Reference

The raw() command activates raw mode.

The noraw() command restores cooked input mode (normal).

Return Value

OK upon success, ERR upon failure.

Notes

The raw mode disables any keyboard buffering done by the terminal, which in effect allows characters to be read more quickly. However, if this is all you're after, I recommend using cbreak() instead of raw().

Raw mode specifically ignores the Interrupt, Quit, Suspend, Killchar, Erasechar, and flow control characters. Knowing which keys are which depends on how your terminal is configured. (Use the command stty -a to determine which keys your terminal uses.) Table A-15 lists common values.

If your keyboard has a Break key, then raw mode may or may not affect it, depending on how the key is mapped.

Table A-15: Keys and codes ignored in raw mode

KEY FUNCTION	NAME	KEY(S)	ASCII	FUNCTION
Delayed Suspend	DSUSP	^Y	0x19	Stops program when character is read (SIGTSTP)
Erasechar	ERASE	^? ^H	0x7F	Back up and erase
Flow control	STOP START	^S ^Q	0x13 0x11	^S pauses text output, ^Q restarts
Interrupt	INTR	^C	0x03	Halt the program (SIGINT)
Killchar	KILL	^U	0x15	Erases the input line, from cursor position to the line start
Quit	QUIT	^\	0x1c	Halts the program (SIGQUIT)
Suspend	SUSP	^Z	0x1a	Immediately stops program and sends it into the background (SIGTSTP)

NOTE Because raw mode ignores the Quit and Suspend keys, be extra careful! Unlike other NCurses programs, when `raw()` is active you cannot "break out" by pressing Ctrl+C or Ctrl+\. When a program runs amok in raw mode, the only way to kill it is with the `kill` command from another terminal window.

The `cbreak()` setting overrides `raw()`. See `cbreak()`.

Examples

```
raw()
```

Here, raw mode is set for the program.

```
noraw()
```

Here, the raw mode is cancelled.

Sample Program

```
1    #include <ncurses.h>
2
3    int main(void)
4    {
5        int ch;
6        initscr();
7
8        raw();
9        mvaddstr(0,0,"Type away, raw mode is on:");
10       while( getch() != '\n')
11           ;
12
13       noraw();
14       mvaddstr(3,0,"Type away, raw mode is off:");
15       while( getch() != '\n')
16           ;
17
18       endwin();
19       return 0;
20   }
```

Sample output:

```
Type away, raw mode is on:
```

Try any of the keys listed in the above table: Ctrl+Z, Ctrl+C, Ctrl+U. You'll see them display ^Z, ^C, ^U instead of performing their normal terminal functions. Press Enter to end the line.

```
Type away, raw mode is off:
```

Typing works as in the terminal. Keys from the above table perform their regular actions.

Also See

`cbreak(),halfdelay()`

redrawwin()

The `redrawwin()` function is used to help force an update of the terminal window when the contents of a window may be corrupted or in need of a complete refresh.

Man Page Format

```
int redrawwin(WINDOW *win);
```

Format Reference

`win` is the name of a window to update. It's a `WINDOW` variable representing a window on the screen, or `stdscr` for the standard screen.

Return Value

`ERR` on failure, `OK` or some value other than `ERR` when things go well.

Notes

This function is equivalent to `wredrawln(win,0,n)`, where `win` is the name of the window and `n` is the window's bottom row.

`wredrawwin()` works by telling NCurses to discard its corresponding data in the current screen, so it is forced to recompute when refreshing that window.

Refer to the entry for `wredrawln()` for more information and notes about this function.

Example

```
redrawwin(boy);
```

The statement directs NCurses to completely update the contents of the window `boy`.

Sample Program

```
1    #include <ncurses.h>
2    #include <stdlib.h>
3    int main(void)
4    {
5        WINDOW *coffee;
6        initscr();
7
8        coffee = newwin(2,40,0,0);
9
10       waddstr(coffee,"I'm just an innocent little program,\n");
11       waddstr(coffee,"minding my own business...");
12       wmove(coffee,0,0);
13       wrefresh(coffee);
14       getch();
15
16       system("echo \"RANDOM DATA\" > `tty`");
17       getch();
18
19       wredrawln(coffee,0,1);
20       wrefresh(coffee);
21       getch();
22
23       endwin();
24       return 0;
25   }
```

Refer to the entry for wredrawln() for sample output.

Also See

wredrawln(),refresh()

refresh()

The refresh() function is used to update the screen in NCurses. Most NCurses output functions require that refresh() be used so that you can see the output on the terminal display.

Explanation

In NCurses, there is the virtual window that exists in memory and then the current screen, which is what's shown on the screen. What the refresh() function does is to check to see which parts of a window have been *touched* (changed) since the last refresh(), then those parts of the window are written to the current screen during the next refresh() operation.

Man Page Format

```
int refresh(void);
int wrefresh(WINDOW *win);
```

Format Reference

The function has no arguments.

Refer to the *w* entry elsewhere in this appendix for information on the win argument.

Return Value

ERR on failure, OK or a value other than ERR on success.

Notes

Next to getch(), refresh() is the most often used function in NCurses.

Internally, the refresh() function is a combination of wnoutrefresh() and doupdate() calls.

It's possible that refresh() alone may not properly update the screen. If so, consider using the clearok() function before calling refresh(). Also see the touchwin() function.

When you are using the following combination:

```
wrefresh(w);
getch();
```

it's okay to replace it with:

```
wgetch(w);
```

which not only waits for a key to be pressed but updates the window w.

You can avoid using refresh() by calling the immedok() function with TRUE as the argument for a given window. If so, all output to that window is immediately and automatically refreshed. There is a performance trade off involved with all that updating. See immedok().

It's possible to optimize screen output, especially when updating multiple windows, by using the wnoutrefresh() function on each window, then a single doupdate() function call to perform the actual screen update. See doupdate().

Examples

```
refresh();
```

The statement updates the standard screen with any information waiting to be displayed.

```
wrefresh(mini);
```

The statement updates the window `mini`.

Sample Program

```
1    #include <ncurses.h>
2
3    int main(void)
4    {
5        initscr();
6        addstr("Goodbye, cruel C programming!");
7        refresh();
8        getch();
9
10       endwin();
11       return 0;
12   }
```

Sample output:

```
Goodbye, cruel C programming!
```

Also See

Chapter 8, `clearok()`, `immedok()`, `touchwin()`, `wnoutrefresh()`

ripoffline()

The `ripoffline()` function creates a special one-line window at the top or bottom of the terminal screen.

Man Page Format

```
int ripoffline(int line, int (*init)(WINDOW *, int));
```

Format Reference

`line` is an `int` value, either positive or negative. When `line` is positive, a single row is ripped from the top of the terminal window. When `line` is negative, a single row is ripped from the bottom of the terminal window.

`init` is the name of a function `ripoffline()` calls to create the line. The function is called with two arguments: first a pointer to a `WINDOW` structure representing the ripped-off line, and second and `int` value representing the number of columns in the ripped off line. (The number of rows is always 1.) The `WINDOW` and `int` values are passed by NCurses to your init function. Your init function must return an `int` value.

Return Value

Always `OK`.

Notes

The `ripoffline()` function must be used before `initscr()` or `newterm()`.
    You may call `ripoffline()` up to five times.
    The function referenced in `ripoffline()` is responsible for placing information inside the line. NCurses passes to your function the name of the `WINDOW` variable used to reference the line, plus the number of columns in the line. Your function can use any of the standard NCurses text output functions to create the line, referencing the `WINDOW` variable, of course. The only two functions not allowed are `refresh()` and `doupdate()`. So be sure to use a `wnoutrefresh()` command to help put the line's text to the screen.
    The size of the standard screen is reduced by one line for each call made to `ripoffline()`. This reduces the value of `LINES` and sets the standard screen's home cursor location down one row for each new `ripoffline()` window created at the top of the screen.
    The line ripped off can be referenced elsewhere in your NCurses program. To do so, save the `WINDOW` pointer to a global variable inside the `init` function. Once saved, you can use that global variable to reference the ripped-off line elsewhere in the program, updating the line via `wrefresh()` just as you would any other window.
    `ripoffline()` is used internally by NCurses to set up the soft label keys. See `slk_init()`.

Example

```
ripoffline(1,setup);
```

The statement removes a line from the top of the screen. The `setup()` function is called to initialize the line.

Sample Program

```
1    #include <ncurses.h>
2
3    static int ruler(WINDOW *w,int cols)
4    {
5        int x;
6
7        waddch(w,'|');
8        for(x=1;x<cols;x++)
9        {
10           if(x % 5)
11               waddch(w,'-');
12           else
13               waddch(w,'+');
14       }
15       waddch(w,'|');
16       wnoutrefresh(w);
17       return 0;
18   }
19
20   int main(void)
21   {
22       ripoffline(1,ruler);
23       initscr();
24
25       addstr("The ruler has been placed atop the screen.\n");
26       printw("The standard screen is now %d rows high.\n",LINES);
27       refresh();
28       getch();
29
30       endwin();
31       return 0;
32   }
```

The sample output is shown in Figure A-11.

Figure A-11: The `ripoffline()` function places a "ruler" atop the terminal window.

Also See

LINES, slk_init()

scanw()

The scanw() function is the NCurses equivalent of the scanf() function. When you need scanf() in your NCurses code, you use scanw() instead.

Man Page Format

```
int scanw(char *fmt, ...);
int wscanw(WINDOW *win, char *fmt, ...);
int mvscanw(int y, int x, char *fmt, ...);
int mvwscanw(WINDOW *win, int y, int x, char *fmt, ...);
int vw_scanw(WINDOW *win, char *fmt, va_list varglist);
int vwscanw(WINDOW *win, char *fmt, va_list varglist);
```

Format Reference

The format for scanw() is identical to scanf(). fmt is a formatting string that describes the type of input. The string is followed by variable pointers in which the input is stored.

Refer to the entries for *w*, *mv*, and *mvw* elsewhere in this appendix for information on the w, mv, and mvw variations to this function.

The vwscanw() functions are comparable to the vscanf() function, where varglist is a va_list (for example, a pointer) representing variable arguments. Refer to the man page for vscanf().

Return Value

An int value is returned, either ERR when things go wrong or a value equal to the number of fields successfully scanned.

Notes

scanw() uses getstr() for input with the string passed internally to the sscanf() function for evaluation.

A variable argument version of scanw(), analogous to vscanf(), is vw_scanw(). Here is the man page format:

```
int vw_scanw(WINDOW *win, char *fmt, va_list varglist);
```

The older version of vw_scanw() was vwscanw(). It carries the same format as vw_scanw() but has been deprecated.

Consider compiling your code with -Wall as an option to help troubleshoot common scanf() and scanw() issues.

Examples

```
scanw("%d",&age);
```

The statement reads an integer value from the keyboard and stores it in the age variable.

```
scanw("%20s",petname);
```

Here, scanw() reads up to 20 nonwhite space characters from the keyboard and stores them in the petname string (char array).

Sample Program

```
1    #include <ncurses.h>
2
3    #define UNI 4.5
4
5    int main(void)
6    {
7        int pieces = 0;
8
9        initscr();
10
11       addstr("SUSHI BAR MENU\n\n");
12       printw("We have Uni today for $%.2f.\n",UNI);
13       addstr("How many pieces would you like? ");
14       refresh();
15
16       scanw("%d",&pieces);
17       printw("You want %d pieces?\n",pieces);
18       printw("That will be $%.2f!\n",UNI*pieces);
19       refresh();
20       getch();
21
22       endwin();
23       return 0;
24   }
```

Sample output:

```
SUSHI BAR MENU

We have Uni today for $4.50.
How many pieces would you like? 3
You want 3 pieces?
That will be $13.50!
```

Also See

Chapter 2, getstr(), printw()

scr_dump()

The scr_dump() function takes a snapshot of the current screen and saves it to disk.

Man Page Format

```
int scr_dump(const char *filename);
```

Format Reference

filename is the name of a file under which the standard screen data will be saved. It is *not* a FILE pointer.

Return Value

OK upon success or ERR on failure.

Notes

The scr_restore() function is the companion to scr_dump(), restoring the image saved to disk and back to the virtual screen.

The file format used by scr_dump() is the same as for putwin(). In fact, the getwin() function can be used to read in the file created by scr_dump().

Remember that the scr_dump() function's argument is a filename, not a FILE pointer!

Examples

```
scr_dump(screen);
```

Here, the `scr_dump()` function saves the current screen to disk using the file specified by the `screen` variable.

```
scr_dump("test.win");
```

The statement above saves the screen to a file named TEST.WIN.

Sample Program

```
1    #include <ncurses.h>
2    #include <stdlib.h>
3    #include <time.h>
4
5    #define FILENAME "windump"
6
7    int main(void)
8    {
9        char word[7];
10       int x,w,r;
11
12       srandom((unsigned)time(NULL));    /* seed randomizer */
13       word[7] = '\0';
14       initscr();
15
16   /* Fill most of the screen with random 6-char words */
17       for(x=0;x<200;x++)
18       {
19           for(w=0;w<6;w++)
20               word[w] = (random() % 26) + 'a';
21           printw("%s\t",word);
22       }
23       addch('\n');
24       addstr("Press Enter to write this screen to disk\n");
25       refresh();
26       getch();
27
28   /* write the window to disk */
29       r = scr_dump(FILENAME);
30       if( r == ERR)
31           addstr("Error writing window to disk\n");
32       else
33           addstr("File written; press Enter to quit\n");
34       refresh();
35       getch();
36
37       endwin();
38       return 0;
39   }
```

The sample output is shown in Figure A-12.

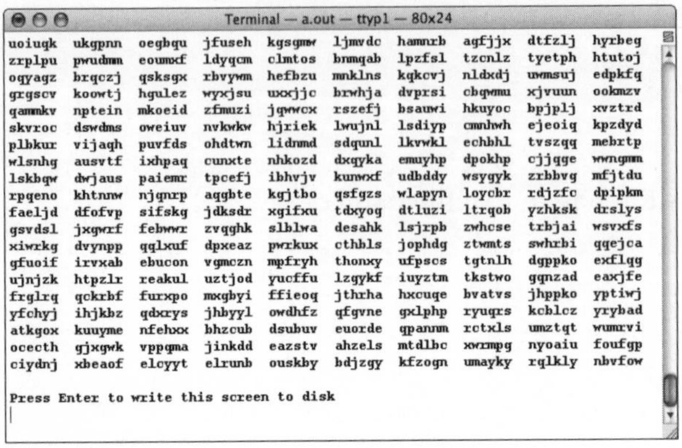

Figure A-12: Random bits of text appear on the screen and are saved to disk.

Also See

Chapter 14, `scr_restore()`, `putwin()`

scr_init()

The `scr_init()` function reads the window data saved to disk by `scr_dump()` and uses information from that file to configure the screen.

Explanation

The `scr_dump()` function writes window data to disk. It writes the visible data to disk (what you see on the screen), as well as various window settings and options.

To restore the visible screen, the `scr_restore()` function is used. However, to restore both the screen and the window settings, `scr_init()` must be used before `scr_restore()`. Or, to make things easier, the `scr_set()` function can be used, which is a combination of `scr_init()` followed by `scr_restore()`.

Man Page Format

```
int scr_init(const char *filename);
```

Format Reference

`filename` is the name of a file in which the standard screen data has been saved. The value is a string, *not* a FILE pointer.

Return Value

OK on success or ERR on failure.

Notes

By itself, scr_init() merely reads window setting information from the named file.

The information scr_init() sets in memory can be updated to the screen by using a wrefresh(curscr) statement.

The scr_init() function pays heed to the terminfo rmcup and nrrmc capabilities. When rmcup exists, the function returns ERR. (Refer to Chapter 1 for a description of rmcup.)

Example

```
if(scr_init("windata.bin") == ERR)
```

The statement checks to see if the scr_init() function returns ERR. If not, information from the WINDATA.BIN file is read from disk and used to configure NCurses window structures.

Sample Program

Refer to the entry for scr_restore() for a sample program and output.

Also See

scr_dump(), scr_restore(), scr_set()

scr_restore()

The scr_restore() function fetches a previously saved screen dump and loads it into memory, replacing the current virtual screen.

Man Page Format

```
int scr_restore(const char *filename);
```

Format Reference

filename is the name of a file to which screen data has been saved. It is *not* a FILE pointer.

Return Value

OK or ERR, based on success or failure.

Notes

The scr_restore() function does not display the screen data. A call to doupdate() is required to display the restored screen.

While the cursor's location is saved in the window file by scr_dump(), the scr_restore() function does not restore the cursor's location. The cursor instead remains at whatever location it was at when scr_restore() was issued. To fix this, scr_init() should be called before scr_dump().

Example

```
scr_restore("windump.dat");
```

The statement restores the screen previously saved to disk in the file WINDUMP.DAT.

Sample Program

```
1    #include <ncurses.h>
2
3    #define FILENAME "windump"
4
5    int main(void)
6    {
7        int r;
8
9        initscr();
10
11       addstr("Press Enter to restore the screen\n");
12       refresh();
13       getch();
14
15   /* restore the window from disk */
16       r = scr_init(FILENAME);
17       if( r != ERR)
18       {
19           scr_restore(FILENAME);
20           wrefresh(curscr);
21       }
22       else
23       {
24           addstr("Error reading window file: press Enter\n");
25           refresh();
26       }
```

```
27        getch();
28
29        endwin();
30        return 0;
31    }
```

Sample output:
The previously saved screen (see scr_dump() *) is restored.*

Also See

Chapter 14, scr_dump(), scr_set(), getwin()

scr_set()

The scr_set() function combines the abilities of the scr_init() and scr_restore() functions.

Man Page Format

```
int scr_set(const char *filename);
```

Format Reference

filename is the name of a screen data file. It is a text constant, *not* a FILE pointer.

Return Value

OK on success or ERR on failure.

Notes

The scr_set() function is equivalent to a call to scr_init() followed by a call to scr_restore(). Refer to scr_init() or scr_restore() for more information.

Example

```
rc = scr_set(fname);
```

The scr_set() function loads window data from a file referenced by the fname (string) variable. Both the window's settings and visual data are loaded. The int variable rc contains either OK or ERR depending on the function's success or failure.

Sample Program

```
1    #include <ncurses.h>
2
3    #define FILENAME "windump"
4
5    int main(void)
6    {
7        int r;
8
9        initscr();
10
11       addstr("Press Enter to restore the screen\n");
12       refresh();
13       getch();
14
15   /* restore the window from disk */
16       r = scr_set(FILENAME);
17       if( r == ERR)
18           addstr("Error reading window file: press Enter\n");
19       wrefresh(curscr);
20       getch();
21
22       endwin();
23       return 0;
24   }
```

Sample output is the same as for scr_restore().

Also See

Chapter 14, scr_dump(), scr_restore(), scr_set()

scrl()

The scrl() function scrolls text in a window up or down a given number of lines.

Man Page Format

```
int scrl(int n);
int wscrl(WINDOW *win, int n);
```

Format Reference

n is an int value indicating the number of lines to scroll the window. When n is positive, n lines are scrolled up; when n is negative, n lines are scrolled down.

Refer to the *w* entry later in this appendix for information on the win argument.

Return Value

Always OK.

Notes

Scrolling must be enabled for the window for scroll() to function properly. See scrollok().

Scrolling does not affect the cursor's location in the window. If the cursor is on row 5, then scrolling the text in the window up or down moves only the text; the cursor remains at row 5.

When text is scrolled up, blank lines are inserted at the bottom of the window; lines at the top are removed. When text is scrolled down, blanks lines are inserted at the top of the window, with lines at the bottom being removed.

Examples

```
scrl(1);
```

The statement scrolls the standard screen up one line, which is the same as the scroll() function.

```
wscrl(viewer,-3);
```

The statement scrolls the text in the window viewer down three rows.

Sample Program

```
1     #include <ncurses.h>
2
3     int main(void)
4     {
5         int ch;
6
7         initscr();
8
9         scrollok(stdscr,TRUE);
10        keypad(stdscr,TRUE);
11        noecho();
```

```
12
13          addstr("Press Enter to quit; Up/Down to scroll");
14          mvaddstr(LINES/2,0,"Scroll me!");
15          refresh();
16
17      do
18      {
19          ch = getch();
20          if(ch == KEY_UP)
21              scrl(1);
22          if(ch == KEY_DOWN)
23              scrl(-1);
24      } while( ch != '\n');
25
26      endwin();
27      return 0;
28  }
```

Sample output:
Use the up/down arrows on the keyboard to scroll the text on the screen. Press Enter to quit.

Also See

Chapter 10, scrollok(), setscrreg()

scroll()

The scroll() function scrolls text in a window up one line.

Man Page Format

```
int scroll(WINDOW *win);
```

Format Reference

win is the name of a WINDOW variable representing the window to be scrolled. Text in that window is moved up one line; the top line of text is removed and a new blank line is inserted at the bottom.

Return Value

Always OK.

Notes

The scroll() function is a macro equivalent to wscrl(win, 1). See wscrl().
Also see scrl() for more notes and information.

Example

```
scroll(main);
```

The statement scrolls the contents of the window main up one line.

Sample Program

```
1    #include <ncurses.h>
2
3    int main(void)
4    {
5        initscr();
6
7        scrollok(stdscr,TRUE);
8        mvaddstr(LINES/2,0,"Watch me scroll up!");
9        refresh();
10       getch();
11
12       scroll(stdscr);
13       refresh();
14       getch();
15
16       endwin();
17       return 0;
18   }
```

Sample output:

```
Watch me scroll up!
```

Press Enter and the line scrolls up one notch.

Also See

Chapter 10, scrollok(), scrl()

scrollok()

The `scrollok()` function enables scrolling in a window.

Man Page Format

```
int scrollok(WINDOW *win, bool bf);
```

Format Reference

`win` is the name of a `WINDOW` variable representing a window created in your code.

`Bf` is a Boolean value, either `TRUE` or `FALSE` as defined in `NCURSES.H`. When `TRUE`, scrolling for window `win` is activated. `FALSE` is the default condition, meaning that the window isn't scrolling.

Return Value

`OK` on success; `ERR` on failure.

Notes

The `scrollok()` function enables scrolling. That means any text displayed after the last line, or a newline or line feed on the last line, pops text up by one row in the window. The top row of text is lost, and a new blank row appears on the bottom to allow for the next text.

The `scrollok()` setting is inherited by subwindows. If you set `scrollok()` `TRUE` for a window, then all its subwindows will also have the ability to scroll. Otherwise, new windows and new subwindows start out with `scrollok()` disabled.

Text can be manually scrolled by using the `scroll()` or `scrl()` functions.

Pads cannot be scrolled. Trying to apply `scrollok()` to a pad returns `ERR`.

Example

```
scrollok(main,TRUE);
```

The statement enables scrolling for the window `main`.

Sample Program

```
1    #include <ncurses.h>
2
3    int main(void)
4    {
5        int x = 0;
6
7        initscr();
8
9        scrollok(stdscr,TRUE);
10       while(1)
11       {
12           printw("%d\t",x);
13           x++;
14           refresh();
15       }
16
17       endwin();
18       return 0;
19   }
```

Sample output:
Incrementing numbers are displayed in columns that scroll up the screen. Press Ctrl+C to halt the program.

Also See

Chapter 10, scroll(), scrl(), setscrreg()

setscrreg()

The setscrreg() function determines which region (between two rows) of the screen will be scrolled.

Man Page Format

```
int setscrreg(int top, int bot);
int wsetscrreg(WINDOW *win, int top, int bot);
```

Format Reference

`top` is an `int` value indicating the top row for the scrolling region. Values range from 0 for the top row, to the value of `bot` minus 1.

bot is in `int` value indicating the bottom row of the scrolling region. Values range from `top+1` to the bottom of the window.

Refer to the *w* entry elsewhere in this appendix for information on the `win` argument.

Return Value

`OK` on success, `ERR` on failure. The function fails when `top` is greater than or equal to `bot`, or when `bot` is greater than the bottom of the window.

Notes

This function works only after scrolling has been enabled for the window via the `scrollok()` function. See `scrollok()`.

Unless `setscrreg()` is used, the top and bottom rows of the window define the scrolling region.

The bottom row of the window can be returned using `w->_maxy`, where `w` is the window's `WINDOW` variable name.

Text can still be written to the window below the scrolling region, specifically by using the various *mv*-prefix text output functions.

Examples

```
setscrreg(5,stdscr->_maxy);
```

The statement creates a scrolling region from line 5 through the bottom of the standard screen.

```
wsetscrreg(options,2,opbot);
```

Here, the statement creates a scrolling region in the window `options`, from line 2 (the third line) of the window through the value represented by `opbot`.

Sample Program

```
1     #include <ncurses.h>
2
3     int main(void)
4     {
5         int x = 0;
6         int stdbot;
7
8         initscr();
9         stdbot = stdscr->_maxy;
10
11        scrollok(stdscr,TRUE);
12        setscrreg(3,stdbot-3);
13
14        attrset(A_BOLD);
15        mvaddstr(stdbot-2,0,"Press Ctrl+C to stop.");
16        attroff(A_BOLD);
17        move(0,0);
18        while(1)
19        {
20            printw("%d\t",x);
21            x++;
22            refresh();
23        }
24
25        endwin();
26        return 0;
27    }
```

The sample output is shown in Figure A-13.

Also See

```
scrollok(),scrl()
```

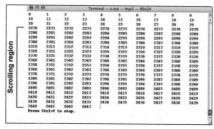

Figure A-13: Only the indicated region of the window scrolls.

setsyx()

The setsyx() function is used to set the virtual screen's cursor location.

Man Page Format

```
void setsyx(int y, int x);
```

Format Reference

y and x are int values used to set the row and column positions of the virtual screen's cursor, respectively. Values range from 0 up through the values of LINES and COLS. When -1 is specified for both y and x, the leaveok() state is set TRUE.

Return Value

setsyx() is a macro and as such its return value should not be used.

Notes

To move the cursor in a window, use the move() function. See move().

   The row, or y, argument comes first.

   Most often setsyx() is used internally in conjunction with getsyx(), which fetches the virtual screen's cursor location. That way the cursor's location can be saved and restored while NCurses is doing something else.

Example

```
setsyx(row,col);
```

The statement places the virtual screen's cursor to the position indicated by the row and col variables.

Sample Program

```
1    #include <ncurses.h>
2
3    int main(void)
4    {
5        int y,x;
6
7        initscr();
8
```

```
 9          setsyx(5,5);
10          getsyx(y,x);
11          addstr("The cursor on the virtual screen is set to 5, 5.\n");
12          printw("And getsyx() reports %d, %d.\n",y,x);
13          refresh();
14          getch();
15
16          endwin();
17          return 0;
18      }
```

Sample output:

```
The cursor on the virtual screen is set to 5, 5.
And getsyx() reports 5, 5.
```

Also See

`getsyx()`, `leaveok()`

set_term()

The `set_term()` function determines which terminal to use for NCurses input and output functions. Used primarily in conjunction with `newterm()` when configuring unique terminal setups for NCurses.

Man Page Format

```
SCREEN *set_term(SCREEN *new);
```

Format Reference

`new` is the name of a SCREEN pointer, returned by `newterm()`.

Return Value

`set_term()` returns a SCREEN pointer indicating which terminal was previously in use.

Notes

This is the only function that manipulates SCREEN pointers. (The `delscreen()` function removes space allocated to the pointers.)

Examples

```
old = set_term(new);
```

The statement activates NCurses I/O on the terminal specified by SCREEN pointer new. The terminal currently used is saved in SCREEN pointer old.

```
set_term(old);
```

The statement transfers NCurses I/O to the terminal identified by SCREEN pointer old.

Sample Program

```
1     #include <ncurses.h>
2
3     int main(void)
4     {
5             SCREEN *s;
6
7             s = newterm(NULL, stdout, stdin);
8             set_term(s);
9
10            addstr("Hello!");
11
12            refresh();
13            getch();
14
15            endwin();
16            return 0;
17    }
```

The program assigns standard input and output to the new terminal s, which is setup by set_term(). The addstr() function in line 10 outputs to standard output.

Sample output:

```
Hello!
```

Also See

```
newterm(), delscreen()
```

slk_attr()

The `slk_attr()` function returns the attributes currently be used to format the soft labels.

Man Page Format

```
attr_t slk_attr(void);
```

Format Reference

The function has no arguments.

Return Value

A `long int` value of the NCurses `attr_t` type is returned, packed with values according to which formatting attributes have been applied to the soft labels. Appendix C describes the bit field.

Notes

This function is the soft label version of the `attr_get()` function. See `attr_get()`.

Examples

```
va = slk_attr();
```

The statement stores attributes used to format the soft labels in the `va` variable.

```
if(slk_attr() & A_BOLD)
```

The evaluation is true when the `A_BOLD` attribute is being used to format the soft labels.

```
if(slk_attr() == A_BOLD)
```

The evaluation is true when only the `A_BOLD` attribute is being used to format the soft labels.

Sample Program

```
1     #include <ncurses.h>
2
3     #define CENTER 1
4     #define LCOUNT 8
5
6     int main(void)
7     {
8         char labels[LCOUNT][19] = { "Help!", "File", "Print", "Text",
9                         "Edit", "Quick", "Config", "System" };
10        char *text;
11        int x;
12
13        slk_init(0);
14        initscr();
15
16        for(x=0;x<LCOUNT;x++)
17            slk_set(x+1,labels[x],CENTER);
18        slk_refresh();
19        if(slk_attr() & A_STANDOUT)
20            addstr("The labels are formatted with the ⤶
standard attribute.\n");
21        refresh();
22        getch();
23
24        endwin();
25        return 0;
26    }
```

Sample output:

```
The labels are formatted with the standard attribute.
```

Also See

```
attr_get(),slk_attron(),slk_attrset()
```

slk_attroff()

The slk_attroff() function is used to remove one or more attributes from the soft label key display.

Man Page Format

```
int slk_attroff(const chtype attrs);
int slk_attr_off(const attr_t attrs, void * opts);
```

Format Reference

`attrs` is a `chtype` variable representing one or more attribute constants. These constants are defined in `NCURSES.H` as listed in Table A-1 under `attrset()`.

`NULL` is used as a placeholder the undefined `opts` argument.

Return Value

`ERR` on failure or `OK` or any value other than `ERR` when things go right.

Notes

The soft key labels are normally formatted with the standout (`A_STANDOUT`) format. `slk_attroff()` can be use to remove this attribute, or `slk_attrset()` can be used to assign new attributes.

Also see the Notes for `slk_attron()` and `slk_attrset()` for more information.

Example

```
slk_attroff(A_BOLD);
```

The statement removes the bold attribute from any text written to the soft labels by subsequent `slk_set()` commands.

Sample Program

```
1    #include <ncurses.h>
2
3    #define CENTER 1
4    #define LCOUNT 8
5
6    int main(void)
7    {
8        char labels[LCOUNT][19] = { "Help!", "File", "Print", "Text",
9                        "Edit", "Quick", "Config", "System" };
10       char *text;
11       int x;
12
13       slk_init(0);
14       initscr();
15
16       slk_attroff(A_STANDOUT);
17       for(x=0;x<LCOUNT;x++)
18           slk_set(x+1,labels[x],CENTER);
19       slk_refresh();
20       getch();
```

```
21
22          endwin();
23          return 0;
24    }
```

Sample output:

The labels are displayed in normal text; the slk_attroff(A_STANDOUT) *function removes the standout formatting normally applied to the labels.*

Also See

attroff(), slk_attron(), slk_attrset()

slk_attron()

The slk_attron() function applies the standard text attributes to the soft labels. It is the soft label key equivalent of the attron() function.

Man Page Formats

```
int slk_attron(const chtype attrs);
int slk_attr_on(attr_t attrs, void* opts);
```

Format Reference

attrs is a chtype variable representing one or more attribute constants as defined in NCURSES.H.

NULL is used in the slk_attr_on() function as a placeholder for the undefined opts value.

Return Value

ERR on failure, OK or some value other than ERR on success.

Notes

As with attron(), the slk_attron() function merely adds attributes to those already set. Setting a new attribute does not affect previous attributes applied to the soft labels.

Soft label keys are normally displayed with the A_STANDOUT attribute applied.

Multiple attributes can be applied by using more than one NCurses attribute constant separated by a logical OR in the slk_attron() statement.

Refer to Table A-1 (in the `attrset()` entry) for a list of NCurses attribute constants.

`COLOR_PAIR(n)` can be specified as a text attribute, where n is a color pair number defined by an `init_pair()` function earlier in the program. Also see the `slk_color()` function.

Individual labels can be assigned unique attributes by using `slk_attron()` or `slk_attrset()` and then issuing a `slk_set()` function to update one or more labels. The updated labels show the newly applied attributes.

Examples

```
slk_attron(A_UNDERLINE);
```

Here, the underline attribute is set in addition to any other attributes already defined for the soft labels.

```
slk_attron(A_BOLD | A_BLINK);
```

This statement turns on the bold and (annoying) blink attributes, in addition to any other attributes previously defined, for the soft labels.

Sample Program

```
1    #include <ncurses.h>
2
3    #define CENTER 1
4    #define LCOUNT 8
5
6    int main(void)
7    {
8        char labels[LCOUNT][19] = { "Help!", "File", "Print", "Text",
9                        "Edit", "Quick", "Config", "System" };
10       char *text;
11       int x;
12
13       slk_init(0);
14       initscr();
15
16       for(x=0;x<LCOUNT;x++)
17           slk_set(x+1,labels[x],CENTER);
18       slk_attron(A_BOLD);
19       slk_refresh();
20
21       refresh();
22       getch();
23
24       endwin();
25       return 0;
26   }
```

Sample output:
The labels appear in bold text (in addition to inverse/standout).

Also See

attron(),slk_attrset(),slk_attroff(),slk_color()

slk_attrset()

The slk_attrset() function discards any previously defined attributes for the soft label keys and defines a new set of attributes. It is the soft label key counterpart of the attrset() functions.

Man Page Format

```
int slk_attrset(const chtype attrs);
int slk_attr_set(const attr_t attrs, short color_pair_number, ⤶
void* opts);
```

Format Reference

attrs is a chtype value representing one or more attribute constants, as defined in NCURSES.H and listed in Table A-1 (under attrset()).

color_pair_number is a short int value representing a color pair number defined by init_pair() earlier in the code. It's the same value as the n used in COLOR_PAIR(n).

NULL is used in the slk_attr_set() functions as a placeholder the undefined opts value.

Return Value

ERR on failure, a value other than ERR (such as OK) on success.

Notes

By default, the soft label keys are displayed in the A_STANDOUT (reverse text) format. They use color pair 0.

Also see the entry for attrset() for more notes, as well as the notes for slk_attron().

Examples

```
slk_attrset(A_BOLD);
```

Here, the bold attribute is applied to the soft labels.

```
slk_attrset(A_BOLD | A_UNDERLINE);
```

The statement here applies both bold and underline attributes to the soft label keys.

```
slk_attrset(COLOR_PAIR(1));
slk_attr_set(0,1,NULL);
```

These two functions are identical; both assign color pair 1 to the soft label keys.

Sample Program

```
1      #include <ncurses.h>
2
3      #define CENTER 1
4      #define LCOUNT 8
5
6      int main(void)
7      {
8          char labels[LCOUNT][19] = { "Help!", "File", "Print", "Text",
9                          "Edit", "Quick", "Config", "System" };
10         char *text;
11         int x;
12
13         slk_init(0);
14         initscr();
15
16         for(x=0;x<LCOUNT;x++)
17             slk_set(x+1,labels[x],CENTER);
18         slk_attrset(A_BOLD);
19         slk_refresh();
20         getch();
21
22         endwin();
23         return 0;
24     }
```

Sample output:
The labels appear in bold text.

Also See

```
attrset(),slk_attron(),slk_attroff()
```

slk_clear()

The slk_clear() function hides the soft labels.

Man Page Format

```
int slk_clear(void);
```

Format Reference

The function has no arguments.

Return Value

ERR on failure; OK upon success (actually, any value other than ERR on success).

Notes

slk_clear() does not need to be followed by a refresh() type command; it's effect is immediately seen.

This function merely hides the labels. To make them appear again, use the slk_restore() function.

Using slk_clear() does not alter the reduced size of the standard screen. The bottom line(s) formerly used by the soft labels still cannot be used.

slk_clear() hides all the soft labels. If you merely want to hide (or remove) one label, use slk_set() to assign that label a null string. See slk_set().

Example

```
slk_clear();
```

The statement removes the soft label key display from the screen.

Sample Program

```
1    #include <ncurses.h>
2
3    #define CENTER 1
4    #define LCOUNT 8
5
6    int main(void)
7    {
```

```
 8          char labels[LCOUNT][9] = { "Help!", "File", "Print", "Text",
 9                          "Edit", "Quick", "Conf", "System" };
10          int x;
11
12          slk_init(0);
13          initscr();
14
15          for(x=0;x<LCOUNT;x++)
16              slk_set(x+1,labels[x],CENTER);
17          slk_refresh();
18
19          addstr("Press Enter to hide the soft label keys:\n");
20          refresh();
21          getch();
22
23          slk_clear();
24          addstr("Press Enter to restore the soft label keys:\n");
25          refresh();
26          getch();
27
28          slk_restore();
29          getch();
30
31          endwin();
32          return 0;
33      }
```

Sample output:
Soft keys are displayed (refer to the figure for slk_set()*).*

```
Press Enter to hide the soft label keys:
```

And the soft labels are gone.

```
Press Enter to restore the soft label keys:
```

And they come back again.

Also See

```
slk_restore(),slk_set()
```

slk_color()

The slk_color() function chooses a color pair for the foreground and background of the soft label text.

Man Page Format

```
int slk_color(short color_pair_number);
```

Format Reference

color_pair_number is a short int value representing a color pair defined by the init_pair() function.

Return Value

The function returns ERR on failure, OK or some value other than ERR on success.

Notes

Only the labels are colored; the spaces between the labels are left as the terminal's assumed default color, such as black. Any color applied to the standard screen extends down to the last row just above the soft labels.

The index line (for slk_init() value 3) is always colored using color pair 0; the slk_color(), as well as other *slk* attribute functions, do not affect the index line.

The slk_color(n) function is equivalent to slk_attron(COLOR_PAIR(n)).

The man page states that slk_color() has effect only when the soft labels are simulated on the bottom of the screen.

Example

```
slk_color(4);
```

Here, the statement applies the foreground and background colors of color pair 4 to the soft labels.

Sample Program

```
1    #include <ncurses.h>
2
3    #define CENTER 1
4    #define LCOUNT 8
5
6    int main(void)
7    {
8        char labels[LCOUNT][19] = { "Help!", "File", "Print", "Text",
```

```
 9                          "Edit", "Quick", "Config", "System" };
10          char *text;
11          int x;
12
13          slk_init(0);
14          initscr();
15          start_color();
16          init_pair(1,COLOR_BLUE,COLOR_WHITE);
17
18          slk_color(1);
19          for(x=0;x<LCOUNT;x++)
20              slk_set(x+1,labels[x],CENTER);
21          slk_refresh();
22          getch();
23
24          endwin();
25          return 0;
26      }
```

Sample output:
The labels appear with white text on a blue background.

Also See

`color_set(),slk_attron(),slk_attrset(),init_pair()`

slk_init()

The `slk_init()` function directs NCurses to configure itself to display soft label keys on the screen.

Explanation

Soft label keys consist of one or two rows of text along the bottom of the screen. Each text label is associated with a function or soft label key, so that pressing that key carries out the function as indicated (or so the theory goes).

NCurses soft label key (*slk*) functions allow for the display of the soft label keys in your program, though programming your keyboard's function keys must also be done to get the things to work.

Man Page Format

```
int slk_init(int fmt);
```

Format Reference

fmt is an int value from 0 through 3. The values specified describe how the soft keys are configured, as referenced in Table A-16 and illustrated in Figure A-14.

Return Value

ERR on failure, OK (or a value other than ERR) on success.

Notes

The slk_init() function *must* be used before initscr() or newterm().

slk_init() decreases the number of lines available on the standard screen by one or two, depending on the format. This affects the value of the LINES constant. See LINES.

The slk_set() function is used to apply text to the labels. To make the labels show up, slk_refresh() is used.

I've found that when specifying 3 for fmt, it's often necessary to use an slk_restore() command just after initscr() to get the index line to display.

There are terminals where the soft key labels are supplied by default; for example, they're not a part of the standard screen. For those terminals, NCurses lets you program the labels. The labels are simulated on other terminals (by removing one or two lines from the standard screen).

Table A-16: Soft label setup for *slk_init()*'s *n* argument

FMT	TOTAL LABELS	CHARS PER LABEL	PATTERN	INDEX LINE
0	8	8	4-4	No
1	8	8	3-2-3	No
2	12	5	4-4-4	No
3	12	5	4-4-4	Yes

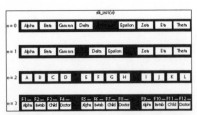

Figure A-14: Soft label key setups

Example

```
slk_init(0);
initscr();
```

These statements set up the terminal for soft key labels. The first line speci-fies 8 labels in a 4-4 pattern. Note that this function must appear before `initscr()`. Further code is required to apply text to and display the labels.

Sample Program

Refer to the entry for `slk_set()` for a sample program and output.

Also See

Chapter 12, `slk_set()`, `slk_reset()`

slk_label()

The `slk_label()` function returns the text assigned to a soft key label.

Man Page Format

```
char *slk_label(int labnum);
```

Format Reference

`labnum` is an `int` value indicating which label to be read. Values range from 1 through 8 or 12, depending on the label configuration defined by `slk_init()`.

Return Value

A pointer is returned, the memory location of the text displayed in the label. On error, NULL is returned.

Notes

Any blanks used to align the label are not returned by `slk_label()`.

If the label's text is truncated, then only the truncated part is returned by the `slk_label()` function.

When a label is not defined (blank), a null string is returned.

Examples

```
lab3 = slk_label(3);
```

The statement places the memory location of the text used in soft label 3 into the char pointer lab3.

```
printw("Label %d is %s.\n",x,slk_label(x));
```

The printw() statement displays the label number and text for the label referenced by variable x.

Sample Program

```
1      #include <ncurses.h>
2
3      #define CENTER 1
4      #define LCOUNT 8
5
6      int main(void)
7      {
8          char labels[LCOUNT][19] = { "Help!", "File", "Print", "Text",
9                          "Edit", "Quick", "Config", "System" };
10         char *text;
11         int x,c;
12
13         slk_init(0);
14         initscr();
15
16         for(x=0;x<LCOUNT;x++)
17             slk_set(x+1,labels[x],CENTER);
18         slk_refresh();
19
20         addstr("Retrieve the text for which label? ");
21         refresh();
22         scanw("%d",&c);
23         text = slk_label(c);
24         printw("The text for label %d is \"%s\".\n",c,slk_label(c));
25         refresh();
26         getch();
27
28         endwin();
29         return 0;
30     }
```

Sample output:
The soft labels are displayed.

```
Retrieve the text for which label?
```

Type a number, such as **7**.

```
The text for label 7 is "Config".
```

Also See

```
slk_set(),slk_init()
```

slk_noutrefresh()

The `slk_noutrefresh()` function finds touched parts of the soft labels and prepares those portions for updating on the virtual screen.

Man Page Format

```
int slk_noutrefresh(void);
```

Format Reference

The function has no arguments.

Return Value

OK, or some value other than ERR, on success; ERR on failure.

Notes

Refer to `wnoutrefresh()` for more information on this type of function and how it can be used to optimize NCurses output.

When you use `slk_noutrefresh()`, as well as other `noutrefresh()` functions, the `doupdate()` function is required to do the actually displaying of text.

Example

```
slk_noutrefresh();
```

The statement scans for any changes (touches) to the soft labels and prepares the updated portions to be written to the screen.

Sample Program

```
1    #include <ncurses.h>
2
3    #define CENTER 1
4    #define LCOUNT 8
5
6    int main(void)
7    {
8        char labels[LCOUNT][19] = { "Help!", "File", "Print", "Text",
9                          "Edit", "Quick", "Config", "System" };
10       char *text;
11       int x;
12
13       slk_init(0);
14       initscr();
15
16       for(x=0;x<LCOUNT;x++)
17           slk_set(x+1,labels[x],CENTER);
18       slk_noutrefresh();
19       addstr("Welcome to your Soft Label Key program\n");
20       wnoutrefresh(stdscr);
21       doupdate();
22       getch();
23
24       endwin();
25       return 0;
26   }
```

Sample output:
Both the text Welcome to your Soft Label Key program *and soft labels appear at the same time, thanks to the single* doupdate() *function.*

Also See

wnoutrefresh(), doupdate(), slk_refresh(), slk_touch()

slk_refresh()

The slk_refresh() function displays the soft label keys on the screen or updates the soft label keys after a change has been made. It's analogous to the refresh() function but specific to the soft label keys.

Man Page Format

```
int slk_refresh(void);
```

Format Reference

The function has no arguments.

Return Value

ERR on failure, OK (or a value other than ERR) on success.

Notes

The slk_refresh() function is specific to the line(s) on the screen containing the soft label keys. Because the line(s) is outside of the standard screen, this special function is required to update the text (labels) displayed there.

Like other refresh() functions in NCurses, slk_refresh() is a combination of two lower-level functions: slk_noutrefresh() and the doupdate() function. See slk_noutrefresh() and doupdate() for more information.

Example

```
slk_refresh();
```

The function updates the soft label key display.

Sample Program

Refer to the entry for slk_set() for a sample program and output.

Also See

Chapter 12, slk_init(), slk_set()

slk_restore()

The slk_restore() function redisplays the soft labels after an slk_clear() command has temporarily hidden them.

Man Page Format

```
int slk_restore(void);
```

Format Reference

The function has no arguments.

Return Value

ERR on failure; OK or any value other than ERR upon success.

Notes

This function is often used in conjunction with slk_clear() to show or hide the soft label keys.

   As with slk_clear(), an slk_refresh() is not needed to follow the slk_restore() and display the soft label keys.

   A call to the slk_restore() function may be necessary right after initscr() to urge NCurses to display the soft label key's index line. See slk_init().

Example

```
slk_restore();
```

   The statement restores the soft label key display to the screen. Presumably they were cleared previously by a slk_clear() function.

Sample Program

Refer to the entry for slk_clear() for a sample program and output.

Also See

Chapter 12, slk_clear()

slk_set()

The slk_set() function applies a text label to a specific soft key.

Man Page Format

```
int slk_set(int labnum, const char *label, int fmt);
```

Format Reference

labnum is an int value representing a specific soft key label. Values range from 1 through 8 or 1 through 12 depending on the number of soft key labels `slk_init()` has created. The labels are numbered from left to right across the screen.

`label` is a string constant or variable representing the text to be assigned a label. When eight labels are displayed, each label can have up to eight characters of text displayed. For the 12 label configuration, each label displays up to five characters. Extra characters are truncated on the right.

`fmt` is an `int` value describing how text is to be aligned within a label's space. Valid values are 0 for left-justified; 1 for centered; and 2 for right-justified.

Return Value

An `int` value: `ERR` on failure, `OK` (or a value other than `ERR`) on success.

Notes

Soft label keys must first be initialized before `slk_set()` can be used. See `slk_init()`.

The `slk_init()` function also determines the total number of labels available as well as how many characters can appear in each label. See Table A-16.

Remember that the labels are numbered starting with 1, not zero.

The labels and their text do not appear until an `slk_restore()` function is used.

To remove text from a label, specify a null string as the `label` argument in `slk_set()`.

A label's text can be changed at any time by issuing an `slk_set()` function with new label text, followed by the appropriate `slk_refresh()` function.

The `slk_label()` function returns text assigned to a given label. See `slk_label()`.

Examples

```
slk_set(1,"HELP!",1);
```

Here, the text `HELP!` is applied to the first soft label. It is centered within the label.

```
slk_set(8,"",0);
slk_refresh()
```

The statements remove the label from soft label key 8.

Sample Program

```
1    #include <ncurses.h>
2
3    #define LEFT 0
4    #define CENTER 1
5    #define RIGHT 2
6
7    int main(void)
8    {
9        slk_init(0);
10       initscr();
11
12       slk_set(1,"Help!",LEFT);
13       slk_set(2,"File",LEFT);
14       slk_set(3,"Print",LEFT);
15       slk_set(4,"Text",CENTER);
16       slk_set(5,"Edit",CENTER);
17       slk_set(6,"Quick",RIGHT);
18       slk_set(7,"Conf",RIGHT);
19       slk_set(8,"Change",RIGHT);
20       slk_refresh();
21       getch();
22
23       endwin();
24       return 0;
25   }
```

The sample output is shown in Figure A-15.

Also See

Chapter 12, slk_init(), slk_label(), slk_refresh()

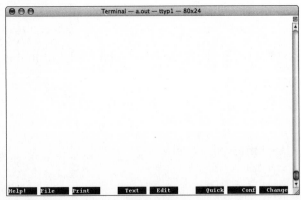

Figure A-15: Soft label keys are set.

slk_touch()

The `slk_touch()` function flags all portions of the soft labels as requiring an update, forcing NCurses to redraw the soft labels on the next `slk_noutrefresh()` or `slk_refresh()` call.

Man Page Format

```
int slk_touch(void);
```

Format Reference

The function has no arguments.

Return Value

ERR on failure, OK or some value other than ERR on success.

Notes

Refer to the entry for `touchwin()` for the lowdown on how NCurses reacts to touched portions of a window and how that relates to information being updated on the screen. The same information applies to the soft labels.

Example

```
slk_touch();
```

The statement flags all of the soft labels are requiring an update with the next `slk_noutrefresh()` or `slk_refresh()` function.

Sample Program

```
1    #include <ncurses.h>
2
3    #define CENTER 1
4    #define LCOUNT 8
5
6    int main(void)
7    {
8        char labels[LCOUNT][19] = { "Help!", "File", "Print", "Text",
9                        "Edit", "Quick", "Config", "System" };
10       char *text;
11       int x;
```

```
12
13          slk_init(0);
14          initscr();
15          start_color();
16          init_pair(1,COLOR_RED,COLOR_YELLOW);
17
18          for(x=0;x<LCOUNT;x++)
19              slk_set(x+1,labels[x],CENTER);
20          slk_refresh();
21          getch();
22
23          slk_color(1);
24          slk_touch();
25          slk_refresh();
26          getch();
27
28          endwin();
29          return 0;
30      }
```

Sample output:

The soft labels appear. Press Enter and they reappear with color applied. If the
slk_touch() *was not issued in line 24, then the new color attributes would not*
have been seen. (Comment out that line, and recompile to see.)

Also See

slk_refresh(),touchwin()

standend()

The standend() function is used to turn off text attributes.

Man Page Format

```
int standend(void);
int wstandend(WINDOW *win);
```

Format Reference

The function has no arguments.

Refer to the *w* entry later in this appendix for information on the win argument.

Return Value

The return value, according to the documentation, is "not meaningful."

Notes

While it would seem that standend() is the logical bookend function to standout(), it does more than just turn off the standout text attribute; it turns off *all* text attributes, even color.

standend() is identical to the following:

```
attrset(A_NORMAL);
```

Example

```
standend();
```

The statement restores the normal text attribute for all text subsequently displayed on the standard screen.

Sample Program

For a sample program and sample output refer to the standout() function's entry (next).

Also See

Chapter 3, attrset(), attroff()

standout()

The standout() function activates the standout attribute for text displayed on the screen.

Man Page Format

```
int standout(void);
int wstandout(WINDOW *win);
```

Format Reference

The function has no arguments.

Refer to the *w* entry later in this appendix for information on the win argument.

Return Value

The return value, according to the documentation, is "not meaningful."

Notes

On most terminals, standout displays text in reverse video, such as black text on a white background.

This function is identical to the following:

```
attron(A_STANDOUT);
```

In fact, the `standout()` function may simply be a macro using the `attron(A_STANDOUT)` function as its definition.

`standout()` is an older Curses function and therefore I recommend avoiding it. Use `attron()` or `attrset()` instead.

Example

```
wstandout(output);
```

The statement activates the standout attribute for any text subsequently written to the window `output`.

Sample Program

```
1    #include <ncurses.h>
2
3    int main(void)
4    {
5        initscr();
6
7        addstr("Yes, I must admit that ");
8        standout();
9        addstr("Chris");
10       standend();
11       addstr(" is my favorite pupil.");
12       refresh();
13       getch();
14
15       endwin();
16       return 0;
17   }
```

Sample output:

```
Yes, I must admit that Chris is my favorite pupil.
```

Also See

Chapter 3, `attrset()`, `attron()`

start_color()

The `start_color()` function is used on those terminals that can display colored text to allow NCurses to access those color abilities. No NCurses text or background color functions can be used until `start_color()` has initialized colors in NCurses.

Man Page Format

```
int start_color(void);
```

Format Reference

The function has no arguments.

Return Value

OK upon success, meaning that your program can use color functions and color attributes. ERR upon failure.

Notes

The `has_colors()` function can be used initially to determine whether or not the terminal is capable of setting text colors.

`start_color()` traditionally appears just after the `initscr()` or `newterm()` function.

The colors applied to text or to a window's background are created as color pairs. See `init_pair()`.

Colors are applied similar to other attributes. See `attrset()`, `attron()`, `bkgd()`. Colors can also be applied directly by using a logical OR to build a `chtype` character, and then using any of the `chtype` character functions to place that text in a window.

Custom colors can be created by using the `init_color()` function, though not every terminal supports it. Also see the `can_change_color()` function.

The number of colors available to a terminal can be found by examining the `COLORS` constant. See `COLORS`.

Also refer to this appendix's COLORS entry for a list of NCurses color constants.

The number of color pairs available is found by examining the COLOR_PAIRS constant.

Example

```
start_color();
```

The function initializes color for the NCurses program.

Sample Program

```
1    #include <ncurses.h>
2    #include <stdlib.h>
3
4    void bomb(int r);
5
6    int main(void)
7    {
8        initscr();
9
10   /* first test for color ability of the terminal */
11       if(!has_colors()) bomb(1);
12
13   /* next attempt to initialize NCurses colors */
14       if(start_color() != OK) bomb(2);
15
16   /* colors are okay; continue */
17
18       printw("Colors have been properly initialized.\n");
19       printw("Congratulations!\n");
20       printw("NCurses reports that you can use %d ⤸
colors,\n",COLORS);
21       printw("and %d color pairs.",COLOR_PAIRS);
22       refresh();
23       getch();
24
25       endwin();
26       return 0;
27   }
28
29   void bomb(int r)
30   {
31       endwin();
32       printw("Color problem %d\n",r);
33       exit(r);
34   }
```

Sample output:

```
Colors have been properly initialized.
Congratulations!
NCurses reports that you can use 8 colors,
and 64 color pairs.
```

Also See

Chapter 3, has_colors(), init_pair()

subpad()

The subpad() function creates and defines a rectangle on a pad as a subpad, much the same as subwin() creates a subwindow.

Man Page Format

```
WINDOW *subpad(WINDOW *orig, int nlines, int ncols,int begin_y, int
begin_x);
```

Format Reference

orig is a WINDOW variable, a pointer, representing the parent pad.

nlines and ncols are int values that set the subpad's size in rows and columns. Values for nlines and ncols cannot be larger than the parent pad.

begin_y and begin_x are int values that set the subpad's position relative to the parent pad. The value 0,0 is the parent pad's upper-left corner.

Return Value

When the subpad() call is successful, a subpad is created in memory and a pointer to a WINDOW structure is returned. When things go awry, NULL is returned and no subpad is created.

Notes

The subpad must fit completely inside the parent pad. Aside from that, like pads subpads can be larger than the standard screen.

As with a subwindow, a subpad shares memory with the pad: Changes to one are reflected in the other.

The best way to put a subpad to use is as a shortcut to reference a specific area in a pad. As such, it's easier to calculate offsets with in a subpad than from the entire pad. Refer to the code for PADDY2.C in Chapter 11 for an example.

As with the pad, the subpad is created off-screen. Use the prefresh() function to display its contents. See prefresh().

Subpads are removed with the delwin() function. Be sure to remove all subpads before the parent pad is removed.

It's possible to have subpads within subpads.

It may be necessary to call touchline() or touchwin() on the pad to update the information on the subpad.

Example

```
s2 = subpad(p,TALL,WIDE+1,TALL,0);
```

The statement creates a subpad s2 inside pad p. The pad is TALL rows tall and WIDE+1 columns wide. It's located at offset TALL, 0 inside pad p.

Sample Program

```
1    #include <ncurses.h>
2    #include <stdlib.h>
3
4    void bomb(char *message);
5
6    int main(void)
7    {
8        WINDOW *pod,*pea;
9
10       initscr();
11
12   /* create a new pad */
13       pod = newpad(50,50);
14       if( pod == NULL )
15           bomb("Unable to create new pad");
16
17       addstr("New pad created\n");
18       refresh();
19
20   /* create a subpad */
21       pea = subpad(pod,20,20,29,29);
22       if( pea == NULL )
23           bomb("Unable to create subpad");
24
25       addstr("Subpad created\n");
26       refresh();
27       getch();
28
29       endwin();
```

```
30        return 0;
31    }
32
33    void bomb(char *message)
34    {
35        endwin();
36        puts(message);
37        exit(1);
38    }
```

Sample output:

```
New pad created

Subpad created
```

Also See

Chapter 11, newpad(), prefresh()

subwin()

The subwin() function creates a subwindow or window within a window.

Man Page Format

```
WINDOW *subwin(WINDOW *orig, int nlines, int ncols,
               int begin_y, int begin_x);
```

Format Reference

orig is a window on the screen, which becomes the parent window of the subwindow.

nlines and ncols are int values indicating the number of rows and columns the subwindow contains, respectively. Values range from 1 to the distance between the window's origin and the bottom and right edges of the window, respectively. When either nlines or ncols is 0, the subwindow extends from its origin to the bottom or right edge of the parent window, respectively. Neither nlines nor ncols can be negative.

begin_y and begin_x give the subwindow's origin, the upper-right coordinate relative to the standard screen. Values for begin_y and begin_x are ints, ranging from 0, 0 (the upper-left corner of the screen) to the maximum number of rows and columns for the standard screen. (See COLS and LINES.)

Return Value

Upon success, a pointer is returned, which is saved in a WINDOW variable declared just as regular windows are declared. On failure, NULL is returned. (See NULL.)

Notes

You shouldn't really think of a subwindow as a real window. In fact, if you need a real window, use newwin() or any of the window creation functions, to make a new window. The features available to real windows over subwindows are far more rich and versatile.

Subwindows are best put to use as a way to access a specific rectangle within a window. For example, you can apply a unique background to the subwindow or use its coordinates as handy offsets that would require more overhead to calculate otherwise. Chapter 9 has more details.

Subwindows can have their own subwindows.

Remember that the begin_y and begin_x coordinates for the subwindow's origin are relative to the standard screen, not the parent window.

As with a real window, a subwindow cannot be larger than the standard screen, nor can any part of the window be off the screen.

The smallest subwindow is one character by one character.

All commands that deal with windows also apply to subwindows. Though:

A refresh() call to the parent window is all that's needed to initially display both the parent and any subwindow(s). After that, however, calls to wrefresh() are required to update a subwindow.

Subwindows do not have their own window data in memory. Instead, they share memory with their parents. This leads to many drawbacks, among them: It's possible for the parent window to overwrite text in a subwindow; and the subwindow must be deleted before removing the parent window. (See delwin().)

Examples

```
footnote = subwin(stdscr,2,COLS,LINES-2,0);
```

The statement creates a subwindow named footnote in the standard screen. The window occupies the bottom two rows of the screen from the left to right sides of the standard screen window. (See COLS, LINES.)

```
menu_edit = subwin(menubar,12,20,2,43);
```

Here, the subwindow `menu_edit` is created in the window `menubar`. `menu_edit` is 12 rows by 20 columns and its upper-left corner is at row 2, column 23, which are screen coordinates and not offsets within the window `menubar`.

Sample Program

```
1    #include <ncurses.h>
2
3    int main(void)
4    {
5        WINDOW *sonny;
6
7        initscr();
8        start_color();
9        init_pair(1,COLOR_WHITE,COLOR_BLUE);
10       init_pair(2,COLOR_RED,COLOR_YELLOW);
11
12   /* create subwindow */
13       sonny = subwin(stdscr,14,50,10,30);
14       if(sonny == NULL)
15       {
16           endwin();
17           puts("Unable to create subwindow\n");
18           return(1);
19       }
20
21   /* color windows and splash some text */
22       bkgd(COLOR_PAIR(1));
23       addstr("Hello, son.");
24       wbkgd(sonny,COLOR_PAIR(2));
25       waddstr(sonny,"Hello, Dad.");
26       refresh();
27       getch();
28
29       endwin();
30       return 0;
31   }
```

The sample output is shown in Figure A-2.

Also See

Chapter 9, `newwin()`, `derwin()`, `delwin()`, `WINDOW`

syncok()

The `syncok()` function directs NCurses to automatically (or not) touch parents of a subwindow when that subwindow's contents are changed.

Man Page Format

```
int syncok(WINDOW *win, bool bf);
```

Format Reference

`win` is a `WINDOW` variable representing a subwindow.

`bf` is a Boolean value, either `TRUE` to touch the subwindows for updating and `FALSE` not to.

Return Value

`OK` on success, `ERR` on failure (though it could be any value other than `ERR` on success).

Notes

The `syncok()` attribute is tied into a specific window; it is not a global attribute in NCurses. Subwindows are created with the `syncok()` attribute disabled (set to `FALSE`).

Seeing as how a subwindow and its parent window share memory, the purpose of this function seems questionable.

Example

```
syncok(subby,TRUE);
```

The statement causes any changes to the window `subby` to automatically be touched in all parent windows. Then again, because the memory is shared, the information is updated regardless.

Sample Program

Not applicable.

Also See

`wsyncup()`, `subwin()`

TABSIZE

NCurses uses the value of TABSIZE to set the position of tab stops on the screen. These stops are used when the \t, or tab, character is displayed; the cursor is advanced on the current line to the location of the next tab stop.

Man Page Format

Not applicable.

Format Reference

```
TABSIZE=n
```

The new TABSIZE value is set to equal n, which is an int value, either a variable or constant.

TABSIZE could also be used in any function where an int value is required, such as:

```
printw("Tab stops are set every %d characters.\n",TABSIZE);
```

Return Value

TABSIZE is set equal to 8 by NCurses. The value is set internal to the NCurses library, not in the NCURSES.H file.

Notes

TABSIZE is a global variable. Resetting its value in a function does not keep the new value local to that function.

TABSIZE is initially set to a value of 8, meaning that the \t character advances the cursor to the next column matching a multiple of 8:

```
8, 16, 24, 32, 40, 48, 56, 64, 72
```

and on up to the far right column on the screen

As a variable, the value of TABSIZE can be reset at any time in an NCurses program. Resetting TABSIZE affects tab positions from that point in the program onward.

Tab characters do cause the cursor to drop down to the next line on the display. That is, displaying a \t character after the last tab stop on a line causes the cursor to drop to the next line and display the character at the first tab stop position on the following line, which is at column 0.

Displaying a tab at the last position on the last row of a window causes a window to scroll, but only when scrolling is enabled for that window.

Examples

```
TABSIZE=10;
```

The statement sets the tab stops to intervals of 10.

```
If( x > (maxx - TABSIZE) )
```

This comparison is made using the value of TABSIZE.

Sample Program

```
1    #include <ncurses.h>
2
3    int main(void)
4    {
5        initscr();
6
7        addstr("Tabs set naturally:\n");
8        addstr("A\tB\tC\tD\tE\tF\tG\tH\tI\tJ\tK\tL\tM\n");
9        addstr("Tab stop set to 5\n");
10       TABSIZE = 5;
11       addstr("A\tB\tC\tD\tE\tF\tG\tH\tI\tJ\tK\tL\tM\n");
12       refresh();
13       getch();
14
15       endwin();
16       return 0;
17   }
```

Sample output:

```
Tabs set naturally:
A       B       C       D       E       F       G       H ⮏
        I       J
K       L       M
Tab stop set to 5
A    B    C    D    E    F    G    H    I    J    K    L    M
```

Also See

addch(), addstr()

termattrs()

The termattrs() function is used to confirm which attributes the terminal is capable of producing.

Man Page Format

```
chtype termattrs(void);
attr_t term_attrs(void);
```

Format Reference

The functions have no arguments.

Return Value

The functions return a long int bit field with bits set according to which attributes the terminal is capable of producing. The chtype attributes are defined in NCURSES.H and are prefixed with A; attr_t attributes are also defined in NCURSES.H and prefixed by WA.

Notes

It's possible to ferret out specific attributes by using a logical OR with the attribute constant and the value returned by termattrs().

The attr_get() function is used to read attributes currently being used in a window. See attr_get().

Refer to Appendix C for more information on the chtype attribute constants.

Examples

```
printw("The terminals attributes value is %X.\n",termattrs());
```

The function displays the termattrs() value as a hexadecimal number.

```
a = termattrs();
```

Here, the attributes bit mask for the current terminal is saved in chtype variable a.

Sample Program

```
1    #include <ncurses.h>
2
3    static void attryn(chtype a, chtype c)
4    {
5        if(a & c)
6            addstr("Yes");
7        else
8            addstr("No");
9        addch('\n');
10   }
11
12   int main(void)
13   {
14       chtype attributes;
15
16       initscr();
17
18       attributes = termattrs();
19       addstr("This terminal is capable of the following ↵
attributes:\n");
20       printw("%14s","AltCharSet: ");    attryn( attributes, ↵
A_ALTCHARSET);
21       printw("%14s","Blink: ");         attryn( attributes, A_BLINK);
22       printw("%14s","Bold: ");          attryn( attributes, A_BOLD);
23       printw("%14s","Dim: ");           attryn( attributes, A_DIM)    ;
24       printw("%14s","Invisible: ");     attryn( attributes, A_INVIS);
25       printw("%14s","Normal: ");        attryn( attributes, ↵
A_NORMAL);
26       printw("%14s","Reverse: ");       attryn( attributes, A_REVERSE);
27       printw("%14s","Standout: ");      attryn( attributes, ↵
A_STANDOUT);
28       printw("%14s","Underline: ");     attryn( attributes, ↵
A_UNDERLINE);
29       printw("%14s","Protect: ");       attryn( attributes, A_PROTECT);
30       printw("%14s","Horizontal: ");    attryn( attributes, ↵
A_HORIZONTAL);
31       printw("%14s","Left: ");          attryn( attributes, A_LEFT);
32       printw("%14s","Low: ");           attryn( attributes, A_LOW);
33       printw("%14s","Right: ");         attryn( attributes, A_RIGHT);
34       printw("%14s","Top: ");           attryn( attributes, A_TOP);
35       printw("%14s","Vertical: ");      attryn( attributes, ↵
A_VERTICAL);
36       refresh();
37       getch();
38
39       endwin();
40       return 0;
41   }
```

Sample output:

```
This terminal is capable of the following attributes:
  AltCharSet: Yes
       Blink: No
        Bold: Yes
         Dim: No
   Invisible: No
      Normal: Yes
     Reverse: Yes
    Standout: Yes
   Underline: Yes
     Protect: No
  Horizontal: No
        Left: No
         Low: No
       Right: No
         Top: No
    Vertical: No
```

Also See

Appendix C, `attrset()`, `attr_get()`

termname()

The `termname()` function returns the terminal name as a string (`char` array).

Man Page Format

```
char *termname(void);
```

Format Reference

The function takes no arguments.

Return Value

The function returns a string in the form of a pointer. It can be used as an immediate value or stored in a `char` pointer variable.

NULL can be returned by `termname()` when there is an error.

Notes

The name returned by `termname()` is the same as returned by the $TERM environment variable.

For a more verbose string describing the terminal, use the `longname()` function. See `longname()`.

Example

```
addstr(termname());
refresh();
```

These statements display the terminal name on the standard screen.

Sample Program

```
1    #include <ncurses.h>
2
3    int main(void)
4    {
5        initscr();
6
7        printw("The term name is %s.\n",termname());
8        refresh();
9        getch();
10
11       endwin();
12       return 0;
13   }
```

Sample output:

```
The termname is xterm-color.
```

Of course, your output may vary.

Also See

`longname(), newterm()`

timeout()

The `timeout()` function sets a variable delay for NCurses text input functions.

Man Page Format

```
void timeout(int delay);
void wtimeout(WINDOW *win, int delay);
```

Format Reference

delay is an int value, either negative, positive, or zero. When delay is negative, input functions are blocking as normal. When delay is zero, input functions are non-blocking and return ERR when no input is in the queue. Positive values of delay represent the number of milliseconds NCurses waits for character input before the input function returns ERR.

Return Value

ERR on failure or OK on success.

Notes

One thousand milliseconds equals one second.

Setting the nodelay() function is the same as timeout(0).

The halfdelay() function is similar to using positive values with timeout(), though halfdelay() uses tenths of a second as its argument, not milliseconds. And halfdelay() is directed at all NCurses input, not window-oriented as timeout() is.

Examples

```
timeout(1000);
```

The statement sets the text input delay to one second. When getch() has not received input after one second, it returns ERR.

```
timeout(-1);
```

The statement activates (or reactivates) the blocking nature of text input functions such as getch(). This could be used in a program to reset a previously set timeout() value.

Sample Program

```
1    #include <ncurses.h>
2
3    #define DELAY 1000
4
```

```
 5    int main(void)
 6    {
 7        int ch;
 8
 9        initscr();
10
11        timeout(DELAY);
12        printw("The timeout delay has been set to %d ↩
      milliseconds.\n",DELAY);
13        addstr("Try to type in your name fast enough:\n");
14        refresh();
15
16        do
17        {
18            ch = getch();
19            if(ch == '\n')
20                break;
21        } while(ch != ERR);
22
23        mvaddstr(5,0,"Hope you got it all in!");
24        refresh();
25        getch();
26
27        endwin();
28        return 0;
29    }
```

Sample output:

```
The timeout delay has been set to 1000 milliseconds.
Try to type in your name fast enough:
```

Try to type quickly; if you pause longer than 1 second, either at first or between any keys, the program is over.

Also See

`getch()`, `nodelay()`, `halfdelay()`

touchline()

The `touchline()` function marks one or more rows in a window as changed, which directs NCurses to update the row(s) on the next call to `refresh()`.

Explanation

Refer to the entry for `touchwin()` for an explanation. The same material applies for the `touchline()` function, though for `touchline()` only specific lines in a window are marked as changed, and therefore written to the screen upon the next `refresh()` call.

Man Page Format

```
int touchline(WINDOW *win, int start, int count);
```

Format Reference

`win` is a `WINDOW` variable representing a window created earlier in this program, or `stdscr` for the standard screen.

`start` is an `int` value representing the starting row to be updated. Values range from 0 for the top row on through as many rows as there are in the named window.

`count` is an `int` value that tells NCurses how many rows to update. Values range from 1 for just the named row, on up to as many rows as there are from the current row to the end of the window.

Return Value

`ERR` upon failure and an `int` value other than `ERR` upon success.

Notes

Remember that `touchline()` requires *three* arguments: window, starting line, and count. It's really a "touch lines" function.

`touchline()` updates lines from the named row *down*.

A common reason for using `touchline()` is when NCurses is having trouble updating the current screen, such as when one window overlaps another.

The `touchline()` function by itself does not update the screen. It merely coordinates between the named window and memory. A `refresh()` or `wrefresh()` function is required after `touchline()` to actually see the updated window.

If you know specifically which lines of text need updating, then the `touchline()` function is more efficient than calling `touchwin()`.

Examples

```
touchline(stdscr,0,10);
```

Here, the top 10 lines of the standard screen are touched, meaning that each and every character will be updated on the next `refresh()` call.

```
touchline(menu,10,0);
```

Here, the `touchline()` function flags line 10 in the window menu for updating with the next `wrefresh(menu)` call.

Sample Program

```
1    #include <Ncurses.h>
2    #include <stdlib.h>
3    #include <time.h>
4
5    #define MAX 23
6
7    int main(void)
8    {
9        WINDOW *alpha;
10       int rows[MAX];
11       int c,r,total;
12
13       srandom((unsigned)time(NULL));    /* seed randomizer */
14       for(c=0;c<MAX;c++)               /* initialize array */
15           rows[c] = 0;
16       total = 0;                    /* initialize counter */
17
18   /* NCurses setup stuff */
19       initscr();
20       start_color();
21       init_pair(1,COLOR_WHITE,COLOR_BLUE);
22       alpha = newwin(0,0,0,0);
23       wbkgd(alpha,COLOR_PAIR(1));
24       untouchwin(alpha);            /* pretend win is updated */
25
26       addstr("Press Enter to touch and display window alpha\n");
27       refresh();
28       getch();
29
30   /* Loop to gradually reveal the blue window */
31       while(total<MAX)
32       {
33           r = random() % (MAX + 1);
34           if( rows[r]==0 )
35           {
36               rows[r] = 1;
37               touchline(alpha,r,1);
38               wrefresh(alpha);    /* update the line */
39               napms(100);         /* pause 1/10 sec */
40               total++;
41           }
42       }
43       getch();
```

```
44
45        endwin();
46        return 0;
47    }
```

Sample output:

```
Press Enter to touch and display window alpha
```

After pressing enter, each row of window alpha is updated one after the other as each is touched. Eventually the entire screen turns blue.

Also See

```
refresh(), touchwin(), wtouchln(), is_linetouched()
```

touchwin()

The `touchwin()` function directs NCurses to treat a window as if every character on the window has been changed or modified since the last refresh, forcing NCurses to redraw the entire window on the next `refresh()` or `wrefresh()` function.

Explanation

Internally, NCurses keeps track of which parts of a window have been updated since the last refresh. For efficiency's sake, only those changed parts of the window are then updated to the current screen on the next refresh. By using `touchwin()`, every single character in the window is flagged as touched, or changed, forcing NCurses to redraw everything from scratch on the next `refresh()` or `wrefresh()` call.

Man Page Format

```
int touchwin(WINDOW *win);
```

Format Reference

```
touchwin(win)
```

`win` is the name of a window to touch. After the call, all locations in the window are flagged as requiring updating for the next call to `wrefresh(win)`.

Return Value

ERR upon failure, or a value other than ERR upon success.

Notes

It's only necessary to use touchwin() when NCurses is having trouble updating the current screen. This happens most often when dealing with overlapping windows.

By itself, touchwin() does not redisplay the current screen or the named window; it merely updates the window's contents. To update the current screen, you must call wrefresh() for the window after using the touchwin() function.

Using touchwin() followed by wrefresh() is similar to using the clearok() function for that window, followed by wrefresh(). Though remember that the clearok() function clears the screen before redrawing the image, and it does not change a window's status from touched to untouched.

Example

```
touchwin(help);
```

Here, the touchwin() function assures that all parts of the window help will be drawn for the next call to wrefresh(help).

Sample Program

```
1     #include <ncurses.h>
2
3     int main(void)
4     {
5         WINDOW *bob;
6
7         initscr();
8         start_color();
9         init_pair(1,COLOR_WHITE,COLOR_BLUE);
10        init_pair(2,COLOR_RED,COLOR_WHITE);
11
12        bob = newwin(0,0,0,0);
13        wbkgd(bob,COLOR_PAIR(2));
14        bkgd(COLOR_PAIR(1));
15
16        waddstr(bob,"Hello from the window bob!\n");
17        waddstr(bob,"I like long walks and romantic candlelit ⮰
dinners.\n");
```

```
18          waddstr(bob,"Press Enter to return to the standard ⤵
screen.\n");
19          addstr("This is the standard screen.\n");
20          addstr("To see the window bob, press the Enter key:\n");
21          refresh();
22          getch();
23
24          wrefresh(bob);
25          getch();
26
27          addstr("Welcome back to the standard screen (kinda).\n");
28          addstr("To see the whole window bob, press Enter.\n");
29          refresh();
30          getch();
31
32          waddstr(bob,"Thanks!\n");
33          waddstr(bob,"Press Enter to see the whole standard ⤵
screen.\n");
34          touchwin(bob);
35          wrefresh(bob);
36          getch();
37
38          touchwin(stdscr);
39          refresh();
40          getch();
41
42          endwin();
43          return 0;
44      }
```

Sample output:
In white text on a blue screen:

```
This is the standard screen.
To see the window bob, press the Enter key:
```

Press Enter to see red text on a white screen:

```
Hello from the window bob!
I like long walks and romantic candlelit dinners.
Press Enter to return to the standard screen.
```

Press Enter to see:

```
Hello from the window bob!
I like long walks and romantic candlelit dinners.
Welcome back to the standard screen (kinda).
To see the whole window bob, press Enter.
```

The top two lines are red on white; the bottom two lines are white on blue. Press Enter:

```
Hello from the window bob!
I like long walks and romantic candlelit dinners.
Press Enter to return to the standard screen.
Thanks!
Press Enter to see the whole standard screen.
```

Press Enter:

```
This is the standard screen.
To see the window bob, press the Enter key:
Welcome back to the standard screen (kinda).
To see the whole window bob, press Enter.
```

Also See

`clearok(), refresh(), is_wintouched(), untouchwin()`

TRUE

TRUE is a Boolean value used in NCurses for setting options, as a value returned by specific functions, or for comparisons.

Man Page Format

Not applicable.

Format Reference

TRUE can be used in one of the following ways:

```
function([arg(s)],TRUE)
```

Here, TRUE is used in the given function to switch some NCurses setting on or activate an option.

```
var = function([arg(s)])
```

In this statement, the value returned by the function can be either TRUE or FALSE and is stored in the var variable. var is declared as a bool value.

```
if( eval == TRUE)
while([eval ==] TRUE)
```

Here, TRUE is used as a comparison to some evaluation eval. Or in the case of the while loop, TRUE can be used by itself to create an endless loop.

Functions that return TRUE can also be used immediately inside comparisons:

```
if( function([arg(s)] )
while( function([arg(s)] )
```

Here, the function returns a TRUE (or FALSE) value, which is then immediately evaluated by if or while.

Return Value

The value of TRUE is set in NCURSES.H to 1.

Notes

Table A-17 shows which NCurses functions use the Boolean TRUE.

The logical opposite of TRUE is FALSE. Functions that use or return TRUE can equally use or return FALSE, depending on the situation.

Table A-17: NCurses functions using TRUE or FALSE

FUNCTION RETURNS T/F	FUNCTION USES T/F
can_change_color()	clearok()
has_colors()	idcok()
has_ic()	idlok()
has_il()	immedok()
is_linetouched()	intrflush()
is_wintouched()	keypad()
isendwin()	leaveok()
mouse_trafo()	meta()
wenclose()	mouse_trafo()
	nodelay()
	notimeout() 486
	scrollok()
	syncok()
	use_env()

Examples

```
if(can_change_color())
```

Here, if evaluates the results of the can_change_color() function. If TRUE is returned, then the terminal has the ability to use custom colors for text attributes.

```
scrollok(stdscr,TRUE);
```

The previous function turns on text scrolling for the standard screen.

Sample Program

```
1      #include <Ncurses.h>
2
3      int main(void)
4      {
5          bool tf;
6          initscr();
7
8          tf =  has_colors();
9          if( tf == TRUE)
10             addstr("This terminal can do colors.\n");
11         else
12             addstr("This terminal cannot do colors.\n");
13         refresh();
14         getch();
15
16         endwin();
17         return 0;
18     }
```

Sample output:

```
This terminal can do colors.
```

Or:

```
This terminal cannot do colors.
```

Also See

FALSE

typeahead()

The `typeahead()` function controls NCurses typeahead feature (see the next section) and determines which input source to monitor for typeahead.

Explanation

`typeahead` is an internal feature NCurses uses to optimize input. When there is keyboard activity during a screen update, NCurses suspends the update to immediately process the keyboard input, specifically if the input is coming from a tty. The next `refresh()` or `doupdate()` call then completes the screen update.

The `typeahead()` function allows you to specify which input source to monitor for typeahead or whether typeahead should be disabled.

Man Page Format

```
int typeahead(int fd);
```

Format Reference

`fd` is a file descriptor or `FILE` type variable, such as `stdin`. It specifies the input source typeahead monitors. When the value -1 is specified, then typeahead is disabled.

Return Value

`OK` upon success or `ERR` on failure.

Notes

The file value `typeahead()` normally uses depends on how NCurses was started. When `initscr()` is used, then the default value is `stdin`, standard input. When `newterm()` is used, then default input is set as the third argument (see `newtertm()`).

The typeahead feature does disrupt screen updates. If you'd rather have your program always and completely update the screen whenever `refresh()` or `doupdate()` is called, then specify `typeahead(-1)`.

Examples

```
typeahead(-1);
```

The statement disables NCurses typeahead optimization during a screen refresh.

```
typeahead(stdio);
```

Here, NCurses `typeahead` is set for standard input, most likely to restore `typeahead` after being disabled.

Sample Program

```
1    #include <ncurses.h>
2
3    int main(void)
4    {
5        initscr();
6        typeahead(-1);          /* Disable typeahead */
7
8        addstr("All this text will be put to the screen without a\n");
9        addstr("keyboard interruption.");
10        refresh();
11        getch();
12
13        endwin();
14        return 0;
15    }
```

Sample output:

```
All this text will be put to the screen without a
keyboard interruption.
```

Refreshing takes place so quickly on x-terminals that you'd really need to hook up a remote terminal, set it to something slow, and then test this function to really see the results.

Also See

`newterm(), flushinp(), intrflush()`

unctrl()

The `unctrl()` function is used primarily to convert control codes to a displayable string using the ^c format, where ^ is the "control" prefix and c is a letter or symbol corresponding to the code.

Man Page Format

```
char *unctrl(chtype c);
```

Format Reference

c is a chtype character representing a character or code plus optional formatting attributes.

Return Value

unctrl() returns a pointer to a character array (string) representing the character or code c. For displayable characters, the character itself is returned in the string. For control codes, the code letter prefixed by a ^ is returned. See Notes.
    On error, NULL is returned.

Notes

Though the ch argument is a chtype and may contain formatting attributes, any attributes present are ignored by the unctrl() function.
    Table A-18 references the ASCII control codes, 0 through 32 plus code 127.

Table A-18: Control keys and codes

VALUE HEX	VALUE DEC	CHAR	CODE	MEANING
0x00	0	^@	NUL	Null
0x01	1	^A	SOH	Start Of Heading
0x02	2	^B	STX	Start Of Text
0x03	3	^C	ETX	End Of Text
0x04	4	^D	EOT	End Of Transmission
0x05	5	^E	ENQ	Enquiry
0x06	6	^F	ACK	Acknowledge
0x07	7	^G	BEL	Bell
0x08	8	^H	BS	Backspace
0x09	9	^I	HT	Horizontal Tab
0x0a	11	^J	LF	Line Feed
0x0b	12	^K	VT	Vertical Tab

(continued)

Table A-18 *(continued)*

VALUE HEX	VALUE DEC	CHAR	CODE	MEANING
0x0c	13	^L	FF	Form Feed
0x0d	14	^M	CR	Carriage Return
0x0e	15	^N	SO	Shift Out
0x0f	16	^O	SI	Shift In
0x10	17	^P	DLE	Data Link Escape
0x11	18	^Q	DC1	Device Control 1
0x12	19	^R	DC2	Device Control 2
0x13	20	^S	DC3	Device Control 3
0x14	21	^T	DC4	Device Control 4
0x15	22	^U	NAK	Negative Acknowledge
0x16	23	^V	SYN	Synchronous idle
0x17	24	^W	ETB	End Transmission Block
0x18	25	^X	CAN	Cancel
0x19	26	^Y	EM	End of Medium
0x1a	27	^Z	SUB	Substitute
0x1b	28	^[	ESC	Escape
0x1c	29	^\	FS	Form Separator
0x1d	30	^]	GS	Group Separator
0x1e	31	^^	RS	Record Separator
0x1f	32	^_	US	Unit Separator
0x7f	127	^?	DEL	Delete

In some localities, codes 0x80 through 0x8f are represented as shown in the table, but prefixed by the ~ (tilde). Code 0xff is displayed by `unctrl()` as ~?.

Examples

```
p = unctrl(x);
```

Here, the `char` pointer variable `p` references a string representing the character's code value of `x`.

```
printw("That character is code %s.\n",unctrl(x));
```

Here, the `printw()` function displays the string returned by the `unctrl()` function.

Sample Program

```
1    #include <ncurses.h>
2
3    #define MAX 0x7f
4
5    int main(void)
6    {
7        chtype ch;
8
9        initscr();
10
11       for(ch=0;ch<=MAX;ch++)
12           printw("%s\t",unctrl(ch));
13       refresh();
14       getch();
15
16       endwin();
17       return 0;
18   }
```

Sample output:

```
^@        ^A        ^B        ^C        ^D        ^E        ^F        ^G ↩
          ^H        ^I
^J        ^K        ^L        ^M        ^N        ^O        ^P        ^Q ↩
          ^R        ^S
^T        ^U        ^V        ^W        ^X        ^Y        ^Z        ^[ ↩
          ^\        ^]
^^        ^_                  !         "         #         $         % ↩
          &         '
(         )         *         +         ,         -         .         / ↩
          0         1
2         3         4         5         6         7         8         9 ↩
          :         ;
<         =         >         ?         @         A         B         C ↩
          D         E
F         G         H         I         J         K         L         M ↩
          N         O
P         Q         R         S         T         U         V         W ↩
          X         Y
z         [         \         ]         ^         _         `         a ↩
          b         c
d         e         f         g         h         i         j         k ↩
          l         m
n         o         p         q         r         s         t         u ↩
          v         w
x         y         z         {         |         }         ~         ^?
```

Also See

```
keyname(), addch()
```

ungetch()

The `ungetch()` function places a specific character back into the keyboard input queue.

Explanation

Characters read from the keyboard are buffered by the terminal, fed one at a time into the various NCurses key-reading functions. So, for example, `getch()` reads the oldest character waiting in the buffer, then the next character and so on. When the buffer is empty, `getch()` waits or returns ERR depending on the `nodelay()` status.

What `ungetch()` does is to place a character into the keyboard input buffer. That character then becomes the next character to be read, unless `ungetch()` is called again with another character.

You can use `ungetch()` to "stuff the ballot box" as it were, but it can also be used in conjunction with `getch()` to preview waiting characters.

Man Page Format

```
int ungetch(int ch);
```

Format Reference

`ch` is an `int` value representing a character to be placed into the keyboard input buffer.

Return Value

OK upon success or ERR on failure.

Notes

When stuffing more than one character into the keyboard buffer, remember to do it *backwards*. For example, to stuff OK into the buffer, you need to do:

```
ungetch('K');
ungetch('O');
```

Remember that `ungetch()` requires an `int` argument, not a `char`.

It's also possible to stuff special keys into the keyboard buffer, such as `KEY_LEFT` or `KEY_F(10)`. Refer to Appendix D for a list of these constants.

`ungetch()` is not a window-oriented function; all windows share the same input queue.

Examples

```
ungetch('\t');
```

Here, a tab character is placed into the input queue. The next time a character-reading function fetches a character from the keyboard, that character will be \t.

```
ungetch('n');
ungetch('e');
ungetch('B');
```

In the previous code, the name `Ben` is stuffed into the input queue by successive `ungetch()` functions.

```
ch = getch();
if(ch != '\n')
{
    ungetch(ch);
    ungetch('\n');
}
```

This code tests to see if there is a newline at the end of whatever text has been input. When there isn't, then the `if` statements are executed and a newline is added to the queue.

Sample Program

```
1    #include <ncurses.h>
2
3    int main(void)
4    {
5        char name[80];
6        char stuff[] = "\nakoozaB eoJ";
7        char *c;
8
9        c = stuff;
10       initscr();
11
12   /* stuff input */
13       while(*c)
14           ungetch(*c++);
```

```
15
16    /* typical Q&A type of code */
17         addstr("Your name: ");
18         refresh();
19         getstr(name);
20         printw("Pleased to meet you, %s.\n",name);
21         refresh();
22         getch();
23
24         endwin();
25         return 0;
26    }
```

Sample output:

```
Your name: Joe Bazooka
Pleased to meet you, Joe Bazooka.
```

No typing necessary!

Also See

Chapter 7, getch(), nodelay()

untouchwin()

The untouchwin() function removes all signs of updates on a window, leading NCurses to believe that the window has been fully updated (refreshed).

Explanation

NCurses keeps track of changes made in a window. For efficiency's sake, only the text changed in a window is written to the current screen during the next refresh() call. By using untouchwin(), you direct NCurses to ignore changes made in a window, and to assume that all text has been updated.

This call can be used when you want only a specific part of a window's update to be displayed. For example, you could use several functions to output text to a window, then use untouchwin(), then output more text. Only the text output after untouchwin() would then be updated at the next refresh() call.

In the sample program for touchline(), untouchwin() is used just after the window is created. This allows subsequent calls to the touchline() function and wrefresh() to reveal the window one line at a time.

Man Page Format

```
int untouchwin(WINDOW *win);
```

Format Reference

win is a WINDOW variable referencing a window to be untouched. After the function is called, NCurses assumes that the window's memory and information on the screen have been synchronized and an update is not needed.

Return Value

ERR upon failure or an int value other than ERR upon success.

Notes

The opposite of the untouchwin() function is touchwin(), which tells NCurses that every possible text position in a window needs updating on the next refresh() call.

There is no untouchln() or untouchline() function corresponding to untouchwin(), but there is the wtouchln() function. In fact, untouchwin() is most likely a macro version of wtouchln().

Example

```
untouchwin(help);
```

The window help is flagged as fully updated, meaning the next call to wrefresh(help) will not update any text written before the previous statement.

Sample Program

Refer to the entry for touchline() for a sample program and output.

Also See

```
touchwin(), refresh()
```

use_default_colors()

use_default_colors() is an extended NCurses function that sets the foreground and background text colors to the same as used in the terminal window when start_color() initializes NCurses text color attributes.

Man Page Format

```
int use_default_colors(void);
```

Format Reference

The function has no arguments.

Return Value

OK is returned when things work; ERR otherwise.

Notes

The start_color() function in NCurses initializes the color functions. It also sets the default foreground and background color for text, which is stored in COLOR_PAIR(0). Normally the colors are set to white text on a black background. The use_default_colors() function, however, resets COLOR_PAIR(0) to match the same foreground and background text colors used in the terminal window. So if you're using xterm and have the text color set to yellow text on a black background, that color combination then becomes COLOR_PAIR(0) for use in NCurses.

The use_default_colors() function is the same as assume_default_colors(-1,-1).

Refer to the entry for assume_default_colors() for more information.

Example

```
use_default_colors();
```

The colors set by start_color() for COLOR_PAIR(0) will be the same as used by the terminal window.

Sample Program

```
1    #include <ncurses.h>
2
3    int main(void)
```

```
4    {
5        int r;
6
7        initscr();
8        start_color();
9
10       use_default_colors();
11       addstr("The default colors have been set to\n");
12       addstr("the same as the terminal's colors.\n");
13       refresh();
14       getch();
15
16       endwin();
17       return 0;
18   }
```

Sample output:

```
The default colors have been set to
the same as the terminal's colors.
```

The text above appears colored the same as text in the terminal window.

Also See

COLORS, init_pair(), assume_default_colors()

use_env()

The use_env() function tells NCurses whether to use the terminal's terminfo definitions of lines and columns or the default LINES and COLUMNS environment variable values.

Man Page Format

```
void use_env(bool f);
```

Format Reference

f is a Boolean value, either TRUE or FALSE. When set TRUE, NCurses uses the values of the environment variables LINES and COLUMNS as the size of the window. When set FALSE, the values for the window size are pulled from the terminfo database. In either case, NCurses also takes into account the terminal's size by asking the system. When using the environment variables, those override the system's size. When using the terminfo database, the system's values (if known) override the database.

Return Value

The function returns nothing.

Notes

The use_env() function must be specified *before* the initscr() or newterm() function initializes NCurses.

If either LINES or COLUMNS is not set in the environment, then NCurses uses the values from the terminfo database by default. If you manually set LINES or COLUMNS in the environment, then *Bad Things* can happen.

A few applications set $LINES or $COLUMNS, and they're not resizeable.

Note that the environment variable is COLUMNS but in NCurses the COLS variable is used instead. See COLS.

Example

```
use_env(FALSE);
```

The statement directs NCurses to use the terminfo database's values for the current screen size.

Sample Program

```
1    #include <ncurses.h>
2
3    int main(void)
4    {
5        use_env(FALSE);
6        initscr();
7
8        printw("LINES = %d\n",LINES);
9        printw("COLS = %d\n",COLS);
10       refresh();
11       getch();
12
13       endwin();
14       return 0;
15   }
```

Sample output:

```
LINES = 24
COLS = 80
```

Also See

`initscr()`, `LINES`, `COLS`

vline()

The `vline()` function draws a vertical (up-down) line from the cursor's current location down a given number of rows.

Man Page Format

```
int vline(chtype ch, int n);
int wvline(WINDOW *win, chtype ch, int n);
int mvvline(int y, int x, chtype ch, int n);
int mvwvline(WINDOW *, int y, int x, chtype ch, int n);
```

Format Reference

`ch` is a `chtype` character used to draw the line. Though typically only a single character, such as |, is used, you can combine characters, text attributes and colors with the `chtype` variable. Refer to Appendix C. When zero is specified for `ch`, the default `ASC_VLINE` character is used. See Appendix B for more information on ACS characters.

`n` is an `int` value that sets the length of the line in rows. Valid values for `n` range from 0 on up to whatever an integer can hold. When `n` is zero no line is displayed. When `n` is greater than the distance between the current cursor position and the bottom of the window, then only as many `ch` characters as can be displayed are shown. (Long vertical lines will not cause the screen to scroll, nor will the line wrap in any way.)

Refer to the *mv*, *mvw*, and *w* prefix entries elsewhere in this appendix for information on the `win`, `row`, and `col` arguments.

Return Value

`vline()` always returns `OK`.

Notes

The line always goes from the cursor's current position down.

Drawing the line does not affect the cursor's location. The cursor remains at its previous location or whichever location was set by the `mvvline()` or `mvwvline()` functions.

The line drawn is not protected against erasure by other NCurses text output functions; the line can be overwritten at any time.

Examples

```
vline(0,10);
```

The function draws a line 10 characters long (tall) from the cursor's current position. The default line drawing character is used.

```
mvvline(y,10,'*',len);
```

Here, the function draws a vertical line using asterisks. The line is len characters long from location row y, column 10.

Sample Program

```
1     #include <ncurses.h>
2
3     int main(void)
4     {
5          int maxy,maxx,halfy,x,len;
6          initscr();
7
8          getmaxyx(stdscr,maxy,maxx);
9          halfy = maxy >> 1;                    /* y/2 */
10         len = 1;
11
12         for(x=0;x<maxx;x++)
13         {
14              mvvline(halfy-len,x,0,len+len);
15              if( !(x % 7)) len++;
16         }
17         refresh();
18         getch();
19
20         endwin();
21         return 0;
22    }
```

The sample output is shown in Figure A-16.

Also See

Chapter 14, Appendix B, box(), hline()

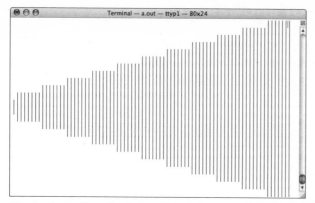

Figure A-16: The vline() function draws a, well, modern art-like thing on the terminal.

vwprintw()

See printw().

vwscanw()

See scanw().

w prefix functions

This appendix lists NCurses' pseudo functions. Internally, most NCurses functions come with the w prefix, which means that the function initially specifies a window argument. This entry covers the common information shared by all w prefix functions; refer elsewhere for the function specifics.

Format

All w prefix functions feature win as their first argument.

win is a WINDOW variable, representing a window created earlier in the program.

Refer to the individual functions elsewhere in this appendix for information on the other arguments listed.

Notes

The WINDOW variable always comes first in those functions that require it. Even with the mvw prefix, win comes first (then the screen coordinates).

The argument win is a WINDOW pointer variable, but do not prefix it with the & operator.

The pseudo functions are macros defined as their w-prefix counterparts with the stdscr, standard screen, argument used for the window.

Also See

addch(), addchstr(), addstr(), and so on

wcursyncup()

The wcursyncup() function sets the cursor position for all ancestors of a window equal to the cursor position in the named window.

Man Page Format

```
void wcursyncup(WINDOW *win);
```

Format Reference

win is the name of a subwindow, a WINDOW variable.

Return Value

The function returns no value.

Notes

wcursyncup() basically fixes the cursors location. The cursor doesn't move when focus is changed from the subwindow to any of its parents.

Each window still maintains its own cursor location; wcursyncup() simply sets them all to the same relative screen coordinates.

Example

```
wcursyncup(little);
```

The statement sets the cursor's location in all parents of subwindow little to the same location.

Sample Program

```
1     #include <ncurses.h>
2
3     int main(void)
4     {
5         WINDOW *sonny;
6         int a;
7
8         initscr();
9         start_color();
10        init_pair(1,COLOR_WHITE,COLOR_BLUE);
11        init_pair(2,COLOR_RED,COLOR_YELLOW);
12
13        bkgd(COLOR_PAIR(1));
14        sonny = subwin(stdscr,5,20,10,30);
15        wbkgd(sonny,COLOR_PAIR(2));
16
17        waddstr(sonny,"This string is written to the window 'sonny'");
18        wnoutrefresh(stdscr);
19        wnoutrefresh(sonny);
20        doupdate();
21        getch();
22
23        wcursyncup(sonny);
24        refresh();
25        getch();
26
27        endwin();
28        return 0;
29    }
```

Sample output:

Two windows appear on the screen, with text written to the smaller, yellow subwindow. After wcursyncup(), the cursor's location on the standard screen is reset to the same location as was set in the window sonny. If you comment out line 23, you can see how the cursor location changes to the home position, 0-0, upon the second refresh() in line 24.

Also See

move()

wenclose()

The wenclose() function determines whether the coordinates of a mouse click are within a given window.

Man Page Format

```
bool wenclose(const WINDOW *win, int y, int x);
```

Format Reference

win is the name of a WINDOW variable representing a window in NCurses.

y and x are int values or variables, representing the vertical (row) and horizontal (column) position of a mouse click or event.

Return Value

The function returns a Boolean value, either TRUE or FALSE whether the coordinate is inside or outside the named window, respectively. Both TRUE and FALSE are defined in NCURSES.H.

Notes

This function works best when you refresh and update the window in question.

Example

```
if(wenclose(menu,me.y,me.x);
```

The if condition tests TRUE when the coordinates of me.y and me.x are within the window menu. Assume that me is an MEVENT structure updated by getmouse().

Sample Program

```
1      #include <ncurses.h>
2
3      int main(void)
4      {
5          WINDOW *target;
6          MEVENT eek;
7          int ch;
8
9          initscr();
10         start_color();
11         init_pair(1,COLOR_WHITE,COLOR_CYAN);
12         noecho();
13         keypad(stdscr,TRUE);
14
15         target = newwin(5,3,9,39);
16         wbkgd(target,COLOR_PAIR(1));
```

```
17          wnoutrefresh(stdscr);
18          wnoutrefresh(target);
19          doupdate();
20
21          mousemask(BUTTON1_CLICKED,NULL);
22          while(1)
23          {
24              ch = getch();
25              if( ch == KEY_MOUSE )
26              {
27                  getmouse(&eek);
28                  if(wenclose(target,eek.y,eek.x))
29                  {
30                      beep();
31                      touchwin(target);
32                      wnoutrefresh(target);
33                  }
34                  else
35                  {
36                      mvaddch(eek.y,eek.x,'*');
37                      wnoutrefresh(stdscr);
38                  }
39                  doupdate();
40                  continue;
41              }
42              if( ch == '\n' )
43                  break;
44          }
45
46          endwin();
47          return 0;
48      }
```

Sample output:

*A small cyan window appears in the middle of the screen. Clicking the mouse inside that window beeps the speaking. Clicking outside of the window displays a * at the click point.*

Also See

```
getmouse(),wmouse_trafo()
```

WINDOW

WINDOW is an NCurses variable type used to reference a window on the screen. Internally, WINDOW represents a structure created in memory and filled with various values and settings according to the window's state.

Man Page Format

Not applicable.

Format Reference

Most of the settings in the WINDOW structure can be adjusted by using standard NCurses functions. Even so, the following references names and values found in the WINDOW structure. In each example, win represents the name of a WINDOW variable.

Cursor's location

```
win->_cury
win->_curx
```

The _cury and _curx elements are variables of the NCURSES_SIZE_T type (int) representing the cursor's location in a window, row and column. These are the same values returned by the getyx() function. (Actually getyx() is a macro that reads the cury and curx values.)

Window size

```
win->_maxy
win->_maxx
win->_begy
win->_begx
```

The _maxy and _maxx elements are variables of the NCURSES_SIZE_T type (short) the representing the maximum values for the placing the cursor in a column or row. The header file says that these are not the window size, but they are one less than the window size. That's because the first row and column is zero. (The getmaxyx() function returns these values *plus one*.)

The _begy and _begx elements are variables of the NCURSES_SIZE_T type (int) indicating the coordinate of the window's upper-left corner. These are the same values returned y the getbegyx() function.

Window state flags

```
win->_flags
```

flags is a short that contains 7 bit flags, as shown in Table A-19.

Testing these values is done with a logical AND. See the Examples for more information.

Table A-19: Window state flags

CONSTANT	BIT POSITION	ON VALUE
_SUBWIN	0x01	Window is a subwindow
_ENDLINE	0x02	Window is flush-right
_FULLWIN	0x04	Window is full screen
_SCROLLWIN	0x08	Window's bottom edge is screen bottom edge
_ISPAD	0x10	Window is a pad
_HASMOVED	0x20	Cursor has moved since last refresh
_WRAPPED	0x40	Cursor was just wrapped

Window attributes

```
win->_attrs
win->_bkgd
```

The _attrs element is an attr_t type variable indicating which attributes are applied to text (non-space characters) in a window. The bit fields in _attrs are filled according to which attributes are set. See attrset().

_bkgd is a chtype() variable equal to the current background chtype (character and attribute) assigned to the window. This value is set by the bkgd() function.

Window options

```
win->_notimeout
win->_clear
win->_leaveok
win->_scroll
win->_idlok
win->_idcok
win->_immed
win->_sync
win->_use_keypad
win->_delay
```

For all Boolean elements, the value TRUE sets the bit and the condition, described below.

_notimeout is a Boolean value which when set directs NCurses not set a timeout for the Esc key press. This value is controlled by the notimeout() function.

_clear is a Boolean value which when set tells NCurses that information in the window needs to be redrawn from scratch. This setting is controlled by the clearok() function.

_leaveok is a Boolean value which when set tells NCurses not to update the cursor's position for the window. This setting is controlled by the leaveok() function.

_scroll is a Boolean value, which when set tells NCurses that the window's contents can be scrolled. This setting is controlled by the scrollok() function.

_idlok is a Boolean value, which when set tells NCurses to use the hardware insert/delete line feature. This setting is controlled by the idlok() function.

_idcok is a Boolean value, which when set tells NCurses to use the hardware insert/delete character feature. This setting is controlled by the idcok() function.

_immed is a Boolean value, which when set tells NCurses to automatically call the wrefresh() function any time the window's image is changed. This setting is controlled by the immedok() function.

_sync is a Boolean value, which when set tells NCurses to automatically update a subwidow's data any time the parent window's data is changed. This setting is controlled by the syncok() function.

_use_keypad is a Boolean value, which when set tells NCurses to interpret the keyboard's keypad, function, cursor and other special keys. This setting is controlled by the keypad() function.

_delay is an int value, which sets the keyboard input delay. Values less than zero turn getch() into a non-blocking call. Zero sets no delay. Values greater than zero set the delay in milliseconds. This setting is controlled by the nodelay() and timeout() functions.

Window data

```
win->_line
```

_line is a pointer to a special structure that holds the window's actual data. NCurses developers really don't want you messing with that data, so this element of the WINDOW structure is undocumented.

Window Scrolling Region

```
win->_regtop
win->_regbottom
```

The two variables _regtop and _regbottom are NCURSES_SIZE_T values that set the top and bottom of a scrolling region of text in a window. These are set by using the setscrreg() function.

Subwindow Data

```
win->_parx
win->_pary
win->_parent
```

For a subwindow, _parx and _pary are int values indicating the upper-left corner of the subwindow relative to the parent. These coordinates are returned via the getparyx() function.

_parent is a WINDOW pointer indicating the parent window. This value is the address of the parent window's structure, not its name. See the Examples.

Pad Data

Data for a pad is kept in a pdat structure within the WINDOW structure. The pdat structure is named _pad and referenced as listed below:

```
win->_pad._pad_y
win->_pad._pad_x
win->_pad._pad_top
win->_pad._pad_left
win->_pad._pad_bottom
win->_pad._pad_right
```

The pad data in the window corresponds to the arguments used for the prefresh() function as shown in Table A-20.

Table A-20: WINDOW pad data related the prefresh() function's arguments

PREFRESH() ARGUMENTS	WINDOW PDAT STRUCTURE ELEMENT
pminrow	_pad._pad_y
pmincol	_pad._pad_x
sminrow	_pad._pad_top
smincol	_pad._pad_left
smaxrow	_pad._pad_bottom
smaxcol	_pad._pad_right

Return Value

Not applicable.

Notes

Obviously, it's preferable to change attributes by using the proper NCurses functions wherever possible.

The subwindow information for a window, win->_parx, win->_pary, win->_parent, is set only when the window is a subwindow.

Note that there is no reference in the WINDOW structure for any subwindows. True, subwindows do link back to their parents (via the _parent element). But there is no element in the WINDOW structure to reference any offspring. (NCurses does maintain an internal list of all windows.)

Examples

```
if(win->_flags & _FULLWIN)
```

The if test is true if the _FULLWIN bit is set for the window win, meaning that window win is full screen.

```
if(sub->_parent == stdscr)
```

The if condition is true when the standard screen has a subwindow named sub.

Sample Program

Not applicable.

Also See

getyx(), getmaxyx(), getbegyx(), attrset(), bkgd(), notimeout(), clearok(), leaveok(), scrollok(), idlok(), idcok(), immedok(), syncok(), keypad(), nodelay(), timeout(), setscrreg(), getparyx(), prefresh()

wnoutrefresh()

The wnoutrefresh() function copies modified (touched) text from a window to the virtual screen.

Explanation

The refresh operation in NCurses consists of two parts:

- First, NCurses takes those portions of a window that have been changed or *touched* and writes those portions from the window data structure to a virtual screen in memory.

- Second, the contents of the virtual screen touched since the last refresh are displayed on the terminal.

The copying of information from a window data structure to the virtual screen is carried out by the wnoutrefresh() function. The updating of the virtual screen to the terminal is handled by another function, doupdate(). Together they form the two components of a refresh() or wrefresh() call.

The advantage of using wnoutrefresh() comes when updating multiple windows. In that case, repeated calls to wnoutrefresh() followed by a single doupdate() call is more efficient than a series of wrefresh() calls, plus it results in less flicker.

Man Page Format

```
int wnoutrefresh(WINDOW *win);
```

Format Reference

win represents the window to update on the virtual screen. It's a WINDOW variable, representing a window created earlier in the code or stdscr for the standard screen.

Return Value

ERR upon failure, OK (or some value other than ERR) upon success.

Notes

wnoutrefresh() has the effect of un-touching a window. See touchwin().

A similar function, pnoutrefresh(), exists for help in updating pads. See pnoutrefresh().

The slk_noutrefresh() function is used for help in updating soft labels. See slk_noutrefresh().

Examples

```
wnoutrefresh(alpha);
wnoutrefresh(beta);
wnoutrefresh(gamma);
doupdate();
```

The three `wnoutrefresh()` functions update information from the three windows, `alpha`, `beta`, and `gamma`. Then final `doupdate()` function updates the terminal. These four statements are more efficient than three corresponding `wrefresh()` functions.

```
wnoutrefresh(stdscr);
```

Here, the standard screen is updated to the virtual screen. A subsequent call to `doupdate()` will update the terminal screen.

Sample Program

Refer to the entries for `doupdate()` and `mvwin()` for sample programs and output.

Also See

`refresh()`, `doupdate()`, `wredrawln()`, `touchwin()`

wredrawln()

The `wredrawln()` function directs NCurses to update specific lines from a window to the terminal.

Explanation

This function, along with `redrawwin()`, operates under the assumption that something has disrupted a program's text on the terminal. In that instance, NCurses may not recognize the corrupted screen or know that its internal representation of the screen (`curscr`) is out of sync. The `wredrawln()` function allows a program to fix one or more lines in a window, forcing NCurses to write those lines and make the `curscr` once again match what the user sees.

Man Page Format

```
int wredrawln(WINDOW *win, int beg_line, int num_lines);
```

Format Reference

win is a WINDOW variable representing a window on the screen.

beg_line is an int value specifying a line on the screen to update. Values range from 0 for the top line, down to as many rows are between beg_line and the bottom of the window.

num_lines is the number of rows to update, from 1 through as many rows are available between beg_line and the bottom of the window.

Return Value

ERR upon failure or some value other than ERR upon success, usually OK but not always.

Notes

wredrawln() does not actually refresh the screen. The next wrefresh() command merely ensures that the lines touched by wredrawln() are fully updated on the terminal screen.

The lines wredrawln() replaces are *completely* replaced.

The redrawwin() function is used to force a re-write of the entire screen. It's equivalent to wredrawln(win,0,n), where win is the name of the window and n is the window's bottom row.

I've yet to see this function work as described. Though it appears to do something, just not what is advertised. A better solution is to use the following as a replacement for wredrawln():

```
touchwin(stdscr);
touchwin(curscr);
wrefresh(curscr);
```

Example

```
wredrawln(stdscr,0,11);
```

The statement describes the top 12 lines of the standard screen as in need of a complete refresh.

Sample Program

```
1    #include <ncurses.h>
2    #include <stdlib.h>
3
4    int main(void)
```

```
 5    {
 6         initscr();
 7
 8         addstr("I'm just an innocent little program,\n");
 9         addstr("minding my own business...\n");
10         move(0,0);
11         refresh();
12         getch();
13
14         system("echo \"RANDOM DATA\" > `tty`");
15         getch();
16
17         wredrawln(stdscr,0,2);
18         refresh();
19         getch();
20
21         endwin();
22         return 0;
23    }
```

Sample output:

```
I'm just an innocent little program,
minding my own business...
```

Press Enter to write text over the program's output:

```
RANDOM DATA innocent little program,
minding my own business...
```

Press Enter to restore the program's output:

```
I'm just an innocent little program,

minding my own business...
```

(Again: This doesn't work on any of the terminals or under any of the platforms on which I've tried it, and it's most likely a bug that will go away in the future. Until then, changing line 17 to refresh(curscr) does fix the program but doesn't address the issue of whether wredrawln() is properly working or not.)

Also See

wredrawln(), refresh()

wrefresh()

See refresh().

wsyncdown()

The wsyncdown() function is called to ensure that locations touched in a window are also touched in any subwindows.

Man Page Format

```
void wsyncdown(WINDOW *win);
```

Format Reference

win is the name of a WINDOW variable representing a window on the screen.

Return Value

The function returns no value.

Notes

This function is called internally by the wnoutrefresh() function. It's unusual to call this function manually.

The wsyncdown() function recursively calls all parent windows of the named window. Therefore, specify the smallest child window to synchronize the refresh to all of its parents.

This function is not related to the wsyncup() function.

Example

```
wsyncdown(pp);
```

The statement touches an changed locations in the window pp, then checks for any parent windows to pp and touches the same changed locations in those windows as well. Again, the wrefresh(pp) command would do the same thing, so there is seldom a need to use this command.

Sample Program

Not applicable.

Also See

```
wnoutrefresh()
```

wsyncup()

The wsyncup() function touches the locations in the parents of a subwindow that have been changed in the subwindow.

Man Page Format

```
void wsyncup(WINDOW *win);
```

Format Reference

win is the name of a WINDOW variable representing a subwindow.

Return Value

This function returns no value.

Notes

wsyncup() is called internally by NCurses whenever the mvwin() function is used to relocate a window.

This function may be called automatically whenever there is a change made to any window. See syncok() for more information.

wsyncup() seems rather redundant, given that a subwindow shares memory with its parent.

Example

```
wsyncup(baby);
```

The statement touches all changed locations in the subwindow baby inside all parent windows as well.

Sample Program

Not applicable.

Also See

syncok(), refresh()

wtimeout()

See `timeout()`.

wtouchln

The `wtouchln()` function flags one or more lines in a specific window as either requiring updating on the screen or as not needing updating. (Refer to the entry for `refresh()` for more information about how parts of windows are *touched* and require updating.)

Man Page Format

```
int wtouchln(WINDOW *win, int y, int n, int changed);
```

Format Reference

`win` is a `WINDOW` variable indicating which window the `wtouchln()` function affects.

`y` is the top row to mark as either touched or untouched.

`n` indicates how many rows, including `row`, to flag as being touched or untouched. Values range from 1 to the number of rows between `row` and the bottom of the window.

`changed` is either 1 or 0. When `changed` is 1, then the rows indicated are flagged as touched and will be updated at the next `wrefresh()` call. When `changed` is 0, then the rows indicated are flagged as up to date or untouched.

Return Value

The function returns `ERR` upon failure; an `int` value other than `ERR` is returned upon success.

Notes

The `touchwin()`, `touchline()`, and `untouchwin()` functions are all macros defined in `NCURSES.H` that use the `wtouchln()` function. Table A-21 shows how they map out.

Table A-21: *wtouchln()* equivalents of other NCurses functions

FUNCTION	WTOUCHLN() EQUIVALENT
touchline(win,row,count)	wtouchln(win,row,count,1)
touchwin(win)	wtouchln(win,0,getmaxy(win),1)
untouchwin(win)	wtouchln(win,0,getmaxy(win),0)

(The getmaxy() macro is defined in NCURSES.H; refer to the Notes entry for getmaxyx() in this appendix for details.)

Examples

```
wtouchln(stdscr,0,halfy,1);
```

The statement flags the top half of the standard screen as being in need of updating on the next refresh() call. This assumes that the halfy variable equals half the window's height.

```
wtouchln(help,13,1,0);
```

The statement tells NCurses to ignore any modifications done on row 13 in the window help.

Sample Program

```
1     #include <ncurses.h>
2
3     int main(void)
4     {
5         int r;
6         initscr();
7
8     /* Write some text to the entire window */
9         for(r=0;r<LINES;r++)
10            mvprintw(r,0,\
11            "This is the fabulous row %d on the standard screen.",r);
12
13    /* Update every other line */
14        for(r=0;r<LINES;r+=2)
15        {
16            wtouchln(stdscr,r,1,1);
17            wtouchln(stdscr,r+1,1,0);
```

```
18          }
19          refresh();
20          getch();
21
22          endwin();
23          return 0;
24      }
```

Sample output:

```
This is the fabulous row 0 on the standard screen.

This is the fabulous row 2 on the standard screen.

This is the fabulous row 4 on the standard screen.

This is the fabulous row 6 on the standard screen.

This is the fabulous row 8 on the standard screen.

This is the fabulous row 10 on the standard screen.

This is the fabulous row 12 on the standard screen.

This is the fabulous row 14 on the standard screen.

This is the fabulous row 16 on the standard screen.

This is the fabulous row 18 on the standard screen.

This is the fabulous row 20 on the standard screen.

This is the fabulous row 22 on the standard screen.
```

Note how the standard screen cursor blinks after the last line printed, line 23, which wasn't refreshed? Cursor movement is independent of characters placed on the screen and is not affected by touch or untouch functions. Also see leaveok()*.*

Also See

refresh(), touchwin(), untouchwin()

The Alternative Character Set

The *Alternative Character Set*, or *ACS*, is defined in the NCURSES.H file. Its purpose is to provide a common set of characters for use on all platforms. The table in this appendix gives the name defined for the characters, as specified in NCURSES.H. The Char column shows what the character commonly looks like. The ASCII column displays the ASCII character substituted when the character isn't available. And the Description column describes the character's appearance or use.

DEFINE NAME	CHAR	ASCII	DESCRIPTION
ACS_BLOCK	▇	#	A solid (100 percent) block
ACS_BOARD	▓	#	A 50 percent shaded block
ACS_BTEE	⊥	+	Line art bottom T intersection
ACS_BULLET	•	o	Bullet
ACS_CKBOARD	▚	:	A 33 percent shaded block
ACS_DARROW	↓	v	Down arrow
ACS_DEGREE	°	'	Degree symbol
ACS_DIAMOND	◊	+	Diamond

(continued)

DEFINE NAME	CHAR	ASCII	DESCRIPTION
ACS_GEQUAL	≥	>	Greater than or equal to
ACS_HLINE	─	-	Line art horizontal line
ACS_LANTERN	§	#	Lantern or section symbol
ACS_LARROW	←	<	Left arrow
ACS_LEQUAL	≤	<	Less than or equal to
ACS_LLCORNER	└	+	Line art lower-left corner
ACS_LRCORNER	┘	+	Line art lower-right corner
ACS_LTEE	├	+	Line art left T intersection
ACS_NEQUAL	≠	!	Not equal
ACS_PI	π	*	Pi
ACS_PLMINUS	±	#	Plus/minus
ACS_PLUS	+	+	Plus
ACS_RARROW	→	>	Right arrow
ACS_RTEE	┤	+	Line art right T intersection
ACS_S1	─		Scan line 1 (top)
ACS_S3	─		Scan line 3 (high)
ACS_S7	─		Scan line 7 (low)
ACS_S9	─		Scan line 9 (bottom)
ACS_STERLING	£	f	British pound
ACS_TTEE	┬	+	Line art top T intersection
ACS_UARROW	↑	^	Up arrow
ACS_ULCORNER	┌	+	Line art upper-left corner
ACS_URCORNER	┐	+	Line art upper-right corner
ACS_VLINE	│			Line art vertical line

The wide or char_t constants are identical to those listed in the table, though with the prefix W added to the defined name. For example, the wide plus/minus character is defined as WACS_PLMINUS.

The *chtype*

In NCurses, `chtype` is a special type of variable that holds a combination of character and attribute information. Those values are stored in a `long int`. (The `chtype` variable in NCurses is `typedef`'d to a `long int`.)

Functions using `chtype` variables include: `addch()`, `addchstr()`, `attroff()`, `attron()`, and `attrset()`, plus a host of others. But more important, each character position in an NCurses window stores a `chtype` value. As a `chtype`, character locations in a window include both character and attribute information. Because of that, when characters are copied or moved in NCurses, the attribute information is copied and moved along with the character.

The `chtype` need only describe characters; it doesn't have to include attribute information. To add the attribute, use the `chtype` in a function such as `addch()`. The attribute can be applied by using a logical OR with the character to display. For example:

```
addch('E' | A_BOLD);
```

This function displays the character E at the cursor's current position, plus applies the bold text attribute to that character.

Attributes for `chtypes` can also be assigned by using any of the attribute functions, such as `attroff()`, `attron()`, or `attrset()`.

The names and values of NCurses text attributes are listed in Table C-1. Also refer to Table 3-1 for information on what each attribute does or how it controls the screen.

Table C-1: Text attribute masking values

ATTRIBUTE NAME	VALUE (HEX)	ATTRIBUTE NAME	VALUE (HEX)
A_NORMAL	0x00000000	A_ALTCHARSET	0x00400000
A_ATTRIBUTES	0xFFFFFF00	A_INVIS	0x00800000
A_CHARTEXT	0x000000FF	A_PROTECT	0x01000000
A_COLOR	0x0000FF00	A_HORIZONTAL	0x02000000
A_STANDOUT	0x00010000	A_LEFT	0x04000000
A_UNDERLINE	0x00020000	A_LOW	0x08000000
A_REVERSE	0x00040000	A_RIGHT	0x10000000
A_BLINK	0x00080000	A_TOP	0x20000000
A_DIM	0x00100000	A_VERTICAL	0x40000000
A_BOLD	0x00200000		

Obviously, it's better to use the attribute name than its value. To further clarify things, Figure C-1 illustrates how the chtype variable is bitmapped to the various attributes.

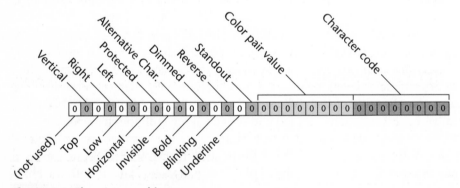

Figure C-1: The chtype bitmap

Note how the A_ATTRIBUTES and A_CHARTEXT attributes (Table C-1) are used in the bitmap. They can effectively mask out either the character or attribute branch of the chtype variable.

Keypad Character Codes

The following constants are defined in NCURSES.H. They're used by those functions that read special keys from the keyboard. The keys are defined in Table D-1.

Table D-1: NCurses keypad codes and values

DEFINE	VALUE (OCT)	KEY NAME / DESCRIPTION
KEY_CODE_YES	0400	A wchar_t contains a key code
KEY_MIN	0401	Minimum key value
KEY_BREAK	0401	Break key (unreliable)
KEY_DOWN	0402	Down-arrow key
KEY_UP	0403	Up-arrow key
KEY_LEFT	0404	Left-arrow key
KEY_RIGHT	0405	Right-arrow key
KEY_HOME	0406	Home key
KEY_BACKSPACE	0407	Backspace key
KEY_F0	0410	Function keys

(continued)

Table D-1 *(continued)*

DEFINE	VALUE (OCT)	KEY NAME / DESCRIPTION
KEY_F(n)	(KEY_F0+(n))	Value of function key n (Space set aside for up to 64 Function keys)
KEY_DL	0510	Delete-line key
KEY_IL	0511	Insert-line key
KEY_DC	0512	Delete-character key
KEY_IC	0513	Insert-character key
KEY_EIC	0514	sent by rmir or smir in insert mode
KEY_CLEAR	0515	Clear-screen / Erase key
KEY_EOS	0516	Clear-to-end-of-screen key
KEY_EOL	0517	Clear-to-end-of-line key
KEY_SF	0520	Scroll-forward key
KEY_SR	0521	Scroll-backward key
KEY_NPAGE	0522	Next-page / PgDn key
KEY_PPAGE	0523	Previous-page / PgUp key
KEY_STAB	0524	Set-tab key
KEY_CTAB	0525	Clear-tab key
KEY_CATAB	0526	Clear-all-tabs key
KEY_ENTER	0527	Enter/send key
KEY_SRESET	0530	Soft (partial) reset (unreliable)
KEY_RESET	0531	Reset or hard reset (unreliable)
KEY_PRINT	0532	Print key
KEY_LL	0533	Lower-left key (home down or bottom)
KEY_A1	0534	Upper left of keypad (see notes)
KEY_A3	0535	Upper right of keypad
KEY_B2	0536	Center of keypad
KEY_C1	0537	Lower left of keypad
KEY_C3	0540	Lower right of keypad
KEY_BTAB	0541	Back-tab key
KEY_BEG	0542	Begin key

Table D-1 (continued)

DEFINE	VALUE (OCT)	KEY NAME / DESCRIPTION
KEY_CANCEL	0543	Cancel key
KEY_CLOSE	0544	Close key
KEY_COMMAND	0545	Command key
KEY_COPY	0546	Copy key
KEY_CREATE	0547	Create key
KEY_END	0550	End key
KEY_EXIT	0551	Exit key
KEY_FIND	0552	Find key
KEY_HELP	0553	Help key
KEY_MARK	0554	Mark key
KEY_MESSAGE	0555	Message key
KEY_MOVE	0556	Move key
KEY_NEXT	0557	Next key
KEY_OPEN	0560	Open key
KEY_OPTIONS	0561	Options key
KEY_PREVIOUS	0562	Previous key
KEY_REDO	0563	Redo key
KEY_REFERENCE	0564	Reference key
KEY_REFRESH	0565	Refresh key
KEY_REPLACE	0566	Replace key
KEY_RESTART	0567	Restart key
KEY_RESUME	0570	Resume key
KEY_SAVE	0571	Save key
KEY_SBEG	0572	Shift+Begin key
KEY_SCANCEL	0573	Shift+Cancel key
KEY_SCOMMAND	0574	Shift+Command key
KEY_SCOPY	0575	Shift+Copy key
KEY_SCREATE	0576	Shift+Create key

(continued)

Table D-1 *(continued)*

DEFINE	VALUE (OCT)	KEY NAME / DESCRIPTION
KEY_SDC	0577	Shift+Delete-character key
KEY_SDL	0600	Shift+Delete-line key
KEY_SELECT	0601	Select key
KEY_SEND	0602	Shift+End key
KEY_SEOL	0603	Shift+Clear-To-End-Of-Line key
KEY_SEXIT	0604	Shift+Exit key
KEY_SFIND	0605	Shift+Find key
KEY_SHELP	0606	Shift+Help key
KEY_SHOME	0607	Shift+Home key
KEY_SIC	0610	Shift+Insert-Character key
KEY_SLEFT	0611	Shift+Left-Arrow key
KEY_SMESSAGE	0612	Shift+Message key
KEY_SMOVE	0613	Shift+Move key
KEY_SNEXT	0614	Shift+Next key
KEY_SOPTIONS	0615	Shift+Options key
KEY_SPREVIOUS	0616	Shift+Previous key
KEY_SPRINT	0617	Shift+Print key
KEY_SREDO	0620	Shift+Redo key
KEY_SREPLACE	0621	Shift+Replace key
KEY_SRIGHT	0622	Shift+Right-Arrow key
KEY_SRSUME	0623	Shift+Resume key
KEY_SSAVE	0624	Shift+Save key
KEY_SSUSPEND	0625	Shift+Suspend key
KEY_SUNDO	0626	Shift+Undo key
KEY_SUSPEND	0627	Suspend key
KEY_UNDO	0630	Undo key
KEY_MOUSE	0631	Mouse event
KEY_RESIZE	0632	Terminal resize event
KEY_EVENT	0633	Some other event
KEY_MAX	0777	Maximum key value

Not every keyboard has all these keys. Some are from the ancient days of computers!

The values specified in the Values column may not be the same for all platforms; they're listed here merely as reference. Be sure to use the symbol defined in your code instead of a value.

Not all keys are defined in all implementations of NCurses.

As a tip, when dealing with the numeric keypad, it helps to use the illustration shown in Figure D-1.

Figure D-1: The NCurses numeric keypad

Index